I Wonder as I Wander

I Wonder as I Wander

The Life of John Jacob Niles

RON PEN

FOREWORD BY
RICK KOGAN

THE UNIVERSITY PRESS OF KENTUCKY

Excerpts of the unpublished autobiography of John Jacob Niles are printed
with the permission of John Edward Niles and Thomas M. T. Niles.

The University Press of Kentucky

Scholarly publisher for the Commonwealth,
serving Bellarmine University, Berea College, Centre College of Kentucky, Eastern
Kentucky University, The Filson Historical Society, Georgetown College, Kentucky
Historical Society, Kentucky State University, Morehead State University, Murray
State University, Northern Kentucky University, Transylvania University, University of
Kentucky, University of Louisville, and Western Kentucky University.
All rights reserved.

Editorial and Sales Offices: The University Press of Kentucky
663 South Limestone Street, Lexington, Kentucky 40508-4008
www.kentuckypress.com

14 13 12 11 10   5 4 3 2 1

Library of Congress Cataloging-in-Publication Data

Pen, Ronald.
   I wonder as I wander : the life of John Jacob Niles / Ron Pen ; foreword by Rick Kogan.
      p. cm.
   Includes bibliographical references and index.
   ISBN 978-0-8131-2597-8 (hardcover : alk. paper)
   1. Niles, John Jacob, 1892-1980. 2. Singers—Kentucky—Biography. 3. Composers—
Kentucky—Biography. I. Title.
   ML420.N694P47 2010
   782.42092—dc22
   [B]   2010020663

This book is printed on acid-free recycled paper meeting the requirements of the
American National Standard for Permanence in Paper for Printed Library Materials.

Manufactured in the United States of America.

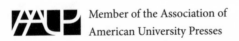 Member of the Association of
American University Presses

In gratitude to
John Jacob Niles
Rena Lipetz Niles
Helen Behr Pen

Never let the dull facts
interfere with a good yarn.

—John Jacob Niles

Contents

Illustrations follow pages 152 and 216

Foreword

Rick Kogan

It was nearly twenty-five years ago, or possibly longer, that my childhood friend Ron Pen took me for a walk that carried me at once into another man's life and into what would become Pen's long-standing and determined and frustrating and now realized passion to put the life and times of John Jacob Niles between the covers of a book, this remarkable book. That day is so colorfully and lovingly and powerfully evoked in the first pages of this book—the gauzy sun, the carvings of "sacred icons and scriptures . . . intertwined with images of the native tobacco leaves and dogwood blossoms"—that not only was I instantly transported back a couple of decades, but I felt immediately compelled to devour every page that followed.

Now, I am not one to be seduced by reading that "the early morning fog is pierced by the call of the brass horn and baying of the hounds as horses and riders pound wildly through fields," though I have spent some enjoyably bucolic and whiskey-peppered nights on the Pen porch, behind the warm place that the author and his wife and daughter have called their Kentucky home for decades.

I am a city kid, "Chicago born," as novelist Saul Bellow put it at the opening of his masterpiece, *The Adventures of Augie March,* before adding, "[I] go at things as I have taught myself, free-style, and will make the record in my own way: first to knock, first admitted; sometimes an innocent knock, sometimes a not so innocent." These words might serve also as apt description of Niles. Rena, his wife of forty-four years, pegs him precisely when she says, "He was strictly an individualist and he only operated successfully when he operated alone." Well, he is no longer operating alone and hasn't been ever since Pen first determined to take the measure of this complex and often contradictory man.

Ron Pen too is Chicago born, and it seems to be a small miracle that he made his way to Niles country from an art-stuffed and music-filled house on Schiller Street, where he lived with his father, mother, and sister. It was in this place that his love for the arts and, indeed, for the unconventional was first planted and nurtured with sufficient love and care that it has lasted a lifetime.

My great friend and mentor Studs Terkel was also a great pal and ardent admirer of Niles. Years before his death in 2008 he wrote his own epitaph: "Curiosity did not kill this cat." And it has been curiosity that has fueled Pen's passion. Niles once said, "Never let dull facts interfere with a good yarn." This, of course, is not the sort of thing any biographer wants to hear, and Pen was wise not to heed those words. He has gathered an astonishing amount of research, of facts, and delivered them so clearly that he makes his subject's life anything but dull. The facts are revelatory. They are entertaining and engaging. They are informative. They explain, definitively I dare say, the complexities of this American original and his great and ongoing and—almost certainly—everlasting influence.

As you read this book, you should know that not every notable person gets the biographer he or she deserves. In Pen, Niles has the good fortune to have "found" a kindred soul—an admirer, to be sure, but one with great knowledge, a clear eye, a good ear (to be expected), and a stylish pen. It has been a long journey, and these two men have walked the same roads. They have shared the land and air and sun. They are tied now forever in words.

Pen writes that Niles lies in a "pastoral graveyard, well shaded by walnut trees and graced by a serene pond," but I beg to differ. Against all the laws of man and eternity, Pen has made Niles live again. He is here, alive in spirit and in words and in song.

Listen!

Acknowledgments

A book that occupies more than a quarter of a century of the author's life owes a great debt to many people who have shared that life and the book's lengthy gestation. First and foremost, I need to express profound gratitude to Hooey, my wife and my life. In every sense, this is her book as well as mine. My family has provided a garden of delight and an oasis of support. I thank my remarkable daughter Robin and my artistic and nurturing parents, Rudolph and Yvonne, who brought me into being and guided me on the adventure. Though we characterize our sibling relationship as "sinister" and "bother," I can scarcely imagine a more engaging and witty sister than Polly. I gratefully acknowledge her and her darling companion Susan Blommaert.

My gratitude also extends to Jack and Barbara Behr, my parents-in-law, who embraced me and welcomed me into their wondrous family, whose members include Barbi and Tommie, Joan and Wells, Ann and Crans (my lifelong friend and best man), Leslie and Robert, Sally and Logan, and a teeming horde of delightful children and grandchildren whom I cherish in my heart.

The Niles family graciously and generously provided encouragement from the very beginning. In particular I am indebted to Rena Niles, whose earthy aristocracy, vision, and grace enabled this book to come into being; it is very much her story as well as Johnnie's. I am indebted to her sons, ardent advocates for the Niles Center for American Music and integral cast members of this book. "The Beezer," Thomas Michael Tolliver Niles, freely bestowed stories and photos; and John Edward Niles, a chip off the old block and a fount of Nilesian lore, contributed valuable perspective. Let me also note Niles's nephew Robert Niles and his wife Ema Jean Niles and Niles's thespian niece Nancy Niles Sexton, who all helped animate the narrative.

I owe much to The Hindman Settlement School at the Forks of

Troublesome Creek, where much of the writing of this book was accomplished through the generosity of a special confluence of people and place. In particular, I wish to thank the indefatigable director, Dr. Michael Mullins, and the wonderful staff, including Doris Miller, Rita Ritchie, Moses Owens, Linda Amburgey, Carolyn Cornett, Ann Ritchie, Rebecca Ware, and James Phelps.

I promised this book many and many a year ago to the University Press of Kentucky. During this time I have been privileged to be the recipient of director Stephen Wrinn's wry wit and wisdom. I have also enjoyed conspiring with former director Ken Cherry, Joyce Harrison, Laura Sutton, Ann Malcolm, David Cobb, and others who magically transformed my thoughts and words into the book that you now hold in your hands. Copy editor Lois Crum skillfully nurtured the manuscript from an ungainly colt into a thoroughbred. Many thanks to Sarah Kehrberg, who graciously and knowingly helped me navigate the mysteries of the index. And with utmost respect and gratitude for wading through an enormous manuscript and contributing invaluable criticism, please let me express my appreciation to Dale Cockrell, Ronald Cohen, and Alan Jabbour.

A scholar naturally develops a particular affection for libraries and librarians that open the portals of knowledge. Please allow me to acknowledge Wayne Shirley at the Library of Congress; the Knott County Library in Hindman, Kentucky, and librarians LaDonna Collins and Tammy Owens; Andrew Leach, Assistant Librarian and Archivist at the Center for Black Music Research, Chicago; Frank Villella, Archivist of the Rosenthal Archives of the Chicago Symphony Orchestra; Sharon Bidwell, Librarian at the *Courier-Journal,* Louisville; the remarkable Lucille C. Little Fine Arts Library and Resource Center, and especially Director Gail Kennedy, and librarians Ron Lloyd and Paula Hickner; Lesley Chapman, Visual Resources Curator at the University of Kentucky; Steve Gowler and Harry Rice at Berea College's (very) Special Collections; Jeff Place at Folkways, Smithsonian Institution; the generous assistance of the John C. Campbell Folk School, including Director Jan Davidson, Archivist and Historian David Brose, and Anna Shearouse, for assistance with photographic archives; Archaeologist Philip J. DiBlasi at the University of Louisville; Gino Francesconi, Archivist and Museum Director, Carnegie Hall; Rabbi Mark Goldman, Rockwell Temple, Cincinnati; the J. Paul Getty Museum; the

Doris Ulmann Photographic Collection of the Special Collections and University Archives, University of Oregon; and Nathalie Andrews, Director of the Portland Museum, Louisville.

Please allow me to acknowledge my heartfelt gratitude to the Special Collections and Digital Programs division of the University of Kentucky Libraries. This wondrous library (home of the John Jacob Niles Collection) and knowledgeable staff served as my very closest ally in the completion of this book. Thanks to Director William J. Marshall (retired), James Birchfield, Claire McCain (retired), Lisa Carter, Kate Black (Appalachian Collection curator), Gordon Hogg, Matt Harris, Frank Stanger, Paul Holbrook, current director Terry Birdwhistell, and the virtuosic digital dexterity of Jason E. Flahardy, who prepared many of the images for this work.

Let me thank those with whom I spend my working days at the School of Music of the University of Kentucky, particularly my colleagues and friends Lance Brunner, Jonathan Glixon, Diana Hallman, and Donna Kwon in the Division of Musicology and Ethnomusicology; W. Harry Clarke and C. Ben Arnold, past and present directors of the School of Music, who supported me in word and deed; and the Dean of the College of Fine Arts, Robert Shay, who kept the faith.

Various friends, musicians, and authors have contributed significantly to this narrative, none more so than Jean Ritchie, my musical and spiritual mother; Jacqueline Roberts, a Kentucky songbird who concertized with Niles for many years and served as his muse for late works, such as the *Niles-Merton Songs;* pianist Nancie Field, who elegantly collaborated with Niles and Roberts; Studs Terkel, a masterful oral historian who cherished Niles's use of the word "ornry"; Bob Dylan, who understood Niles; Rick Kogan, who has always had my back and who has remained a constant friend through it all; Philip Walker Jacobs, who generously shared all that he learned with me as we examined the intertwined lives of Doris Ulmann and John Jacob Niles in tandem; the Red State Ramblers family, to whom I am indebted for much music and mirth; and Rick and Debbie Sipe, whose gracious and generous hospitality made my writing a joy in their lovely cabin in Desbarats, Ontario.

It is a pleasure to acknowledge the Sinfonia Foundation Fellowship that generously supported a portion of the sabbatical spent writing the manuscript.

I Wonder as I Wander

Niles at age forty in 1932, at Berea, Kentucky. Photo by Doris Ulmann. Doris Ulmann Collection, PHO38-13-1583, Special Collections and University Archives, University of Oregon Libraries.

Overture

Sunrise in Clark County

Every man, woman and child on the top side
Of the earth has a God-given right to come
Into contact with and be enlivened, uplifted,
Entertained, refreshed, and perhaps educated
By music, poetry, and art of the race in which
They belong.

—John Jacob Niles

The sun creeps over the mist-shrouded hills of Kentucky's rolling blue-grass and ignites the amber and scarlet leaves clinging to the autumnal trees. From my upstairs porch, you can just make out the silhouette of the first wave of mountains beyond the snaky green Kentucky River. Looking out over the rugged fieldstone walls hugging Grimes Mill Road, it is less than a mile to John Jacob Niles's Boot Hill Farm, cradled in a bend of Boone Creek. The same creek that was home to frontiersman Daniel Boone in 1773 was Niles's home from 1939 until his death in 1980.

From Boot Hill Farm, it is but a brisk hike winding up the hill to St. Hubert's Episcopal Church, the little country church whose front doors were lovingly crafted by Niles. Sacred icons and scriptures adorn the doors, but these carvings are also intertwined with images of the native tobacco leaves and dogwood blossoms that bind the church to the surrounding countryside. Inside the church, deer antlers surmount the hymn board. While this symbol might seem extravagantly pagan for staid

Episcopal worship, the antlers are there to remind the congregation that Saint Hubert, patron of the hunt, miraculously witnessed the appearance of a crucifix between a stag's horns.

The choice of Saint Hubert as the church's patron is particularly apt, because the parish is centrally situated within the verdant countryside known as "hunt country." Just a little farther down the road along Boone Creek rests old Charles Grimes's Mill, hewn from native creek limestone and reinforced with heavy timber beams. Originally built in 1807 to grind wheat bound for New Orleans, it became the home of the 120-year-old Iroquois Fox Hunt in 1928 when the mill ceased to operate.[1]

The hunt club's great feudal hall is warmed by a huge old stone fireplace that casts flickering shadows on the weathered ceiling beams. The air bears the scent of well-waxed wood and generations of leather mingled with oak smoke. After a raw autumn day spent riding through fields and splashing across streams, the club's members, including the Nileses and neighborhood companions, such as Charlotte and Fauntleroy Pursley and Winnie and Ed Madden, enjoyed many a convivial evening in the welcoming space.[2]

Back up the hill behind the church is a pastoral graveyard, well shaded by walnut trees and graced by a serene pond. Here John Jacob rests next to his wife, Rena Lipetz Niles, under a simple granite marker that lies flush with the lush bluegrass. The stone reads simply: "John Jacob Niles 1892–1980." Here, at the end, is where the story of John Jacob Niles begins.

Thirty years after Niles's death, this is still very much John Jacob Niles's hunt country, where the early morning fog is pierced by the call of the brass horn and the baying of hounds as horses and riders pound wildly through fields, dash across creeks, and vault fences hard on the scent of a fox or coyote. Niles would recognize the sounds of clawhammer banjo and old-time fiddle that still ring out across the rocky palisades of the Kentucky River. And he would be at home strolling through the tobacco fields turning a hazy gold as workers top the yellow flowers in the heat of Indian Summer. This is the land where Niles built his home place, raised his family, farmed his fields, rode upon his land, and created his music.

His music:

Oh beloved one, if I die with music in my mouth,
Choked as 'twer by the very sounds of heaven,
If I die with music in my mouth,
Remember that I have lived with it anon,
Have tuned my many strings to augment my voice,
And offered song to raise your sagging spirit,
And subtly wedded word with intangible sound
To brush away frustration's bitter hand.

If I die with music in my mouth,
Remember that I have lived with it anon.[3]

John Jacob Niles, "dean of American balladeers," lived and died with "music in his mouth," yet folklorists and musicologists alike were more than reluctant to acknowledge Niles's extraordinary life and career upon his death March 1, 1980.[4] There is a glaring dissonance between the dearth of scholarly respect accorded Niles and the wealth of coverage lavished on him by the popular media. The charismatic performer who was featured in *Life* magazine, who recorded on RCA's prestigious Red Seal label, who performed in celebrated venues such as Carnegie Hall and the White House, and who composed and arranged nearly one thousand songs was generally shunned by academia.[5]

Folklorists accused Niles of fraudulent collection methodology and suspect scholarship, while dismissing his performance style as eccentric and "inauthentic." Musicologists and music critics found it difficult to reconcile the diverse aspects of Niles's varied compositional repertoire, which freely intermingled arrangements of traditional music, songs composed in the manner of folk music, and purely original compositions that included larger-scale works such as oratorios and song cycles. There seemed to be an unbridgeable gulf between Niles's "folk" repertoire created for his own idiomatic performance and a completely separate "art" music repertoire intended for performance by other musicians.

Niles's transgression and subversion of the imagined boundaries articulating traditional, normative, and elite culture confounded critics and frustrated folklorists. He was very much an American original who succeeded in transcending that very fine line between cultural contexts by appearing on stage attired in white tie and tails but wrapped in the folksy persona of "Johnnie Niles—Boone Creek Boy." His dulcimer-accompanied performance *repertoire* may have been derived from the folk music world, but his performance *style* belonged to the art music stage. Academic critics were partially correct in characterizing Niles as a singer of folk music but not a folksinger.[6] However, once one understands Niles in terms of American institutions such as the Chautauqua and vaudeville, rather than traditional folk context, the contradictory facets of his narrative begin to resolve themselves.

Niles's career unfolded against a vivid backdrop of live performance—at the medicine show, the Chautauqua, and vaudeville; in salons and at women's clubs; on college campuses; in churches; under tents; at celebrated concert halls around the world; for a circus; on the radio; at festivals; and on countless mountain cabin porches. He lived within the living oral tradition of balladry and square dances as well as the art-music conservatory tradition of composed music. He learned to shape his performances to suit the demands of the nascent radio and recording industries, remaining professionally active well into the age of television and rock and roll by negotiating the communication skills necessary to survive in popular media. He succeeded in acquiring a unique personal style and artistic context that carried him through a career of seventy-one years.[7]

In the process, he made the transition from folk to folk revival. Niles was, perhaps, the quintessential "poplorist," according to Gene Bluestein's characterization of the relationship between cultural "tradition and transformation": "Unlike patterns of folk expression in older societies, for us the balance between the individual and the community is often tipped in favor of the individual and the community is often tipped clearly toward the former; poplorists, however, deliberately emphasize the collective values of the society that do not vanish into the anonymity folklorists have led us to expect when the folk process operates. . . . In poplore the balance shifts toward the individual."[8] Niles's unique high-pitched singing style and dramatic presentation reconfigured folk music on his own terms. He was not singing *to* the folk, but he adapted their voice to tell his own story. As Bluestein observed: "The American folk tradition does not involve 'submission of individuals to culture' as Glassie has suggested;

rather creative individuals use folk styles to make major changes in cultural materials. . . . The folk process, which has been seen as centering on the disappearance of the individual artist into a communal tradition, must be reconceived to recognize the contribution of known individuals to folk legacy."[9]

Niles was very much an individual and very conscious of his individuality. As Rena Niles, his wife of forty-four years, put it: "He was strictly an individualist and he only operated successfully when he operated alone. It would have been a mistake for him to be a member of an orchestra or a singing group in which he would have had to share the spotlight with others. The spotlight, as he saw it, belonged exclusively to Johnnie Niles."[10] Niles's colorful personality was drawn irresistibly to the limelight like a moth to the flame. He was the consummate showman all his life; his life and work became a seamless unity in which anything could be converted to a stage prop and anybody could become his audience. Family and friends were the supporting cast in the drama scripted and performed by John Jacob Niles.

The Families Gather at the River

The drama unfolds in the former city of Portland, Kentucky, in the early years of the nineteenth century.[1] Portland was strategically located right below three miles of rocky shoals known as the Falls of the Ohio and just to the west of the neighboring city of Louisville.[2] During summer months, when the Ohio River was at low stage, boats going upstream from ports along the Mississippi and the Ohio were compelled to disembark at Portland's Commercial Street (now Thirty-fourth Street) wharf and move overland around the falls to Louisville. Likewise, boats headed downstream from Louisville had to transfer their goods overland and reembark at Portland to continue their trip.

Portland sang in a vivid welter of contending voices: the penetrating whoosh of whistles as steamboats navigated the locks in the canal; the clamor of stevedores shouting to one another as they worked the rasping block and tackles; the hollow cacophony of horses' hooves on the cobblestone wharf; the great iron lungs of the Fischer-Leaf Foundry echoing across to the din raised by the Louisville Cement quarries strung out along Shippingport Island, and the grinding and halting of locomotives as they hauled their goods through the rail yards and clattered across the bridge to New Albany, Indiana.

Portland was becoming a thriving community whose economic opportunity and river access enticed many immigrants from Germany and Ireland to settle there. Grand homes such as magistrate Squire Earick's house on Commercial Street or steamboat captain William Campbell's house along Rudd Avenue gazed out over the river, while brick and frame shotgun houses with side porches lined streets such as Portland Avenue or Bank Street. The grand St. Charles Hotel dominated the bustling waterfront, where the cobblestones were stacked with bales of cotton and tobacco, hogsheads of molasses and sugar, and crates of factory-produced wares. The city was a hive of distilleries, foundries, convents, saloons, schools, churches, mercantile shops, banks, warehouses, a vast cement factory, rail yards, lumberyards, furniture factories, and a horse-drawn ferry that crossed the river to New Albany.

The very success of the port sowed the seeds of its demise. The inconvenience and financial cost of transportation to circumvent the falls finally compelled the city to build a canal around the falls connecting Portland directly to Louisville. The project, spearheaded by James Guthrie, was chartered in 1825, and construction began a year later. On December 22, 1830, the first boat passed through the 1.9-mile-long canal. In 1871 the canal was enlarged to accommodate the volume of traffic and the expanded size of the ships, but this also had the unfortunate effect of eventually bypassing Portland entirely. As the waterfront wharves and warehouses gradually became silent, John Jacob Niles's ancestors started assembling in Portland.

The Ancestors

At his seventy-seventh birthday concert in Cincinnati, Niles spoke of his great-grandfather Adams, "a piano manufacturer and a player of Bach and Buxtehude. He moved up and down the Ohio Valley, from Pittsburgh to Cairo. He tuned organs and pianos after the War Between the States had destroyed his business. He tuned, and he played Bach and Buxtehude [and] he made a magnificent piano."[3] This great-grandfather was born Jhan Engelbert in Prussia in 1808. A musician, woodworker, and carver, he immigrated to the United States and settled in Portland, Kentucky, where he established a piano building and tuning business as early as 1832.[4] He met Sarah Graff, who had been born in Alsace-Lorraine in 1826, and on February 15, 1848, the two were married by Joseph Potter at Louisville.[5] By then, Engelbert had Americanized his name to John E. Adams; he retained his surname as a middle initial and took Adams as his last name, in a nod to President John Quincy Adams (1767–1848). Sarah had previously altered her last name from Graff to Craft. One year later, in 1849, they had a daughter, Louise Craft Adams.

John and Sarah settled on Portland Avenue, a broad thoroughfare that had once served as the turnpike connecting Portland to Louisville. John's shop and residence at 615 Portland, between Eighth and Ninth streets, was beyond the Louisville Railroad Bridge across the river and at the very eastern edge of the city. By 1882, however, he had moved toward "Portland Proper" and lived in a new residence next to Mount Olivet Presbyterian Church, at Twenty-fourth Street. The house was a modest one-story dwelling of brick with a frame cornice and four windows facing the church.

In John Adams, some of the seeds of his great-grandson's future development were perhaps already sown. Adams was a piano and harpsichord builder whose woodworking skills were reputedly showcased in elaborately carved casework. Perhaps the ancestral combination of woodcraft skills and musical instrument manufacture presaged the construction of John Jacob Niles's unique dulcimers or his carved doors and furniture. Certainly an artistic and craftsmanlike approach to wood was a family tradition. Robert, Niles's younger brother, became a respected finish carpenter and cabinet maker.[6]

In the same neighborhood, several blocks west of the Adams family, another German immigrant, Jacob Augustus Reisch, owned a grocery and saloon. Jacob was born in Bavaria in 1837 and immigrated to the United States sometime between 1851 and 1861.[7] Niles's flamboyant account of his grandfather presents Reisch as an improbable Forest Gumpian character on a stage with Kaiser Wilhelm, P. T. Barnum, and "Jeb" Stuart. Although this colorful narrative is a little reckless with the truth, it reveals the central role that Reisch occupied in the family mythology and manifests Niles's own love of a well-embroidered tale.

My grandfather . . . left Germany in a great rush one night late in the year of 1849 after his military unit (he was an Uhlan) had revolted and tried to kill the grandfather of Kaiser William II.[8]

After that it was walking the roads of Germany by night and finally slipping over the frontier into Holland, and then a sailing ship (name by legend the Graf Frederic) and more than four weeks at sea, and finally in borrowed clothes he carried hod for P. T. Barnum. Mr. Barnum, (according to grandfather) was building a concert hall entitled Castle Garden, in which he hoped to present the Swedish nightingale, Jenny Lind.

In 1856 Jacob Augustus Reisch started south and settled in Richmond. Then like a bolt out of the sky came the news that a war was imminent. "*Ganz Gut*" cried Jake, for had he not been looking for a war this many a year? He did not know exactly why they were fighting or precisely who the enemy was. But all of a sudden, his unit, made up of local cavalier types, galloped away to the North. Grandfather fought in both battles in the Bull Run area. After the death of J. E. B. Stuart,[9] grandfather's unit was sent west and fought in the Battle of Chickamauga with General Hood.

In 1867, after wandering through Tennessee and Kentucky, he found himself in Louisville, where he pawned his thoroughbred, bought a team of Percherons, and went into the cartage business. He carted freight around the falls of the Ohio River. After that everything he touched turned to gold.[10]

Other family accounts painted Reisch's past in somewhat more muted tones, saying that he probably entered the Union Army by accident when he signed an army recruitment form rather than an immigration document. Instead of having a career as a dashing Confederate cavalry officer, he was a baker in the Union Quartermaster Corps, family members believed. It is doubtful that Reisch had a cartage business around the falls, since the canal made this service obsolete by 1830. Robert Niles (John Jacob Niles's nephew) told an alternative version of the family story that has a ring of veracity to it. Surely, it was the kind of story that was replayed many times by European immigrants during the Civil War:

I was told that Jacob Reisch came to this country in 1861 after having trouble with the German Army. When he got to Ellis Island, he didn't have any papers, spoke no English, and wanted to go to Cincinnati as he heard there was a large German population there. At this time, a New Yorker offered him $15.00 to take his place in the Union Army. He was really pleased because, by being a soldier, he could get by without speaking much English. When the army moved through Louisville, he realized that the west end of the city had a large German colony. He decided to come back to Louisville after the war.[11]

Reisch became a prosperous grocer, a saloon owner, a prominent local politician, and a successful entrepreneur. He ended up owning quite a bit of property as well as a major share of the German Bank, which later became the Portland Building and Loan Company.[12]

One story circulating among the Niles family links a substantial part of Jacob Reisch's fortune to his sales of whiskey to the workers who built the Portland canal. Although Reisch came around too late to sell laborers liquor during the initial construction of the canal, his grocery and saloon were certainly in operation during the 1871 expansion, and he could have accrued a tidy profit by supplying thirsty Irish canal workers with food and drink. The family store and residence located at 355 Portland would have been well situated in this regard, since it is but a few blocks away from the canal. Jacob was undoubtedly frugal with his money and property. One of the stories told about him was "that he always kept a guinea hen tied to his coal pile. In those days he would sell coal by the bucket, and every time he would hear the guinea hen start to make noise, he would grab his meat cleaver and run out back to catch people stealing coal."[13]

Jacob Reisch met and subsequently married Louise Adams, who lived three blocks away on Portland Avenue. Most probably they attended the same church and had many friends in common, although Louise was twelve years younger. Certainly Reisch would have been regarded as a very eligible bachelor, since he owned his own business. The terse language of an 1870 census record for Reisch notes: "Grocer, age 30, value of real estate $2,500, personal estate $1,000. Born in Bavaria. Louise is 21, keeping house, born in KY of foreign parents, a daughter Louisa born 9/12/70."[14]

The Reisch saloon must have served as a convivial, even raucous, community center. Years later Niles lovingly recalled the colorful roster of bartenders who kept folks well lubricated at the long bar: "Puss Eldridge (He'd been hit in the face sometime), Whole Hog Charlie (That's a kind of sausage you know), Bicycle Bill (he rode one of those tall bicycles with the big wheel), Tilepipe Leonard (God knows where that came from), Sinkhole Beasley (a sinkhole is something they have in this part of the country), and Slackjaw McGee (surprised in his early youth and never quite recovered)."[15]

While "Old Jake" Reisch is enshrined in family lore, Niles's paternal grandparents are but dimly recalled: "I never knew my paternal grandfather. He died long before I was born, and my father gave up going to school (he was twelve years old) and went to work in a broom factory where he sized broom straws for two dollars a week. Everyone said he was well paid. His mother went to reading to him. She actually was reading him an education of sorts. Before she married a Niles, her name was Nancy Tolliver Randolph. There were those who claimed that her family name was Renouff. They were most likely mistaken."[16]

In fact, it was Niles's account that was in error; he probably wished to claim that aristocratic Virginia Randolph lineage rather than the less distinguished Renouf surname. Niles's paternal great-grandparents were of English stock. Philip Renouf emigrated from England to Canada and then moved to the United States. By 1860 he was described as a forty-one-year-old carpenter with real estate valued at one thousand dollars and a personal estate worth forty dollars. He was married to a Canadian, Anna Renouf, who was thirty-nine years old.[17] The couple had a daughter, Ann Elizabeth, in Canada in 1845; a year later another daughter, Mary; and finally a son, John, born in New York in 1853. By 1860 the Renouf family was living in Portland at 1605 Portland Avenue and Philip was working as a driver at the Fischer-Leaf foundry.[18]

The Fischer-Leaf plant was in a busy industrial section of town where several furniture-making companies, tobacco warehouses, a fertilizer company, the Louisville Bridge Company, and a hominy mill clustered around the railroad bridge over the river. The grounds, between Fifteenth and Seventeenth streets on High Street, included a foundry, a coal yard, a tin shop, storage, and a slate cutting and marble area. Incidentally, the plant was just a few blocks away from the Reisch saloon.

The Niles family itself, according to family legend, stretched back five generations in Kentucky. John Jacob claimed that "five generations back, a man named John Niles looked an Indian in the face, fired his rifle, and at the same time received an arrow to his heart. John Niles and the Indian were buried in the same grave."[19] Nancy Niles Sexton said that John Tolliver Niles "came up the river from parts unknown," but she felt that the family originated on the Isle of Jersey.[20]

John Tolliver Niles, born in Kentucky about 1839, eventually met Ann Elizabeth Renouf (Runoph). The two were married March 22, 1863, at Louisville in a ceremony witnessed by Mary Niles and Philip Renouf.[21] By 1870 John Tolliver was a tobacconist and his family was living just about a block away from the Fischer-Leaf plant at Seventeenth Street between Portland and Baird streets. John and Ann had three children, Ida L. Niles in 1867, Mary E. Niles in 1868, and John Thomas Niles on May 11, 1869. By 1873 the Niles family lived just around the corner, at 203 Portland Avenue, near Seventeenth Street, but one year later John Tolliver had died; Ann, now a widow with three young children, moved to 32 Baird Street, near Eighteenth Street. Their home was a frame shotgun duplex with a tin roof, behind the Henry Nadorff Brewery and Ice Factory.

An amusing family anecdote confirms Ann's residence near the brewery: "Anna Niles had several geese and one day she looked out her back door and they were lying dead in the middle of winter. Being very poor and not one to waste of anything, she went out, got them, and plucked them for their feathers. In the process of doing this, to her surprise, the geese started to move around. She lived on Portland Avenue that backed up to the brewery, and a vat had leaked some beer in her back yard. Her geese were just so drunk, so she had a lot of geese for dinner."[22]

Life must have been difficult for Ann; she moved the family to two different meager frame shotgun homes on the same block, first 1715 and then 1711, before settling down at 1703 Portland Avenue. Her daughter Ida lived at home and worked as a seamstress for J. Newberger. John Thomas, as soon as he grew old enough, also took a series of jobs to help support the family. He is first listed as a barkeeper at the tender age of fourteen in 1883. Since the neighborhood saloon belonged to Jacob Reisch, it is likely that John Thomas first met Jacob's daughter Louisa there. He took other jobs, as a laborer in 1884 and one year later as a clerk; the following year he was working at the same Fischer-Leaf plant where his father had once been employed.

Thursday night, March 27, 1890, in Portland was much like any other, though it was particularly humid, a little too warm for early spring, and the sky glowed ominously. Folks had finished supper when the tornado struck sudden as a hammer blow. The next morning's *Courier-Journal* newspaper shouted headlines such as "Death and Disaster from Above," "Louisville Visited by the Storm Demon Last Evening," "The Greatest Calamity That Has Occurred in Its History," "The Path of the Tornado through the City Marked by Death," and "The Horrors of Conflagration Added to the Other Fearful Destruction." Although the tornado damaged the Seventh Street depot, tore ships from their moorings, and totally destroyed the recently completed Sawyer-Wallace tobacco warehouses, the worst of it struck the Falls City Market Building and orphaned John Thomas Niles. The second name on the *Courier-Journal*'s list of victims was "Miss Annie Nyles," Portland Avenue between Sixteenth and Seventeenth. Ann ("Annie") Niles was buried that Sunday, a day the paper characterized as the "saddest Palm Sunday that ever was passed in Louisville. So many were buried that the horses were driven at a trot."[23]

Intersecting Families

The Reisches had a comfortable German-American middle-class household in riverfront Portland in the Victorian era just following the Civil War. Their two-story brick home was heated by shallow, ornate coal-burning fireplaces manufactured by the local Fischer-Leaf Company. In the evening, gas lamps cast a warm golden glow on the dark wood burnished furniture, which included overstuffed and uncomfortable but very fashionable horsehair sofas. Outside, there was the smell of humid river air and dogwoods, redbud, and magnolias in fragrant bloom.

Inside, the Reisch family is gathered about an ornately carved square grand piano crafted by local maker John Adams. Young Louisa Sarah is playing a fashionable parlor song and singing; perhaps it is Henry Clay Work's "Come Home, Father." The family in the parlor is gently conversing, Jacob is contentedly smoking his clay pipe, Louise is humming along, and Louisa's brother Gustave is lying on the carpet recreating the battle of

John Jacob Niles Family Tree

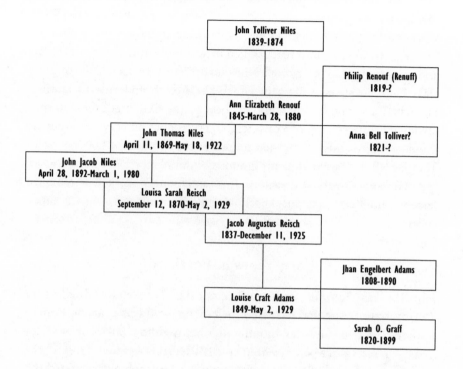

Gettysburg with his lead toy soldiers, while the old grandfather clock in the hallway paces off the seconds.

A knock at the door interrupts this tranquil scene. It is John Thomas Niles, hat in hand and dressed in his clean but threadbare best outfit. He is a little daunted by the relative opulence of the home and the stern, disapproving glance of old Jacob, but Louisa bounds off the piano stool, gently takes his arm, and guides him into the parlor. Her mother graciously inquires whether young Mr. Niles has dined and offers him refreshment. After some polite, if strained, conversation about Benjamin Harrison's tariff policies, Niles sits down next to Louisa on the piano bench and adds his strong, rough tenor to hers in the chorus of Foster's "Hard Times Come Again No More."

One year after his mother's funeral, John Thomas married Louisa Sarah Reisch on June 9, 1891, in a ceremony witnessed by George Mintz and Lucie Despair. There might well have been considerable opposition to the wedding on the part of the Reisch family. It is somewhat telling that the wedding was not witnessed by any family members. Louisa Sarah was educated (at St. Benedict's Academy, located between Thirty-fifth and Thirty-sixth streets), well read, skilled in accomplishments such as piano, and was expected to marry well. Niles, an orphan, was outside the middle-class German social milieu in which the Reisch and Adams families circulated. With no formal schooling beyond the sixth grade and few professional prospects, it took considerable persistence and courage to court the daughter of this established family. Forced to live by his wits, John Thomas Niles, described by his granddaughter Nancy Niles Sexton as an "artist dreamer," worked at various times as a foundry worker, a fireman, a farmer, a politician, a deputy sheriff, an entrepreneur, and a square-dance caller.

Early Years in Portland

John Thomas "Tommie" and Louisa Sarah "Lula" moved to a dwelling on Twenty-sixth Street that bordered the city line and was near the Roman Catholic Cemetery. Just ten months after her wedding, Lula delivered her first-born son at her parents' home on 121 North Twentieth Street.[24] On the morning of April 28, 1892, at 2:20 A.M., John Jacob Niles entered the world, crying out with a voice that would someday be characterized as the "electrifying C# alto."[25] Lula and Tommie had a daughter, Irene L. Niles, in 1894 and three more sons, Leland G. Niles in 1897, Robert J. Niles in 1903, and Charles R. Niles in 1906. During this time Tommie worked as a molder for the Fischer-Leaf Company until 1899, when he became employed as a fireman at the Customs House. For most of the shotgun houses crowding Portland's low-lying areas, sanitation was a real problem. Water was obtained from outside pumps, drains led out into open ditches, and many homes had outhouses located in the back part of their property. It was scarcely surprising that cholera epidemics swept through the community in the late nineteenth century. At age three, John Jacob (Johnnie) fell ill and nearly died. Back in 1886, Jacob and Louise Reisch's three-year-old son Jacob had died of cholera. Although Niles survived, he appears to have been a somewhat frail youngster, not physically robust;

he was inclined to be thoughtful and sensitive and was more introverted than socially effusive.

In the fall of 1897, five-year-old Niles was sent to the nearby Duncan Street School. Niles recalled his earliest school experiences: "The very first day I attended that 'institution of higher learning,' I was treated so badly by the big Irish boys of the community that I have never been able to forget it. They hated me because my father was a Republican and a Protestant. . . . As I grew up I began to realize that those school yard battles had very little to do with religion, but that the real reason for my troubles arose from the fact that I was a little bit different. I was odd, I was strange; and being different is dangerous."[26] Clearly very unhappy at the Duncan Street School, Niles attended another school the next fall; this one was on Montgomery Street, just west of the large Marine Hospital. He remained there for third and fourth grades and then returned to Duncan Street for the final two years of elementary school. Although formal education was not always a pleasant experience for him, Niles acquired a much more enjoyable and valuable education at home from his mother, who read literature to him in both English and German.

Musical Encounters

Niles's music education continued outside of school as well. He first encountered the orchestral and chamber-music world as an eight-year-old, in an experience that greatly affected the course of his career and eventually shaped the function and sound of his hand-crafted dulcimers. While there is little external evidence to support Niles's recollection of the Chicago Symphony Orchestra's 1900 visit to Louisville, the vivid accounting in Niles's autobiography reveals an event that must have been profoundly important to him. In fact he wanted to title his autobiography "Tympani on the Dulcimer" in an echo of this experience. As Niles reports it, his school principal called him into her office and announced that he had been chosen to sing in the children's chorus with an orchestra. He later learned from newspaper accounts that it was "the Chicago Orchestra" and that Theodore Thomas was the conductor. "I sat among the tubas and percussion," Niles writes, "and I could hardly watch the conductor for watching the players. The fifths and fourths in the kettle drums delighted me. Their effect I hoped to transfer to the dulcimer."[27]

That same year, after his ninth birthday, he was exposed to very different music, in an encounter that helped to shape his attraction to the full range of the cultural spectrum: he attended a hybrid medicine-minstrel show managed by a friend of his father, Melrose D. Pankhurst. In an early field notebook, he drew a diagram of the stage and noted, "Bony Miser Rockfish and Professor Pankhurst—medicine show—had about ten negro players and singers—stage four feet high—musicians were in costume."[28] This concise diary entry was amplified years later in his autobiography:

> The Pankhurst operation was set up very near my home, on a vast open lot bounded by 20th Street on the east, 22nd Street on the west, Bank Street on the north, and Rowan Street on the south. Pankhurst's show was actually a black-face minstrel show, except that all the performers were truly negroes, all males and all very talented. There were singers, pantomimes, a small group of actors who performed a hilarious after-piece called "A Wedding Break-fast in the Congo," and some expert soft-shoe dancers. And everyone, including the professor himself, could and did "double in brass" when the band played "Dixie."[29]

Louisville's entertainment scene was humming at the turn of the century; the coarser medicine and minstrel shows were elevated as vaudeville and Chautauqua, and the potent rural-urban brew of the jug band was just starting to distill. The riverfront nurtured a vibrant cultural exchange in which black and white cultures promiscuously shared ideas along class lines.

Minstrelsy developed in the streets of Louisville in 1870. According to Dale Cockrell, Thomas Dartmouth "Daddy" Rice probably first encountered the African American laborer who was the model for the character of "Jim Crow" there during the summer of 1870. Soon thereafter Rice developed a blackface act based on Crow's extravagantly leaping dance and catchy song and unleashed it on the stage of the Southern Theatre.[30] In much the same way, Niles and his future collaborator Marion Kerby appropriated facets of black culture in the name of popular culture by recontextualizing African American musical expression on the concert stage from 1928 to 1933.

Jug bands, though more commonly associated with Memphis, originated in Louisville right at the turn of the century as bands centered around Clifford Hayes melded rural blues styles and traditional string-band music with urban ragtime and early jazz.[31] Growing up in the city, Niles was steeped in the ragtime-like sounds of jug-band music, but he did not consciously collect it or perform it. Nevertheless, the fusion of urban and rural music would have resonated with him, and echoes of jug-band syncopations occasionally permeate his piano accompaniments.[32]

Vaudeville, which exerted a defining impact on Niles's career, also traced its American origins to Louisville. Borrowing the "variety show" approach of traveling medicine, minstrel, circus, and wild west shows, vaudeville institutionalized these itinerant performances in a more urban and urbane setting within established theaters. Vaudeville was founded on the pretensions of class upward mobility: impresarios hawked entertainment as high culture rather than huckstering snake-oil panaceas. The music, comedy, dance, acrobatics, and novelty acts of the earlier traveling shows were now larded with speeches and scenes from Shakespeare, and the general tone was elevated "to educate, edify, amaze, and uplift" the audience.[33]

The centrality of the vaudeville experience in Niles's life is tellingly reinforced by Niles himself. He elected to use an extended anecdote recounting his first paid performance to set the tone for his entire autobiography. In some ways; this account encapsulates Niles's "middlebrow" navigation of high and low art expression that is the hallmark of vaudeville intent. A short entry of June 1907 in his notebook provides a concise summary: "Saturday afternoon to Amusement Park to hear entertainment. . . . Performers drunk. Luncheon with bourbon—was called on to play piano. Was picked out of house. Filled in for drunken cast. Piano terrible. Manager sent out of town for anybody who could play piano or sing. Picked me out of the house. . . . Barber shop quartette, I sang tenor. Blossom Quartette was greatest success of the afternoon. After the Ball. $1.50."[34] Niles's autobiography vividly fills the narrative gaps, describing his experiences of improvising, singing, and accompanying a variety of acts on the piano before closing: "I had not untied the fabulous winds of change, but I had made a dollar and fifty cents at the chosen profession of my life. And I had held an unruly audience in my hand—forever after that wonderful afternoon nothing ever pleased me quite so much."[35] That intoxicating afternoon firmly pointed Niles to a stage career, where his charisma, bravado, and showmanship were valued assets.

Collecting and Preserving

Several years earlier, Niles had encountered the very different world of folklore in an initial song-collecting experience. This pursuit demanded very different skills to accurately document a musical event and faithfully notate and analyze the context. Charisma, bravado, and showmanship merely distract from the objective transcription and reflection necessary for examining oral culture. A faithful rather than a fanciful ear and an observant eye rather than a storyteller's tongue are essential qualities for a folklorist.

Niles's role as a folklorist poses one of the more problematic aspects of his career. Scholars have been justifiably suspicious of his methodology, his commentary, his transcriptions, and his sources. The colorful raconteur who never let the "dull facts interfere with a good yarn" certainly embroidered stories concerning the people and places of his music-collecting adventures. There is also no doubt that he "borrowed" phrases of text or tune and created new songs based on the original skeleton. Furthermore, in his early publications with Carl Fischer and G. Schirmer, Niles was somewhat disingenuous with attributions, ambiguously claiming some of his original songs to be folk songs yet citing the same songs as his original compositions for copyright and royalty consideration.[36] These two contradictory impulses—creating and collecting, presenting and preserving—were successfully resolved in Niles's composition in the style of folk music and fully integrated in his performance manner and repertoire. However, they consistently remained an obstacle to his later efforts to be taken seriously as a folklorist and scholar.

Niles's narrative concerning his first collecting experience revealingly demonstrates the way in which his documentation is entangled with his song-writing. The goal of his collecting was not to preserve the music for posterity but to provide grist for his own imagination and a source for his personal performance repertoire. He explains that it was the late summer of 1899 when he first "came into contact with the magical process of folklore recording." While he and his mother were visiting the Graham family, his mother learned that the great-grandmother of the Graham family, along with three siblings, "used to sing a little family song at Christmas time." He listened as

> Granny began singing in a wavy, indefinite ancient voice. The lack of teeth did not improve her diction, and all the while my mother did her best to get something down on paper. . . . The old granny repeated the same line several times:
>
> Jesus, Jesus, rest your head
> You has got a corn-shuck bed.
>
> My mother took it all down very carefully and put it in her pocketbook. For the next nine years, this precious piece of manuscript rested among her handkerchiefs.[37]

The manuscript at some point was moved to the piano bench, where it lay forgotten until Niles finally retrieved it in December 1906. As documented in his second field notebook, Niles overlaid the Graham family's folk fragment with his compositional artifice, completing the tune and expanding the text. Eventually, the song born of Niles's first folk collecting experience was published as "Jesus, Jesus, Rest Your Head" in 1922 and became one of his most enduring compositions.

2

The Move to Rural
Jefferson County

On September 22, 1902, Niles's father moved the family away from Louisville to Inverness Farm in rural Jefferson County. There are various possible reasons for this change in lifestyle. It might have been an attempt by Tommie Niles to improve his financial affairs. John Jacob Niles indicated that his father had "a huge load of debts" at this time.[1] Or perhaps it was an attempt to escape the cholera epidemics. Probably it was the best way to provide a larger space for the rapidly expanding family. This must have been a challenging move, away from the close-knit Reisch family, away from friends and relations, away from the neighborhood, and away from the culture and comforts of the city. For Niles, who was ten, this must have been a particularly difficult transition to a completely different life style; piano lessons in the city were exchanged for daily chores such as milking cows.

As difficult as the transition was, the move to rural Jefferson County provided Niles with a range of experiences that were later useful. Life lived in both city and country prepared Niles for folk collecting experiences at isolated mountain farms as well as for elegant receptions following Women's Club concerts. In the future he proved to be equally comfortable in rural or urban settings, whether it be the rustic John C. Campbell Folk School in the North Carolina mountains or New York City's bohemian Greenwich Village. Later in life, gatherings at his Boot Hill Farm in Clark

County reflected a remarkable mix of elegant earthiness in which local farmers freely mingled with sophisticated European émigrés. Boot Hill conversations could run the gamut from blue mold on the tobacco crop to the latest opera production in Paris. Symbolically, the elevated wooden floor in the farmhouse's spacious living room served as both a salon stage and a root cellar.

Growing up on the subsistence farm, Niles had his feet solidly planted on the earth, but his head still floated in the clouds. In between chores and schoolwork, he found ample time to dream, invent, and follow his musical instincts. In 1905 he left school for a year to work the farm, but he also devised a perpetual motion machine, successfully implemented a crop-fertilization technique, collected ballads and composed anthems for church, constructed an airplane, and developed plans for an automobile brake light. Niles's inventive ability to create whatever was needed from the materials at hand is reflected in his brake-light anecdote. His note-book 45/1 presents a detailed diagram for constructing the light, and he explains in his autobiography:

> Two early-model Cadillac automobiles arrived in Louisville. . . . Not far from the Confederate monument on south Third Avenue, the first of the Cadillacs stopped suddenly, and the second one (following too closely) crashed into it with a resounding bang. Parts of both bodies were bent, and the drivers bawled at one another. I joined some of the curious public.
>
> About sundown that afternoon I went out with an apple and a carrot to bait my rabbit traps. They were box traps, the kind with a small door sliding up and down at one end. The door is held up by a fulcrum that is released if a rabbit or other unfortunate smallish creature happens to go into the trap and nibble on the bait. The automobile accident I had observed a few hours earlier flashed before my eyes. I realized that I could contrive a lightweight wooden box quite like my rabbit trap, put an oil lantern in it, provided with a red lamp shade, which would be covered by the lowered door in normal driving and exposed in emergencies, by attaching the fulcrum to the foot and/or hand brake. Later that evening I explained my plan to my father, who

encouraged me to make such a signal box and send it to Mr. R. E. Olds, who was then one of the leading automobile makers in the country.

The "signal box" was sent off, and about a month later a letter arrived from the great Mr. Olds. He congratulated me because I had come upon the idea at such an early age, and advised me to go to engineering school and become an accredited mechanical engineer. He said the invention showed real thinking on my part but said there would never be enough automobiles on our highroads to make such a refinement valuable or necessary. My father read the letter to me several times. Then he wadded it up in the palm of his hand and threw it into the fireplace.[2]

After his year of freedom from school, Niles returned to Louisville's DuPont Manual Training High School, at the corner of Brook and Oak streets. The school's mission complemented Niles's interests, since it sought "to provide young men with a system of education which would fit them, in a more direct and positive manner for the actual duties of life." The curricula consisted of a three-year program that would "prepare a large number of boys with skills to earn their living in industrial pursuits." Given Niles's evident disinterest in school and his passion for inventing and designing, Manual seemed a good choice.[3]

Niles described himself as a first-year student at Manual in the following terms:

In 1906 I had almost reached my full height and although my weight was only 128 pounds, I could work beside any farmhand we had. I usually played piano at night when the house was quiet, and then again after breakfast, with a clean mind, my milking and my early chores done. During the day I usually worked on an acre of land, and from it I extracted rations for the family. . . . Here I was, nearly full grown, playing piano and/or organ with reasonable skill, bringing home a fair report from Manual Training School, working diligently at whatever farm work was required, bringing in Siberian kale and wild greens, walnuts, late mushrooms, persimmons, and wild game occasionally. But I gave the

appearance of being a pure clodhopper though it did not occur to
me that there was anything the matter with that.[4]

First Fieldwork and Song Composition

Although Niles might have regarded himself as a "pure clodhopper," as
a high school student he was precociously engaged in some decidedly
sophisticated musical activity. The years 1906 to 1909 mark an initial period of folk music collecting that provided him with some of his earliest
performance repertoire as well as ballads that were published years later
in *The Ballad Book*. He was also writing his first original compositions,
several of which became the most popular and successful of his career.

In summer 1906, Niles started collecting folk songs in his little notebooks. That July he transcribed a family version of "I Had a Cat and the
Cat Pleased Me," a variant of "Old McDonald Had a Farm" that he had
learned from his father. This charming children's song, with the cumu-
lative verses simulating different animal sounds, remained a part of his
repertoire for the rest of his life and ended up on recordings for both
the Folkways and Tradition labels.[5] A year later, he accompanied his father to Manchester, Kentucky, in Clay County, where he met "Granny"
Cilla Baker of Redbird Creek and notated her singing of the Child ballad
"Lord Bateman." At this point he was already aware of the subtle social requirements of fieldwork; for example, a subject had to be made comfortable with the process of recording. Mastering the art of "palaver" opened
doors and loosened tongues. Niles recounts the visit:

> I got on with this grand old woman without the slightest diffi-
> culty. As soon as we got through the usual palaver (which I was
> beginning to understand), Granny Baker asked me what songs
> I sang, and where I had learned them. Then I sang a shape note
> hymn to the accompaniment of a smallish dulcimer I spied hang-
> ing on the wall. . . . Before the evening was out Granny Baker sang
> all twenty-five verses of what she called "Bateman and Suzie." She
> was in her eighty-second year and she never missed a verse, nor
> had to go back and repeat. I took down the text as she sang and
> then wrote down her music.[6]

In June 1908 Niles collected "Way Down Yonder and a Long Ways Off," which he titled "Jaybird" when he reworked it for inclusion in the Niles-Kerby repertoire of 1928. His notebook also recalled the source: "Mrs. Stewart and Liz Smith (sister). Jaybird Song of Dick Stewart lazy loafer who never works—lives off his old mother and father at Valley Station Farm—a great family gone to pot—once owned all of Kenwood Hill area." Niles even attached this family's family tree in his notebook.[7] At a time when the process of folk collection in the southern Appalachian region was still very much in its infancy, it seems remarkable that this farm boy and high school student saw the value of preserving the old-time songs. It was even more remarkable that he took such care to record details about the people from whom he was collecting the music.[8]

The Dull Facts and a Good Yarn

John Jacob benefited musically by accompanying his father on trips such as those to Manchester or to Reelfoot Lake, which sprawled across northwestern Tennessee into Fulton County, Kentucky. There he documented the five songs that were eventually arranged as the set of Gambler's Songs.[9] Niles also had the presence of mind to realize that music could be collected closer at hand as well. In the summers of 1908 and 1909, he documented songs in the southeastern portion of Jefferson County from Pete Mullenoux, Harkus and Tillie Whitman, Carter and Brother Patterson, and Kate Stewart. During these sessions he took down numerous texts and tunes in his notebooks, including "Two Old Crows," "Pretty Polly," "The Jeweled Ring," and "Robin Hood and the Old Maid" from Mullenoux; "The Parsley Vine," "The Shirt of Lace," "Oh Judy, My Judy," and "Barbara Allen" from the Whitmans; and "The Dreary Dream" from Kate Stewart. An account of his work with the Pattersons is representative of these experiences. In each case, the journal notebooks document a text and a tune and append some brief commentary. The notebook accounts provide grist for anecdotes that marry the song and the source for the next seventy years. The autobiographical accounts garrulously expand those in the journal, whereas *The Ballad Book* presents a more restrained and objective narrative. Consider the different versions and voices that

Niles adopted over the years in depicting an encounter with the Patterson family on July 5, 1908.

The original journal entry tersely notes, "Uncle Brother Patterson is the most down trodden of all the down trodden Pattersons—a very interesting melodic line—music came from Patterson grandmother from Virginia."[10] Years later, in the autobiography, Niles wrote an amplified, dialect-laced, fully developed story complete with moral, just as though he were presenting a spoken introduction to a song in a performance:

> Being that young, I thought I understood squalor. A sixteen-year-old boy should understand squalor, particularly if his mother is a do-right. But to the Patterson family, squalor was no novelty. Indeed, the Pattersons simply thrived on squalor, and very few of them were the slightest bit literate. . . .
>
> Twenty years previous, Uncle Brother was a rich and wide-swiping spender; his enterprises were farming and herding. One night in a Hay market brawl, blood was spilled, and when the law had done with him, Uncle Brother was on his way to prison. My father had observed the trial and tried to benefit this flamboyant farmer, but to no avail. Once Uncle Brother was in close confine (prison) my mother began writing letters. She knew well that Uncle Brother could neither read nor write, but when this unfortunate was freed, he carried a neat bundle of letters tied with a greasy piece of hemp string, many of which had never been opened. They were his treasure trove. . . . Once when father visited him, I was taken along.
>
> We arrived on a Sunday and discovered that the Pattersons lived in a series of tin shacks on the side of a smallish creek in eastern Jefferson County. . . . Both Carter Patterson and Brother Patterson sang and I wrote both of these items in my little black book and, as fate would have it, they turned out to be "The Parsley Vine" and "The Shirt of Lace," and were published in *The Ballad Book of John Jacob Niles* fifty-two years later.[11] Of course, I sang. It had to be unaccompanied. . . . They wanted us to stay for a meal of victuals, but my father, being wiser than we all, thanked them "no" and told them we had to get home to our own victuals. Then Brother said, "As a fellow says, you got a dinner at home

cooked up by your mommie, the one that wrote me all those letters whilst I was in close confine." I was at once on the verge of tears, and when my father shook endless hands and thanked them all and told them goodbye, his voice was a bit clouded with emotion. Just before we left, Carter Patterson said, addressing my father, "Tommie, might as well let the boy enjoy hisself, the whilst he's young, 'cause a man-person ain't much use to himself oncet he's dead." Father nodded and shook the reins. We moved off.[12]

If the journal account is etched in black and white, the autobiography account sings in living color with 3-D glasses. Finally, the *Ballad Book* recounts the experience more directly and economically.

Uncle Brother Patterson (that is the way his name appeared on the county engineer's paybook) was Carter Patterson's brother. He was much older than the other men in the family and he was much more silent. The others were full of fun but Uncle Brother was on the sad side as a rule. He had been a cattle drover as a young man, and had once owned a very fine farm; but he ran afoul of the law and lost it all. It seems that there was some bloodshed in a saloon in the old Haymarket section of Louisville, KY in the winter of 1880. According to Uncle Brother's story, it was a sort of drunken brawl over some strayed cattle. Uncle Brother came out alive, but when the law took leave of him, the century had turned. He spent the remainder of his life living as a vagabond, doing occasional odd jobs and working in the forests. He had heard his noisy relatives sing the rather uninteresting "Parsley Vine" song, and to establish his position as a singer he took me aside and sang "The Shirt of Lace." Very quietly and accurately. None of the Patterson men could read or write.[13]

These three intersecting yet wildly divergent perspectives on the same story raise interesting yet troubling issues concerning Niles's intentionality and veracity. From a vaudevillian vantage point, it was wonderful for Niles to have such vibrant stories available to sell the songs that he made his own in performance. Surely it enhanced the somewhat abstract dramatic narrative of a Child ballad to invest the ballad's provenance with the story of a vagabond from a fine but fallen family who had been imprisoned for a crime of passion. Presenting both the ballad story and the source's story was like the literary device of a "play within a play" of complementary narratives. Furthermore, coupling the song with a story added credibility to the ballad story by authenticating the source and certifying the pedigree of the song's transmission lineage.

In the world of folk orality, it is also well within established tradition for a storyteller to relate the same tale over and over again, embroidering the core of fact with new elaborations each time. In fact, this very ornamentation and variation is the hallmark of a skillful raconteur. Curiously, such layering of fiction on fact often serves to reveal truth more clearly, like a Halloween costume that reveals far more than it conceals.

Niles's collecting anecdotes were not much different from traditional "Jack Tales" for him. They were just entertaining stories that he could employ to entertain and enlighten an audience. More pragmatically, the patter also served as a bridge between songs and provided "cover" while he changed instruments or retuned his dulcimers. Given his father's reputation as a storyteller and Niles's own dramatic flair, the dual role of storyteller and musician was far more suited to his temperament than a potential career as a "pure" interpretive pianist or opera singer.

While folklorists *study* folk tales and the process of storytelling, a folklorist would hardly confuse the role of a scholar with that of the storyteller itself—but that is exactly what Niles did. Because his stories were larded with fiction, his versions of the ballads were also dismissed as willfully "doctored up," or they were perceived as instances of Niles's own composition being falsely passed off as folk expression.[14] If Niles had been content to limit his creative impulses to his charismatic performance style and his original composition, he would never have engendered this criticism; but in fact he incited it through the academic contexts he eventually sought for his music in lectures and publications.

In the Field

This initial period of Niles's folk collecting, bounded by his high school years (1905–1909), produced an interesting mix of repertoire. While

Child and native American ballads certainly dominated, there were also lyric folk songs, recreational songs, carols, and even street cries. The generation of music collectors who preceded Niles into the field concentrated almost entirely on the ballads, avoiding the other musical forms that were just as surely a part of the folk repertoire. But Niles recorded whatever was at hand. His collecting agenda was not yet shaped by external prejudices; instead, he was guided by curiosity and an ear for what might prove to be a useful contribution to his personal performance and composition repertoire.

Cecil Sharp (1859–1924) and Maude Karpeles (1885–1976) did not collect dance music because they felt that "the instrumental tunes which were played as accompaniments to the dance were of little value."[15] Niles made no such cultural value judgments—he failed to collect dance tunes for pragmatic reasons. He was a pianist rather than a fiddler, and he usually did not play for dances. Similarly, Niles had no aversions to collecting sacred music. He collected none at this time just because the music he heard in church already existed in published Lutheran and Baptist hymnals. Collecting music was not a goal in itself; it was merely the means for creating a useful personal performance repertoire.

Even the most insignificant musical expression could prove valuable in this regard. For instance, in 1905 he documented a short "street cry," noting: "Black Tom pushes a little cart—Horseradish, horseradish, Old Black Tom never lies, ground horseradish for yo' eyes, horseradish, horseradish."[16] Twenty-five years later this cry and several others were described in an article published in *Scribner's Monthly* and woven into a musical arrangement that was recorded by Niles on RCA.[17] Niles's activity predates Alan Lomax's 1937 street-cry recordings (on Archives of American Folksong 878–944) and Herbert Halpert's extensive fieldwork conducted in March–June 1939 (AFS 3624–3672), but there is also a world of difference in purpose. Whereas Lomax's and Halpert's documentary recordings were strictly preservationist, Niles's street-cry collecting was directed toward personal performance and composition; his work is really in the lineage of Elizabethan settings, such as the *Street Cryes of London* by Orlando Gibbons (1583–1625). It is safe to assume that Niles's original "horseradish cry" was collected naively, whereas his later arranging and composition activity with the street cry was influenced by familiarity with the Elizabethan genre encountered during his music studies in France at the Université de Lyon (1918) and at the Cincinnati Conservatory (1920–1922).

In Church

The sacred music Niles composed during this period consisted of original hymns and anthems that were written for specific churches upon specific occasions. He had been singing and playing in church since he was a child, but one gets the feeling that he was drawn to the musical and aesthetic aspects of worship far more than the mystical aspect of liturgical religion. His garden provided a source for his spiritual refreshment, while the church contributed a social community and a convenient stage and audience for his musical development. In later years he called himself a Buddhist, but he also was closely associated with the Episcopal Church and its grand musical tradition.[18] Notebook entries indicate that his first sacred music compositions were completed during his senior year of high school. In April 1908 he wrote a hymn for the Beechmont Baptist Church;[19] this incident was significant because the organist there was Roberta Voorhies (1895–1919), his future wife. One month later he wrote a new hymn but noted, "It is a bit complicated for singers—mother thinks Chopin has gotten into the accompaniment."[20] Niles's autobiographical account of these early anthems reflects on his longstanding Marian devotion.

> One choir director gave me $1.50, while the other (from a poorer group) gave me a dollar. To say that I was delighted no end would be an understatement. . . . I found the original sketches of the two pieces tied up in a great bundle with many others, where they had been gathering dust while I made the war. I burned them, so no one could discover how tiresome a composer, poet, and arranger I was when rising fifteen. The text of one of these Christmas anthems concerned the birth of our Lord and Master, Jesus Christ, and of course, there were references to the Blessed Mother. My wife, Rena, whose judgment is of the best, declares that I fell in love with the Blessed Mary when I was fourteen years of age; and

have never been able to tell of all my adoration and affection in all the complicated versions of what happened in Bethlehem of Judeah two thousand years ago. This is perchance why preachers and priests have tried, in spite of the limits of my faith to recruit me as a member of their orders. They have failed in every way and meanwhile made me into a hand-hammered Zen Buddhist.[21]

Despite Niles's "limits of faith," he embraced a passionate interest in the Nativity during the rest of his life, as reflected in his composition or arrangement of at least sixty-two carols.

Go 'Way from My Window

In some ways, a look at the genesis of "Go 'Way from My Window" provides a most revealing window on Niles's entire life and career up to 1909. The ability to fuse the roles of collector and composer was invaluable to Niles's compositional and performance repertoire. He had a talent for "recycling," by taking a small fragment of song or text and developing a whole new work around the core, like creating a pearl around a grain of sand. Niles referred to this impulse to create something new out of what was at hand when he said on one occasion, "I'm convinced that a concert singer who is not also a composer and poet is at a distinct disadvantage. Perhaps this point of view goes back to my early years: when I was a child growing up in Kentucky, we made what we needed."[22]

"Go 'Way from My Window," Niles's first original "song in the style of folk music," springs from a collecting experience during his high school years. In 1907 he recorded a single line of text from an African American worker: "A powerful black man named Objerall Jacket (that is how he appeared in the weekly paybook) had been working on a trenching operation, and I worked some of the day beside him. He grunted out a piece of folk work-song all day long to lighten his labor with the pick and long-handled shovel. I took the words of a portion of his song and turned them around in my mind, then proceeded to compose four additional verses."[23] This account is largely buttressed by evidence contained in Niles's notebooks. His earliest entry documents this as "a song for Heidy" (Moore) and notes the text "Go way from my window, go way from my door" set to a seven-note melody line.[24] The next entry expands the poem in the following passage: "Blanche Juckett—pretty girl. . . . I had written a poem for her and was setting it to music. Poem for Blanche: I'll walk by your window, I'll walk by your door, I'll walk by your bedside, And bother you no more."[25]

A sketch dated June 17, 1908, and marked "A" presents a developed form of the tune and the text. There are two different melody sketches here, one based on a simplistic repetition of minor thirds and another marked "or perhaps" that mirrors the final form that the tune took except for a different final phrase. Niles also experimented with several versions of the first verse. This is version A:

> Please go way from my window,
> Please go way from my door,
> Please go way from my bed,
> And bother me no more.
>
> If I walked by your window,
> And asked you to go from my door,
> As I walked by your window,
> And said don't hunt me no more.[26]

A sketch dated May 1909 and marked "B" transposes the tune to the key of D and presents three stanzas and the first line of a fourth stanza. It is interesting to compare the working version of the second stanza with its final form. The subtle change of "But you I never will forget" to "I'll ne'er forget my own true love" removes the grammatical clumsiness and also universalizes the statement to make it relevant to any singer or listener.

> I'll give you back your presents,
> Your slender golden ring,
> But you I never will forget,
> As long as songbirds sing.[27]
>
> I'll give you back your letters,
> I'll give you back your ring,

But I'll ne'er forget my own true love,
As long as songbirds sing,
As long as songbirds sing.[28]

In a subsequent sketch labeled "C" and dated September 26, 1908, Niles completed the entire melody and the first two stanzas of text. The melody is in the same key as the original fragment, and the second stanza of text is essentially the same as what eventually became the third stanza. The pages following "Sketch C" reveal Niles's methodology for working with rhymes. Here he lists all the letters of the alphabet and then proceeds to list rhymes for "door," "ring," and "too." In this way, he crafted the rhymed text for the second and fourth lines of each strophe.[29]

Sketch C also notes Blanche Juckett's rejection of the song as a gift. "There is no use offering a song to some young ladies. They simply want it all—wonderful tune and perfectly clear text—I mean the poem. So I shall put it down and forget it. Blanche is so easily offended."[30] This rejection is intensified in another field notebook:

Go Way from My Window is a great disappointment. Blanche won't take it as a gift. She laughed and laughed.
  1) I am no good as a beaux
  2) I am not a very good dancer
  3) and always poor mouthed
  4) no musician (can't play fiddle)
    Put Go Away in piano seat to forget. Am going to try for a job with county survey.[31]

Niles's autobiography recast this rejection in a narrative form based on his spoken introductions to the song in concert situations.[32]

The disappointments of my fifteenth and sixteenth years piled up when, a few days after Christmas, Miss Blanche Juckett handed me a rather rumpled copy of my first opus, "Go Way from My Window." Along with the music she delivered herself of a rather insulting speech in which she said I was no composer, no singer, no poet; and as I was more than a year younger than she (and broke in the bargain), I was naturally no "sort of catch" for a girl to consider. . . . At that time we had a piano bench like many another, with a seat that could be lifted up, covering a space usually full of discarded music. Into this "cold storage" I threw my precious MS, where it remained nearly twenty-two years.[33]

Like the parallel narratives that introduced his ballads, this anecdote concerning Juckett's rejection of both his love and his song ingeniously fulfilled the "play within a play" purpose. On one level, the girl's rejection of his gift parallels the unrequited love of the song's subject, who sings, "I'll give you back your letters, I'll give you back your ring." On a deeper psychological level, the rejection could even refer to critics' spurning of Niles's gift of song—with the "last laugh" tag ending "they were mistaken, of course."

Despite the popularity of "Go 'Way from My Window," there was an undercurrent of negative criticism.[34] Niles was accused of plagiarizing the Elizabethan English love song "Goe from My Window" that was represented in several theme and variation works by Thomas Morley and John Munday contained in the *Fitzwilliam Virginal Book*.[35] The song survived as a "folk" song recorded by revival singers such as Ronnie Gilbert and was also documented in African American tradition by Alan Lomax.[36] However, these versions share no text commonality with Niles's composition beyond the similarity of the first line. Musically, they are totally distinct, so there is no reason to doubt the origin of Niles's collection, adaptation, and composition of his song. In fact, the opening motif, "Go away from my door," was in such common currency that Bob Dylan even incorporated it into his "It Ain't Me Babe."[37] Comparing the following three versions of the first stanza should make it obvious that there was no plagiarism afoot in the use of the common verse. The first version is Niles's, the second Ronnie Gilbert's, and the third Bob Dylan's. In fact, if there was plagiarism, it was by folksingers who later recorded Niles's original song and claimed that it was "traditional" or "anonymous."

Go 'way from my window,
Go 'way from my door,
Go 'way, way from my bedside,
And bother me no more.

Go from my window, my love, my love,
Go from my window, my love,
Oh the wind is blowing high,
And the ship is lying by,
And you cannot get a harboring here.

Go 'way from my window,
Leave at your own chosen speed.
I'm not the one you want, babe,
I'm not the one you need.

Graduation

Niles's comments regarding his graduation from Manual High School present a glance over his shoulder to the past and a confident glimpse ahead to the future. As might be expected, the occasion was mostly another opportunity to appear on stage, and Niles evinces considerably more interest in his costume and performance in the Shakespeare play than in anything else having to do with graduation. The commencement exercise and reception are just a sideshow for the theatrical event. His plans for the future include working for a surveying crew. Since his family was financially insecure, Niles was always careful to plan and document all his expenditures. He wrote in his notebook:

> McCauley's Theatre, Walnut Street between 3rd and 4th. I played the soothsayer in Julius Caesar and wore a wonderful costume. I had only a few lines but they were delivered well Prof. Jones said. Later we received our diplomas. This is the end of my schooling in Louisville. I am sad to leave these wonderful boys—the ones I have been with so long. I am 17. I have a good job with in the civil engineering dept. of the city and county. I will get $40 dollars a month—10 cents carfare 20 cent lunch 30 X 24=720 so I shall have 32 and 80 left each month.[38]

Here, at the end of June 1908, the world begins to unfold for young Jack Niles.

3

Independence and Adventure

With his diploma in hand, Niles immediately started work with the county survey crew, cutting brush, dragging chains, and driving stakes. The hard labor was not much more challenging than work on the family farm, but unlike farm work, it provided an income—most of which went to his family to help pay off his father's debts. By the end of the summer, Niles had worked his way into more of a desk job.[1] Once in the main office, Niles went to work in the calculating department, where he soon put his practical skills to work repairing Brunsviga adding machines.[2]

Niles's talent for fixing the machines caught the attention of the Burroughs Adding Machine Company, which hired him in August 1910 and retained his services for the next six years.[3] Burroughs at this time was beginning to extend its tendrils into a society that required fast new ways of calculating the business concerns of rapidly expanding industries and mercantile operations. Burroughs was based in Detroit, where its 70,304-square-foot plant manufactured just under a thousand machines per year. *Modern Business* lauded the product: "It brings mechanical skill almost to the point of human intelligence . . . it is amazing, but true."[4]

Niles worked as a "mechanical inspector" for a year in Louisville, during which time he traveled about central Kentucky repairing machines. These travels also conveniently served as an excuse to collect songs. At Christmastime 1910 he recorded a sketch of "Ef I Had a Ribbon Bow," taken from the singing of a young mother living in Ebenezer, Mercer County, along the Kentucky River. He eventually adapted the tune and text, added a piano accompaniment, and published it in his collection *Seven Kentucky Mountain Songs.*[5] At the same time he also transcribed a sketch of "How Old Are You My Pretty Little Miss"—a different and earlier version than the one he eventually collected from Anne M. Hensley in the early 1930s.

In the Bluegrass

Niles was growing ever more independent through his job and work-related travels, and in 1912 he moved completely away from home for the first time. The Burroughs Company decided to relocate Niles to their Lexington office, thereby introducing him to the city where he eventually resided from 1937 until his death. On May 2, 1912, Niles boarded the Chesapeake and Ohio train for the eighty-mile trip from Louisville to Lexington and settled in at his boarding house and his office in the very heart of town, facing the courthouse. He described his boardinghouse as "high class" with excellent food and soft beds. "But," he lamented, "the piano was out of tune."[6]

Throughout his life, Niles made notes about the condition of the pianos with which he was confronted. Given the quantity of terribly tuned pianos that he was compelled to play, it is little wonder that he seized on the idea of using the dulcimer for his accompaniment rather than rely on instruments that he could neither carry nor tune himself.

Lexington was a fortuitous choice for Niles's first move. It was a much smaller city than Louisville, but it maintained a thriving cultural life, reflected in its sobriquet "Athens of the West." Lexington served as a bustling agricultural market for the surrounding bourbon, tobacco, and horse industries. The town was particularly lively during "Court Days," when rural folks congregated in the city's central market for trading, gossip, and entertainment. Niles's portrait describes the lively scene just outside his office door right after moving to Lexington: "I was introduced to Lexington in a glamorous manner on Fayette County Court day. It seemed to me that the entire county had turned out, men women, children, grandfathers, grandmothers, whites and blacks, preachers and fakers and sharpers, interlarded with a goodly number of plainclothes police. Of course there were horse traders and hound swappers, pocketknife traders, peddlers of cures, nostrums, love powders, old household articles and new. Children cried almost continuously."[7]

The move to Lexington also served to expand Niles's music repertoire by placing him near a variety of rural communities. Collecting folk music was an exceedingly challenging process at the onset of the twentieth century. Once in a community, Niles had to ascertain who the local musicians were. Simply identifying a subject was problematic because there was no public forum for performance; they could be located only by reputation and word of mouth. There was also a certain moat of distrust that had to be bridged, since Niles was a stranger and his motives for collecting music were unclear. Most of his informants had never sung for anyone other than family, and they were understandably uncomfortable or even hostile. Niles had to gain the confidence of the singer and make him or her feel relaxed enough to sing while Niles took down the music through dictation. Finally, there were simply the physical challenges posed by locating and arriving at the destinations. Travel by foot, mule, horse, or automobile was usually difficult and sometimes dangerous when one was following vague directions to a remote settlement down a holler or up a mountain, or fording a stream into deep woods.

Surmounting all the adversities, Niles was able to note several carols that he later incorporated into his publication *Ten Christmas Carols from the Southern Appalachian Mountains*. "See Jesus the Savior" was acquired from a "tall beautiful dirt poor woman deserted by her husband" at Index, Morgan County, Kentucky, and he transcribed "Come Sing All Men 'Tis Christmas Morning" from the singing of Amanda Hogarthy, a "cook in Lexington's outskirts on Georgetown Pike."[8]

Niles was particularly vigilant in his search for ballads. During this year he collected the text for "Lord Thomas and Fair Ellender" from Betty May Smathers of Mount Sterling, "The Old Woman and the Devil" from a "granny woman at Jackson," and "The Bold Peddler" from the singing of Aunt Etta Smithy at the "fork of road between Corbin and Middlesboro."[9] But perhaps the most valuable experience for him occurred closer to home, on a trip back to Louisville to visit his parents in August. While down at the river, he met Augusta Singleton, who was fishing from a houseboat, and collected a version of "The Hangman." "She sang a version of 'The Maid Freed from the Gallows' to an unforgettable tune," he explains in his autobiography. "Naturally, I took down her song as fast as she sang it, and this pleased me and surprised her no end. She called her version 'Granny and the Golden Ball.'"[10]

In addition to the collecting activities in and around Lexington, several performance opportunities presented themselves. Niles started playing piano in a saloon on Limestone Street off Main Street. The owner wanted dinner music, and so he hired Niles along with a trumpet player, a "very versatile drummer who could double with the comb and xylophone," and an old-time fiddler.[11] This regular gig paid a dollar for an evening's work and furnished Niles with dinner and beer as well. It also led to an intriguing opportunity to perform at Kentucky's most infamous brothel, Belle Brezing's establishment.

Belle Brezing (1880–1940) bought the three-story house at 59 Megowan and Wilson streets, near Transylvania University, in 1894 and established an elegant bordello that attracted a wealthy and powerful clientele until the U.S. Army closed it in 1917. It is commonly asserted that Brezing served as the model for Belle Watling in Margaret Mitchell's *Gone with the Wind*. Having heard of Niles, Brezing invited him to gather a vocal quartet to sing carols at her Christmas morning breakfast. Niles was not above singing in the whorehouse, and his notes record that he sang "Jesus, Jesus, Rest Your Head," "The King Shall Come," "Silent Night," "Joy to the World," "O Come, O Come Emmanuel," and "Go 'Way from My Window." He also noted, "Very pretty whores at breakfast (good table manners) 25 dollars etc. Mrs. Belle said come back anytime."[12] Niles certainly had no problems intertwining the sacred and profane, singing his carols like a fox set loose in a henhouse. With the twenty-five dollars Brezing paid him, Niles bought a fine winter coat that kept him stylish and warm throughout that first winter in Lexington.

In the spring of 1913, Niles was sent to Detroit for training at the Burroughs Company factory. One year earlier, the company had begun giving its salespeople a four-week training program in the application, repair, and sales of its machines. Niles spent only three weeks, and according to him, it was a very unproductive exercise. Niles failed as an adding-machine representative, simply because he had little or no interest in the adding-machine business. He readily acquired the mechanical skills to repair instruments, and he relished the focused engineering problems that challenged his creativity. However, he possessed none of the business-management and organization acumen required for the job. Furthermore, he passionately desired to be a musician and was obviously not the least bit attracted to a career as an adding-machine sales and re-pair agent. However, the Burroughs job did provide a steady income, opportunity for travel, and enough free time to continue his music col-lecting and performance activities.

Into the Mountains

After a short visit home to Louisville for his twenty-first birthday, Niles set off on his first trip into the mountains of East Kentucky to make a se-ries of Burroughs repairs in and around Hazard, the county seat of Perry County. Situated at a large bend in the Kentucky River, Hazard was just starting to boom when the railroad went through on June 17, 1912. By the time Niles arrived in 1916, it was a lively, rough-and-tumble town. The muddy main street was lined with haphazard board sidewalks and strewn with posts set into the ground for crosswalks. Because the town sprawled up from the river into the hills, floods were a constant threat.

In the course of fixing several adding machines in town, he met Mrs. L. C. "Ma" Hibler, manager of the Beaumont Hotel, who put him in touch with various singers.[13] Niles had a knack for identifying local people who were willing and able to help him meet community musicians. In this case, Hibler steered him to "Red" Jules and "Black" Jules Napier, who were working at the blacksmith shop. Niles collected from them a version of the ballad "William and Ellen" that was later published in his *Ballad Book*.

Leaving Hazard, Niles traveled to Cannel City, near the border of Morgan and Magoffin counties, then up to Index, near West Liberty, the county seat of Morgan County. There, he spent the night at a cabin before setting out for the train back to Lexington from West Liberty the next day. His account of the evening drips with the hyperbolic dialect and ro-manticism that infected the writing of so many local-color authors and folk music collectors of the period 1910–1930. The "local color" style sells books, but the "outsider" narratives too often sacrifice the Appalachian land and people on the altar of commercialism. A short excerpt from an account of Niles's first mountain excursion captures the histrionic flavor of his narrative, "underscored," as in a cinematic soundtrack, with dulcimer and ballad music and strains of a popular gospel hymn:

> A jolt-wagon, two very unwilling mule-animals, and one of the most widely-known jokers in the entire community carried me on the last leg of my journey. The driver's name was Froggie Benton. He was as tongue-tied as a human person could be, and he had the added disadvantage of having adenoids and a tic. He advised me by all means to stop at Miss Ellie Claybourne's cabin. Miss Ellie, whom I found to be a penitentiary widow with three young boys, had inherited about 200 acres of scrub land only to discover that she was, according to Froggie Benton, "sittin' on top of a cool fortune in coal royalties." The royalties hadn't appeared as yet; the mining had just begun. Froggie told me that there was a narrow-gauge connection in the morning, a snake-handlin' preachin' about 7 o'clock tonight, and, smirking as only his type can smirk, "they ain't no use of runnin' out on as pretty a gal as Miss Ellie."[14]

He continues to spin the yarn in the same vein:

> It was growing dark when there was a knock at the screen door. "Come in," said Ellie, "Whoever you be, take cheers or set. . . ." It proved to be Preacher Geezil and two of his young relatives. "No, thankee very much, but we can't stop 'cause we'uns got to get on to church and spread the word of God. Be you all a-comin' with us?" "No, Preacher Geezil," said Ellie speaking very sweetly. "I have an outlander here with us tonight, and I don't think it would serve any purpose for me to bring 'im. He has his own strange way of worshipping God, and I don't reckon that a collection of snake handlin' moonshiners and bootleggers will change him a bit or benefit him at all."
>
> Several women outside began to sing just outside Ellie's cabin: "We will gather at the river. . . ." Additional worshippers increased the volume of sound. Meanwhile, one of the copperhead boxes had fallen sideways. Preacher Geezil was in a panic. Some-

one righted the copperhead box, and the rattlers went right on; sensing the pressure of the moment, they rattled at a still higher note. Finally, Geezil realizing that the danger was past, turned to Miss Ellie and literally screamed: "Your Chicago mail-order dresses, your lies about your poor jail-hampered husband, your unwillingness to humble yourself . . ."[15]

And Back to Louisville

Returning to Lexington, Niles learned that the Burroughs Company was transferring him back to Louisville. In some ways, this mandated return to his hometown was like the strategic retreat of a pawn in a chess game. For the next four years, Niles settled into a routine that included work, brief travels associated with his job, a social life centered on church and music performance, and evenings spent composing or rehearsing music. While still close to his family, he maintained some measure of independence by living in an apartment in the Beechmont area from which he could easily commute to the Burroughs office at 119 S. Fourth Street.

His proximity to home facilitated collection of music from his father. Between 1915 and 1917 he collected "Turtle Dove" ("one of father's best") and the ballads "Bugle Britches," "Lord Lovel," and "Mary Hamilton."[16] Shortly before leaving for France in 1917, Niles took down the words for "The Shepherd's Daughter and the King" that his father's father had learned from broom makers in a Portland factory when Tommie was just twelve years old.

During this period Niles also reworked a murder ballad, "Anne Moore," collected earlier from his father. Niles's journal noted, "This is father's text of 1909 but the tune was made over by me a lot in 1915."[17] Even at this early point in his career, he exhibited a penchant for recrafting traditional music to suit his own vision of how he felt the song should be sung. His father played another important role in one last song from this period, although in this case, neither tune nor text was recorded directly from Tommie's singing.

In 1916 Niles recorded a version of the traditional lyric folk song "Black Is the Color of My True Love's Hair," but at the request of his father, he completely recomposed the tune. The original sketch, dated July 16,

1916, documented a melody line and lyrics for one strophe collected at Ary, a hamlet along Troublesome Creek between Lost Creek and Rowdy, Kentucky.[18] Niles appended the note, "Father thinks this is terrible as a tune, but a great idea worth working out."[19] A later sketch, dated August 1, 1916, recorded a similar version of "Black Is the Color" from the singing of "a politician named Combs in Hazard, KY. Father did not like it. Hotel Lobby."[20] Presumably, this "hotel lobby" was located in "Ma" Hibler's establishment at the base of Hazard's Main Street, where Niles had stayed during his earlier Burroughs service call.

Several additional sketches written in December show Niles's efforts to please his father by creating an entirely different melody from the one represented in the initial sketches. An entry dated December 12, 1916, contains the melodic contour of Niles's new melodic line, although the rhythm is not fleshed out yet. Evidently, he pleased Tommie Niles at last, for this effort has the appended comment: "Father likes this much better." A final sketch made one day later changes the key from E minor to G minor, adds a slight melisma to fill in a third on the word "love," experiments with substituting the word "very" for "rosie," and changes the word "ground" to "grass." The ghost of Tommie Niles is still looking over his shoulder, for he adds the remark "Father likes this one—but no one else will even listen."[21]

Like his earlier efforts "Go 'Way from My Window" and "Anne Moore," "Black Is the Color of My True Love's Hair" is the product of Niles's transformation of tradition—his desire to create original songs in the style of folk music, by fusing elements of traditional material with musical elements drawn from his own imagination. Since it was frequently unclear where the line between plagiarism and artistry was drawn, Niles was often compelled to defend his compositional practices. In the case of "Black Is the Color," there were critical as well as legal challenges to be answered years later, as demonstrated in this exchange of correspondence printed in *Sing Out* magazine in 1962.[22]

Niles received a letter from Elias B. Bull:

Dear Mr. Niles,

A friend of mine and I are having an argument which we are in hopes you can settle. It involves the ballad "Black Is the

Color of My True Love's Hair." I say that you are the author and quote your article in the tenth anniversary issue of *Sing Out;* my friend says the author is unknown and quotes Lomax's *Folksongs of North America,* pp. 197 and 206. I would greatly appreciate your clearing up this matter for us.

Niles responded as follows:

Dear Mr. Bull,

Your letter of August 15th has been forwarded to me here. Having clarified the problem of "Black Is the Color of My True Love's Hair," officially, legally, and otherwise, I see that confusion still exists, and am glad to clarify the problem once again.

Of course confusion has been valuable to those who were inclined to publish already published and copyright material. Please understand that I'm not implying for a moment that you belong to that category. I feel sure you simply want to know the facts, and here they are:

I wrote the present, widely used and popular tune known as "Black Is the Color of My True Love's Hair" to please my father, God rest him, who was dissatisfied with the tune then existing in oral tradition. The date was 1916. The tune my father disliked was not unlike the one reported by Cecil Sharp in *English Folk Songs of the Southern Appalachians.*

Please note: I do not claim to have written the text of "Black Is the Color." It is in public domain. The tune is my composition, and it is copyright by G. Schirmer, Inc. as such.

I was amused one time to hear a folk-singer tell me he thought it was a "dirty trick" on my part to have written the tune of "Black Is the Color." Personally, I do not feel that my having written some of the most widely used songs in American folk music today should be held against me.[23]

Niles's version of the text *is* closely related to the lyrics collected contemporaneously from Lizzie Roberts by Cecil Sharp in 1916 as well as a version maintained in oral tradition by the Ritchie family of Kentucky.[24] The only substantial alterations that Niles made consist of the elimination of the third and fifth stanzas and the return of the first stanza to conclude the song rather than employ the sixth stanza found in the folk version. Niles also shifts the persona from the original female to a male point of view to match his own narrative voice. Other less significant variations include the substitution of "grass" for "ground" and the localization of "Troublesome" for "Clyde."[25] A comparison of the first stanzas of the Roberts-Sharp version (the first one below) and the Niles version reveals their close correspondence.

> But black is the color of my true love's hair,
> His face is like some rosy fair;
> The prettiest face and the neatest hands,
> I love the ground whereon he stands.

> Black, black, black is the color of my true love's hair.
> Her lips are something rosy fair,
> The pertest face and the daintiest hands—
> I love the grass whereon she stands.

The Ritchie family and Lizzie Roberts versions of the tune are also very similar. In fact, it is highly likely that the Ritchie family learned the song from a source in proximity to Roberts. According to Jean Ritchie, "My older sisters learned this song while attending the John C. Campbell Folk School in Brasstown, North Carolina, and they brought it back to the family. We have loved it ever since."[26]

These versions are both pentatonic (no fourth or sixth) with a seventh degree that exists in both raised and lowered forms. The strong presence of a major third and a triadic outline creates a "major" feel. There are four phrases, with the first and fourth phrases being similar in contour and the second and third phrases nearly identical. The melodic essence of the first and fourth phrases features a triadic ascent and descent based on a D major chord. The contrasting phrases are built around an ascending and descending minor-chord emphasis on a blues-inflected minor seventh degree. Formally, the song is strophic with a phrase structure of *abba*.

By way of contrast, Niles's melody is cast in the Aeolian mode. The first phrase begins with an ascent on an E minor triad (matching the threefold repetition of the word "black") and a descent on a B minor chord. The second and fourth phrases are nearly identical except for the cadence point and are characterized by a beginning strong upward leap of a fifth. The third phrase is new, although it serves melodically and harmonically as a consequential phrase in relationship to the initial phrase. Formally, Niles's version is strophic with an *abab* sort of phrase structure. Thus, the tonality, the formal phrase structure, and the melodic contour of Niles's version appear to have no real points of correspondence with the two traditional versions of Ritchie and Roberts, confirming Niles's claim to have composed a new melody to accompany his adaptation of traditional words.

In addition to his composition and collecting activity, Niles continued to hone his performance skills at church and on the stage. The program of a November 1914 concert at Kelly's Hall reveals a vaudeville-style repertoire composed of sentimental Irish airs coupled with Stephen Foster parlor and minstrel songs involving soloists and a vocal quartet.[27] In Niles's role as "Jebediah Christopher Hodge, ye famous high-voiced singer," he sings "Believe Me," "If All Those Endearing Young Charms," "Killarney," and "Mother Machree." With the quartet he sings "Forsaken," "Soldier's Farewell," "Uncle Ned," "Old Folks at Home," "Old Black Joe," and "Bonny Eloise." Niles also gave a dramatic reading of Rudyard Kipling's poem "On the Road to Mandalay."

Snatches of diary comments from January 1915 portray a quotidian life torn between unsatisfying job demands and fervid involvement in music study and performance. At this time, Niles was engaged in church music composition and performance and was becoming ever more involved in the world of voice and opera. His friends all appear to be chosen because of their shared passion for music. These are some of Niles's thoughts:

January 1: "Worked 1/2 day today. Went to dinner and then to the show. . . . This is the first time since last winter that I have gone to the theatre."

January 2: "Worked 1/2 day today. . . . I sang over a lot of new music."

January 3 (Sunday): "Bert [Roberta Voorhies] and I looked over some anthems I brought with me and she was pleased with them. I practiced all evening. . . . I went down to see Peggy after supper. We sang over everything and enjoyed a very pleasant evening."

January 4: "To work as usual—practice tonight—read some of the operas as there will be an opera company in town this week. I am going."

January 5: "Tonight I went to Peggy's home for supper and after that we arranged a program for the performance. We sang everything they had and all of my music."

January 6: "This was one of the hardest days I have ever had for a long time. Garner (Rowell) and Lee and I went over to New Albany tonight and the other members of the orchestra were not there to practice."

January 7: "Worked today as usual and tonight I went to the opera *Lucia de Lamermoor* [*di Lammermoor*]. Lee and I and Garner and Jessie and Mary went together. We enjoyed the opera very much. Particularly the last song by Sir Edgar. This is one of my songs and that probably led me to like it better."[28]

4

Jack Niles Goes Off to War

Niles's diary reveals the narrowly circumscribed world of family, music, and work in which he dwelt. Events in the outside world, however, underscored his daily activity like an ominous pedal point. Given the complexity of his family's strong German lineage, his father's vocal politics, and his own vulnerable draft status, Niles found it increasingly difficult to balance daily life with the impending world events.

The Russian czar Nicholas II abdicated on March 15, 1917, and the U.S. Congress ratified President Wilson's Declaration of War on April 6. One month later John Jacob Niles found himself a cadet in the U.S. Army.

In a gesture duplicated by many of his contemporaries, in April 1917 Niles married his sweetheart, Roberta Voorhies, the organist at Beechmont Baptist Church, whom he had known for nine years. The two enjoyed only a few days of married life, for Niles left for the army in May. After he finally was released from service, September 14, 1919, they shared only a hasty reunion before Roberta died of the "Spanish" influenza on October 18, 1919.[1]

This first marriage appears to have been based more on familiarity and exigencies of the moment than on love and desire. Niles preserved no letters, photographs, or other evidence of their relationship. The few diary notes seldom refer to Roberta (Bert) as anything but an organist. This account of March 6, 1915, provides some insight into their tepid relationship: "I worked 1/2 day today and hurried home, buying some things for mother. I practiced and read and then fixed up and went to Bert's home to practice the song for tomorrow. We practiced it over and several others. I always enjoy visiting Bert although this was supposed to be all business."[2]

A passing comment in the autobiography also indicates this lack of passion, not even referring to her by name. "Meanwhile, in spite of my half-hearted love affair with a church organist and my utter boredom, I was fortunately in touch with several high school and university English teachers who talked of the beauty and immediacy of the Georgian poetry."[3] Niles and Voorhies spent less than two months together as a couple—she was simply a war bride and he became a war widower. No children resulted from this brief union.

After enlisting, Niles boarded the interurban train headed to Fort Benjamin Harrison in Indianapolis. The fort, a central mustering point for recruits, teemed with a population of twelve thousand soldiers, who were processed, given inoculations, and trained for three months. At the end of boot camp, Niles applied for, and was accepted to, the Army Signal Corps, that branch of the armed services that served as home to the fledgling air force.[4] Niles was elated to be chosen for this service, since he could finally consummate his dream of flying that had been sparked by the Wright brothers' initial Kitty Hawk flight on December 17, 1903.[5]

Captain Crittenberger asked Cadet Niles to sing at the boot-camp graduation celebration; he willingly consented and was accompanied by Cadet Wright on piano. Niles reported that "Rudolph's narrative (*che gelida mannina* [sic]) came off smooth as glass. My high C-natural was accurate and full of sound. Rogers' 'Star' was like eating pie compared to the first number. I stumbled all over myself trying to sing 'There Is a Long, Long Trail A-Winding into the Land of My Dreams,' I think it was a little too near me and my own problems. Then I sang Cavaradossi's lament in the last act of *La Tosca*, 'Eluce van le stele' [sic]. The applause was terrifying."[6] Niles's program was an interesting mix of popular song and operatic aria, the same high art–low art vaudeville combination that had informed his musical training and performance up to this time. "There Is a Long, Long Trail" was a particularly appropriate choice, because it tapped into the doughboys' nostalgia for home and loved ones as they departed for war in Europe:

There's a long, long trail a-winding
Into the land of my dreams,
Where the nightingales are singing
And a white moon beams:
There's a long, long night of waiting
Until my dreams all come true;
Till the day when I'll be going down
That long, long trail with you.

France

From Fort Harrison Niles traveled to the Columbus, Ohio, Ground School for several months of officer training before being sent by rail to Hoboken, New Jersey. On October 18, 1917, Niles joined thirty-five hundred other soldiers, along with stores, munitions, and artillery, on board the *Covington,* formerly a Hamburg-America cruise liner named the *Cincinnati.* After weeks of rolling slowly through the sea, the transport ship finally landed at St. Nazaire on November 3. It was a long, hard voyage salted with overcrowded conditions, terrible cooking, plenty of seasickness, and the constant fear of a German attack.

Niles remained in port for several days and then took a train to the air base at Issoudun, midway between the cities of Bourges and Châteauroux, about one hundred fifty miles south of Paris. There were thirteen fields at Issoudun, but during the time that Niles was stationed there, only eleven were in use; each field was dedicated to a special training activity or reserved for various models of Nieuport aircraft. This was a large facility, and twenty-five American squadrons were stationed there.[7]

Despite the demands of army life, Niles continued to seize opportunities to perform his music. On his second night at Issoudun, he presented a concert, though it appears his choice of songs was hardly suited to the audience. "I sang my spirituals," he said, "and my setting of 'Black Is the Color'—the Americans, except a few, would rather hear 'Good Bye Millie' and 'On the Banks of the Wabash.'"[8] This inauspicious concert was notable only as the first public performance of "Black Is the Color," which has since remained one of Niles's most popular and enduring compositions.

Within a month Niles was entrusted with various music and writing responsibilities at Issoudun. He served as the associate editor for the base's new newsletter, originally called *What Shall We Call It* and waggishly renamed *Plane News*. In addition, Niles received orders to start a marching band to accompany military functions. Despite never having directed or played in a band, he arranged some music and rehearsed the newly constituted post brass band. One week later, they were called upon to solemnize an aviator's funeral with Niles's arrangement of Chopin's *Marche funèbre*.

In early December, Niles was ordered by Captain Kearney to board the Paris, Lyon, and Mediterranean Express en route to Paris on a mission to buy a printing press, music, and other provisions for Christmas. It is hard to imagine the wonder and awe the Kentucky youth must have experienced, traveling to this grand European capital for the first time. All the culture and history that he had devoured as a student suddenly enveloped him in a sensory overload of art, architecture, fashion, music, and cuisine.

Niles reveled in the bounty of cultural opportunities presented by Paris despite the war, or perhaps in defiance of it. He also enjoyed meeting Lafayette Escadrille flying ace Bert Hall, an encounter that led to publication of Hall's memoirs recounted by Niles in *One Man's War*.[9] After three delicious days, Niles returned to the routine life of guard duty, training, and preparations for the Christmas program at Issoudun that ended up being something of a disaster for Niles, with intoxicated singers pouring milk punch into the open piano.

On January 20 Niles returned to Paris to gather "power equipment, broadcasting and receiving devices, four motorcycles, tires and repair parts, and many things not procurable in Italy." It was all to be transported by rail to the Eighth Aviation Instruction Center at Foggia, Italy. After several days, an evening spent attending a performance of *Tosca*, and another meeting with Bert Hall, Niles accompanied the train, with his rail car filled with ordnance, through Lyon to Modane, where the car was transferred to an Italian train headed to Genoa, Rome, Caserta, and finally Foggia.[10]

In the Air

Niles began actual flight training at Foggia, practicing with Farman (French) and Colombo (Italian) aircraft under the instruction of Italian aviators. Despite the demands of an intensive training regimen, he managed to steal some time for his music at Foggia. Listed as "Nyles Y. Yhon" on the program, Niles participated in *Un concerto vocale e strumentale* (A vocal and instrumental concert), directed by Professor Signor O. Ligi, at the hotel Alberto Dei Piccoli in Rome.[11] His repertoire included Massenet's *Elegia*, the traditional Scots song "Annie Laurie," and the aria *Che gelida manina!* from *La bohème*. Surprisingly, none of his own compositions were listed on the program, though it is likely that "Black Is the Color" might have been used as an encore.

By May 7, 1918, Niles was flying solo, and on May 17 he received his wings and his commission as a First Lieutenant in the Allied Expeditionary Force. Shortly afterward he was headed by train back to Issoudun for additional training, but since Issoudun was overcrowded, the unit spent ten days at St. Maxeuce-deux-soeurs. This short layover allowed Niles to meet and share music with a unit of Polish grenadiers who were also stationed there. In exchanging music at a final farewell concert, Niles sang "Solenne in quest' ora" from *La forza del destino,* while a Polish soldier sang a carol, "Keep Jesus Warm," that Niles transcribed and many years later published in a four-voice SATB (soprano, alto, tenor, bass) choral arrangement as "Carol of the Polish Grenadiers."[12]

Niles arrived at Orly July 14. He was assigned as a taxi and reconnaissance flier and charged with flying a great variety of planes to airfields in France and England.[13] His flight log tersely recorded a mission on September 13: "Ordered to fly a Spad type 13, unequipped to Colombey-les-Belles, stopping first at Vinets for oil and gas." But the amplified version in the autobiography provides a more vivid tale of the danger and excitement accompanying these daily brushes with mortality:

> I drew a brand new Spad, just delivered from the Duperdessen plant a few kilometers away. It developed 180 horsepower and was said to possess all the latest improvements. Never having taken a Spad off the ground before, I was a little apprehensive.
>
> My motor started the very first time we tried it. I revved up my engine to be sure it would give the plane enough thrust, or rather ground speed, to lift off, and signaled the "chock-holders" to release the wheels on the undercarriage. Suddenly I was mov-

ing away. In my lap I had attached a map of the country over which I must fly. My destination was Colombey-les-Belles, a few kilometers from Toul and the front line.

Once I was airborne, I was totally lost. The situation terrified me no end. The Nieuports I had flown were on the slow side, while my Spad seemed to be flying fast as lightning. There was no time for mistakes. The Seine flashed under me. In vain I looked for a railroad line that was to be one of my landmarks. There was no railroad line; only pleasant green fields of growing crops and tiny knots of farmers' villages. Then I tilted my Spad enough to see the ground clearly. There before my surprised eyes, was the little city of Melun. I was many kilometers off track. One of the older pilots, who had been standing around in the dispatch office, had told me, "When in doubt, always come home." And that is exactly what I tried to do.[14]

On September 30, 1918, Niles was flying his Camel from Lympne, England, to Orly. Halfway over the Channel, a violent storm developed and he was forced to land at Marquis. Along with some other grounded fliers, Niles was transported to Boulogne, where he was lodged in the Café de la Mer until the rains stopped and he could complete the flight to Orly. This proved to be a fortunate change of itinerary because on October 4 Niles was introduced to another fragment of folk music, which he reworked as the song "Venezuela." He explains in his autobiography:

I had observed a sailing ship moored quite near the door of the Café de la Mer, from which Barbados Negroes were carrying sacks of grain, some wheat, some Kaffir corn, and some rye. After dinner, I realized that the rain and the dark had stopped them for the night.

[The next day] In spite of the fog, the Barbados Negroes were carrying bag after bag of grain out of the five-master and into waiting lorries. I stopped to watch and mostly listen to their sing-song kind of music. It was, of course, a work song, somewhat on the order of the pulling and working chanties of earlier times.

The love song about the sailor and the girl in Venezuela was the oldest plot going around. Sailor meets girl, girl falls headlong in love with seaman, seaman's leave runs out and he departs quite gaily, saying "There'll always be sailors ashore in Venezuela." I used the last phrase of the final verse, wrote the remaining three verses on short notice, made over the tune, and created a reasonable accompaniment to give it what I hoped would be a dramatic quality.[15]

While it is no longer possible to verify Niles's narrative detailing the collecting experience, his notebooks do provide some evidence of the genesis of the song. An entry dated April 26, 1918, titled "I met her in Venezuela," contains three measures of the tune. It also appears that the location was noted as "Le Havre" rather than Boulogne. A sketch dated April 27 contains a completed version of the melody. A final entry of April 28, 1918, presents a complete version of the melody and a first stanza of text. There is also a date of October 4, 1918, on this sketch, which would corroborate the date and place where he originally recorded the song. Unfortunately, the original holograph manuscript is no longer available; it was among the items taken in a theft at Boot Hill Farm in 1967.

Shortly after Niles collected the sketch that became "Venezuela," the skies cleared and he returned to the airbase at Marquis to fly the Camel to Gamache and on to Orly. Somewhere south of Amiens, Niles's plane was hit by German antiaircraft fire and he was forced to crash land his burning plane. The trip that began on October 5 in Boulogne was Niles's final wartime flight; he ended the day in critical condition at the Third American Red Cross Hospital at St. Denis, France. After nine days in the hospital, Niles was discharged and returned to Orly, where he now walked with a pronounced limp and the aid of a cane.[16] There was little need for him to return to flying, however, because within a month Marshall Foch met with German leaders in rail car 2419d to sign the Armistice agreement. Niles had survived the dangers of war, lived through a nearly fatal airplane crash, and was now poised to enjoy a period of study and enlightenment in France as part of the army of occupation.

La Vie de Paris

Niles claims that while in Paris he visited the famous salon of poet Gertrude Stein on various occasions during November and December 1918. It is difficult to verify these accounts now, because the only communication from Gertrude Stein to Niles that survives is a letter postmarked September 13, 1934, addressed to his wife, Rena Lipetz [Niles], from Alice B. Toklas on behalf of Stein.

Perhaps Stein was willing to respond to the young Rena Niles on account of her earlier relationship with John Jacob Niles, or perhaps she was just politely responding to Rena's earlier inquiry. In any event, there is nothing other than Niles's autobiographical reminiscences to document his claims of reading poetry at Stein's apartment. Nevertheless, Niles's accounts *sound* convincing, and they do provide some understanding of the role that French culture played in expanding his horizons. This passage may simply be a flight of Niles's fancy in retrospect, a bit of historical revisionism that placed him at the center of a world to which he desperately aspired. In that case, it is beside the fact whether the account is factually true or not. In Niles's mind, this was the beginning of the world of arts and letters for him. This salon provided a model for all his aspirations, and Gertrude Stein—whether real or virtual—supplied the inspiration for the next chapter of his life. His final publication, a collection of poems titled *Brick Dust and Buttermilk* (1977), noted in the dedication, "I have been encouraged and spiritually supported by some of my friends and faulted by others. Among those who were kind enough to help me are the following," and included in the list of ten names is that of Gertrude Stein.

A journal entry from the early 1920s provides one of the poems that Niles allegedly read for Stein. "She seemed to like them very much," he says, though they were a new genre of poetry for him; before this occasion he had written only sonnets. This is one of the poems he refers to:

I closed my window against the boistrious [*sic*] wind
But the wind came regardless of my pains.
The wind knew every crack ever so well
The wind knew the way from coming oft before.
The wind was no child, Indeed the wind was very old.

See how I have sprinkeled [*sic*] both of my wings
Sprinkeled them with a sparkling glinting dust
A dust made of perfumed and poweded [*sic*] moon beams.

Pray my love loosten [*sic*] your shutter latch
That I who love you may enter with the moon light,
Enter and trace in faint silver shadows
The legend of my affection on your floor.

My love if you would lower your silken coverlid
And open your arms a-welcoming me to come in
How soon I would answer your sweet summons
And cover you from every shaft of moonlight
Cover you with the shadow of my bod.

I know the beating of your wings will fan the fires,
That smolder in my sleeping heart
I know that my hand will eloquently sing
If you will but touch it with your lips.[17]

Music Studies Abroad

Niles received a very special gift that Christmas of 1918. The army granted him a six-week "sick leave" to remain in Paris, where he was allowed to enroll in classes at the Schola Cantorum. When his orders came through, on December 28, Niles left Orly and moved into a small basement apartment in the Boulevard Saint-Michel neighborhood not far from the Seine River. The Schola Cantorum, at 269 Rue Saint Jacques in the Montparnasse District, was a good choice for Niles, who at age twenty-nine was largely self-taught. Unlike the Paris Conservatoire, which emphasized performance technique, the Schola attempted to develop the whole musician through a curriculum that included music history, theory, form and analysis, and harmony.

Through the introduction of his landlord, Professor Picot, Niles began taking private piano lessons with Clothilde Marcel, who instructed him in the art of collaborative performance.[18] This instruction proved most valuable to Niles in the not-too-distant future, when he found himself serving as an accompanist for Marion Kerby. Professor Picot also introduced him to the noted composer Vincent d'Indy (1851–1931), with whom Niles took two composition lessons each week.[19] Niles said one of his greatest benefits during that period came from d'Indy's criticism when he heard "Black Is the Color." He told Niles, "Lieutenant, I see that you are a man of few notes, that is in your accompaniments. This is all very well. I like to think of myself as being the same way. Yes, it is all very well to be meager with your accompaniments. You may employ one note per measure if you wish, but God have mercy on you if it is the wrong note! Many a composer has fooled the ear of the public with an avalanche of notes, but with one note per measure—no."[20] The earliest published version of "Black Is the Color" (1936) features an economical accompaniment consisting of a doubled melodic line buttressed only by occasional simple chords and a somewhat independent bass line. Evidently, Niles heeded d'Indy's sage advice.

Life in Paris gave Niles equal measures of ecstasy and frustration. He experienced the elation of an opera or theater performance nearly every evening. He was in the company of stimulating teachers and challenged by his music studies. He had the run of a city teeming with art and museums. He appears to have enjoyed the company of several beautiful and talented women. And yet he was also increasingly depressed by his lack of career progress. Niles had a passion for theater, a strong voice, and some piano experience, but it was becoming increasingly clear to him that he was not cut out for a career as an opera singer or a concert pianist. At nearly thirty, he was far behind the development of younger students with whom he would be competing. At this point in his life he saw no other options for a performance career; he still lacked a vision of what new opportunities might possibly be created to tap into his unique set of talents. The diversions, the delights, and the emotional roller coaster of his Paris sojourn came to an end on February 24 with the receipt of Special Order 25 from Brigadier General Harts of the American Expeditionary Forces, District of Paris. Niles was ordered to report to the Université de Lyon to pursue a course of studies. Arriving by rail on March 2, 1919, in Lyon, Niles registered the next day and began classes in French language, history, and geography on March 6. Sharing an apartment on Avenue

Ramparts Deniers with five other soldiers, he quickly discovered that he also needed a studio to practice piano and compose, so five days later he rented a spacious studio equipped with a piano at 8 Rue du Plâtre.[21]

The five months spent in Lyon were dominated by a passionate relationship with a French woman identified only as "Brigitte." Niles was apparently guilty of desultory attendance at classes and lectures in government and history but more assiduous in his attention to piano lessons with a Spanish musician he identified as F. Via.[22] Musically, he appeared to be particularly focused on composing and arranging traditional music for several salon performances given at the home of Brigitte's Uncle Daniel. A list of song texts pasted in his notebook that was begun in Lyon represents a clear portrait of his repertoire—an eclectic mixture of popular songs, spiritual arrangements, art songs, arias, and his growing opus of original songs.[23]

In some ways, the time spent in Lyon amounted to a lovely but unsubstantial little coda appended to Niles's extraordinary European adventure. Between November 3, 1917, when he first stepped ashore in France, and August 10, 1919, when he boarded the ship *Cap Finisterre* headed for the United States,[24] Niles lived a lifetime of experiences that he could never have conceived of within the confining embrace of his Kentucky home. He experienced both the horrors and the joyous camaraderie of war. He realized his dream of flying free of the earth. His intellectual and emotional horizons were exploded by his exposure to the pleasures of European culture—art, music, cuisine, theater, and poetry. He continued his collection and adaptation of music in oral tradition. He made some important contacts that continued to be useful in the future. He gained an introduction to the formal discipline of music study. And most importantly, he went to war and lived to tell the tale.

5

Life after the War

Landing at Hoboken Harbor on August 20, 1919, Niles began the gradual and uncomfortable transition back to civilian life. He was formally demobilized from the U.S. Army, with a clearance of money and property accountability, at Camp Sheridan, Ohio.[1] Free of obligations and entanglements, and with nothing but uncertainty ahead, he returned to his parents' home in Louisville. Although there is no record of it, there must have been an uneasy reunion with his wife Roberta that served only to remind him of how he had been transformed by the war. He chose to move in with his parents rather than initiate a new life with her; and then she was dead of influenza a month later.

Surely, Niles felt a little like Rip Van Winkle, returning to find the world had changed in his absence. The countryside around Inverness Farm must have seemed dull and distant compared with the vibrant life of Paris and the adrenaline-charged wartime experiences. How could Niles have attempted to explain the person he had become to those who had known him in sunnier and slower times? Fortunately, musician Garner Rowell, an old friend, happened by and provided Niles with some direction by steering him to the Cincinnati Conservatory.[2]

Cincinnati, Chicago, Cincinnati

Niles registered as a full-time student and enrolled in piano, voice, harmony, composition, opera, and French. The Veterans Bureau supported his education by providing one hundred dollars each month to cover tuition and expenses. He supplemented this small income by singing in various area church choirs, including the Jewish K. K. Ben "Rockdale" Temple.[3]

Niles had his heart set on an opera career, and though he was beginning to realize that his light tenor voice might limit him to comprimario and chorus roles, he immersed himself in voice and opera classes and within a week was already rehearsing for a production of Massenet's opera *Manon.* During the summer opera season, Niles performed several small roles, including second tenor in *Pagliacci,* at the Cincinnati Zoological Gardens. On May 25, 1920, he appeared as Chevalier des Grieux in *Manon,* a production accompanied by the Cincinnati Orchestra and performed at Emory Auditorium.[4] Enthusiastic about Ralph Lyford, director of the opera workshop, Niles wrote: "My work with the opera department was by far the most interesting of all. Ralph Lyford was a great conductor, teacher, humorist, and accompanist. He helped me greatly with the problems I had in playing accompaniments."[5]

Niles was considerably less enthusiastic about his voice and composition lessons. While he had an affinity for operatic arias and French art song, he was really focused on composing and performing his own songs based on folk materials. Quite naturally, conservatory-trained faculty saw Niles's interests as tangential to the canon of appropriate vocal literature. His direct expression, modally tinged tonality, and simplistic accompaniment were light years distant from the musical complexity and vocal challenges posed by German lieder and oratorio passages. It is little wonder that Niles's voice professor Daniel Beddoe, a Welsh tenor, was unsympathetic to Niles's songs and that Niles, in turn, dismissed Beddoe's tutelage.[6] Composition and history with Edgar Stillman Kelley was equally tedious to Niles, who simply noted, "I met with Dr. Kelley about five times and got nothing for my time. He had wasted his time too."[7] Influenced by his study in Stuttgart, Kelley's music was strongly European in flavor. Understandably, Niles's American folk music–influenced songs failed to impress him.

In October 1921 Niles withdrew from Cincinnati Conservatory upon the advice of his mentor Ralph Lyford, who wrote him a letter of introduction to Mary Garden, director of the fledgling Chicago Opera Association. He then successfully appealed to the U.S. Veterans Bureau for a transfer to Chicago and its Veteran's Bureau Music School there. When the paperwork was completed, Niles packed up his few possessions and boarded the Illinois Central train bound for the city that was gaining an unsavory reputation as the "hog butcher to the world." He settled into his apartment in a rooming house at Thirty-fifth and Michigan on the city's South Side, just a few blocks from the old brownstone on Indiana Avenue that served as the music school. It was an ethnically diverse neighborhood populated mainly by eastern European immigrants who were drawn to work at the vast stockyards just to the west.[8]

Niles's audition at the Veteran's Bureau School immediately welcomed him to the spectacularly poor caliber of performance and education that constituted his school experience for the next six months.[9] Fortunately, he had other avenues and resources for continuing his musical education. He took his letter of introduction downtown to the Auditorium Theatre, where the Chicago Opera Association was engaged in rehearsal for *Tales of Hoffman,* and he met Mary Garden. She auditioned him and allowed him the privilege of attending rehearsals and taking lessons with opera coach Hermann Devries.[10]

It was a long, cold winter in the windy city for Niles. While he had the opportunity to experience wonderful productions at the Civic Opera, he was not making much musical progress of his own, aside from singing in church choirs, presenting a few concerts in Cicero, and dutifully participating in the unsatisfying activity associated with the Music School. Fortunately, his career warmed up as a new opportunity—radio—presented itself. Niles happened to be just at the right place and time; his connection to the Civic Opera yielded an introduction to the year-old Westinghouse Radio Station KYW.

KYW, the first Chicago-area station, went on the air at 4:30 P.M. November 11, 1921, with Mary Garden's words "My God, it's dark in here!" spoken as she felt her way through the darkened stage, not knowing that the microphone was live. The station, located on the sixteenth floor of the Commonwealth Edison Building, was conceived by Samuel Insull as a vehicle for transmitting Civic Opera performances, and beginning with the broadcast of *Samson and Delilah* several days later, the entire opera season was broadcast throughout the Chicago area. On January 18, 1922, the station augmented its opera broadcasts with a more popular format on a midnight revue that featured performers such as the Duncan Sisters and Little Jack Little.[11]

Niles was perfectly suited to the station's mission, possessing the vaudevillian showman's mix of operatic and popular repertoire. His early involvement with radio showmanship paid him three dollars per fifteen-minute session, but more importantly, it gave him valuable experience that he applied in the future to broadcasts with New York's WFBH, with the pioneering Kentucky Educational Radio Listening Post project, and in his radio scripts written for Louisville's WHAS. Niles wrote in his autobiography:

In a little room at the top floor of a solid city block of buildings belonging to Westinghouse Electric, I received my instructions and warnings. I was assured that there was no danger of electrocution. I was told that everything I sang should be in the key of G, because that key was most certain to activate the microphone, and that if the young man behind a double sheet of thick glass made motions by passing his hands horizontally, I was to quit singing quickly, and if the young man moved his hands up and down, I was to proceed with my performance.

The first thing I sang on the air was "Barbary Ellen." I had arranged it in the key of B. Then I had the song "The Frog in the Spring." This, too, was set in B. And I had several French songs prepared. One was in G minor, and the other was in A minor. The young man behind the pane of thick glass seemed greatly pleased.[12]

The next week Niles returned to the studio with a fresh repertoire, consisting largely of World War I songs such as "The Long Trail," "Hinky Dinky Parlez Vous," and "If You Want to Know Where the Privates Are," and walked away with another three dollars. Before long, he had a daily twenty-minute segment at three o'clock in the afternoon. This experience allowed him to try out his own arrangements of folk and wartime songs and tested his ability to convincingly project a song without seeing or being seen by the audience.

As the long Chicago winter melted into spring, Niles felt the call to return to Cincinnati to prepare for the summer opera productions at the zoo. His six months in Chicago had provided him with little schooling, precious few opportunities to perform opera, some interesting radio experience, enough free time to complete the first sketches for several wartime writing projects, and a serious, undiagnosed vocal condition that made his voice "sound like a frog suffering from laryngitis."[13] Ralph Lyford advised Niles to stop singing temporarily and devote his time to compiling his soldier songbook.

Lyford's advice to Niles was apt, but bitter. He could not go home to the family farm. Without a voice, he could not find work as a singer, and no one was interested in his song collection. The days stretched on dismally as he labored over his song arrangements or hung around the opera rehearsals. Poverty was a constant companion; he was completely dependent on Lyford's generosity in allowing him to remain employed with the opera chorus.

Death Visits the Niles Family

As Niles was living in his basement apartment in the Mount Auburn area of Cincinnati and attending classes, the rest of the Niles family still resided down the river in Louisville at Inverness and Taylor roads, an intersection that had once been farmland but was now perched on the edge of Iroquois Park and increasingly absorbed within the city.[14] Tommie Niles was listed as a "stockman" at Peerless Manufacturing Company, and with the exception of the youngest son, Charles, who was a student, the children were all employed. Irene was still working as a nurse, Leland was a bookkeeper, and Robert was a carpenter, busy constructing houses on Inverness Avenue with his brother Leland.[15]

Suddenly and surprisingly, Tommie Niles, just fifty-four years old, died at 12:15 A.M. on April 18, 1922. The cause of death was officially "acute dilatation of heart," brought on by the shock caused by an operation at Jewish Hospital for gallstones. After being taken to the John Miller Funeral Home in Louisville, he was interred at Evergreen Cemetery in Jefferson County. The loss of Niles's father compounded the frustration and depression Niles was experiencing and intensified introspection about his future.

Niles dutifully continued to rehearse for the summer's opening performance of *Carmen,* in which he had the role of El Remendando, but
he also began assembling sketches for a collection of soldier songs tentatively titled "We Sang Our Way through Hell." This was a critical turning
point in Niles's career, for the notion of creating books of song collections offered a viable career path beyond opera. Up to this point, Niles
had conceived of his collecting activity only as a means of enlarging his
own personal repertoire. He understood that songs could be collected
and transformed (such as "Go 'Way from My Window" or "Black Is the
Color") or arranged and performed (such as his father's version of "Little
Mohee"). For the first time, however, he began to realize that they could
also be valued in themselves and presented as a historical document in
notated form.

It is difficult to ascertain whether Niles encountered other similar
collections at this time. He might have come into contact with at least
several early folk collections, such as Cecil Sharp's *English Folksongs
from the Southern Appalachians* (1917) or Loraine Wyman and Howard
Brockway's *Lonesome Tunes* (1916), but he probably would not have seen
these until late in 1922 when he moved to New York City. Through a
week of study with George Saintsbury in London during July 1919, Niles
had examined Francis Child's collection of balladry (and even owned
a handsome ten-volume, leather-bound 1882 edition signed by the author), but Child's work hardly provided a model for the project that Niles
conceived.[16] There simply was no other collection of wartime songs with
commentary, illustrations, and musical transcriptions out there to guide
Niles's imagination. The only other work that was even closely contempo-
raneous with the two books that he eventually published was *Songs and
Slang of the British Soldier,* which appeared in 1931, four years later than
Niles's first collection.[17]

Helen Babbitt, Hélène Babbitt, Mrs. John Niles, 1922–1933

During the challenging and uncertain days following his return from
the war, some of the few bright moments must have been provided by
Niles's burgeoning romance with Helen Babbitt. After several years spent

as a widower, Niles met Babbitt, an aspiring twenty-six-year-old actress who had served as a Red Cross nurse during the war.[18] She was working in Cincinnati with the Little Theatre Movement at the time. Surely her beauty, her sense of style, and her interest in the arts would have caught Niles's attention.[19] It is unclear exactly when and how they met, but the earliest record is a diary entry noting that Niles had accompanied Babbitt on piano during a fashion show held at Tattersall's Tobacco Warehouse on April 18, 1922—the very same day that his father died.[20]

It was becoming apparent to both Helen and Niles that their ambitious career plans were not being furthered by life in Cincinnati. Fortuitously, two of Niles's acquaintances from the opera, Henrietta Wakefield and Greek Evans, asked him to join them that fall at their home in Wilton, Connecticut. Niles gratefully accepted their offer to let him earn his keep by serving as a chauffeur, farmhand, opera coach, and general handyman—this was exactly the sort of "jack of all trades" job that he could handle. In fact, it was just the kind of position he famously filled a decade later for the celebrated photographer Doris Ulmann.

Niles and Babbitt moved to New York together in 1922. At this time she changed her name from "Helen" to the more colorful "Helene," which was eventually graced by French accent marks to become "Hélène." That they were married at least by 1925 is indicated by a music dedication. Niles dedicated each of the eight selections of his first music collection, *Impressions of a Negro Camp Meeting* (1925), to a different person, and the final song, "Heaven," was inscribed to Helene Babbitt Niles.

In 1926 the couple lived in Nyack, New York, on the Hudson River, just over the Tappan Zee Bridge from New York City. During the summer Helene took a summer course of study, as evidenced by her notes on acrobatics and imagination from June 19 through August 14. She commented, "The universal law is the result of observation made on nature, time, phrenology, and physiognomy."[21] Niles made at least one trip to his wife's hometown of Des Moines in 1927, listing his address for two weeks as 4115 Hickman Avenue.[22] A Syracuse, New York, newspaper dated January 27, 1929, featured a picture of a pretty and fashionable Mrs. John Niles flanked by her more drab companions, Janet Spencer and singer Marion Kerby, with whom Niles was now performing regularly.[23]

The next mention of Helene Niles appears in a 1929 society column noting the couple's return to Cincinnati as the weekend guests of Mr. and Mrs. Ernest Bruce Haswell and praising both Niles's literary activity and Helene's theatrical work.[24] Two other collections of music published in 1929 by Niles, *Seven Kentucky Mountain Songs* and *Seven Negro Exaltations*, are dedicated to Helene with the new spelling, and presumably the new pronunciation, "Hélène." *The Songs My Mother Never Taught Me*, also published that year, also carried Hélène's name on the dedication (along with Emily, Florence, and Blanche).

The Nileses lived together three more years, first at Nyak, New York, and then back to Manhattan; first at 150 West Fifty-fifth Street, then 155 West Twelfth. In 1932 Niles moved to 259 West Eleventh, and the marriage came to an end.[25] There was little to keep the couple glued together in the face of Niles's frequent performances, including several extended European concert tours, coupled with Hélène's active theater career. The tone of a letter written by Niles in 1932 to his friend Roy Flanagan in Richmond, Virginia,[26] reveals some of the ambivalence caused by his separation in mixed doses of freedom and self-pity. At the head of the letter he wrote, "Today is Tuesday but it won't matter tomorrow."

Dear Flannagans,

I have been separated from my wife . . . she thinks I am a dud. . . . I said yes and found myself a new place to lay my head . . . also my hips. . . . Helene Niles is really a swell one . . . but its hell being married to a so called artist. . . . More of that later or none of it as you all see fitting. . . . My voice is as a broken reed now that I am thrown upon the cold unfeeling world by my woman (we are still friends, understand)
I have no ideas today
Just an old worn out bunch of vocal cords . . .
Better luck next time. . . .
I'll be a Pagliacci and sing tho my heart is breaking. . . .
But I'm free as air.

Love to you both.[27]

The final mention of Niles's ex-wife appears in a letter from him to his future wife, Rena Lipetz, on October 23, 1933: "You didn't know it but my ex wife was there and she looked simply swell. . . . She was with Mr. Eric Hodjins who is said to be one of the few people who have a chance to be another O. Henry. . . . God can he write, and my Ex wife adores people who can swing words."[28] After this Hélène Niles simply appears to disappear from the Niles narrative completely, replaced on the stage by Marion Kerby, replaced professionally by Doris Ulmann, and replaced amorously by his future wife, Rena. Hélène died in Albany, New York, in November 1967.

6

Creating a Life in the Big Apple

In fall 1922, after the final opera performance in Cincinnati, Niles packed up his few possessions and traveled to Wilton, a small, quiet town in the Norwalk River Valley, just fifty miles away from the throbbing heart of Manhattan. There was little about this placid bedroom community to retain Niles's interest, however, so after a few months, he moved to the city itself and settled into a dingy basement apartment located on Washington Place, just off Washington Square in the center of Greenwich Village.

The next day, Niles hit the pavement, attempting to parlay letters of introduction provided by a wartime acquaintance from Italy to gain access to the forbidding New York publishing houses of Charles Scribner's Sons, Carl Fischer, and G. Schirmer. Niles had been compelled to learn the subtle art of social networking as a matter of necessity. In the uncertain world of art and entertainment, personal contacts were absolutely essential to pave the way for opportunity. He was very fortunate with this particular contact, for it opened the doors to interviews that soon enabled him to write a series of articles for *Scribner's Monthly* magazine and a collection of spirituals for Carl Fischer. Although Gustave Schirmer was not receptive initially, his publishing company eventually proved to be Niles's most important outlet for his musical compositions and arrangements.[1] With the renewed incentive provided by the possibility of actually publishing his work, Niles dedicated much of his time during the next few years of his New York life to writing stories and books and arranging music.

The Electrifying Effect of the Male Alto C Sharp

The Veteran's Bureau continued to send Niles a nine-dollar monthly disability check, but more importantly, it also made arrangements for him to take lessons from Juilliard School faculty member Alberto Bimboni.[2] The day Niles set out for his first lesson with Bimboni was the day his singing voice finally returned. But the restoration carried with it a remarkable transformation. The lyric tenor voice that Niles had worked so hard to develop had now become a much different instrument, one that might be characterized more as a male alto or countertenor. Suddenly, Niles possessed that quirky, distinctive sound that would indelibly stamp performances and recordings with his unique style. This was an "inauthentic" caterwauling, yodeling voice that could grate on your ears, but it was also a charismatic voice that demanded your attention. It could soar or whisper with drama. Love it or hate it, few listeners could remain neutral when confronted with the sound that Niles himself described as the "electrifying effect of the male alto C sharp."[3] On that pivotal February morning in 1923, said Niles, "I opened my mouth and tried my voice. That moment was the beginning of a new life for me. I sang my entire scale from top to bottom, and the top was far and away higher than it had ever been before. I then stood before my mirror and sang the highest notes in my scale. I sang with the ease of a bird. To me this was a miracle."[4]

Miracle or not, Niles now gained access to a unique and peculiar instrument shaped by operatic training, molded by vaudeville showmanship, and infused with the easy delivery of folk music. The distinctive timbre and range were perfectly complemented by the crisp enunciation of Niles's dramatic declamation. Like Bob Dylan several generations later, Niles considered his voice merely a vehicle for vividly depicting the text narrative. The medium was servant to the message. One critic, Ronald D. Scofield, described Niles's "persuasive" voice in these terms: "As record fans are well aware, Niles has a strangely persuasive voice that ranges from a husky whispering baritone to a fragile but beautiful round and limpid falsetto that could match many a coloratura soprano for quality— though he needs and reveals only a limited volume."[5] In a record review, Oscar Brand (1920–), a celebrated folk revival singer and a longtime New York radio host, painted Niles's voice in these colorful terms: "The weird, hoarse falsetto of John Jacob Niles adds a strange power to some of his renditions. . . . In a few of the songs, the queer delivery often overpowers the material. . . . Yet listening to Niles is a fascinating experience; certainly no one will be bored."[6] And critic Paul Hume cited Niles's own assessment of his voice in an obituary for Niles in the *Washington Post.*

> He [Niles] once gave the best of all descriptions of that voice. "The nature of my voice has much to do with the material of my performance. In the lingo of the concert stage, I did not live in the lower registers. I soon discovered the electrifying effect of a male alto C sharp, and this led me to compose a melodic line involving the highest notes in my range." Thus, long before the era of the first famous countertenors of this century, Alfred Deller and Russell Oberlin, John Jacob Niles was singing in heights that most males consider astronomical.[7]

For years, Niles had been gathering a repertory of traditional music drawn from rural, mountain, and African American sources. Now he had the instrument to sing that repertoire. In the irreducible triangle that binds the singer to the song and to the audience, what was still missing was the appropriate venue to reach his audience. That missing link was revealed at New York City's Princeton Club in December 1927.

Show Business and Radio

Buoyed by his Westinghouse Radio experience in Chicago, Niles began searching for a station in New York where he could resuscitate his broadcasting career. The opportunity presented itself in 1925, when he rejoined Mildred Gardner, a pianist whom he knew from the Cincinnati Conservatory. Through a connection at Carl Fischer's, Niles met with the staff of the Concourse Radio Corporation, which was starting up a five-hundred-watt station on the roof garden of the Majestic Hotel. On June 30, 1925, WFBH, "the Voice of Central Park," went on the air, with Niles and Mildred Gardner featured in a daily live show. Niles also served as an announcer and the music director. A 1925 New York newspaper column by Gerard Sheedy titled "Southern Accent Distinguishes Niles at

Station WFBH" was accompanied by a caricature of Niles complete with slicked-back hair parted down the middle and a natty bow tie. Sheedy commented, "Jack Niles is the only announcer in the metropolitan district with a real southern accent," and concluded: "Radio fans who tune in on 278 meters and hear a soft Southern voice saying 'you all' may be disappointed that it is not some southern station that is hard to get, but Jack Niles at WFBH."[8]

Unfortunately, this station and Niles's repertoire were a poor match. Over the years Niles had developed a real antagonism for popular music. As a classically trained musician, he sought to elevate public taste rather than pander to it. WFBH was more interested in selling songs and products—what Niles characterized as "quickery and quackery." As a result, Niles and the station parted after about four months. He did not return to radio until he moved back to Kentucky, where he worked with the University of Kentucky's fledgling public radio station WBKY (now WUKY) and with Louisville's powerful station WHAS.

Niles also entered the world of show business, with gigs at several nightclubs. He worked various jobs both backstage and onstage at Jimmy Durante's club, the Silver Slipper, just about the time that the fifteen-year-old Imogene Coca was working there. Several years later he moved to the Chez Helen Morgan Lounge, the first of a series of cabarets that featured Morgan singing her torch songs seated on the piano.[9] These clubs had opened up in Manhattan following Prohibition in 1920 as a way of making the lounges appear more respectable by featuring celebrity entertainers.

New York had a thriving "follies" scene in the early 1920s, featuring revues such as the Ziegfeld Follies, the Grand Street Follies, and the Garrick Gaieties. Niles found his way into the cast of the Grand Street Follies in 1924 through the recommendation of a theatrical lawyer, Helen Arthur, whom he met at WFBH. Arthur was a member of the opening-night cast of the Follies and worked for producers of both the Follies and *The Dybbuk*.[10] After auditioning, Niles was cast as Abie in a burlesque version of *Abie's Irish Rose*. The role was perfectly suited to his operatic training, because it was created as a parody of a Metropolitan Opera tenor.[11] The job, paying fifty dollars per week, supported him while he was working at his various writing projects. The performances also gave him valuable live stage experience that helped him transcend the footlights and create an intimate bond with the audience.

The Publishing Career Unfolds

Finally, with the Carl Fischer publication of Niles's first music collection, *Impressions of a Negro Camp Meeting* (1925), the lean years of writing and collecting started to bear fruit. *Impressions* contained eight spirituals, although Niles was always careful to avoid referring to his arrangements of African American music as *spirituals,* preferring instead to use the terms *exaltations* or *jump ups.* He was very clear on this point, as his foreword notes: "They are based on traditional tunes but are absolutely not the so-called spirituals." In part, Niles was probably trying to distinguish his versions from the wave of spiritual arrangements that were being issued by composer-arrangers such as Clarence Cameron White and Harry T. Burleigh and in anthologies such as *The Book of American Negro Spirituals* (1925) and *The Second Book of American Negro Spirituals* (1926), published by brothers James Weldon Johnson and John Rosamond Johnson.[12]

The initial 1871 tour of the Jubilee Singers of Fisk University, under the direction of George L. White, had sparked an interest in artfully arranged and carefully rehearsed concert performances of African American spirituals. By the turn of the century, most historically black colleges had choirs or quartets that regularly toured the United States and Europe. The spiritual was accorded even more respect in the 1920s, when it became featured as a symbol of African American heritage by writers and musicians of the Harlem Renaissance. This was a most flexible symbol, because the spiritual's meaning could be subtly manipulated by its performance context and stylistic arrangement. The sacred folk expression of "brush arbors" and camp meetings characterized by Burleigh as "an outburst of intense religious fervor" might represent the traditional heritage of the African American slave, but the spiritual could just as easily be dressed up in art music guise and presented in concert to represent the cultural aspirations of the "New Negro."[13] Clearly Niles and his publisher, Carl Fischer, were tapping into a rich commercial vein—the release of *Impressions* during the same year the *Book of American Negro Spirituals* was published was anything but coincidental.

The title of Niles's *Impressions of a Negro Camp Meeting* contains a bit of unintended wordplay on the term *impressions*. As Niles noted in his foreword, the cycle of eight songs was intended to present "a record of some of my *impressions* gained while attending Negro camp meetings in Kentucky."[14] At the same time, the harmonic style is heavily influenced by *Impressionist* composers, particularly Henri Duparc's *mélodies* (1848–1933), which Niles experienced directly while studying in Paris. Niles's Impressionist harmonic palette is distinguished by the ubiquitous use of seventh and ninth chords, sometimes in a parallel or "planing" motion that seems purely coloristic, as in the songs "Humility," "John's Done Come Down," and "Drinkin' of de Wine." At other times, his harmonic progressions are strengthened by higher-order tertian chords that serve as secondary dominants and by diminished seventh chords, increasing tension toward the tonic resolution. In an obvious nod to the composer Debussy, "Next Came Sunday" features arpeggios composed largely of fourths and fifths. Accompaniment figures, as in the song "Humility," are often composed of ostinati that oscillate between two chords, much as in Duparc's song "L'invitation au voyage."

There is a delicious tension between the lushness of Niles's harmonic idiom and the simplicity of his melodic lines. "Next Comes Sunday," one of four pentatonic melodies in the cycle, has a simple, vigorous call-and-response shout of a camp meeting tune, but it is beautifully contrasted with arpeggios, thick seventh chords, and instances of planing. "Pray On Brother" has the simplistic directness of a repetitive shape-note hymn in the vein of "Hebrew Children," but the accompaniment features vivid seventh chords that contrast with the characteristic hollow-sounding dispersed harmony of a shape-note hymn.[15] These arrangements represent sterling examples of French *mélodie* style in the tradition of Duparc, Chausson, and Fauré. While the simplicity and vigor of the melodic lines is unmistakably American, the sophisticated piano accompaniment is very French. *Impressions* was created by a mature composer who was equally at home with the folk music of camp meetings and with art music of the Parisian salon.

Niles wrote in the foreword, "I have rewritten and adapted the text where necessary to more closely conform to the demands of meter and the particular treatment I have given the melodies. The negro would not recognize all these songs, but some of them he would."[16] Indeed, there is little that an African American would recognize or lay claim to in Niles's arrangements. There are few instances of syncopation other than the dotted-rhythm-ostinato in "Daniel." Only one or two melodic notes could be characterized as blues-inflected tones (on the one stressed note with a fermata in "John's Done Come Down" and over a chromatic accompaniment setting of the line "When St. Peter calls you home" in the song "Pray On Brother"). Some of the sound of the language is faintly retained in the occasional dialect references, such as "ob" for "of" and "de" for "the." Even here, there is a "correct" pronunciation provided as an option for the dialect. There is little here that suggests the brush arbor. These are stylized settings tailored for the intimacy of a chamber stage. In fact, Niles discovered exactly the right showcase for them in his performances with contralto Marion Kerby two years hence. Unfortunately, the publication was not financially successful; Niles's royalty check for the first year was only twenty-two cents.

Local Color Artist

In 1927 Niles inaugurated his writing career when *Scribner's* magazine published his "Hill Billies," a partially fictionalized account of music, moonshining, and myth in the Southern Appalachian Mountains.[17] The article consisted of two sketches, the first of which presented the Dauther Family: Pet Dauther, the mother of this brood; Emmet, her half-witted son, who wrote reams of four-line rhymes and periodically had to be chained inside the chicken coop; his siblings Sni and Minor; and Gimpsen, a hell-fire preacher. All in all, it was a family straight out of Faulkner's Yoknapatawpha County, with a tale of murder and suicide and a few songs thrown in as lagniappe. The second sketch, "Moonshine," brought Niles himself into the story as a war veteran from "up Louisville way" visiting the Bradley family, who had a still on a little island on the Ohio River. Within the narrative, Niles finds a way to depict a barbecue and a square dance and concludes with a snatch of song.[18]

A parade of subsequent articles devoted to mountain topics and wartime experiences followed in the next few years. In 1928 "In Defense of the Backwoods" appeared in an issue of *Scribner's* that also included a photo essay of Appalachian photographs by New York pictorialist Doris Ulmann. In fact, it is likely that Niles and Ulmann met initially through their mutual editor, Robert Bridges, at Charles Scribner's Sons.[19] "In Defense of the Backwoods" makes an impassioned case that the traditional rural music of Kentucky depicts the authentic "land full of beautiful situations and time-honored traditions"—the antithesis of the artificiality of Tin Pan Alley with its synthetic "mammy" and "coon" songs. Niles presents the texts (without music) of various songs and surrounds them with engaging anecdotes that animate the lyrics with colorful context. He artfully weaves a web of stories interspersed with songs—exactly the technique that he is developing for use on the concert stage.

Niles concluded the article with a short paragraph that neatly encapsulates his emerging philosophy concerning the importance of folk culture to national heritage. Here is the engine that drove Niles's performance and publication for the next fifty-some years of his life: "So you see, by drawing on the subject-matter nearest at hand, the mountain man, the hillbilly, the black man, and the clodhopper brighten a few of their dull moments with a natural gift of song—a gift very seldom found among the highly educated classes, where culture has robbed the individual of a beautiful and unrestrained form of expression, and developed an unfortunate self-consciousness in its place."[20]

Niles's other articles, drawn from his wartime experiences, were based on equally entertaining, yet more accurate, stories that were well documented in his notebooks. "The Sixth Hangar" (1928) was an account of German airplanes bombing the airfield at Colombey and mistakenly killing all the German prisoners of war who were temporarily being housed in "hangar six." "Hedge Hoppers" recounted the daredevil exploits of pilots who often crashed while attempting stunts such as landing on a moving train. And "Eleven a.m." is an account of the signing of the armistice agreement of November 11, 1918, followed by reactions of white and black soldiers, each group singing a characteristic song.[21]

Niles's final *Scribner's* article, "The Passing of the Street Cry" (1929), presented a more scholarly examination of the vending calls of traveling street merchants, complete with musical examples reproduced from his field notebooks. He also published "Shout, Coon, Shout!" an article about African American music, in *Musical Quarterly*, a music journal established by G. Schirmer and edited by Carl Engel, who served both as director of the Library of Congress's Music Division (1922–1934) and as editor of *Musical Quarterly* from 1929 to 1944.[22] Niles was paid $175 for each article, but more important than the income the articles produced was that they helped to authenticate Niles's credentials as both a collector and a raconteur.[23] The process of writing them served as valuable calisthenics for the more arduous exercise of writing a full-length book.

One Man's War

Niles first met Lieutenant Bert Hall on January 25, 1919, at American Aviation General Headquarters, 45 Avenue Montaigne in Paris.[24] Several days later they shared dinner at the "Ratt-Jazz" restaurant near the Richelieu Hotel, where Niles was staying. Hall was a seasoned and colorful fighter pilot who had made a name for himself as one of the original seven members of the Lafayette Escadrille. Over an evening's gracious candlelit dinner and too many drinks, Niles and Hall swapped tall tales of wine, women, and war. Hall, a flamboyant figure, had survived any number of martial and amorous encounters, and Niles was the perfect foil for these stories. As an aviator, he understood the details and technical nuances of flying; as a colorful raconteur himself, he could appreciate Hall's vivid anecdotes and embroider them in his own fashion. Furthermore, they were both native Kentuckians. Following this first dinner, Hall and Niles met again January 26 for drinks at Harry's New York Bar and dinner at L'Auberge du Clou. Hall began sharing his diaries with Niles, with the understanding that they would write a book together that would narrate Hall's memoirs. The larger-than-life accounts of Hall's adventures were perfectly suited to Niles's "local color" writing experience that broadly ambled between fact and fiction. And so was born a lively, tempestuous relationship that held together just long enough for Hall and Niles's book *One Man's War* to be published on April 27, 1929. Weston Bert Hall was born in 1886 at Bowling Green, Kentucky, but he soon moved to Page City, Lafayette County, Missouri, in the Ozark Mountains. He started flying a Farman plane in France in 1910, and by 1913 he made up the entire Turkish Air Force. When the Turks stopped paying him regularly (in gold coin), he transferred his services to the Bulgarian side. At the onset of

World War I, he enlisted in the French Foreign Legion and then became one of the founding members of the Lafayette Escadrille (originally called the Escadrille Américaine) when that unit was activated in April 1916. While Hall was an adept fighter pilot, credited in various accounts with either four or nine enemy planes shot down, he was more notorious for his extracurricular activities. Newspaper and magazine titles invariably described him with terms such as "scoundrel," "bad boy," and "rogue."[25] A current Web site devoted to the Lafayette Escadrille uses less savory language, saying he was "regarded by many as a boorish braggart, a soldier of fortune."[26]

Despite this reputation, or perhaps exactly because of it, Hall managed to parlay his wartime experiences and his charismatic persona into several books and a silent film starring Hall as Hall. The movie, *A Romance of the Air,* was directed by Franklin B. Coates and released in November 1918. Modeled on Hall's book *En L'Air! (In the Air) Three Years On and Above Three Fronts,*[27] the tangled, nearly operatic adventure plot breathlessly unfolds:

> Lieutenant Bert Hall, an ace American flyer serving in World War I as a member of the French Lafayette Escadrille, is wounded in an aerial battle and forced to land behind enemy lines. Finding his German opponent dead, Hall exchanges uniforms with him and is taken to a German hospital to recover. There he meets his old Kentucky sweetheart, who was unable to escape Berlin when the war broke out. Accompanied by the Countess of Moravia, who claims sympathy with the Allied cause, but is actually a German spy, they escape to France in a German plane. Through the countess' duplicity, Hall is accused of betraying the French government and sentenced to be shot, but his American lover uncovers evidence that saves him at the last moment.[28]

The film was actually something of a propaganda piece, conceived by the Air Service General Headquarters and designed to be shown in the States as a recruiting tool for the new American Air Section. There was a good deal more fancy than fact in the plot, though there are some tantalizing references to Hall's work in counterespionage and his close personal relationship with Marguerite "Maggie" Zell—known more commonly as the notorious spy Mata Hari. The German-uniform episode was actually based on an adventure Hall experienced while picking up and delivering French spies behind enemy lines. Once he landed for his appointed rendezvous with the spy but was surprised to see a German soldier running out to the plane and jumping in. Just as Hall turned around to shoot him, he realized the soldier was actually the French spy, who had disguised himself as a German.

Although Niles started writing the Bert Hall manuscript while living in Cincinnati and Chicago, it was not until he moved to New York City that he initiated the publishing contacts that spurred him to complete the writing. On May 19, 1928, he received a letter of agreement from Charles Colebaugh, the managing editor of *Collier's* magazine, which sought to publish three articles from the preliminary manuscript on Hall that Niles had written, under the title "Wings, Gasoline, and Gunpowder." Colebaugh offered Niles eight hundred dollars for each article and promised, "If Lieutenant Hall undertakes the flight across the Pacific, and is successful, we shall increase the number of articles used to seven, to be paid at the same rate—$800.00 each." So a portion of the manuscript in this early form was released as an appetizer—the first of several *Collier's* installments designed to whet the public's appetite for the future book.[29]

During much of the time that Niles and Hall were working together, Hall was abroad, traveling through Asia and living in China, where he became known as "General Chan," chief of the air force at Canton. Communication between the two collaborators eventually turned acrimonious, soured by dissension over the financial arrangements. Evidently, the original informal contract between Niles and Hall was superseded by a formal document drawn up between Niles and Holt while Hall was in China. Hall was upset with the content and merchandising of the book, unhappy with the financial arrangement, and irate because he was denied an advance on the sales.

In preparation for his attempted flight over the Pacific, Hall flew to San Francisco in January 1930 and had his specially designed airplane shipped to him from a hangar on Long Island. A friend of Hall's took the plane for a test flight before Hall was scheduled to make his trans-Pacific flight. Unfortunately, the plane's left wing buckled on takeoff, and Hall returned to China without having successfully crossed the Pacific Ocean. Sometime later he reappeared in the United States and "became a vaudeville star, recounting his exploits while wearing both medals he earned and some he did not."[30] Hall died December 6, 1948.

Although sales from the book were not all that Niles and Hall had anticipated, the literary reviews were glowing. For example, the *New York Times* reviewer was impressed with the absorbing nature of the narrative: "Frank and intimate are really rather mild adjectives to apply to this book, which is a tale fit to keep the reader on the edge of his chair with his breath short and his eyes un-winking from beginning to end. . . . Makes any high-colored novel of adventure look pale." And from the *New York Evening Post* came a similar evaluation: "Most vernacular diaries, when served up in print, have the stale flavor of warmed-over victuals; but Hall's courses come hot and hotter from the range. He has the born talker's capacity to take you with him, make you see through his eyes, yearn over what tugs at his entrails, laugh at what tickles his funny bone."[31]

One Woman's War

Hoping to ride on the coattails of *One Man's War*'s success and Niles's name recognition, the Macaulay Company published an interesting follow-up titled *One Woman's War* in 1930. It is unclear just who the author is—it was published anonymously with a "Publisher's Note" that ambiguously explained the manuscript's provenance:

> The manuscript was put in the hands of Lieutenant John J. Niles, author of "Singing Soldiers," and "Songs My Mother Never Taught Me"; these books constitute the first comprehensive collection of songs sung by American soldiers in a major war.
>
> Lieutenant Niles, who was in the aviation service, was in a position to give personal corroboration to many of the episodes treated in this book. Through inquiry and research he was able to secure a point-by-point verification of those sections of the book not covered by his own experiences.

The author, whose name we are not now in a position to di-
vulge, further presented us with documentary evidence of her
wide and varied war work.[32]

There are precious few clues concerning the real identity of this author.
It is probable that it was written by Niles himself, although nothing in
his notebooks or other writings substantiates any of the stories. The
few references to its composition are in his autobiography, where he
noted: "Out of the remains of Bert Hall's book I was working on an
idea involving a Red Cross nurse. I planned to offer the book to be
published anonymously by Macaulay."[33] Later he added: "I had been
working on the remnants of One Man's War and at long last had turned
these fragments and many interviews into One Woman's War. However,
no matter what anyone did about it, One Woman's War was never a
profitable venture. In my contract I was as lucky as any writer had ever
been, because I reserved the rights to all reprints and to all mechanicals
and movies."[34]

Although some of the writing style is reminiscent of Niles's technique
and vocabulary, it seems a stretch to imagine him writing this whole book
in a first-person female voice. It is far more likely that he compiled it,
by assembling and editing a manuscript and interviews. One Woman's
War might also have been written by his wife, Hélène Babbit Niles. She
had served in the Red Cross during the war, though what little is known
of her background does not seem entirely consonant with the history
given in the book of the anonymous daughter of Countessa de Placer-
villers (formerly Mrs. Randall Pierce), who was born in Richmond, Virginia, and lived in Belgium. Nevertheless, her name appears several times
as "Hélène" in the book, and there are several references to a Hélène in
One Man's War, where Hall describes meeting her at the conclusion of his
book.

The final possibility is that it was a manuscript submitted to Macaulay
anonymously to protect the author from repercussions of her "kiss-and-
tell" revelations. Niles may then have been simply credited as the source
of the manuscript as a way of piggybacking on his reputation as a World
War I authority and author of the similarly titled work, in order to sell the
book.[35]

Singing Soldiers

While Niles was collaborating with editor Robert Bridges on the *Scribner's* magazine articles, he was also working with Maxwell Perkins, Charles Scribner's Sons editor in chief, on a book-length collection devoted to World War I soldiers' songs. The idea of compiling wartime songs first occurred to Niles in Paris in December 1917, when he chanced upon Théodore Botrel's 1914 book *Les Chants du Bivouac,* which contained French songs and poems with pen-and-ink illustrations by Carlélie.[36] Niles played through the music at his hotel lobby and ambitiously decided that evening that he would attempt something similar. By the time he was in Cincinnati in 1920, he had compiled the first musical arrangements, but his mentor, Ralph Lyford, advised him to couple the music transcriptions and arrangements with more substantial narrative. In New York, Niles discarded all the earlier sketches and began anew under Perkins's guidance.

Niles made the critical decision to focus solely on the music of African American soldiers. He had earlier, in 1917 while he was in France, consciously chosen to concentrate on black musical expression, so when it came time to organize the collection, he realized that the most "authentic" and characteristic songs that he had gathered were from black tradition. Certainly it would have been far easier for him to collect the music that was closest at hand, but Niles had the acumen and sensitivity to realize that black Americans in the American Expeditionary Force (A.E.F.) were far more likely to adapt traditional songs and create new music in response to the new wartime environment.

Black soldiers played a critical role in the war effort, but they were generally relegated to support rather than combat missions. More than 350,000 African Americans served in segregated units within the Ninety-third Division (placed under command of the French Army) and the Ninety-second Division, which was under the command of the American Army. Although blacks were usually assigned to logistical roles—loading and unloading ships and supply trains, building fortifications and digging graves, some black soldiers had the opportunity to participate directly in combat; the 369th Infantry Regiment distinguished itself by being the first unit to reach the Rhine River, in 1918. The 369th also made a name for themselves as exceptional musical ambassadors. Their band, led by James Reese Europe, was largely credited with introducing jazz to Europe.[37]

Questions naturally arise concerning Niles's intent and methodology regarding his relationship to African American culture. Without a doubt, Niles is guilty of condescending paternalism toward the black soldier and of racism. Without a doubt he is guilty of commodifying black culture so that he could use it for personal profit; he is guilty of perceiving and romanticizing individual African American people as an exotic "other"; occasionally he was guilty of insensitivity—for instance, he saw little irony in his detailed description of a blackface minstrel show that he directed on Christmas Eve 1917. Without a doubt, Niles resorted to stereotypes of language and situation in the use of dialect, such as "ob" for "of" and "de" rather than "the." Although Niles generally eschewed resorting to caricature rather than character in describing physical features, he is guilty by association of employing Margaret Thorniley Williamson's illustrations, which occasionally cross the line into the realm of blackface cartoons.

At the same time, Niles and his book *Singing Soldiers* must be considered in the context of early-twentieth-century cultural thought. This work is a celebration of inclusivity for a culture marginalized by institutional racism. The U.S. Army was highly segregated at this time. In some ways it is astonishing that a white rural southern man could portray black culture with such an attempt at dignity.[38] It is telling that this book, alone in Niles's output, is not dedicated to friends and family but is simply and eloquently inscribed "To the American Negro Soldiers who made this writing possible."

Upon completion of the book, Niles wrote to the National Association for the Advancement of Colored People (NAACP) on June 20, 1927, in an effort to interest the group in his work. While some of his motivation appears to be self-promotion, an attempt to sell copies of the book, a more idealistic, though naive, motive shines through in his attempt to assist in educating African Americans about themselves in the name of "progress."[39] Whatever the motivation, it is fortunate that Niles preserved so many of the texts and tunes with such apparent fidelity. These songs are not derived from white culture in the style of coon songs, minstrelsy, or Tin Pan Alley parodies of black style. Neither are they pale imitations of spirituals, rags, or blues, although many of the songs are related to those genres. These are clearly ephemeral fragments of black culture that would have vanished without a trace if someone like Niles had not been there to document and preserve the songs. As in *Impressions of a Negro Camp Meeting*, Niles successfully managed to convey the essential nature of African American melodies and texts by transforming them through arrangements that sought to retain the integrity of the original performances. Although the arrangements should never be confused for the real thing, they do present a stylized version that elegantly and economically represents the original songs with the respect they richly merit.

By November 1926 the manuscript was finished, and a year later *Singing Soldiers* was finally on the shelves. The book played to Niles's strengths as both a storyteller and a musician. As a narrative, *Singing Soldiers* presented a web of vivid anecdotes that bound the songs together in a context of flesh-and-blood scenes fraught with all the danger and excitement of the recent war. Musically, *Singing Soldiers* highlighted Niles's ear for fieldwork and his economical Impressionist musical settings and revealed his genuine sympathy for African American expression.

Niles navigated the dual nature of this book, both song collection and engaging wartime account, with great skill. The general reader could easily become absorbed in the narrative without being distracted by the musical arrangements. Since a number of the songs merely presented the lyrics or reproduced the lyrics coupled with an unobtrusive melody line, the general reader could appreciate the complementary song dimension of the book without being bogged down in music notation. At the same time, the musical arrangements were carefully designed to be appropriate for modest performers, yet they were sufficiently musically intriguing to be attractive to professional musicians.

Niles was careful to allow the music to speak for itself. These songs are not over-arranged. Of twenty-nine songs, eleven were presented simply as melody-line transcriptions that strike a balance between being prescriptive and descriptive. In the versions with a melody line plus a piano accompaniment, there is a real economy of means coupled with a variety of subtly different approaches. Some songs, such as "Diggin'" or "Crap-Shootin' Charley," rely on only one or two chords (although they are often chromatically inflected or higher-order tertian chords). One song, "He's a Burden Bearer," is based on an arpeggio figure, and one, "I Don't Want

Anymore France," has some of the rhythmic characteristics of ragtime. Although the harmony and texture are considerably more reserved than in *Impressions of a Negro Camp Meeting*, there are a few instances of Impressionist figures that enhance the sparse texture, such as the string of parallel augmented fourths in "Ghost Song" (bar four) or the "planing" fourths of bar six in "The Gimme Song."

There are few gratuitous references to stock African American musical gestures. Where a call-and-response texture is present, it is subtly implied by an accompaniment texture change, as in "Lordy, Turn Your Face," where the "call" is doubled in a single-note bass line while the "response" is accompanied by homorhythmic chords. In "Goodbye Tennessee," there are small notations in the lyrics where an "uhm hmm" response is interjected. Niles seemed to take unusual care to reconcile the problems of notation with oral tradition in this song. He instructed at the bottom of the page: "The little responsive 'uhm hums' were either sung by some one near by or by the soloist himself. Once the assisting singer sang 'I says goodbye . . .' The form of the song varied with the verses. One might say that the singers defied form and note value in an attempt to gain an unusual rhythm and tell their story at the same time."[40]

Although Niles recorded numerous blues-related songs, he generally avoided the obvious opportunities for blues scale inflections. Since his harmonic palette was already highly colored by the frequent use of seventh, ninth, and augmented sixth chords, Niles's use of blues notes was sparing and judicious—as much structural as melodic, as in the blues thirds employed in the beginning of the chorus of the "Gimme Song."

Book reviews were unanimous in their endorsement of Niles's effort. Olin Downes (1886–1955), one of the country's most respected music critics, began his *New York Times* column: "Correspondents of the music page of *The Times* have in recent weeks discussed the origins of negro folk music and the question of the musical originality of the negro. A new phase of this subject, one fascinatingly related and corroborative of the generally accepted estimate of the negro's extremely creative musical nature, is illustrated by the book, 'Singing Soldiers,' recently come from the press, compiled by John J. Niles and dedicated to the 'American negro soldiers who made this writing possible.'" Later in the article, Downes added that "the melodies quoted are excellently treated by the collector.

Moreover the book carries in it the savor of the place and time where the songs were sung."[41]

Robert A. Simon, writing in the *Evening Post,* addressed the dual nature of the audience for the book and cited its value as an anthology of previously undocumented folk music: "Among the negroes, Lieutenant Niles found a kind of folk music, brought up to date and adapted to war situations. 'Singing Soldiers' is a short compilation of such songs, threaded together with agreeable tales of the author's martial adventures. As a war book it is what might have been expected from an aviator who had a flair for setting down entertaining or dramatic episodes, but as a source book it is of great importance."[42]

An extensive *New York Times* book review by S. T. Williamson described the book as "hell-roaring verses and measures born of men tried in battle, an unexpurgated doughboy hymnal." The reviewer praised the narrative as well as the musical contents: "Each addition to his collection was an adventure in itself, and the telling of the circumstances leading up to the procurement of the new verses makes Mr. Niles's book of far more interest to the general reader than had he kept it merely an anthology."[43]

John Thomason Jr., reviewer for the *New York Herald Tribune,* presented a most thoughtful and critical approach, founded on his status as a captain in the U.S. Marine Corps and as a Texan. While he "authenticated" Niles's war experiences and lauded the veracity of Niles's transcriptions and repertoire, the most important part of the review delved into the essential question of a white man writing about black culture. Thomason touched upon challenging racial constructs here, intuitively comprehending a sense of "dual consciousness" as W. E. B. Du Bois (1868–1963) might have used the term in *The Souls of Black Folk* (1903). Thomason rightly perceived that the intersection of African American "two-ness" as an American and as a Negro, can be revealed in the African American's song:

> You never know what the Negro is thinking about; reared myself among Negroes in Texas, I do not believe that many white men know how his head works. For his contacts with the whites he has a special set of manners; inside, and with his own people, he is something else again. Only when he sings does one catch a

glimpse of that other self which is perhaps the real one. And these songs ring true. . . . Finally, Lieutenant Niles has approached the subject sensibly, which can not always be said of white folks who write of Negroes. He has handled it with sympathy, and without sentimentality, and his touch is sure and firm from first to last. The fact that he is a Southerner may account for this—for the fact that he is able to consider Negroes as Negroes, and not as pegs whereon to hang ideas created in the writer's own imagination.[44]

The *Hartford Courant* was less insightful but more laudatory, praising the book as both a music anthology and an entertaining wartime account: "It isn't a dainty chronicle, but neither is it top-heavy with rank detail—it conveys to the reader the impression that he is getting, so far as that is possible, the truth of things as they were."[45]

Niles's wartime experiences were purchased at a great price—privation, homesickness, and serious injuries resulting from his flirtation with death in flimsy airplanes. Ten years later, however, the investment yielded substantial dividends in terms of the success of his publications that capitalized on the war. Lieutenant Niles was gaining a reputation as one of the leading authorities of wartime song, and he was not about to stop publishing now that he had an audience.

Hell on Wheels

Niles's rising star was manifest in the fast literary and musical circles in which he was moving. He began collaborating on a work for musical theater with a group of Pulitzer Prize–winning writers, directors, and musicians, who gathered about the famous Algonquin "round table." A *New York Times* theatrical column of September 1, 1928, announced the projected work with the headline "'Hell on Wheels,' a Comedy of War, Promised—Maxwell Anderson Has Hand in It" and commented that "Hamilton McFadden, who made his debut as a Broadway producer last season, is to vouchsafe a third [war play for the season], to be called 'Hell on Wheels.' It is described as a 'war comedy filled with favorite soldier songs of the war.'" Its authors were named as Maxwell Anderson, Jack Niles, and Douglas Moore.[46]

This production attracted an exceptionally talented creative team. Maxwell Anderson (1888–1959) was a prominent journalist who wrote for the *New Republic,* the *New York Evening Globe,* and the *New York World.* While at the *World,* Anderson collaborated with book reviewer and war veteran Lawrence Stallings to write *What Price Glory?* a play that enjoyed an extended Broadway run in 1924. Eventually Anderson won a Pulitzer for *Both Your Houses* in 1933 and New York Drama Critics' Circle Awards for *Winterset* (1935) and *High Tor* (1936).

Niles had most likely met Douglas Moore (1893–1969) when they were both students at the Schola Cantorum in 1919. Moore served as a lieutenant aboard the destroyer USS *Murray* until the armistice allowed him to continue his music studies in Paris with Vincent d'Indy and Nadia Boulanger. Returning to the States, Moore was first appointed music director at the Art Museum of Cleveland and then, after studying with Boulanger for a year on a Pulitzer Traveling Fellowship, he joined the music faculty at Columbia University. Eventually he wrote the opera *Giants in the Earth* (which received a Pulitzer in 1951) and the folk opera *Ballad of Baby Doe* (1956), which has subsequently been embraced within the standard repertoire. Niles and Moore came from vastly different social and educational backgrounds: Niles from rural Kentucky roots and Moore from a venerable ninth-generation Long Island, New York, family with ancestral ties to Miles Standish and John Alden. Yet their common wartime experiences and complementary musical training brought them together in harmony.

It was probably through Douglas Moore's connection to Robert Sherwood (1896–1955) that George S. Kaufman (1889–1961) was drawn into the project. Moore had previously collaborated with Sherwood, who was drama editor for *Vanity Fair* and a member of the Algonquin round table, on the production of *The Road to Rome* (1927), so it is likely that Moore also came in contact with Kaufman, another longstanding member of the table. Kaufman served as drama critic (and later drama editor) for the *New York Times* and was coauthor of a number of plays, including the Pulitzer Prize–winning *You Can't Take It with You* (written with Moss Hart). While the *Times* announcement for *Hell on Wheels* didn't mention George Kaufman by name, Niles noted that he was also part of the effort. It is highly likely that he was brought in to work with this high-profile project, since he was often hired by producers to develop scripts into hit plays.[47] The producer, Hamilton McFadden, soon left New York and the Broadway stage and moved to Hollywood, where he directed and produced a string of forty films, including *Cheer Up and Smile* (1930), *Black Camel* (1931), and *Charlie Chan in Paris* (1935).

Niles was not entirely at home in the company of the razor-witted folks at the Algonquin, but he had served in the war with two round-table regulars who had written for the *Stars and Stripes,* Franklin Pierce Adams and Alexander Woollcott. Adams, who was now author of the column *The Conning Tower,* published in the *Herald Tribune,* the *World,* and the *New York Post,* invited Niles to join him at the Algonquin. Niles commented, "I had lunch with the Round Table group three times at the Algonquin Hotel, and then decided it was not for me, in spite of the gaiety, the wise-crackery, the influence of the other members, and the charm of Miss Dorothy Parker. There was a hovering kind of bitterness in the ridicule they employed. After three lunches (which I could hardly afford) I realized that I was too much of a country boy for all this sophistication."[48] Unfortunately, all the wit and wisdom of the round table could not make a hit production out of the ungainly premise of *Hell on Wheels*— the wartime saga of a vast naval artillery weapon. The project was wisely scrapped before it ever went into production.[49]

The Songs My Mother Never Taught Me

Any list of popular songs from World War I would probably include "Over There," "It's a Long Way to Tipperary," "Goodbye Broadway, Hello France," "K-K-K-Katy," "Pack Up Your Troubles in an Old Kit Bag and Smile, Smile, Smile," "Oh, How I Hate to Get Up in the Morning," "There's a Long, Long Trail," and "How Ya Gonna Keep 'Em Down on the Farm (after They've Seen Paree?)," and yet not a single one of these hit songs is found between the covers of *Songs My Mother Never Taught Me,* the next wartime song collection connected with Niles.

The favorable reception of *Singing Soldiers* had taught Niles that there was a substantial audience with an appetite for wartime songs and stories. In addition, he still possessed a quantity of soldiers' songs that had been recorded but were not included in the first book. It was only natural then, that Niles and the Macaulay Company, which had published *One Man's War*, would consider producing a sequel to *Singing Soldiers*. So *The Songs My Mother Never Taught Me* came into being, although this time Niles called in some reinforcements, including coauthor Douglas Moore and illustrator Abian A. "Wally" Wallgren (1892–1948).

Following the demise of the *Hell on Wheels* project, Niles sought Moore's compositional expertise in this new collaborative venture. Moore, described by Niles as "a truly great musician," contributed some of his own songs to the book, although they are not credited as such. He is definitely the author of the naval songs, particularly the more extended works with introductions and key changes, such as "Destroyer Life" (which was credited to the singing of the officers and crew of the USS *Murray* between 1917 and 1919) and "The Shore Navy." In contrast to the raucous tone of many of the book's songs, some of Moore's lyrics would feel more at home in a sophisticated Cole Porter song. Consider the witty internal rhymes and polysyllabic vocabulary of this stanza of "The Shore Navy," which differs wildly from the earthy savor of songs in *Singing Soldiers*.

Oh, the shore navy, the shore navy,
How tedious the work of the staff.
There's innumerable luncheons and similar functions
And oceans of tea to quaff.
There's a sweet yeomanette for each office to pet,
Conversational, banter and chaff.[50]

It is difficult to disentangle Niles's contributions from Moore's, since all of the song types and arrangements in *Songs My Mother Never Taught Me* are so different from those in *Singing Soldiers*. While Niles and Moore shared a common vocabulary of French Impressionism, gained from their shared experiences at the Schola Cantorum, this book reveals little of the Impressionist influence found in *Singing Soldiers*. Both the harmonies and the rhythms of the accompaniments are sturdy, uncomplicated, and designed for ease of performance. In fact, the piano parts of this book appear to be conceived with the technical facility of amateurs and boisterously inebriated plunkers in mind. There is a consistency in arrangement style that reflects the smooth articulation between Niles's and Moore's contributions. The narrative anecdotes appear to be mostly Niles's handiwork.

Wallgren was invited to collaborate on a book tentatively titled "The Songs My Mother Never Taught Me" via a letter Niles sent him on February 20, 1929. It is clear that Niles had not personally met Wallgren yet, but Niles had already tried to interest Lee Furman, president of the Macaulay publishing house, in the idea of asking Wallgren to contribute illustrations to accompany Niles's music.[51]

A contract from the Macaulay Company of April 8, 1929, formalized Wallgren's participation in the book; for $250 he consented to provide ten full-page black and white illustrations and "such other cuts for chapter-heads and tail-pieces as you may consider advisable."[52] Wallgren, described by Niles as "unpredictable, though delightfully humorous . . . with all the benefits and disadvantages of being a one-time marine . . . and also inclined to the bottle,"[53] was the perfect choice for this project. As one of the original staff members for the *Stars and Stripes,* he had gained widespread name recognition.[54] Furthermore, his earthy sense of humor, formed in the frontline trenches, was perfectly wedded to the bawdy character of the songs.

Before enlisting in the U.S. Marines, Wallgren had enjoyed a successful career creating cartoons for the *Philadelphia Public Ledger* and then the *Washington Post.* During the war he was assigned to the Fifth Marines of the First Division and remained a private until the conclusion of the war. His cartoons, appearing in every issue of the *Stars and Stripes,* saw the war through the eyes of the common soldier in the field, satirizing officers and regulations and commenting wryly on the conditions of daily life with lice, poor food, muddy trenches, drinking, and, of course, women. These were just the ingredients of *Songs My Mother Never Taught Me.*

Although this new work superficially resembled the format of *Singing Soldiers,* with song arrangements for piano and voice, anecdotal narrative context, and illustrations, there were some critical differences in the content and intent. The primary difference was that the focus was now on white soldiers. Out of fifty-eight songs, there were now just six songs identified as African American in origin, and these were all segregated in the back of the book, where they were as ghettoized as blacks were in the army (there were a few songs associated with black tradition, such as "Frankie and Johnnie" and "Sallie Brown," that were without dialect and placed in the "white section" of the book). In a way, *Songs My Mother Never Taught Me* was more of a response or reaction to *Singing Soldiers* rather than a sequel, since it set out to demonstrate that white soldiers and sailors could be as creative as blacks. The foreword noted, "Sailors and soldiers sent [these songs] to us from everywhere; some in answer to the statement made by the author in 'Singing Soldiers,' that negroes were the only soldiers who sang anything original; and some out of a desire to have the music of the war recorded and kept for future generations."[55]

Symbolically, the most popular song of the war, "Mademoiselle from Armentières," existed in two different forms and appeared in two different sections of the book. The white version was positioned first in the collection, an indication of the primacy of this song's importance among white doughboys. The version that developed among African American soldiers, known as "Tell Me Now," was nearly at the back of the bus, among the black soldier's songs. Here, Niles appended a headnote explaining the difference between the two versions: "This is what the negroes did to 'Mlle. From Armentières.' 'Mlle. from Armentières' was a white man's song. The negroes would have very little of it. Why should they? Their ancestors had been inventing better songs ever since they learned the English language. But the colored boys took the form of 'Hinky Dinky Parlez-Vous,' and with the idea of repeating the first statement several times, they got to work and 'Tell Me Now' was the result."[56] "Tell Me Now" presents a trenchant perspective of the war as a "white man's war" in which black soldiers merely got ensnared. Consider the unresolved implied question of the third stanza:

> I don't know why I totes dis gun,
> Tell me, oh, tell me now,
> I don't know why I totes this gun,
> 'Cause I ain't got nothin' 'gainst de Hun,
> Tell me, Oh, tell me now.

The provenance of the songs altered the complexion of the repertoire considerably. Many of them were not personally documented by Niles but were received from a host of solicited and unsolicited sources and then arranged by Niles or Moore, or both.[57] It is revealing that this collection, unlike *Singing Soldiers,* contained none of the single-melody-line transcriptions characteristic of field transcriptions. *Songs My Mother Never Taught Me* is really more of a songbook devoted to musical parody, in which white soldiers adapted popular song as a way to remain sane in an insane world of death and violence. By satirizing the experience, soldiers had some release from the stress, built the camaraderie essential to survival, and achieved some illusion of control over the absurdities of daily life in the trenches.

If *One Woman's War* was Niles's way of presenting a female voice to balance the male adventures of *One Man's War,* there was no counterpart in his musical collections. Women are frequently the *subject* of songs, but they are nowhere evident as the *source* of songs. Females occasionally make an appearance in Wallgren's illustrations, but they are usually depicted as ravishing, leggy, buxom dames surrounded by a horde of admiring soldiers (see "Mademoiselle from Armentières," page 19, or "Madelon," page 97) or as a bevy of beauties in the rum-addled imagination of a sailor (see "The Waitress and the Sailor," page 147). However, one of the few illustrations that appears twice is an achingly true sketch of a melancholy French woman in wooden shoes holding a squalling baby and waving goodbye to a departing soldier who loved and left her.[58]

Females were an essential part of the war, whether maintaining the home front, serving in war-related industry, or volunteering in various service agencies—particularly the Red Cross, where eventually eighteen thousand women served in army and navy hospitals. The French and the English were compelled to include women more directly in the war effort as truck and motorcycle drivers and even as aviators. Niles and Moore briefly acknowledged this involvement in the foreword: "Women had to do with the madness that was war. Many of them had their first opportunity to prove a previously unexpressed nobility. Many of them were brave beyond the usual understanding of the term, but somehow they seldom got into the original song creations that became a part of our army and navy's kit and baggage."[59] Women might be brave and loyal, but they were still not welcome in the boy's club that is war. Women are object not subject, and in this book they are very much two-dimensional objects of desire and a nuisance when men are gathered to sing their bawdy songs for "stag consumption" only.

There are bawdy, boisterous "unexpurgated" songs in the book, many of them armed with "sing-along" choruses and performance notes, such as: "Don't try to sing this song in a state of cold sobriety. . . . It won't go that way. . . . The time of night has something to do with it too. . . . The ideas in the 'Limey Sailor Song' go best after midnight, the neighbors notwithstanding."[60] *Singing Soldiers* indicated some congregational participation through subtle call-and-response cues, whereas *Songs My Mother Never Taught Me* used the chorus form and provided explicit performance directions to guide audience participation.

Much of the repertoire of this book developed as improvised parodies of well-known songs. It was only natural for soldiers to comment on the matters closest to them, and the most natural vehicle were those tunes that were also closest at hand—well-known folk and popular songs. Parodies in which the original tune was outfitted with a new set of lyrics included "Heligoland," "The Sergeant," "Louse Song," "The Corporal," and "Home Boys, Home," all sung to the tune of "Son of a Gambolier." "Allentown Ambulance" is set to the tune of "The Infantry," and "De Six Bit Express" is based on a variant of Stephen Foster's "Camptown Races." "The Waitress and the Sailor" is based on two tunes sung by Niles's father, "Abe Lincoln Was a Farmer's Lad; He Lived in Illinois" and "And She Gets There Just the Same." "The Ki-Wi Song," poking fun at aviation officers who do not actually fly, is sung to the folk tune commonly associated with the words "The old grey mare, she ain't what she used to be." And while not exactly a parody, additional wartime verses are appended to "The Hearse Song," which is more often sung with the lyrics "The Worms Crawl In."

In addition to the parodies, there are several well-known songs with their lyrics intact, most prominently "The Marine Hymn" and "The Caisson Song." The only anomaly is the inclusion of Niles's "Venezuela," which was problematic since the song was disingenuously identified as "music that was collected from traditional singing." Niles later addressed the inclusion of "Venezuela" in an article for *Atlantic:*

When I offered the manuscript of *Songs My Mother Never Taught Me* to a New York publisher, he was aghast to discover that "Venezuela" was not included. "But 'Venezuela' is composition," I said, "words and music. It is not folk music." (I had learned to use the term by then.) "Folk music be damned," said he, striking the desk a resounding whack, "You want to sell your book don't you?" Yes, I said, I did want to sell the book. Verily, I did. "Well then, put 'Venezuela' in the book. And some of those others I've heard you sing around town. And let me tell you another thing, young man: if you want the New York publishers to take your stuff, you'd better label it all folk music."[61]

The 1918 notebook entries are consonant with Niles's depiction of the song's origin in *Atlantic,* but there is no substantiation for the conversation with the New York publisher, who was probably Lee Furman of Macaulay. In any event, Niles's original song was not identified as his song, in much the same way that "Black Is the Color" was ambiguously attributed to "Ary, on Troublesome Creek" in the original G. Schirmer publication. The cachet of "Folk" proved to be a powerful marketing tool.

Hinky-Dinky Barley Brew

Niles collaborated with his second wife, Hélène, and illustrator Bob Dean to publish a little illustrated book (thirty-two pages) of anti-Prohibition verses set to the popular World War I song "Hinky-Dinky Parlez Vous," or, as it was usually known, "Mademoiselle from Armentières." Published in 1932 under the tortuous title *Hinky Dinky Barley Brew: A Cry from the Heart: Being the Reincarnation of the Justly Famous Song Entitled Mademoiselle from Armentière,* the book was dedicated to D.U. (the photographer Doris Ulmann), which must have been somewhat problematic, since Niles's marriage to his editor, Hélène, was unraveling at this point and he was now involved in a professional and personal relationship with Ulmann.

With its catchy tune and two-line structure interspersed with the ubiquitous "parlez vous" refrain, the song was the perfect vehicle for expressing an improvised commentary on any and every wartime sentiment, from love to drink to politics. *Hinky Dinky* carries this song's history one step further with Niles's collection of verses lampooning Prohibition.

Hinky Dinky was a frothy little publication, an attempt to provide the public with a spirited response to the bleak implications of Prohibition.[62] Just as "Mademoiselle from Armentières" served as the perfect vehicle for doughboys to lampoon the war, so Niles transformed it to serve a similar purpose in the war against the war against John Barleycorn:

> If you're going to drink this bath tub gin, parlez-vous,
> If you're going to drink this bath tub gin, parlez-vous,
> If you're going to drink this bath tub gin,
> Just reinforce your gut with tin.
> Hinky Dinky, parlez-vous.

Niles had intended *Hinky Dinky Barley Brew* to be just the first in a series of complementary publications, but no subsequent volumes ever appeared because of his separation from Hélène and a busy schedule that included concertizing with Kerby, travel through the mountains with Doris Ulmann, and music publication with G. Schirmer.

Carl Engel and G. Schirmer Publications

Although Niles was originally snubbed by Gustave "Gus" Schirmer, president of G. Schirmer Inc. (and son of the Gustave Schirmer who founded the music publishing house in 1848), he was eventually embraced by the new president of Schirmer, Carl Engel (1883–1944), who developed a cordial relationship with Niles that blossomed into a long-term professional association with G. Schirmer Inc.

Engel, born in Paris July 21, 1883, studied music composition in Strasbourg and Munich before immigrating to the United States in 1905. He served as music editor for the Boston Music Company from 1909 to 1920 and was appointed president of G. Schirmer Publishing in 1929. Though European born and educated, Engel developed an appreciation of American music, primarily through his close relationship with Oscar G. T. Sonneck, head of the Music Division of the Library of Congress and the first serious scholar of American music.[63] Engel and Sonneck, G. Schirmer, the Library of Congress's Music Division, and the *Musical Quarterly* were all woven together in an inextricably tight little web. Engel succeeded Sonneck as chief of the Library of Congress's Music Division, served as president of G. Schirmer, and also served as editor (from 1929 to 1944) for the *Musical Quarterly*, a journal founded by Sonneck and published by G. Schirmer.

While serving the Library of Congress, Engel was responsible for two particularly important developments. In 1925 he inaugurated the Elizabeth Sprague Coolidge Foundation, devoted to sponsoring music concerts at the Library of Congress. Engel also initiated a program of recording folk music for the Library of Congress in 1928.[64]

Given Engel's interest in folk music advocacy—both at the Library of Congress and at G. Schirmer, it is scarcely surprising that he and Niles developed a close working relationship. Engel appreciated Niles's French-influenced arrangements of African American folk music. Engel's own background as an Impressionist-influenced composer of art song, coupled with his burgeoning interest in American vernacular music—both jazz and folk styles—were in harmony with Niles's own interests.[65]

It is not difficult to imagine the two of them collaborating to develop Niles's long-term catalog of Schirmer compositions. Engel's musical sensitivity, social purpose, and business acumen provided direction in terms of format and arrangement style, while Niles contributed a repertoire and the ability to craft playable and effective arrangements. The first collection to emerge from this partnership, *Seven Kentucky Mountain Songs*, was completed in fall 1928 and published in 1929; *Seven Negro Exaltations* was finished in summer 1929 and published later that same year.

These two collections devoted to marginalized American cultures bore many similarities. Superficially, they shared a common look and common dimensions, belonging to an extensive Schirmer Folk Song series that had African, American, British-Irish, Dutch, French, German, Italian, Russian, Swedish, and miscellaneous contributions.[66] Both collections featured cover illustrations by C. M. Sutherland depicting scenes suggested by the songs, and both included prefaces by Niles. For *Seven Kentucky Mountain Songs*, Sutherland created twelve sketches containing the full range of stereotypical Appalachian images, including a moonshine still, women gossiping over a fence, a pastoral cabin on a hillside, a hayseed riding a mule, and a sheriff with a shotgun under his arm. The drawings are all encased in circles as though glimpsed from afar through a telescope. Similarly, Sutherland's cover illustration for *Seven Negro Exaltations* wove a continuous frame—a border of sketches depicting Noah with ark and animals, a black preacher, African American angelic figures in each corner, a farmer tugging at his resolutely stubborn mule, a minstrel-show-like dandy rolling dice, and a street vendor with his cart.

Between the covers, the books' formats mirror each other as well. They both open with a prefatory statement, they both contain seven arrangements for piano and voice, and they both provide critical notes that contribute conversational, contextual information concerning the singer, the song, and the circumstances under which the collecting was done.

The *Seven Kentucky Mountain Songs* preface conveys Niles's romantic conception of Appalachia in eloquent and nearly poetic terms. He attempts to establish a visual context for the music, compounded of all the people and places Niles has experienced in his search for mountain songs. This is a Kentucky, an Appalachia, that never was but should have been, a construction of various outside narratives imposed on the region. Niles's Appalachia is an exotic "other" populated by "our contemporary ancestors," who are tied to Elizabethan ways because of the impenetrable isolation of the mountains. For Niles, Appalachia *is* a ballad—a "great classic legend" inhabited by folks "killing their razor-back hogs, stilling their liquors, cultivating their corn crops, collecting tan bark, weaving the home-spun, shooting out their feuds, singing their unbelievable music"— rather than a real place inhabited by real people engaged in the process of adapting to the forces of industrialization.[67]

The language of the preface to *Seven Negro Exaltations* is more reserved, because Niles is not as personally involved with the people and the culture. His introduction serves as an encomium praising the enduring creativity of African American musicians who spontaneously and naturally composed their music in response to oppression. However well intended these generous comments are, this conception of music is just as frozen in time and just as isolated as Niles's notion of mountain music. There is not a whiff of the "New Negro" inhabiting Niles's Old South; there is not a hint of the Harlem Renaissance and its creative explosion of jazz, even though the author was living right in the middle of it in New York City.

Niles crafted entertaining and educational notes for both collections. These generally captured the collecting experience with short sketches of the people and places in sufficient detail to establish the "authenticity" and context of the song. While the notes are similar in form to those of *Songs My Mother Never Taught Me,* they differ significantly in content. Niles appears to be specifically focused on providing evidence of the song's provenance, sometimes even referring to publications of other collectors. The notes for "The Cherry Tree Carol" are representative, but they also reveal Niles's simultaneous attraction to folklore scholarship and his rejection of it, as revealed in the self-deprecating comment about too much "reading of books": "Recorded from the singing of Charles Mulleneoux at Lexington, Kentucky, during the Trotting-Horse Race Meeting, in the autumn of 1912. Mulleneoux was born in Breathitt County, Ky., near the village of Hardshell, on Troublesome Creek. He was a trotting-horse trainer and a singer of much rare mountain music. He sang the Cherry-Tree song as a humorous piece. When I explained to him that it was an ancient English Christmas carol, he merely smiled and classified me with all people who go in for too much reading of books."[68]

The role of these notes becomes critical, for Niles stood at a career crossroads between the conflicting forces of preservation and of transformation. In fact, Niles's activity reflected the larger tension in the South between tradition and progress, between older agricultural models and industrialism, and between nostalgia and change. On the one hand, Niles was engaged in actively collecting music and text from folk sources. On the other hand, he was equally busy creating arrangements from these folk sources and writing original songs in the style of the songs he had been collecting. There would be nothing wrong—indeed, much that is right—about both preserving folk song and creating original song based on the model of folk song. There is only a problem when the collector-composer is less than scrupulous in declaring which is which.

The publication of "Venezuela" in *Songs My Mother Never Taught Me,* falsely attributing the song to folk sources rather than crediting Niles with composing it as an original song, pointed him in a direction that hounded his career for the remainder of his life. He was perched at the edge of a dilemma. If he wanted his music to be heard and to be published, it appeared necessary for him to associate it with folk music, but if he wanted the copyright and recognition for his original songs, he needed to claim what was rightfully his own as his own. Unfortunately for his reputation as a folklorist, he chose to dwell on both sides of the dilemma; subsequently he ambiguously labeled some of his work as the product of folk collection rather than personal invention. This appears to be the case already in these first Schirmer publications.

In *Seven Kentucky Mountain Songs,* Niles presented arrangements of some widely disseminated songs, the lyric folk song "Come All Ye Fair and Tender Ladies" (also commonly known as "Little Sparrow"), the carol-ballad "Cherry Tree Carol," and the ballad "The Legend of Fair Eleanor and the Brown Gal" (Child ballad 73). In each case, the text seems to be closely related to that found in other sources, although in the "Cherry Tree Carol" there are troubling instances of what might be considered colloquial Appalachian dialect interspersed with the more conventional language. The use of "hit" for "it" is a warning sign, because its frequent, and frequently incorrect, use suggests that Niles may have been attempting to make traditional text appear more "authentic" and "backwoodsy." Consider the following stanzas of the "Cherry Tree Carol":

Then Joseph sat and wondered
How hit had come to be,
An' he said, "Mistress Mary:
Yer babe haint nothing to me."

Then Joseph flew up in anger,
In anger flew up he:
Let the pappy of your baby
Climb the cherry-tree for thee (ye).[69]

The tunes for these three songs, however, are all very different from any of the other tune families that have been documented. While this may certainly be just the result of fortuitous collecting in which Niles found unique sources, another possibility asserts itself. As in the case of "Black Is the Color," Niles may have retained the texts that he collected and then composed or "improved" the original melodies. He may actually have broached this possibility in the preface, where he stated: "with every transmission there had been a change . . . perhaps an improvement."[70] The version of "The Cherry Tree" published in *Seven Kentucky Moun-*

tain Tunes disappears thereafter from Niles's repertoire. A substantially different version is published by Niles in *Ten Christmas Carols from the Southern Appalachian Mountains* in 1935 and reproduced or rearranged in various other publications and recordings, including the *Ballad Book,* where it appears as Niles 23. This version, taken from the singing of "Aunt" Becky Sizemore of Breathitt County in 1934, bears a much stronger resemblance to other traditional tunes and also has a text that is stylistically more in conformance with other documented versions.[71]

The tune for "The Legend of Fair Eleanor and the Brown Gal" does not resemble any traditional source, nor are there any notebook sketches to buttress Niles's claims concerning its collection. By the time Niles published "Fair Eleanor" again, in *Ballads, Carols, and Tragic Legends from the Southern Appalachian Mountains* (1937), he had replaced his "father's version" with one that was collected from the singing of Hannah Smith on February 26, 1936, at Willscott Mountain in Cherokee County, North Carolina. This version is reproduced as Niles 28 in the *Ballad Book,* along with three other variants—none of which is the one collected from his father.

Similarly, Niles's tune for "Fair and Tender Ladies" does not resemble other versions, nor is there any documentation in his notebooks for the source; he claimed to have learned it from "the singing of a group of little girls at a Saturday night dance in West Liberty, Kentucky." This melody, while undeniably beautiful, is not typical of folk style. The tune is surprisingly disjunct, with a number of uncharacteristic leaps. There is also an artistic, but uncharacteristic, ornamental melisma over the words "cloudy morning." Like "Fair Eleanor" and "The Cherry Tree," "Come All Ye Fair and Tender Ladies" does not appear again in his published or recorded output.

The other songs, "Ef I Had a Ribbon Bow," "Hi Ho the Preacherman," "In My Little Cabin," and "When I Lays Down and I Do Die," appear to be even more likely the product of Niles's imagination rather than his preservation. Although his critical notes provide an anecdote in connection with each song, the stories are less than convincing by themselves without any clear antecedents of tune or text and without any of Niles's own notebook entries to buttress his account.[72] In fact, the gorgeous song "Ef I Had a Ribbon Bow" was eventually published in *The Songs of John Jacob Niles,* where he finally took complete credit for the words and music without any mention of the "twenty-three year old mother of three children in Ebenezer, Kentucky."

In each of these songs it is more than possible that Niles's imagination was sparked by a morsel of song or story collected from an informant. However, these pieces appear to be instances of "original song in the style of folk music" masquerading as traditional music in a collection that purports to be composed of folk music. This is not to deny the beauty of Niles's composition—quite to the contrary. In particular, "Ef I Had a Ribbon Bow" and "In My Little Cabin" possess a sure sense of melodic invention, a genius for setting the text with economy and grace, and lyrics that tell a story with the directness characteristic of folk expression. It is just a pity that contemporary attitudes concerning American music drove Niles to dissemble about his creations.

Seven Negro Exaltations mimics *Seven Kentucky Mountain Songs* in content as well as format. Once again, there appears to be a whole range of songs that are drawn from tradition, others that are loosely based on tradition, and some that are completely original. Songs such as "Hold On" (usually under the title "Keep Your Hand on the Plow") appear to be accurate transcriptions of spirituals widely found in African American culture. Other pieces, such as "My Little Black Star," seem to be solely the product of Niles's composition and are not found anywhere outside of his collections and recordings. Unfortunately, there are no contemporary notebook sketches that document any of these songs—the earliest holographic sources for all of them are manuscript versions dated 1929 that were clearly prepared for performance and publication. Further, it is nearly impossible to discern what is original and what is not, based on Niles's published critical notes. Consider the narrative appended to "My Little Black Star":

> Recorded from the singing of Aunt Sarah Bramlett (colored) in Danville, Boyle County, Kentucky, during the early spring of 1913. In 1913 Aunt Sarah was said to be 93 years of age. Her calculations were based upon the return of Halley's comet. She called it Halley's "Comic." At the close of the Civil War she was living with her people in Northern Tennessee. The song about the little black star was a lullaby sung by a Tennessee negress whose husband had

been taken away to the penitentiary. Aunt Sarah said that the song came with her into Central Kentucky about 1870.[73]

It is certainly possible that there was an Aunt Sarah Bramlett living in Danville, Kentucky. It is probable that Niles could have met her there in 1913, because he was living nearby in Lexington at the time. The comments about Halley's Comet are unclear, since the comet made an appearance in 1835 and again in 1910. If Bramlett was 93, she would have been born in 1820, considerably before the comet's previous appearance. What is certain is that the next time the song was published (in *The Songs of John Jacob Niles*), the words and music were unequivocally attributed to Niles without a mention of Aunt Sarah Bramlett. Likely we will never know what role, if any, Sarah Bramlett played in the composition, arrangement, and publication of this song.

In the same way, it is difficult to untangle whether the convincing call-and-response exhortation of "Does Yo' Call Dat Religion" was truly heard at the "little negro church across the road from the main campus of the Kentucky University at Lexington" (the University of Kentucky). Niles has a diary account of the church, with a map of its location, and the church is still there today. There is a spiritual recorded under the title "Do You Call That Religion" or "Scandalize My Name" that is closely related, so this one appears to be collected from the source, just as Niles claimed. "Trip to Raleigh," claimed by Niles to have been collected from a "Negro bootblack at the Seven Gables Hotel of Burnside, Kentucky," is a variant of "Shoot dat Buffey," recorded by Milton Metfessel and published in 1928, so it appears likely that this song was also recorded from traditional singing.[74] In fact, it appears that almost all of the songs that Niles claimed he had taken from African American sources were actually in currency in black tradition. Of the fifteen songs published in *Impressions of a Negro Camp Meeting* and *Seven Negro Exaltations,* only "My Little Black Star" appears to be original composition, and "John's Come Down" and "Next Come Sunday" are ambiguous. Perhaps in testament to the more traditional character of *Seven Negro Exaltations,* compared to *Seven Kentucky Mountain Songs,* Guthrie Meade and Richard Spottswood elected to cite the former, and not the latter, in their scholarly and popular-collections index in *Country Music Sources.*[75]

7

Kerby and Niles Present Folk Music on the Concert Stage

Even while *Seven Kentucky Mountain Songs* and *Seven Negro Exaltations* were still on the drawing board, the songs from the collection were already being given a trial run in rehearsals for Niles's new performance initiative, the duo of Marion Kerby, contralto, and John Jacob Niles, tenor.

Marion Kerby (1877–1956) was already a veteran actress by the time she met Niles in December 1928 at the Princeton Club of New York. She inaugurated her stage career at the turn of the century, and by 1922 she had made her reputation in the role of Nana, the "mean sister," in the original theatrical production of *Seventh Heaven*. In 1926 Kerby stepped away from the Broadway stage and redirected her dramatic expertise toward interpreting African American culture. The *Social Notes* column of the *New York Times* included notice of a 1926 Palm Beach, Florida, performance of stories and spirituals: "A dinner dance was given by Mrs. William Randolph Hearst last evening at the studio apartment of Addison Misner in Via Misner. . . . Two orchestras played, and Miss Marion Kerby and Miss Marjorie Lambkin entertained with negro spirituals and stories."[1]

After working with Lambkin, Kerby initiated a new partnership with Marie Cecelia "Cissie" Loftus (1876–1943), who was renowned as an impersonator both in the United States and in Britain. Cissie was comfortable with both vaudeville and legitimate theater and had a wealth of social and artistic connections, which made her an ideal complement for Kerby. Together they performed in London and Dublin and subsequently made their American debut at New York's Selwyn Theatre on May 15, 1927. A preview was printed in the *New York Times:* "Miss Loftus will present impressions of the popular stars of the moment and will likewise be heard in children's songs. Miss Kerby will confine herself to negro melodies and anecdotes."[2]

Kerby and Loftus continued to perform at joint recitals, particularly during the summer months, when regular Broadway work was light. On August 23, 1927, they presented a benefit for the Soldiers and Sailors Club of New York at "The Orchard," the home of Mr. and Mrs. Charles E. Merrill at Southampton, Long Island. On this occasion William Walker was their piano accompanist. In 1928 Kerby appeared on Broadway in a revival of *John Ferguson* at the Theatre Masque but continued her performances with Cissie Loftus. In the summer of 1929, they were joined by pianist John Jacob Niles. The recital at New York's Barrymore Theatre headlined Loftus and featured Kerby for the sake of variety.[3]

Niles was not content to merely serve as Kerby's accompanist, however. He envisaged a more equal partnership in which Kerby would present her character sketches, Kerby and Niles would each be featured in solo songs, and then they would sing some songs in duet. Niles would also serve as both accompanist and arranger. While it was useful to be connected to Cissie Loftus initially, it was clear that the team of Kerby and Niles would be too much in her shadow if they continued to share the bill with her, so in the fall of 1929 the pair went on the road without Loftus.

Niles and Kerby's decision to perform folk and traditional music in a concert-hall situation was not unusual at this time. By the 1920s a substantial repertoire of artful spiritual arrangements was published by composer-arrangers such as Harry Burleigh (1849–1966), so that the music was readily available to both white and black performers. Baritone Oscar Seagle (1877–1945) presented a whole program of spirituals as a solo performer in a recital context on April 14, 1917, and for his annual New York recital he programmed a set of Burleigh arrangements of spirituals along with a group of Dvorak songs and a set of "patriotic songs" written by French composers in response to the war in Europe.[4] The remarkable singer, athlete, actor, and activist Paul Robeson (1898–1976) performed what may be considered the first program consisting of entirely African American works on the concert stage; it took place on November 2, 1924, at Boston's Copley Plaza Hotel. Robeson followed that performance with a series of concerts and recordings with arranger-accompanist Lawrence Brown.

What made Kerby's approach to the spiritual, or "exaltation" as she termed it, different was her incorporation of the music within a dramatic context. The songs were woven into a tapestry of folk stories, "preachings," and anecdotes, largely lifted from her experience at Stovall Plantation in Mississippi. As a character actress, her sense of timing and drama was essential to enfolding the music into a larger narrative. As she put it, she aimed to "transfloat" her audience through Aunt Dilcey's eyes—to convey plantation life through a seamless web of impersonation, gesture, movement, and song.

Upon hearing Kerby and Niles at the Library of Congress Festival of Chamber Music, the noted American composer Amy Beach (Mrs. H. H. A. Beach) praised their interpretation of African American song in a letter written to Kerby in 1929:

> I can not tell you how deeply I was impressed by the character of your work, so ably seconded by Lieutenant Niles who seemed your second self. The enormous variety of the songs and their interpretation by you both seemed astounding, and your program actually produced *living glimpses* of the many-sided musical and spiritual natures of the negro race. It was great dramatic power which you showed and such power must win success. Your singing haunted me day by day on the ocean where one has time to think, and I shall never again read Negro stories or hear their songs without having you in my thoughts.[5]

Despite Mrs. Beach's lavish praise, the Niles-Kerby performances of African American culture were far more concerned with showmanship than with simulation of authentic performance practice. While the two certainly felt that they were sympathetically representing black people and their music, they essentially purveyed a "whiteface" parody of African American culture strongly influenced by minstrelsy.

Niles provided the core of their African American song arrangements and held the entire show together with his piano accompaniment, but the most distinctive aspect of Niles's performance was the contribution of his Kentucky music. This repertoire was romantically characterized as "mountain music," even though at this point much of his collection was actually recorded in the Bluegrass region—six of the songs in *Seven Kentucky Mountain Songs* were attributed to sources living near Lexington.

Although Appalachian folk collecting can be traced to "Songs from the Mountains of North Carolina" (1893),[6] collecting activity was really sparked by publications of Transylvania University professor Hubert G. Shearin (1878–1919) in collaboration with his student Josiah Combs of Hindman, Kentucky (1886–1960). Shearin sounded a poetically worded call to folklorists entreating them to travel to the Appalachian Mountains in order to preserve the valuable body of Anglo-American folk song that was rapidly vanishing in the face of twentieth-century progress: "The clank of the colliery, the rattle of the locomotive, the roar of the blast-furnace, the shriek of the factory whistle, and alas, even the music of the school-bell, are already overwhelming the thin tones of the dulcimore and the quavering voice of the last Minstrel of the Cumberlands, who can find scant heart to sing again the lays of olden years across the seas."[7] Shearin's call was amplified by the subsequent publication of Cecil Sharp's *English Folk Songs of the Southern Appalachians* (1917).

There was a world of difference between documenting folk song for scholarly preservation and arranging it for presentation, however. Collectors such as Hubert Shearin, Cecil Sharp, Elmer Sulzer, Dorothy Scarborough, Olive Dame Campbell, Katherine Pettit, Henry Mellinger, Josiah Combs, and Harvey Fuson were essentially preservationists who notated melody lines and texts in a descriptive format. Mary Wheeler, Susannah Wetmore, Loraine Wyman and Howard Brockway, Josephine McGill, Carl Sandburg, and Niles were more concerned with performance and presentation; their notation was prescriptive, usually featuring piano with voice arrangements. Alan Lomax (1915–2002) and his father, John (1867–1948), though, who were arguably the most wide-ranging and important collectors of all, presented their repertoire in versions targeted at both audiences. Alan's headnotes could be either scholarly or garrulous, and the music could be presented in skeletal form or fleshed out with piano arrangements of Ruth Crawford Seeger that are every bit as "lush" as those of Niles or Brockway.[8]

While there were many other collectors trolling the cultural head-waters of Appalachia for ballads, there were far fewer musicians actually performing Appalachian mountain music on the concert stage, as Niles and Kerby were doing. The single most important precedent was the team of singer Loraine Wyman (ca. 1885–1937) and pianist-composer Howard Brockway (1870–1951). In spring 1916, Wyman, a performer of French folk songs, and Brockway, a composer and pianist at Juilliard, spent six weeks centered at the Pine Mountain Settlement School in Harlan County, Kentucky. They traveled widely through the region, collecting what they referred to as "lonesome tunes" (ballads), "love songs" (lyric folk songs), and "fast music" (play party songs). Upon returning to New York City, they transformed their collection into arrangements suitable for both performance and publication.

As Niles was also learning, the art of transcription and the art of composition were closely related but contradictory practices. Fidelity of text and tune was sometimes at odds with the collector's anticipated results. In some cases artistic intent could lead to an entirely different note choice from that demanded by folkloric integrity. Transcribing music by ear was very different from the process of documenting it with electronic reproduction. The ideal compromise often lay between the two competing forces of subjectivity and objectivity. Brockway commented on this tension in an article for *Art World*:

> The writing of the melody was often an affair of puzzling diffi-culty. The melodic intervals were frequently of an unusual and curious character. To add to the difficulty, there was the fact that the voices, while excellent as natural voices, were untrained, and this made the question of intonation in the case of certain steps an important one.
>
> In Knott County, for instance, we found a man who came from a neighborhood famous for singers. He was born on "Carr Creek," referred to as "Singin' Carr." Amongst the lovely melodies

which he gave me, with a zest which I revered in him, there was one of such haunting and pathetic beauty that it seemed too good to be true. I wrote it down very carefully and the longer I considered it, the more worried I became lest my desire had lent cunning to my ear and had even led my pencil to write the intervals which I fain would have come true![9]

Wyman and Brockway made some thoughtful compromises in crafting their *interpretation* of folk material. Wisely, they made no attempt to recreate the performance practice of the "natives" from whom they collected the music. Instead, they elected to transform tradition through an arrangement style that allowed the unadorned melody and text to be complemented by a largely unobtrusive, yet musically engaging, piano accompaniment. In the process, the musical ambience was caught somewhere between the domestic intimacy of a parlor and the artistic conventions of an urban concert hall. The *New York Times* captured the essence of Wyman and Brockway's debut performance: "There was no attempt at exact reproduction in the manner of the folk singers, though both of the concert givers gave brief specimens of that manner. Mr. Brockway's accompaniments, about which and his manner of treating them there might be debate, are for the most part highly developed in form and harmony, his playing of them exquisite; and Miss Wyman's singing is that of an artist in vocal technique, style and finish, with something of the illustrative manner added—It is indeed extremely charming, ingratiating and exactly adapted to her purposes."[10]

Almost thirteen years to the day later, Niles and Kerby took to the stage in a program format that was strongly reminiscent of Wyman and Brockway's performance. Conceptually, Niles and Kerby were undoubtedly influenced by Wyman and Brockway's model for presenting folk culture in an art-music context. However, Niles and Kerby contributed five additional ingredients to their predecessors' recipe that enhanced their own popular success. First, they expanded the performance patter and commentary that positioned the songs within a cultural context, thus helping the audience experience a personal connection with "exotic" material that was disconnected from them by both class and race. Second, Niles and Kerby created a complementary mix of diverse African American and Appalachian Mountain repertoire in contrasting sets, which heightened the effect of each. Third, the addition of dramatic presentation, incorporating Kerby's impersonations and monologues, established a narrative component. Fourth, the idiosyncratic and exaggerated vaudeville-like performance approach of Niles and Kerby projected the repertoire more effectively than the more reserved recital style of Wyman and Brockway. And finally, Niles and Kerby were *both* singers. Consequently, they could feature the contrast of two voices in solo songs in addition to the harmony of their voices in duets.

The team of Niles and Kerby made their first major appearance on October 8, 1929, at the Library of Congress Festival of Chamber Music in the Music Room of the Congressional Library, Washington, D.C. This gala event, attended by First Lady Mrs. Herbert Hoover, featured Niles and Kerby's mountain and spiritual songs, followed by a jazz-oriented set that included Werner Janssen's "Obsequies of a Saxaphone: Or the American Mercury." Olin Downes wrote a review in the *New York Times* that praised Niles and Kerby's performance but was critical of the light, entertaining quality of their African American material compared with the "archaic simplicity and beauty" of the southern mountain repertoire.[11]

The pair's first real public concert, presented at the Barbizon Hotel in midtown New York City on January 15, 1930, garnered a short but complimentary notice from the *New York Times:* "Marion Kerby, contralto, and John J. Niles, tenor, gave a first public performance at the Barbizon last evening, presenting with rare humor and sympathy, old Southern negro 'exaltations' and Kentucky mountain songs which they had collected at the source. Their entertainment was enjoyed by one of the largest audiences in the hotel's two seasons of musical recitals."[12] Just a little over a week later, Niles and Kerby were the featured entertainment of a soirée held at the home of Mrs. M. Crouse Klock in Syracuse, New York.[13] Niles and Kerby continued to polish their act and presented salon concerts at social gatherings during the winter in order to perfect the act for a planned spring concert tour in England.

Niles and Kerby departed from New York on April 10 aboard the *Minnekada,* a ship with "the lingering odor of a mule stable," according to Niles. Eleven days later they landed at London and prepared themselves for their British debut at Grotrian Hall on Wigmore Street. The concert, on May 1, 1930, was a great success. Herbert Hughes, reviewing the performance for the *Daily Telegraph,* observed:

> At the Grotrian Hall last night Miss Kerby reappeared with a new collaborator in Mr. John J. Niles. The result was interesting—and surprising. For at one moment the voice of Mr. Niles was a rather thin, high tenor; at another a low, husky baritone; at another he was yodeling—all the time playing the piano with a fine musical touch. Miss Kerby herself is the very embodiment of rhythm (and despite a manner distinctly free-and-easy) of religious sentiment and fervour.
>
> Together these singers made the Negro "exaltations" (as Miss Kerby has named them) extremely impressive, and the Kentucky mountain songs, denuded of any pedantic implications, very homely and natural.[14]

After the critical success of the Grotrian Hall concert, Niles and Kerby's manager at the Imperial Concert Agency started receiving requests for performances. One week later they appeared at a dinner entertainment at the home of Lady Mendl, then traveled up to Stratford-upon-Avon to perform for a gathering of Christian Scientists. Next they performed a second concert (of, eventually, four in all) at Grotrian Hall, which was just as enthusiastically received by the press. Hughes, writing in the *Daily Telegraph,* again lauded their performance:

> The authority, the experience, of these artists none of us would challenge. They have brought something to us that has the true ring of authenticity. We know they have absorbed the tradition, the idiom, of the mountains and the plantations; their knowledge is not merely acquired, it is inherited.
>
> The beauty of most of the songs no one will dispute; and no one could dispute the technique of their interpreters. The indisputable thing was their charm. "He's a Burden Bearer," "Little Black Star," and the "Wash Blue" from Louisville, belong to the impressions that remain.[15]

Basil Maine of the *Morning Post* echoed the *Telegraph*'s praise: "At a time when our appetite for Negro Spirituals had almost sickened, it is surely something of a feat for two singers to revive the earlier enthusiasm. That is what Marion Kerby and John Niles have done here in London during the past two weeks."[16]

The success of Niles and Kerby was a reflection of the harmony created by the warmth of their onstage collaboration. However, this partnership was merely a fragile facade that threatened to explode at any moment. Niles and Kerby were consummate professionals, but once they were out of the footlights, they fought nearly continuously. Niles's notebooks and autobiography are laced with story after story relating their stormy arguments.

Despite the tensions, the partnership held together through the last of the four concerts at Grotrian Hall, and the pair returned to the States, where they prepared new material for another round of concerts. On December 6, 1930, they made a return appearance at the Barbizon Hotel. In the audience was the noted Columbia University scholar and "song-catcher" Dorothy Scarborough (1878–1935), who was moved by the concert to write Niles a glowing epistle the next day:

Dear Lieutenant Niles:

I am still stepping high to music after your and Marion Kerby's songs last night. You can't think how I envy you your ability to sing so delectably the wonderful songs you collect as a folk-lorist. It seems to me that you should devote your whole time to collecting folk-songs and putting them over in music. And in our wide country there are so many songs dying for want of a recorder, that you are definitely needed. What are the Guggenheim fellowships and awards like that for if not to make possible such creative work on the part of talented young people? I urge you to look into the matter. There are only a limited number of persons among us qualified by temperament and training to collect our folk-songs in a scientific way and to make them known to the people. You are emphatically of that number and I should like to see some arrangements made whereby you could give your time to that research for a while.

Carl Sandburg came just after you left last night and I was ever so disappointed that the four of us couldn't have had a session together. He spoke appreciatively of the work you are doing.

Thank you a thousand times for the pleasure you and Miss Kerby gave us by your singing. If there is any way by which I could be of service to you at any time, please let me know. I am tremendously interested in the work you two are doing.

Cordially yours,
Dorothy Scarborough[17]

The enthusiasm expressed in Scarborough's letter stems from a shared vision of African American and Appalachian folk music. Her collections, *On the Trail of Negro Folk Songs* (1925) and *A Song Catcher in Southern Mountains* (1937), resembled Niles's repertoire.

Kerby and Niles closed out the year with some warmly received concerts presented in some cold venues. For example, on December 11 they appeared at an afternoon concert at Hart House Theatre in Toronto, Ontario. The program now included a set of "Street Cries" collected and arranged by Niles. A critic for the *Evening Telegram* praised the concert, drawing attention to the new "street cries" set.

They call their offering "Negro Exaltations and Kentucky Mountain Songs." The exaltations are what are known as spirituals, the mountain songs are what have been in circulation amongst Kentucky folk since earliest settlement times. Some of them are almost Tudor madrigals in form and freedom, and some are Scotch as bagpipes. Mr. Niles sang a number of Kentucky and New York street cries and one of Miss Kerby's solo numbers was an unaccompanied monologue, an ancient negress' vision of the "Lam o' Gawd." For the rest, the recital was shared equally by the two artists—Mr. Niles keeping up a richly musical and spontaneous fire of ejaculation and antiphon at his associate, playing the piano meanwhile and throwing every ounce of his enthusiasm into his work.

It is impossible to mistake the downright earnestness of the two singers, and everything they do is beautiful.[18]

Niles returned to New York City for the holidays, but shortly thereafter he joined Kerby on the road for a hectic schedule of concerts that took them back and forth across the country. Their first appearance was on January 15 in Lansing, Michigan, at the Agricultural College (now Michigan State University); then they drove down to Chicago, where Niles attended the opera. The next day he and Kerby presented a concert in Oak Park that he characterized as the "worst show we ever gave and dullest house."[19] They drove back to New York City and the very next day entertained at the Orange Tennis Club. On January 21 he was home for a day spent at dinner and the theater with his wife, Hélène, and then he packed for a cross-country rail trip on the Canadian Pacific to Vancouver. Niles and Kerby arrived at Vancouver on January 25 and went immediately down to Seattle, where they performed at the Sunset Club on January 28. The next day found them at the Cornish School, and the following day they performed a salon concert at the Corbetts' home before getting on the train to San Francisco.

The matinee performance on February 2 at Alice Seckel's Musicale, held at the Gold Ballroom of the Fairmont Hotel in San Francisco, received yet another rave review: "The work of these two artists is unique, defying classification and description. It is the sort that 'gets' you, holds you spellbound, and leaves an indelible impression upon your memory."[20] The next several days were spent performing at private gatherings—at Louise Boyd's home in San Rafael and for Mrs. George Cameron at Burlingame—before closing out the tour in Los Angeles.

Less than a month later, Kerby and Niles had a return engagement in Toronto, this time performing at Hygeia Hall in a concert sponsored by the Toronto Social Hygiene Club, as part of their celebration of Health Week. Again, the newspaper review appearing in the *Evening Telegram* was highly complimentary of Kerby's "superbly dramatic effect" and characterized the evening as "unique and altogether fascinating."[21]

Back in New York City, Kerby and Niles prepared themselves for another European tour, this time adding appearances in Germany and Holland as well as a return visit to England. They arrived in Cherbourg, France, on April 18 and left right away for Paris to catch an express train to Berlin, where they performed at Wigman Scule on the evening of April 19. The concerts in Berlin were well received, as evidenced by Anton Mayer's critique in the Berlin *Acht Uhr Adenblatt:*

> The singers do not imitate the negro, but they have concentrated themselves so entirely on their art, that we clearly see before us the intuitive artistic talent of the negro.
> The rare love songs charm us with their beautiful melody, especially "Go Way from My Window," a song of unbelievable sweet melancholy. The voices of the interpreters, the deep alto of Miss Marion Kerby and the falsetto tenor of Mr. Niles combine themselves with the most wonderful results, which reminds us of bells and high string notes.[22]

They left for Amsterdam on April 24 and gave a concert at the Muzic-lyceum on April 25, which was followed by an important performance at Amsterdam's venerable Concertgebow. The next day they went to Den Haag to perform at the Diligentia Hall on Niles's fortieth birthday. Then the duo went on to Rotterdam for another recital. In each city they were received with numerous laudatory reviews. One reviewer in Amsterdam's *Algemeen Handelsblad* raised an interesting point of interpretation and performance practice, observing, "We have heard negro songs sung in different ways by Roland Hayes, Edna Thomas, Layton and Johnson, the Fisk Jubilee Singers and the Utica Singers, but so realistically and so negro like we have never heard it yet." This is a revealing comment: the reviewer is crediting Kerby and Niles with being more "black" than actual African Americans. At a time when soloists like Robeson and groups such as the Fisk Jubilee Singers were attempting to "pass" in their performance style and repertoire, Kerby and Niles were attempting a "reverse pass" by simulating African American style.

After their last performance in Holland, they sailed for London, landing on May 8, and gave a matinee concert at Grotrian Hall on May 14. Niles was critical of the performance, commenting: "Performance was a great mistake—I shall oppose matinees in the future." Nonetheless, the critics loved it. Even though the duo had played this venue a number of times, the reviewer for the *Daily Telegraph* still found the material fresh: "Remembering the happy impression made by Miss Kerby and her colleague on previous visits, a large audience greeted them back at Grotrian Hall yesterday and found in their delightful 'negro exaltations,' nursery rhymes, Kentucky mountain tunes, and the rest no less characteristic charm and freshness than before. Some of them were new; others pleasantly familiar—'Rabbit, Rabbit!' especially among the former and 'Uncle Norah' among the latter. And among 'Folk songs of the Birth and Youth of Jesus' there were none more enchanting than 'C'est La Mode' (from the Marne Valley) and the Polish lullaby 'Keep Jesus Warm.'"[23]

Niles and Kerby played at Grotrian Hall twice more, on May 19 and May 26, before Niles crossed the channel to Paris, where he remained from June 8 to 15, "mercifully free of Kerby for a few days," and "visited by flocks of Americans in Paris." Returning to London, he and Kerby performed for several private gatherings, including an appearance at the home of Lady Astor; played a BBC broadcast on July 7; and then closed out their European tour with a concert for the North Court Musicales on Wood Street. On July 11 they boarded the *Bremen,* a "one-time palatial German liner captured by the English at the end of World War I, and put into transatlantic service by the White Star Line."[24]

There was little time to relax, however. By August 2, 1931, Niles and Kerby were back on the road, appearing at various New York locations, including Cooperstown, Rome, Millbrook, and Essex, for concert fees that averaged three hundred dollars. Finally, Niles returned to New York, where he spent the fall settled in at his apartment at 155 West Twelfth Street. Even off the stage, he remained active, working for photographer Doris Ulmann and completing a large suite for two pianos and two solo voices titled *Africa to Harlem.*

The wintry thrall of January's snow and ice sent much of the social elite in search of sun, sand, and surf. Those who were wealthy enough and idle enough to be listed in the little red and black *Social Register* migrated south to the gracious warmth and genteel civilization of Palm Beach, Florida. Here, members of prominent families from Chicago's Gold Coast and North Shore; Grosse Point, Michigan; Philadelphia's "Main-line"; Greenwich and Darien, Connecticut; and New York's Park Avenue, Tuxedo Park, and Hudson River Valley mingled in evenings of elegant cocktail parties, dinners, and special entertainments.

Kerby had already participated in this social scene in 1926, so she had both the savvy and the connections to exploit her successful musical partnership with the country club set. Niles and Kerby were the darlings of the scene that January, entertaining at dinner at the home of Mr. and Mrs. Sidney Homer on January 26 and giving an afternoon recital at the Everglades Club on the twenty-eighth for "a gathering of prominent colonists." On the thirty-first, the New York Times reported that Niles and Kerby were at the Winter Park home of Mr. and Mrs. Irving Bacheller for the weekend.[25] On February 3 Mrs. Willey Lyon Kingsley hosted a dinner party in honor of Niles and Kerby, who were her house guests.[26]

The team of Kerby and Niles provided a novel recreation for members of Palm Beach society by allowing their audience to experience the exotic allure of African American culture without exposing the audience to actual African Americans. Like a roller coaster, this entertainment was simultaneously exciting and racy, yet safe. Niles and Kerby were cultivated, well groomed, and socially adept, a far cry from the actual plantation blacks and Appalachian hillbillies whose cultures were being co-opted and interpreted.

Their residence in Palm Beach was certainly a lovely way to escape the winter; but, more importantly, the intimate association with socially prominent families helped Niles and Kerby to establish connections with potential patrons that paved the way for future club and private party engagements across the country.

Niles and Kerby finally left Florida and took off across the country, performing in Chicago between February 7 and 13 at the University Club, the exclusive Casino Club, and the Caxton Club. On February 15 they were in Buffalo, New York, to present a concert at the State Teacher's Club Auditorium under the auspices of the Buffalo Philharmonic Society. A day later they were at the Chromatic Club. Then they boarded the train for California and played a string of concerts from February 26 to March 12 at venues such as the Beverly Hills Hotel, the Pasadena Community Playhouse, the Santa Barbara Boy's School, and Alice Seckel's Matinee Musicale (a return engagement). On the way home, they performed at a private gathering at Mrs. Kate Callahan's 1325 Astor Street home in the heart of Chicago's Gold Coast. Once at home in New York, they unpacked their bags and presented a show at the American Women's Clubhouse, just down the street from Carnegie Hall. The performance was reviewed by both the *Musical Courier* and the *New Yorker;* the *Courier* praised the performance and carefully distinguished Kerby and Niles's presentation of mountain music from hillbilly music: "The tunes are haunting and appealing, utterly unlike the nasal, monotonous brand of 'mountain song' familiar to radio habitués."[27]

Niles and Kerby relaxed their schedule in the spring. It was probably a good thing for their professional association, since their personal relationship appeared to be particularly strained; Niles noted on his copy of a Wells College program: "Kerby is no doubt insane."[28] Fortunately, Niles's attention was now focused on his upcoming trip into the southern Appalachian Mountains to work with Doris Ulmann. He was in the mountains from July 1 through at least July 12 and returned to New York, where he and Ulmann met with Dr. Orie Latham Hatcher, president of the Southern Woman's Educational Alliance.

Back in New York, he quickly returned to the stage with Marion Kerby, performing at the same mix of venues—private entertainments, clubs, hotels, and concert halls, including the Westchester Playhouse, the Hyde Seminar, and the Century Theatre Club Meeting at the Commodore Hotel, all in New York City; and at Mrs. Taylor's home at 2008 Delancey Place in Philadelphia. By this time, Niles was growing particularly weary of the social demands of performing at private dinners.

One reason Niles had grown increasingly disenchanted with the small social engagements was his dawning awareness of the possibilities for his music, both in terms of larger concert venues and expanded musical forms. The opportunity to perform at prestigious halls, such as Amsterdam's Concertgebow or London's Grotrian Hall was much more artistically satisfying and financially rewarding than the burden of entertaining at small dinner engagements and women's clubs. Niles was well aware that his bread was buttered at these small social engagements, but he was really beginning to chafe at Kerby's frequent programming of small salon recitals. His commercial survival was at odds with his creativity and threatening to "cure him of art."[29]

From the time he had first started composing and arranging, Niles had worked consistently as a vocal miniaturist, a creator of songs. As a singer, he was pragmatically most focused on creating a personal repertoire for himself, and later for the duo of Kerby and Niles. In the early 1930s, however, Niles started expanding his sense of musical form to encompass larger works. *Africa to Harlem,* a suite written for two voices and two pianos, represented his first extended compositional effort. It was a natural outgrowth of the Kerby-Niles performances. Its melodic material was lifted from their repertoire (along with some music collected by Niles's wife, Hélène, in Birmingham, Alabama), the vocal lines were tailored specifically for their voices, and the two piano parts largely mirrored the accompaniments that Niles had already been providing for their song arrangements.

Like a railroad train composed of interconnected cars, the suite represents a compromise between small form and larger architectural order. By juxtaposing short works in sequence, a suite creates a larger unity. In this manner, *Africa to Harlem* surveyed the whole span of African American musical culture through four programmatic movements: "A French Holiday in Old New Orleans," "Sanctified," "Picnic on Oyster Island," and "Night Club." The explicitly programmatic intent is manifest through annotations in the score, such as the one appended to "A French Holiday in Old New Orleans": "This movement must have a fantastic quality about it—it is intended to represent the French civilization on the verge of its decline in the new world and the negro just beginning to take part in political and literary musical life. The use of the minuet is intended to give the impression of a ball in one of the old French mansions. Outside, French military stand and, refusing to join the ladies, they sing the music of the barracks. Nearby are negroes who do odd jobs and sing the while." Niles completed four movements of the manuscript in October 1931.[30] One year later *Africa to Harlem* received its premiere at New York's Beethoven Hall on October 13, 1932, with Mary Howe and Anne Hull on piano and Kerby and Niles performing the vocal parts.

Niles also began composing both the libretto and the music for a full-scale grand opera, "The King of Little Italy," on June 22, 1932.[31] The plot was based on "an exposition of the prodigal son theme," and it was set in "New York's Bleeker St., with its underworld rumblings against old-world piety and new world ambition, the prodigal son gets killed on his return instead of the fatted calf."[32] Much of Niles's New York world was woven into the libretto, from the Italian-laced speech of his grocer friend Umberto to the street cry of Angelo, the flower vender who died of tuberculosis. Niles continued working on the opera every time he was back at home, but his interruptive concert schedule and the Appalachian expeditions with Doris Ulmann hindered sustained composition. The opera was never completed.

Ten days after the *Africa to Harlem* premiere, Niles and Kerby traveled back to Toronto for a performance at Toronto's Eaton Auditorium on November 26. They closed out the year with New York concerts at the Greenwich House Music School and at the home of Susan B. Weld. Then they boarded the train for Chicago, where they performed on December 16 at the Winnetka Woman's Club and two days later at the home of the Wells sisters in Lake Forest. On the nineteenth they drove into Chicago to perform at the Fortnightly social dance entertainment held at the Contemporary Club. Returning to New York, they performed at a holiday party for Mrs. Schirmer at her home on 212 E. Sixteenth Street. In a bit of end-of-the-year self-reflection, Niles recorded, "I took in $1,046.65 this year which is about $80 a month—not enough to get very far on."[33] It was not a bad living in depression times, but critical and popular success were not making him a rich man, either.

Niles and Kerby returned to the concert circuit January 12, 1933, with three New York appearances: an entertainment at Jackson Heights Road, at Strawberry Mansion on the twenty-ninth, and at the Century Club on February 1. Then they traveled over the border to Canada and played at the Heliconian Club in Hamilton, Ontario. The political and economic situation in the United States was deteriorating, however, and bookings for Niles and Kerby were becoming more difficult to obtain. Fortuitously, they were booked for another European tour.

Niles crossed the ocean on a Red Star liner, landing in Antwerp by the first of March. He traveled to Brussels, where he delivered Doris Ulmann's check for twelve hundred dollars to M. Gaevert, a maker of photographic paper. Then he proceeded to meet up with Fredericks' Circus and Wild Animal Show, with which he was booked to play harpsichord from March 3 to April 9. Traveling through the towns of Malonne, Vilnoorde, Leuven, Tervuren, Namur, Dinant, Rochefort, Saint-Hubert, and Arlon,

Niles accompanied the animal show on an old Pleyel harpsichord. He also became romantically involved with Clara Fredericks, the daughter of the circus owner. Inspired by her, he wrote the song "Unused I Am to Lovers" for her to perform. Niles recalled the song, with its graceful, melismatic cadential arabesques, in his autobiography:

> It was at the little town of Vilnoorde that we concluded "Unused I Am" and looked forward to the "world premiere" of this number in Louvain [Leuven]. After endless repetitions, we decided we were ready. By that time I had played the accompaniment so often that I had it quite memorized. Indeed, I had used it several times to accompany the dance of the animals. Any fairly simple piece of music in 4/4 can be made to do just that. But Mlle. Clara was considerably more than a simple piece of music in 4/4, and when she appeared in the costume of a shepherdess, crook and all, and declared, singing, that she was very young and knew nothing of lovers but was somehow hoping to find out about them, the young men in the nearest seats threw their hats in the air and cried delight.[34]

Niles reluctantly left the joys of the circus and the "unbelievable erotic heaven"[35] of Clara Fredericks to rejoin Marion Kerby, meeting her in Den Haag for their concert at Diligentia Hall on April 19. Niles had little but contempt for Kerby at this point. Still, as unpleasant as their personal relationship was, their professional association continued to survive because they complemented each other so well on stage.

They continued on to Hilversen, where they performed for the radio, and then moved on to Amsterdam for a return engagement at the Concertgebow on April 22. The concert was received by a "smallish but enthusiastic" house, according to Niles.[36] Unfortunately, because of the cost of the hall rental, the only profit realized was fifteen guilders each from the concessionaire, who returned 10 percent of his profits to the performers. If not a financial success, the concert was at least critically embraced. The *Algemeen Handelsblad* described the event:

> It happens only once in every music-season, at the utmost twice, that a crowded house in genuine and stirred enthusiasm, simply

refuses to leave, after an evening of artistic emotion. Moments in which the audience, seized by a collective elation wants to hear more and more.

Such an aspect the small Concert Hall offered last night, after Marion Kerby and John Jacob Niles had given us five groups of Negro Exaltations, Kentucky Mountain Tunes, Negro Nursery Rhymes, etc. And this enthusiasm, this emotion are understandable, born as they were out of the emotion which the song and interpretation of these two artists created among an intensely-attentive audience. . . . Thanks for this evening, for these beautiful and stirring experiences, for all this true and honest art.[37]

On April 27 Niles and Kerby performed at Nymingen, and a day later Niles celebrated his forty-first birthday by performing again at Den Haag. Several days later, Niles caustically recalled their final Amsterdam performance on May 1: "Of this final exhibition, I think that the least said will be the greatest favor. The diva vomited energetically during the short intermission. She said I caused it by looking at her in a belittling manner."[38] Somehow, the team of Kerby and Niles limped onward to London, where Niles stayed at 2 Bedford Place while trying to teach Kerby new spirituals arrangements for the upcoming Grotrian Hall concerts. Since they had performed there at least four times each year for the past three years, it was important for Niles to continue developing enough new material to keep their act fresh for repeat audiences.

On May 19 Niles and Kerby performed at Grotrian Hall and then traveled southeast to the village of Totnes, where they presented three concerts at Dartington Hall. While there, Niles fortuitously encountered the Indian poet and philosopher Rabindranath Tagore (1861–1941), whom Doris Ulmann had photographed in the 1920s. Tagore was a remarkable "renaissance man"—a poet, a novelist, an artist, a composer, and an educator. A major influence on Mahatma Ghandi, Tagore was awarded the Nobel Prize for Literature in 1913.[39] Niles was deeply moved by his brief yet intense relationship with Tagore. In some ways, the experience helped prepare Niles for his future collaboration with the author, philosopher, and monk Thomas Merton.

Back in London, Kerby and Niles presented a matinee for the American Woman's Club on May 27. Niles noted that it was an unremarkable concert except for the fact that among the audience were two nannies in whose care were the Princesses Elizabeth (now Queen Elizabeth II [1926–]) and Margaret (1930–2002).[40] Niles and Kerby performed at a private home on June 16 before giving their final concert at Grotrian Hall on June 20. A little over a week later, on June 29, they entertained forty guests at Montrose House, the home of the American ambassador. This proved to be both the final concert of their European tour and their final performance together.

Niles returned to the United States in time to attend a Music Teachers convention in Atlantic City on July 5. On July 22 Kerby sent Niles a typewritten letter closing out their affairs:

Dear Jack,

I'm sure this will be no surprise to you, for after our unhappy experiences at each concert abroad (and for two years before) it would be useless for us to continue together, and judging from the inference of Mrs. Chase [their manager], which she got from your letters to her while abroad, you have been just as miserable with me. So, I feel sure this decision to part will be a relief to you, too.[41]

Doris Ulmann, who now provided much of Niles's financial support, wrote to Olive Dame Campbell concerning Niles's performance future without Kerby:

You will be pleased to know that Jack and Marion Kerby have severed partnership—Jack had this suspicion but now a letter from Miss Kerby has given him this information. This means that Jack can sing without being hampered by her presence. I am pleased—Jack is, in a way, but the way it happened does not please him. I believe that Jack can develop something most unusual by himself—of course, he can sing for you when you lecture without any heartbreak or scenes.[42]

For her part, Kerby wasted little time before returning to the stage with a new musical partner. On November 4, 1933, she appeared at a benefit entertainment for the Campfire Girls at Table Rock, the country estate of Mrs. Morgan Hamilton in Sterlington, New York. The *New York Times* noted she was performing "Negro Exaltations" accompanied by Hamilton Forrest.[43] Forrest (1901–1963) was an appropriate replacement for Niles. In fact the two musicians shared an association with opera and most likely became acquainted in Chicago. At age twenty-seven, Forrest had his opera *Camille* championed by Mary Garden, who produced it for the Civic Opera and sang the lead role in 1930. Forrest was a most capable pianist, composer, and vocalist, though he had no experience and little sensitivity for Kerby's African American and Appalachian repertoire.

When Forrest initiated his partnership with Kerby, he contributed new arrangements, although their program was nearly identical to the earlier Kerby-Niles sets of "Negro Exaltations" and "Kentucky Mountain Songs." A glance at the February 5, 1934, program (attended by Niles and Carl Engel) at the Woman's Club in New York City reveals the similarity of the program. It included many of the same works that were collected and arranged by Niles, including "I'm So Glad Trouble Don't Last Always," "Ef I Had a Ribbon Bow," "Paper of Pins," "Go 'Way from My Window," "Jaybird," "Mister Rabbit," "Old Man Norah," and "A Manger Lullaby" ("Jesus, Jesus, Rest Your Head").

One essential addition to their act was the presence of a piano accompanist, Lloyd Browning, which freed Forrest from the piano bench. Kerby and Forrest performed in many of the same social venues where Kerby and Niles had performed, including Palm Beach, Florida, and Great Barrington, New York, although, with the exception of one New York Town Hall concert November 25, 1935, the new duo languished in small salon entertainments and garnered little of the critical and popular attention that Kerby and Niles had attracted.

Kerby moved to Hollywood, California, and maintained her act through the 1950s, although her performances grew increasingly anachronistic.[44] A 1947 review of a concert at New York's Times Hall noted: "Miss Kerby still 'pretties' up the spirituals a little, gives each a long spoken introduction which would be tiresome if she were not so good an actress and elocutionist. In this day of Marian Anderson, Roland Hayes,

Richard Dyer-Bennet and Tom Scott, who present the songs as they are and not 'dressed up,' Miss Kerby's manner seems a little dated."[45]

Niles and Kerby exchanged several letters over the intervening years, mostly about copyrights and the use of Niles's arrangements. In general, it appears that Niles was relatively generous with her in the use of his songs and arrangements, but the tension between Niles's composed and collected songs was, and remained, a contentious and sometimes litigious issue.[46] In Kerby's case, the recurring use of Niles's repertoire was problematic because she had access to numerous songs that Niles had variously written, collected, and arranged. When accused of recording "Go 'Way from My Window" in 1951, Kerby muddied the song's origins in her response to Niles:

Dear Jack,

. . . Regarding the LP record your friends heard, it's a privately made record and *not for sale*. Mrs. Upham paid for them and gave ten of them to her friends. And, of course, it was at her instigation that I made them. After you and I separated, Sally Kerby took Hamilton Forrest and me to Ashland, Kentucky where we stayed at the Clay Hotel for three weeks. While there Granny Buskirk and Jean Thomas sang "Go Way From My Window," which Hamilton tookd [sic] down and arranged. That is what I used on this record, but it is not published. I remember distinctly the first time you brought "Go Way From My Window" for us to sing, you told me that you got it from Jean Thomas, and that was the first time I had ever heard of Jean's name.

As always,
Marion Kerby

Rena Niles responded on behalf of her husband on December 20, 1951:

Dear Miss Kerby,

Your infringement of the copyright of "Go 'Way from My Window" is so serious that I am answering your letter in my husband's place—because he is preparing a Christmas radio broadcast, and this is no time for him to be disturbed.

First, to state the facts of the case: "Go 'Way from My Window" is composition, copyright by G. Schirmer Inc. None of it ever came from Jean Thomas or any of her people. The original version was written in 1907, and re-ritten [sic] for the Kerby-Niles concerts in duet form. It was later published by G. Schirmer. You could not have taken it down from granny Buskirk by way of oral tradition; if she or any other person sang it, she or he must have learned it from the Niles records or the Niles published music.

Apparently, the music you have recorded is the same, essentially, as the version of 'Go 'Way from My Window" which you sang in the first concert you did with Hamilton Forrest. My husband and the late Carl Engel witnessed this concert, and after your performance of this particular song, Carl Engel said: "This is emasculated John Jacob Niles."

The point at this time, however, is this: every infringement of copyright, whether the records are sold for profit or not, raises the question of the validity of the copyright, and opens the way to other piracies. RCA Victor, after having employed all their legal skill to get around the copyright, is now paying G. Schirmer the legitimate mechanicals on the performance done by Susan Reed.[47] Like yourself, Miss Reed tried to claim that she "collected" "Go 'Way from My Window" in some lonesome valley. Which was a stupid thing to do, since it is the recording company, and not the recording artist, who pays the mechanicals—and they are small, in any case.

We want "Go 'Way from My Window" sung and recorded, but we want it done legitimately and with proper credits and, in the case of recording, under license by the publisher.

There is only one authentic version of "Go 'Way from My Window." That is the Niles song, as published by G. Schirmer. There is no such thing as the Hamilton Forrest version or the Marion Kerby version—any more than there could be a

John Dee version of Brahms' Lullaby. After all, composition is composition, and cannot be treated as public domain material.

Sincerely,
Rena Niles [signed][48]

For several years Kerby sang from the Niles-Kerby mountain song repertoire at Jean Thomas's American Folk Song Festival at Ashland, Kentucky, and after her death December 19, 1956, she was honored at the festival with a "funeralizin" featuring her favorite hymns and a spoken tribute by Marian Anderson.[49]

8

Doris Ulmann

A portrait of Ulmann emerges through the lens of her contemporaries' recollections and from the few photographic images she permitted. Slim, elegant, frail, and pale, she had short dark hair, partially concealed under an array of fashionable hats, and was attired in billowy dotted Swiss summer dresses or scarlet silk. She was uncertain and unsure of herself, humble, and yet fiercely determined—absolutely driven by the purpose of her art. Her hands must have been scarred by her work, by soaking in harsh photographic chemicals, and her fingertips stained umber by the cigarettes. Her intense eyes, later set inside dark circles, gazed out on the world with determination, sensitivity, and artistic vision.[1]

Biographer Philip Jacobs characterized Doris Ulmann (1882–1934) as "a short, dark-haired, dark-complexioned woman [with a] frail physical appearance, refined manners, elegant dress, and New York accent."[2] Niles commented that "she stood 5′ 4 1/2″ inches tall and never weighed over 105 pounds. She moved with a quiet kind of grace and always wore the loveliest clothes . . . looking like some dark-complexioned princess from one of the southern European countries . . . that white angel with the black eyes."[3] Photographer Clarence White described her as "shy and retiring," and Allen Eaton depicted her as "an American artist of ability and devotion who found in the people of her country, regardless of their station and circumstances, inspiration and hope which she has interpreted through a medium that we can all understand." Her friend the author Julia Peterkin characterized her this way: "Poor little underdeveloped child. Kind little Doris. Consumed with ambition. Devouring her very soul with it. Never living, never experiencing. Lonely, unhappy. Wearing Rambora gowns and hats at her work here in the heat and dust, blistering her heels with beautiful shoes." And Olive Dame Campbell, director of the John C. Campbell School, noted: "Mrs. Ulmann looks very exotic in her scarlet silk dress with a natty little red, New York hat on her head. She is quite likely to smoke her gold-tipped cigarettes at any moment but would refrain it if you asked her to do so. . . . She is a most understanding person and appreciates character wherever she sees it."[4]

The few years that John Jacob Niles shared with Doris Ulmann completely transformed his life and career. Her financial support and artistic guidance enabled Niles's major folk-song collecting activity (1932–1935) and nurtured his career as a folk-song interpreter, collector, and composer. Through Ulmann, Niles was introduced to a wide circle of acquaintances, including presidents, leading literary and arts figures, mountain workers, and the social elite. At her death, she bequeathed a generous allowance that continued to support him for the rest of his life. As Niles stated in his autobiography, "She had a vision of her life and my life together, and the direction of my life after her death."[5]

It is unclear when Niles first met photographer Doris Ulmann. Niles's "Blue Notebook" records the year as 1925, which is seconded in an autobiography account in which Niles recalls meeting her in New York City while performing at the Grand Street Theatre.[6] Niles's recollection that Ulmann attended the Grand Street Follies with the intention of seeing the *Dybbuk* could be accurate. If they did meet at this theater, it had to have been in the summer or fall of 1925, since the *Dybbuk* opened on December 15, 1925. While they may have met initially at this time, it is extremely unlikely that Niles went to work for her until later, perhaps following a subsequent meeting spurred by the publication of an article by Ulmann and one by Niles in the same issue of *Scribner's*: "Robert Bridges [editor of *Scribner's*], in his great wisdom, had not placed . . . [Ulmann's article] on facing pages with my article 'Mountain Life and Customs' [wrong title] but we were in the same magazine, not far from one another. Later he said that if I had the nose of a foxhound I would pick up the scent quite quickly."[7] It is also possible that they became acquainted through Carl Engel, who was a family friend of the Ulmanns as well as Niles's editor at

G. Schirmer. In evidence, there are Ulmann photographs of Niles posed with Engel's daughter, Lisette. Unfortunately, the photographs cannot be specifically dated.[8]

Niles's claim of meeting Ulmann in 1925 sounds reasonable, but he also stated that he had started working for Ulmann shortly thereafter, upon finishing a road tour with the Ziegfeld Follies to Boston and Chicago in 1925. This date appears to be far too early—he was probably actually employed by her some time between September 1931, when he was back in Manhattan after his European concert tour, and June of 1932, just before his and Ulmann's initial trip to Kentucky.

Perhaps a clue to when their working relationship began is found in the correlation between a passage of Niles's autobiography and a letter from Ulmann to Carmelite "Cammie" Henry (1871–1948), owner of Melrose Plantation in Natchitoches, Louisiana. Both writings focus on Ulmann's August 1931 injury and recuperation. Niles recollects in his autobiography that he "first got to know" Ulmann after her injury: "When I first got to know Miss Doris Ulmann, she walked a halting step, if walked at all, not because she was ancient of days but through her falling on the concrete sidewalk between her door and the door of her car."[9] This is undoubtedly the accident that occurred in mid-August of 1931 when Ulmann fell on the street and fractured her knee. Writing to Cammie Henry in August 1931 from Lenox Hill Hospital in New York City, Ulmann described her injury and expressed her frustration with its effect on her work. "They have not been able to do much because the surgeon must wait—until it is in condition to operate,—he will operate on Tuesday and then I hope that it will be less painful. . . . I had planned to do so much work for August and September and now I am here not able to move, not able to do anything."[10]

It is likely that Niles was actively involved with Ulmann during the fall and early winter of 1931, while he was living in New York and composing *Africa to Harlem*. With the exception of a short concert swing through Canada, he was basically settled at home until he left for Palm Beach, Florida, with Marion Kerby in January 1932. This would have been the same period when Ulmann was convalescing from her surgery.[11] There would hardly have been much room in Niles's life for full-time work with Ulmann before that year. He was still married to Hélène and was seldom home in New York City, since he was frequently touring with Marion Kerby. By 1932, however, Niles was divorced, and his relationship with Kerby had soured to the point where the dissolution of their concert act appeared inevitable.[12]

When Niles's employment actually began, it rapidly became personal as well as business, and his intimate relationship with Ulmann excited a certain amount of gossip and hostility. Niles noted that within Ulmann's own household, "her German maids looked askance," and he observed that "her German chauffeur, an ex-army man and the former driver for a German general fighting in Silesia, compared me almost noisily with a hog." Niles developed a particularly contentious relationship with the chauffeur, George Uebler. Philip Jacobs characterized their animosity: "It was predictable, of course that . . . Uebler would have difficulty with Niles. It was inevitable that he would look upon Niles as a usurper—not only because he and Niles had been on opposite sides in World War I, but particularly because Uebler had been with Ulmann for many years and had always fulfilled his responsibilities in a dutiful and respectful manner. . . . The fact that Ulmann was willing to permit Niles to take responsibility for matters that had long been under Uebler's charge troubled her employee greatly." Uebler may have been "dutiful and respectful," but, as Julia Peterkin observed, he also had a bullying manner that could threaten his mistress and others. In a letter to author Irving Fineman (1893–1976), Peterkin wrote about her 1932 ride to South Carolina with Ulmann, "Doris is afraid of George, obeys whatever he says, and he, German that he is, scorns women and their orders. I wanted to kill him, but was too weak."[13]

Uebler barely concealed his contempt for Niles, bitterly calling him a gigolo in a letter to writer Lyle Saxon (1891–1946): "Mr. Niles was Miss Ulmann's friend 2 and 1/2 years, the right name of this Gentleman is Gigolo, and you know why. This man takes all money, automobile, apartment for $125.—a month, telephone, all food, clothing, neckties, shoes, and a charge account on Miss Ulmann's bank, from Miss Ulmann's money. That's a gigolo."[14]

Outside of the household, Niles was also regarded with suspicion and tarred with the reputation of a gigolo because Ulmann was both wealthy and ten years his senior. Julia Peterkin referred to him in precisely those terms in a letter to Cammie Henry following Ulmann's death, "Doris left a will within an hour of death leaving all she had to the gigolo."[15] The subject even came up in a conversation between Niles and Carl Engel. Niles recorded, "Engel . . . asked me about Miss Ulmann. I told him as much as I thought he ought to know, and then he told me something that rather shocked me. It seems that some days previously, a female person, who seemed to have an axe to grind, told all and sundry at the Beethoven Club that I was no doubt a gigolo. Mr. Engel's comment to me was, 'Gigolo or not, just be sure you are a working gigolo.'"[16]

Ulmann and Niles's relationship flourished despite the gossip; their independence provided immunity to social criticism. Ulmann's wealth and adventurous nature insulated her; Niles was already twice-married and accustomed to living life on his own terms. So in the summer of 1932 they were poised to set off together on their first joint expedition.

In the spring of 1932, Dr. Orie Latham Hatcher, president of the Southern Woman's Educational Alliance, had contacted Ulmann and asked her to do a series of portraits of mountain people. According to Philip Jacobs, Hatcher had originally recommended the areas around Alpine and Baxter, Tennessee, for Ulmann's work, but Dr. Arthur Estabrook of the Carnegie Institute in Washington, D.C., recommended that she begin in Ashland and then travel to the Cumberland Mountains of East Kentucky instead. In a letter to Hatcher, Ulmann noted the change of locale and provided evidence that Niles was ready to accompany her on the trip. It is likely that Niles also influenced Ulmann's decision to focus her work in Kentucky, because he was already familiar with portions of the mountains through earlier travels.[17]

Upon concluding the last of his summer concerts with Kerby at Wells College in June, Niles returned to New York while Kerby went to Lake Placid, New York, for the remainder of the summer. Niles then traveled to Chicago by rail to work with the illustrator on his new book, tentatively titled "Prohibition and to Hell with It" (published the next year under the title *Hinky Dinky Barley Brew*). Leaving Chicago, Niles took the train to Louisville and then went on to Ashland, Kentucky, where he met Doris Ulmann at the Henry Clay Hotel on Saturday, July 2. They relaxed on Sunday and then, beginning Monday, they took the next few days to photograph the Big Sandy River area around Rowan County, Kentucky. Here they met Jean Thomas and the blind fiddler Jilson Setters (James William Day).

Jean Bell Thomas (1881–1982), a "folk impresario" and author, originated the American Folk Song Festival held in and around Ashland between 1932 and 1972. Through her experience as a script girl with Cecil B. DeMille's production of *The Ten Commandments* (1923) and public relations work for New York socialite Gloria Gould Bishop and nightclub owner Ruby "Texas" Guinan, Thomas had sharpened her promotional skills. Upon returning to Kentucky, she applied those skills to promoting the blind fiddler James William Day (1861–1942), whom she met in 1926 when he was playing at the Morehead courthouse square. Thomas renamed him Jilson Settles (later "Setters") and created a whole new image, dressing him in homespun and posing him in a rustic ladderback chair. In 1928 she gained an RCA recording contract for him, and in 1931 Thomas published a book, *Devil's Ditties,* that imaginatively dramatized his life. Dubbing him the "Singin' Fiddler from Lost Hope Hollow," Thomas took him to London, England, to perform at Royal Albert Hall.

In 1930 Thomas hosted a small music festival in the backyard of her Ashland home. The next year she incorporated the American Folk Song Society and expanded the festival. By June 12, 1932, now styling herself the "Traipsin' Woman," Thomas presented the first American Folk Song Festival; in 1938 the festival featured forty acts and played to an audience of twenty thousand.[18]

United by a commonality of background and purpose, Niles and Thomas appeared to get on well. They were both native Kentuckians who had experienced showmanship in Hollywood and on Broadway and who shared a flair for the dramatic presentation of folk culture. Thomas's breathlessly excited letter to Niles of August 11, 1932, responds to Niles and Ulmann's visit by lauding Ulmann's photographs and then following up with a host of potential collaborative ventures involving a book publication, a future music and photograph collection, and arrangements for the festival. The communication is a particularly revealing record of how folk culture was in the process of being commodified, through publications, festivals, broadcasts, politics, and music copyrights; Thomas displays a real sense for ownership and profits.[19]

After a few days Niles and Ulmann moved south from Ashland to Louisa, Martin, Hindman, Hazard, and then Whitesburg. During this short time they covered quite a bit of territory and took copious photographs. From Martin, they drove on to Hindman, where they took a few pictures at the Hindman Settlement School, met the author James Still (1906–2001), and decided to move on because Hindman "was such a big operation we could not cover it in the time we had allotted, and decided to return later."[20] They moved on to nearby Hazard, a booming coal and logging center that was the seat of Perry County. There they met with Mrs. L. C. "Ma" Hibler, who generously provided Niles with a list of names of local musicians and people she thought would prove to be interesting photographic subjects. By July 5 Ulmann and Niles arrived in Whitesburg (Letcher County) and settled in at the three-story, brick Daniel Boone Hotel.[21]

Even today, Letcher County is rugged and beautiful terrain, though its features have been maimed by strip mining and mountaintop removal. The roads cling to pinched bottomlands along creeks. The hills and hollers snake every which way, with homesteads strung out from the mouth all the way to the head of the holler buried back in the hills. In the spring, magenta redbud and crabapple blossoms glow brilliantly on the steep mountainsides. Highway 119 twists and turns precariously upon itself over the crest of Pine Mountain from Whitesburg to Oven Fork. The vast mist-shrouded peak of Black Mountain sits between Kentucky and Virginia. Line Fork winds through the old-growth forest at Lilley Cornett Woods to Kingdom Come country, situated along the Little Shepherd Trail celebrated by writer John Fox Jr. Rickety plank bridges and shallow-water fords precariously connect homesteads to the winding road.

Extended families still gather to play old-time fiddle and banjo music at community square dances at places such as Carcassonne or share the work, such as potato diggings at harvest time. When Niles and Ulmann traveled to these parts, their car could take them only so far—most travel was along rough creek beds that served as roads, and the only way to get about was by mule, horse, jolt wagon, or foot. Niles was very much a packhorse for Ulmann, carrying the big camera (a Corona 6½-by-8½-inch view camera) attached to a tripod on one shoulder and an oilcloth bag containing twelve plate-holders on the other.

Niles and Ulmann commenced their work in the town of Whitesburg on July 6. A few excerpts from Niles's notebooks convey the flavor of their days in the mountains:

Whitesburg, Ky July the 6th 1932 . . . rain. . . . Took about 15 shots of Adams family. . . . Mrs. Ben Adams works in the local jail . . . that is she cleans the jail. Her house burned down about 6 months ago and she lost everything. . . . Her man Ben Adams has not worked a lick in 18 months. . . . He was a fairly nice looking fellow who seemed to be younger than Mrs. Adams. . . . The oldest daughter "bertha" was a very sad example of mountain girl. . . . She has no friends. . . . The only form of fun she has is going to church, which she does nearly every night. . . . She has managed the household for her mother now for a long while. . . . She is now 20. Miss Ulmann bought her several pairs of very nice silk stockings. . . . Bertha is pretty in a strange way . . . and if she were washed up and cleaned up and dressed up she would make a fair match for most city bred gals. . . . She wants to go into the out side world, but she must help her mother look after the 11 little ones. . . .

Grace Combs . . . is 21 yrs . . . born in Knott co[unty] . . . Carrie Ky. . . . Is already a teacher has been a short while to Richmond Ky. . . . Wants to continue and be really learned. . . . Was perhaps one of the most beautiful things in Ky. . . . Does not sew nor weave nor make baskets. . . . The outside world attracts her very much. . . . Her beauty is of a rather definite type. . . . She is quite tall and very stately. . . . She seems not to belong to any [o]ne around her.[22]

Ulmann and Niles worked at an exhausting pace. On July 6 in Whitesburg alone they photographed four groups of people. There were the fifteen shots of the Adams family, shots of the William Williams family, various generations of the Hughes family, and then thirty-six shots of Solomon and Beth Holcolmb of Kingdom Come. From the Holcolmbs Niles also collected music.

Niles's notebook accounts reveal a great deal about the people whom they photographed. His descriptions are not just factual and descriptive records; there is also an extraordinary amount of personal information and psychological conjecture as well. While Ulmann captured their portraits, Niles grasped much of their life story in a few succinct words. How he was able to learn so much—or surmise so much—based on these brief encounters is hard to imagine. It is difficult to assess just how accurate much of his commentary was, but out of it, in combination with the pictures and the music sketches, an engaging and sympathetic portrait of mountain life emerges.

While the expedition was focused on Ulmann's photography, Niles also found the time to collect music every day. He took down "The Lady and the Gypsy" from Pete Carter at Louisa; "The Pale Ring" from fiddler James Duff on the courthouse lawn of Hazard; "Lady Margot and Sweet Willie" and "Brother's Revenge" from "Granny" Holcolmb; and "The Fine Lady Gay" from Tillie Cornett and "The Fency King and the English King" from "Aunt" Flory French, both at the Daniel Boone Hotel, where they were staying in Whitesburg. The Holcolmbs at Whitesburg were a particularly important source, contributing "Jimmy Randall," "The Sinful Maiden," "The Death of Queen Jane," and others. Each day Niles added new songs to his notebook, although his collecting almost entirely focused on balladry, to the exclusion of other "less prestigious" genres.[23] By July 12, Niles and Ulmann returned, very exhausted, to New York City, stopping in Richmond, Virginia, to meet with Dr. Hatcher, who was delighted with all that they had accomplished in their fieldwork.

During the fall, Niles returned to the stage with Kerby, but he joined Ulmann for a presentation of their work at the annual board meeting of the Southern Woman's Educational Alliance, held at the St. Regis Hotel in New York City on October 31.[24] The intensity of their mountain trip and the frantic pace at which Ulmann worked to develop photographs seriously affected her already frail health. She was obliged to spend a month in bed that fall, and her condition continued to deteriorate through the winter and spring. Letters to friends, such as Lyle Saxon or Cammie Henry, listed a litany of ailments ranging from the grippe, to fatigue, to bronchitis.

Although Niles was back on tour with Marion Kerby in January 1933, he spent his available time at home with Ulmann, and the two developed a deeper and romantic attachment that was facilitated by Niles's divorce from Hélène. It is clear that Ulmann was very much in love with Niles. Her fascination with him is reflected in the many intimate photographs of Niles that playfully study his image. Getty Museum curator Judith

Keller describes a photograph of Niles's hands at the door of Ulmann's apartment: "The erotic tone of Steiglitz's photographs of his lover can also be found in this study; it has been suggested that the forceful, grasping pose of Niles's left hand and the forward gesture of his right hand as he inserts the key into the lock are both heavily laden with intimations of sexuality."[25]

Ulmann also began posing tableau photographs incorporating Niles with a female subject that are suggestive of a certain sexual tension. The subjects can be interpreted as a surrogate for the photographer herself. The photograph of Niles with Blanche Scroggs at the John C. Campbell Folk School reveals this scenario in the posed drama at the laundry house. According to Keller:

> The superficial intent, at least, appears to be that Niles is working with Scroggs, an accomplished singer, to copy into his notebook the lyrics of folk songs passed down to her. In many instances Ulmann did record Niles, notebook in hand, with local musicians. In this series, however, the interest in folklore has to be read as secondary. A more significant and complex explanation offered recently is that Niles, through Ulmann's manipulation, is standing in for the artist, who gazes at her model. Also provocative is the sexual tension it communicates[;] this series may thus be seen as autobiographical on several levels.[26]

As Ulmann increasingly relied on Niles for physical support and emotional affection, this had the unfortunate effect of straining her relationship with close friends, in particular, Julia Peterkin. Peterkin viewed Niles as an obstacle to her close relationship with the photographer; she was jealous of the time Ulmann shared with Niles rather than herself. Caustic comments in Peterkin's letters to novelist Irving Fineman reveal her disdain for Niles: "Poor thing, she knows I loathe Jack and wants to spare me a spell of cursing him, I guess. Women in love are such utter idiots. I often wonder why the creator made them so they cannot tell gentlemen from other men. None of us can where our emotions are involved. It's pathetic."[27]

Those thoughts were echoed in another letter written to Fineman just after Ulmann died. In part, Peterkin may be expressing some of her own amorous frustrations, since her relationship with Irving Fineman was never consummated in marriage; in fact he had recently taken up with a beautiful twenty-seven-year-old divorcée named Helene Hughes:[28] "Poor Doris. Women in love should be jailed, fed on bread and water until they recover from their insanity. Men not in love should be shot."[29]

Shortly after meeting Peterkin in February, Niles journeyed overseas on his final tour with Kerby while Ulmann began documenting dancers in New York, including Doris Humphrey, Martha Graham, and Agna Enters. This was challenging work for her because her experience and technique were dedicated to still-life poses, and dance is such a kinetic art form. Her images are devoid of motion, yet they are reminiscent of graceful classical statuary.

Ulmann also developed plans to fashion a book of photographs depicting Appalachian Mountain arts and crafts for Allen Eaton (1878–1962), an officer of the Department of Surveys for the Russell Sage Foundation and field secretary for the American Federation of Arts.[30] Ulmann and Eaton had been in contact since Eaton had requested the use of her photographs in an exhibition of handicrafts of the region organized by the Southern Mountain Handicraft Guild (now called the Southern Highland Handicraft Guild) for the April 1930 Conference of Mountain Workers at Knoxville, Tennessee. Ulmann's photographs made a strong impression on people who were present at the conference. William J. Hutchins, president of Berea College, sought to mount an exhibit at his college and wished to purchase some of her prints. Olive Dame Campbell wanted Ulmann to come to the John C. Campbell Folk School to document work there. Eaton was interested in having her contribute to a "survey of the handicrafts in the schools and homes of the Southern Mountains"[31] for the Russell Sage Foundation and the Southern Mountain Handicraft Guild. Ulmann was ready and willing to do so.

Ulmann's letter of July 5, 1933, to Lyle Saxon made it clear that she intended to return to the mountains, this time in concert with Eaton's agenda: "I am planning on going to North Carolina and Kentucky in July because there [is] work that I must do. Allen Eaton of the Russell Sage Foundation is making connections for me so that my trip will be as easy as possible in this respect—probably he will use some of my pictures for a book which he is planning."[32]

Eaton was anxious for Ulmann to focus her work at the John C. Campbell Folk School. He had been associated with the school from its origin, having been part of a grant that led to its creation at Brasstown, North Carolina. The director of the school, Olive Dame Campbell (1882–1954) had followed her husband into Appalachia when he served as secretary of the Southern Highland Division of the Russell Sage Foundation. Upon his death in 1919, she continued much of the work he had started, completing his book, *The Southern Highlander and His Homeland* (1921), serving as executive secretary to the Conference of Southern Mountain Workers, and establishing a school in his name built on the model of Scandinavian folk schools.

In 1922 Campbell and Marguerite Butler, of the Pine Mountain Settlement School in Kentucky, traveled through Scandinavia under the auspices of the American Scandinavian Foundation. The folk schools they visited in Denmark, Norway, Sweden, and Finland influenced the design and mission of the school they intended to start back home in Appalachia. After looking at sites in West Virginia and North Carolina, Campbell settled on Brasstown, North Carolina, because of the enthusiastic support of the local community.[33] In December 1925 the school was incorporated, and in 1927 the first classes began. Six years later, when Niles and Ulmann came to visit, the school was functioning as a community center for adult education and recreation and also served as a center for a thriving handicrafts industry.

At dawn on July 13, 1933, Niles contemplated the array of supplies and belongings he had to pack before he and Ulmann could set off for the mountains of North Carolina. In addition to clothing, mountain-climbing gear, and medications, there were "bolts of black cloth to make ordinary hotel rooms into darkrooms, with a small claw hammer and a box of nails to attach the cloth to the window frames. Then there were boxes and boxes of 6 1/2 X 8 1/2 DC Ortho plates, a Corona-view camera, 6 1/2 X 8 1/2, a smaller camera (my camera) 4 X 5 and plates for it, two tripods, a smallish box of tools and repair parts, a small hand drill and a set of very tiny drills (for pinhole exposures), a food-box, an electric water heater, and a water container." On the front seat of the 1929 Lincoln, next to Doris's chauffeur, were stashed repair parts for the car and new rubber tires, uninflated.[34] They set off early in the morning, with George Uebler behind the wheel, and arrived in Washington late that afternoon, staying at the Raleigh Hotel. The next day they continued their journey down the broad swath of the Shenandoah Valley, bounded on one side by the Blue Ridge and on the other side by the Appalachian Mountains. They continued on south and west to Asheville, North Carolina, where the roads grew ever more twisty and treacherous, winding through the edge of the Smoky Mountains and the dense Nantahala Forest of the westernmost part of North Carolina. Finally, they arrived at Murphy, North Carolina, the small county seat of Cherokee County, and settled in at the Regal Hotel, at the south side of the town square.

Olive Campbell was expecting them, because Eaton had written her on July 13 to give her notice of their arrival and also to provide some instruction as to the kinds of contacts and photographs he sought. In his tactful manner, he conveyed to Campbell an ambiguous assessment of Niles's character that is simultaneously an endorsement and a veiled caution: "John Jacob Niles is a nice fellow at times, is particularly interested in mountain music, and is a little more aggressive on some matters than I am—all this you will find out. He is a professional musician, has just been in Holland, I think specializes in mountain music, and is interested in mountain folks generally. . . . Mrs. Ulmann does not seem to me any too strong and I am glad she has such a husky young man to help her in her work."[35]

On July 16, Niles and Ulmann drove the six and a half miles from Murphy to the hamlet of Brasstown, following the Hiwassee River. From there it was just a few minutes' drive into Cherokee County to the campus of the John C. Campbell Folk School. The two set to work that morning, photographing subjects directly connected with the school, including Olive Dame Campbell and Marguerite Butler. Ulmann was simply delighted with Brasstown and quickly established a deep mutual bond of friendship with Campbell.[36] Campbell glowed effusively on behalf of both Niles and Ulmann in a letter to a faculty member at Berea College:

> We are having a very interesting visit from Mrs. Doris Ulmann who takes marvelous mountain pictures of which you have doubtless heard. We had an exhibit of some of them at Knoxville two or three years ago. With her is a professional musician by

the name of John Jacob Niles. He is from Kentucky originally, brought up on the edge of the mountains, or at all events in close touch with mountain people. He learned folk song from his own father and mother. During the years he has gone on collecting and harmonizing not only mountain songs but negro and others wherever he comes upon them. He sings abroad every year. We have been enchanted with his singing and playing, with which he is most generous.[37]

Niles and Ulmann slipped into a routine for the daily excursions into the surrounding mountains. The evening before, Campbell would help schedule the itinerary for the day's excursion. The school's kitchen staff awakened early in the morning to pack a substantial hamper with plenty of fried chicken for the noontime dinner. Then Niles would pack the three cameras, tripods, and glass plates into the small car rented from a garage in Murphy. Niles would usually drive, with either Robert or Mercer Scroggs (1923–) in the seat beside him to serve as a guide, while Ulmann reclined in the backseat. Starting off from the gentle valley of the school, they followed the rude dirt roads and creek beds out into the coves, driving as far up into the mountains as possible. Frequently they would be forced to park the car and walk the rest of the way over footpaths, fording creeks and rivers as necessary. Mercer, an eight-year-old boy when he first met Ulmann and Niles, remembers being amused at the way Ulmann would have to ball up her ankle-length skirts to get through the creeks and underbrush.

They would finally arrive at a cabin way up in a cove, where they would have to "break the ice" before they could get to work. Mercer recalled that Ulmann was a "witch doctor"; she would set to work right away mending some of the scrapes and cuts of the young ones with salves and strips of bedsheets that she carried with her. She would "make her point" by doctoring the kids. Then Niles would get them playing and singing with the " 'tater bug" mandolin, and soon they would all be singing together and getting along fine. At that point Ulmann would begin the photography work, sometimes showing them a portrait of neighbors that she had previously taken and printed so they would understand what she was doing with the camera.

Niles sometimes resorted to plying the subjects with a little moonshine to make them feel more at ease. Although Ulmann did not approve, Niles quietly made his arrangements and kept pint bottles hidden about. He grew to know all the corn liquor artisans in Tusquitee. As Mercer put it, "Jack knew every bootlegger. You didn't say who's bootleggin', you'd usually say who's got the *best*. He'd get 'em all a dancin' on that porch. Jack was a good'un."[38] Between Niles's singing, Ulmann's doctoring, the presence of local boys like Robert and Mercer, and good corn liquor, folks were willing to trust Niles and Ulmann and willing to accommodate themselves to their desires. In return, Niles and Ulmann treated their subjects with respect and Ulmann made every effort to ensure that they eventually received copies of the photographs.

"I Wonder as I Wander"

Niles and Ulmann were highly productive at the school, taking hundreds of photographs while Niles transcribed dozens of ballads from singers such as Hugh Stalcup (Ulmann photographed Pauline Stalcup) and Mr. and Mrs. Carston Geer.[39] The most important find for Niles, however, happened that first day, July 16. Purely by accident, he encountered a small fragment of tune and text that he had the intuition to collect from an itinerant family that was temporarily camped in the town of Murphy. Over the years, Niles recounted the story of "I Wonder as I Wander" many times, embellishing the account in each successive reiteration until the song's genesis achieved nearly mythic status.

The most complete account of Niles's encounter with Annie Morgan, the reputed singer of the folk fragment that became "I Wonder as I Wander," is found in his autobiography. With a Saturday afternoon free to himself, Niles had begun to wander about Murphy, notebook in hand. He later wrote:

> I heard singing coming from the other side of the town square. On investigating, I discovered a revivalist group about to start a street preaching. But in spite of the singing on and on, there was no preaching. It proved that the police (the county sheriff and the local "lawman") had taken the matter in their own hands

and given the revivalist and his group until sundown to "get the hell out of town" or else. The law had also confiscated a huge pile of canned goods. Because of the depression, the local population, having no actual cash-money, had contributed to the cause by bringing cans of vegetables, or sometimes potted meat, and dropped them in the collection bucket. But the sheriff and the local "lawman" had discovered that Preacher Morgan was a "low dog and a simple thief" and was not to be trusted any longer, nor allowed to prey on the simple-minded locals with "his noisy hell-fire-and-damnation kind of preachin'."

The sheriff had said that the Morgans could sing and preach one more afternoon service and collect what funds they could (Morgan had declared that they were utterly penniless without the pile of canned goods). Thereupon they had begun to "whoop-it-up" by way of banjo and voice, preparatory to the preaching and pleading for cash donations. They had opened their meeting with a blowsy female-person who said she was the wife of the great divine, Preacher Morgan. She sang lustily, "Let the Church Roll On, My Lord, Let the Church Roll On. . . ." But no one was ready to help grease the wheels of the carriage on which the church rolled, and it took quite a lot of gasoline to motivate their broken-down Ford, the tailgate of which served as a pulpit.

I sauntered over to get a closer look at Preacher Morgan and his entourage. A girl had stepped out to the edge of the little platform attached to the automobile. She began to sing. Her clothes were unbelievably dirty and ragged, and she too, was unwashed. Her ash-blond hair hung down in long skeins, uncombed, and as I came closer and stood beside the fantail, I discovered that her young hands were lovely, save for the unkempt, broken fingernails. If she had been made up by Hollywood experts, she could not have looked her part more effectively. But, best of all, she was positively beautiful, and in her untutored way, she could sing. She smiled as she sang, smiled rather sadly, and sang only a single line of song. The burden of her song had to do with wandering and wondering and the reasons for Christ's birth and death: "I wonder as I wander out under the sky. . . ." And then she stopped, although I had thrown a silver quarter at her feet which Preacher Morgan picked up, I thought rather greedily. That quarter would have purchased enough low-grade gasoline to carry the entire Morgan clan out of Cherokee county and into the state of Georgia. That was exactly what the lawmen wanted so dearly.

Preacher Morgan hissed a few words into the frightened girl's ear. He seemed to be saying, "Sing it again. This fellow is ready and willing to pay for it." I was truly willing. It may have been my clairvoyance. It may have been my stubborn nature. But, whatever it was, I see by my dim records that I went on paying for a single sentence of words and music for eight times. Once it seemed to me that she added the words "how Jesus our Saviour. . . ." Finally, I folded up my notebook. It was too thick a book to close with a snap (as notebooks usually do).

The next morning, "the only evidences of the Morgan family," Niles continued, were "a short washline strung between one of the forelegs of Stonewall Jackson's horse and the tip of his saber. There were several articles of female clothing on the line. They were grey from too many washings in cold water and home-made soap."[40]

Niles's colorful account sings in mythic tones, but the actual story whispers a more complex and nuanced narrative. Critic Nelson Stevens wrote: "One hears stories going around to the effect that John Jacob Niles, emulating Johannes Brahms, has quietly put some of his own inventions among his folk songs. If so, he is a genius. I think he has genius of some kind anyway, whether one calls it critical or creative; his tunes and text are in my opinion superior to anything else of their kind. I know a score of persons who would be overjoyed to see an example of what he started with and what he made of it."[41] What did Niles start with? What did he make of it? For earlier songs in the style of folk music ("Black Is the Color," "Jesus, Jesus Rest Your Head," and "Go 'Way from My Window"), it is possible to identify a surviving tune or text of a traditional song closely resembling the fragment collected by Niles, but not for "I Wonder as I Wander." There is simply no way to verify his vivid narrative save for the evidence preserved in the notebook that presents an outline of the event. No longtime residents of Murphy, North Carolina, remember Annie Morgan, but this is scarcely surprising, because Niles claimed that she was merely traveling through; consequently she would be unknown to local residents. Certainly the phenomenon of itinerant musicians and preachers busking in town squares is a venerable tradition in the South.[42] There would be nothing exceptional about a Preacher Morgan and his family performing in the town square, passing the hat, and subsequently traveling on to the next town.

Some details of this account are certainly fabricated. There was never a statue of Stonewall Jackson—or any other Civil War statuary—in any part of the town. The only monument in the town square was the Bull Moose Pen fountain dedicated to the memory of Archibald D. Murphey.[43] The portion of the story regarding the laundry hanging on the monument appears to be entirely fictional, but this is really only an embellishment. Niles's account of the Regal Hotel on the square does correspond to the large L-shaped brick hotel that stood at the south end of Duke Park, as the tree-shrouded town square was once known. There was also a large open space on Valley River Avenue toward the distinctive Methodist Church where cars parked right in the middle of the street, so the general landscape of the encounter with the Morgans appears accurate.

In examining the origin of "I Wonder as I Wander," we can choose either to accept or reject Niles's claims on the basis of his own documentation. It is possible that he fraudulently forged the contents of his notebook, but this scenario seems extremely unlikely, since he would have to have had the prescience to willfully fabricate these sketches years in advance of a completed, successful song. To conceive of creating such fraudulent sketches would require prodigious foresight and an unbridled imagination for forgery. In fact, these sketches are unremarkable within the context of the contents of his assorted notebooks. The music notation and commentary are entirely consistent with the collecting methodology evidenced in notebooks that he maintained for most of his life from 1908 onward.

Further, Niles's description of the development of "I Wonder as I Wander" from the embryonic stage of the fragment to an original song is in harmony with his previous compositional process and style. In several instances, Niles collected or adapted a fragment of traditional tune or text, or both, and then created an entirely new work based around the core of that original idea.

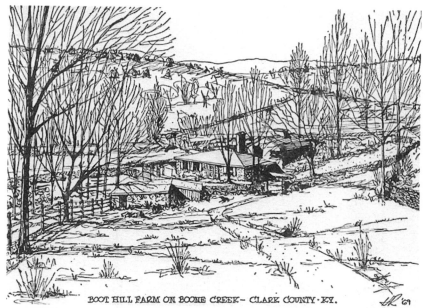

Boot Hill Farm on Boone Creek. Christmas card sketch by Helm Roberts, 1969. John Jacob Niles Photographic Collection, 82M9, Special Collections and Digital Programs, University of Kentucky. Courtesy of Helm Roberts.

St. Hubert's Episcopal Church, Clark County, Kentucky, 2010. Photo by the author.

(*Above*) Charles Grimes's Mill (est. 1807), on Boone Creek at the border of Fayette and Clark counties, Kentucky. The mill became the location for the Iroquois Hunt Club in 1928. Photo by the author.

(*Left*) Niles's gravestone in the cemetery of St. Hubert's Episcopal Church, Clark County, Kentucky. Photo by the author.

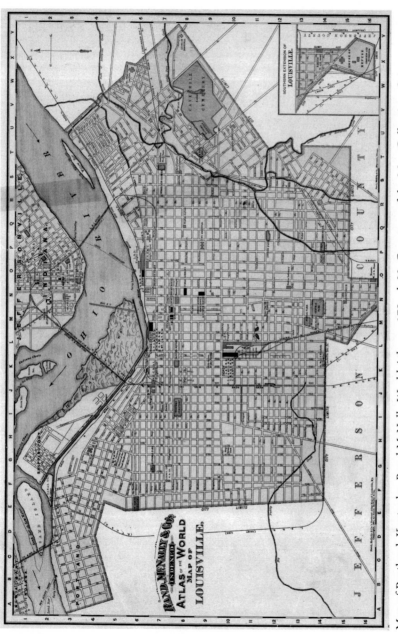

Map of Portland, Kentucky. *Rand McNally World Atlas*, p. 178, pl. 22. Courtesy of the Map Collection, Science Library, University of Kentucky.

Young Thomas Niles, father of John Jacob Niles. John Jacob Niles Photographic Collection, PA82M9385.

John Jacob Niles at age two. John Jacob Niles Photographic Collection, PA82M9179.

Notebook sketch of "Jesus, Jesus Rest Your Head," ca. 1906. Personal Series: Journals, Notebooks, Scrapbooks, 45/1/7, John Jacob Niles Collection, 82M9, Special Collections and Digital Programs, University of Kentucky.

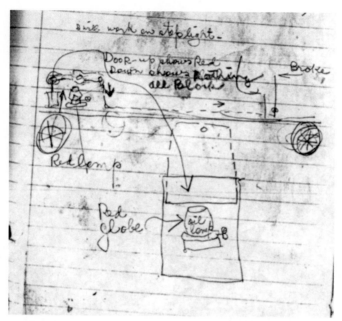

Sketch for a brake light invented by Niles and drawn in a field notebook, ca. 1905. Personal Series: Journals, Notebooks, Scrapbooks, 45/1/7, John Jacob Niles Collection, 82M9.

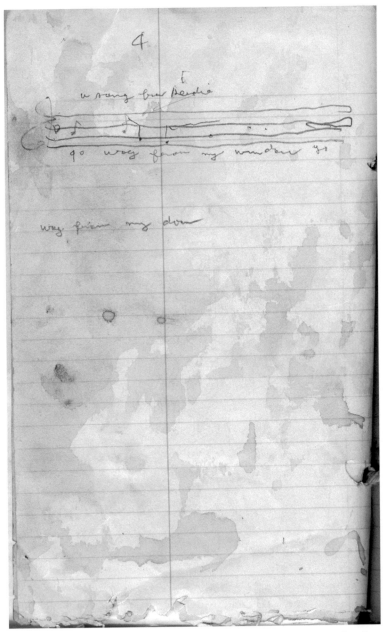

Original transcription of the first line of "Go 'Way from My Window,"
documented in a notebook, ca. 1905. Personal Series: Journals,
Notebooks, Scrapbooks, 45/1/4, John Jacob Niles Collection, 82M9.

(Above) Graduation picture of Niles (*fourth row, fourth from left*) and classmates at Manual Training High School, 1909. John Jacob Niles Photographic Collection, PA82M9499.

(Left) Thomas Niles (*seated*) as assistant deputy with Deputy Mattie Sternburg at Camp Zachary Taylor, six miles southeast of Louisville, Kentucky, 1918. John Jacob Niles Photographic Collection, PA82M9386.

Niles as a World War I aviator at Issoudun air base, France, 1917. John Jacob Niles Photographic Collection, PA82M9186.

(Above) Niles (*on left*) writing for the air base newspaper *Plane News* at Issoudun, France, 1917. John Jacob Niles Photographic Collection, PA82M9500.

(Left) John Jacob Niles as a lieutenant at Foggia air base, Italy, 1918. John Jacob Niles Photographic Collection, PA82M9190.

Niles in uniform with cigarette at Foggia air base, Italy. John Jacob Niles
Photographic Collection, PA82M9189A.

(Above) Niles's studio in Lyon, France, where he rehearsed while attending the Université de Lyon, 1918. John Jacob Niles Photographic Collection, PA82M9169.

(Left) Helene Babbitt Niles, pictured between Janet Spencer and Marion Kerby (*right*) in publicity for a concert at Mrs. M. Crouse Klock's home, 1929. *Syracuse Post Standard,* January 27, 1929. The original newspaper clipping is in the John Jacob Niles Collection.

Quand la guerre est finis . . .

les Americans parti . . .

Laissez les pauvres
Françaises

Un souvenir Bébe. . . .

Illustration in John Jacob Niles, *The Songs My Mother Never Taught Me,*
p. 57.

Niles and Marion Kerby at the Barbizon Hotel, New York City, 1930.
John Jacob Niles Photographic Collection, PA82M9504.

"Sandwich board" men advertising a concert by Niles and Marion Kerby at Grotrian Hall, London, England, 1930. John Jacob Niles Photographic Collection, PA82M9018.

Doris Ulmann with her 6½-by-8½-inch Corona view camera attached
to a tripod, 1934. Photo by John Jacob Niles. John Jacob Niles
Photographic Collection, PA82M9568.

A rare portrait of the photographer Doris Ulmann, 1934. Photo by Carl Van Vechten. John Jacob Niles Photographic Collection, PA82M9563.

Jean Thomas and Niles, posed in front of her cabin near Ashland, Kentucky, site of the American Folk Song Festival, 1932. Photo by Doris Ulmann. J. Paul Getty Museum, 95.XM.26. Courtesy of the museum.

Niles carrying Doris Ulmann's photographic equipment, ca. 1934. Photo by Doris Ulmann. J. Paul Getty Museum, 87.XM.89.21. Courtesy of the museum.

Hands of John Jacob Niles at a door in Berea, Kentucky, ca. 1932–1934. Photo by Doris Ulmann. Doris Ulmann Collection, PHO38-15-1589, Special Collections and University Archives, University of Oregon Libraries.

Niles with Blanche Scroggs at John C. Campbell Folk School, Brasstown, North Carolina, ca. 1933–1934. Photo by Doris Ulmann. J. Paul Getty Museum, 8.7.XM.89.4. Courtesy of the museum.

Olive Dame Campbell and Niles at the John C. Campbell Folk School, ca. 1933–1934. Photo by Doris Ulmann. John C. Campbell Folk School Archive, JCCFS U5 204. Courtesy of the John C. Campbell Folk School.

Niles's original sketch of "I Wonder as I Wander," transcribed in his notebook at Murphy, North Carolina, in July 1933. Personal Series: Journals, Notebooks, Scrapbooks, 46/4/49, John Jacob Niles Collection, 82M9.

Niles with Balis Ritchie, father of Jean Ritchie, and dulcimer, Viper, Kentucky, 1933. Photo by Doris Ulmann. Doris Ulmann Photographic Collection, 1178pa101, Special Collections and Digital Programs, University of Kentucky.

Dulcimer maker Jethro Amburgey (*right*) with Niles at Hindman Settlement School, Hindman, Kentucky, 1933. Photo by Doris Ulmann. Doris Ulmann Collection, PHO38-14-1730, Special Collections and University Archives, University of Oregon Libraries.

Mr. JOHN JACOB NILES

PROGRAM

Negro Songs of a Religious Nature . . *to the Pianoforte*
   a. "I'm So Glad Trouble Don't Last Alway"
   b. "Gambler Don't You Lose Your Place at
      God's Right Hand"

Ballads from the Southern Mountains . *to the Dulcimer*
   a. "My Little Mohee" (Kentucky)
   b. "You Got to Cross that Lonesome Valley"
      (North Carolina)
   c. "The Lass from the Low Countrie" (North
      Carolina)
   d. "Geordie" (Virginia)

Love Songs from the Southern Mountains . *to the Pianoforte*
   a. "One Morning in May" (Kentucky)
   b. "Down in That Valley" (Kentucky)
   c. "Go 'Way from My Window" (Kentucky)
   d. "My Horses Ain't Hungry" (Tennessee)

Three Hundred Years of the Frog and the Mouse
   a. "Down By a Corn Shock"
      (Kentucky) . . . . *Pianoforte*
   b. "Posheen Posheen Posho" (North
      Georgia) . . . . *Dulcimer*
   c. "There Was a Frog Lived in a Spring"
      (Kentucky) . . . . . . *Pianoforte*
   d. "Three Little Pigs in a Stew"
      (Kentucky) . . . . *Dulcimer*

"He's Got the Whole World in His Hands"

Thursday, March 22, 1934
THE WHITE HOUSE

Niles's musical program printed for performance at the White House on March 22, 1932. Career Series: Concert Programs, 1:2, John Jacob Niles Collection, 82M9.

Niles carrying Doris Ulmann piggyback across Cutshin Creek in Leslie County, Kentucky, 1934. Photo posed by Ulmann, photographer's name unknown. J. Paul Getty Museum, XM.89.21. Courtesy of the museum.

Notebook 7 strongly corroborates the process of collection leading to the subsequent process of composition.[44] In a sketch on page 49 dated July 16, 1933, Niles notated two lines of text underlying an accompanying melody line: "I wonder as I wander out under the sky,/How Jesus our saviour did come for to die." The melody for the initial phrase appears just as Niles later published it, but the second melodic phrase was apparently only mumbled indistinctly, as Niles said, for the melody set to the second line of text consists solely of a reiterated pitch A. Niles identified the sketch in a comment at the top: "This is what I got out of Annie Morgan's singing." He then commented on the additional performances following the double bar: "Repeated eight times more or less the same way—Doris [Ulmann] is ill."

Pages 50 and 51 of Notebook 7 continue the documentation in more detail. The performance of "Let the Church Roll On" by Preacher Morgan's wife is recorded at the top of page 51 with one line of text and tune transcribed. There is also a comment appended that qualifies the performance and dates the event: "Sung with a heart broken quality that is quite thrilling. Morgan family, Murphy, N.C. July 16, 1933." Following this is a series of eight sketches for "I Wonder," corresponding to the eight times that Niles claimed to have heard Annie Morgan sing the fragment. The way in which these sketches progressively reveal more of the text and tune of the fragment reflects both the difficult process of capturing oral performance in notation and the problems inherent in compiling a single version from multiple, variable repetitions.

On hand-drawn staves, the first sketch merely marked out the contour of the melody and noted the text "I wonder as I wander out under the sky." The second sketch reveals a little more—most of the initial melody phrase is transcribed and the text includes one additional word: "I wonder as I wander, out under the sky—How." Following the music, Niles appended a comment about the event itself: "Time out for an argument with the chief of police." The argument must have been resolved and Annie must have been permitted to continue singing, for three additional sketches appear on the page. These flesh out more details of the melody and complete the text as far as "I wonder as I wander out under the sky, how Jesus our saviour did come for to die." There is also, written at the bottom of the page, a short text fragment without melody that provides an extra line of text: "For poor onry people like you and like I." A final comment on the page presents Niles's thoughts on the origin of the song: "I believe the song, such as it is, is a statement by her preacher father set to a tune."

The series of sketches continues on the facing page (page 50), with three final attempts at notating the song. In each case, Niles is unable to transcribe more than the original line of melody and the three lines of text. There are, however, some interesting comments that lend further credence to Niles's account of the whole experience. His description of the singer reads: "Singing of a girl who calls herself Annie Morgan about 16 or maybe younger, very pretty—very unwashed." Again, referring to the intervention of the police, he notes: "Sheriff wants to arrest them all." Finally, he refers to the quarter paid for each performance: "This is the sixth time (twenty-five cents each performance.)" Very likely, the fragment of song heard by Niles consisted of just these three lines of text and a melodic phrase. Subsequent sketches in later notebooks reveal the compositional process that completed the melody and filled out the text.

Not long after Niles returned to New York City in the fall, he began developing "I Wonder as I Wander." There is a sketch dated September 26, 1933, and titled "N.C. song—I Wonder or Why Jesus Died?"[45] Only the first line of tune and text are notated here, but there is also a note indicating that Niles has shown the sketches to Carl Engel, who continued to serve as a critical sounding board for Niles's compositional efforts. "Carl E. wants at least three verses—and the title should have I Wonder in it— he rejected the music I submitted today." Additional sketches of September 29, October 1, and October 3 continue the development of the song, which now has a melody worked out in nearly complete form and a text that consists of two complete stanzas:

I wonder as I wander out under the sky,
How Jesus our saviour did come for to die,
For poor onry people like you and like I,
I wonder as I wander out under the sky.

When my brother Jesus was in a cow's stall,
With wise men and farmers and shepherds and all,
But he from God's heaven as star's light did fall,
And the promise of ages he then did recall.

Evidently, Engel was not satisfied with the song in this form, for Niles had added the comment "Carl E. will not take it this way (the ending is wrong)." A sketch made one day later presents four stanzas, although no text is provided for the third stanza.[46] Concerning the fourth stanza, Niles wrote: "Last verse about Jesus again in the same vein as second verse." He subsequently altered this to read "repeat first verse," which is the stanzaic scheme that he eventually settled on in the published form. Carl Engel's guiding hand continues to be present in these sketches, as Niles noted: "Carl E. says the influence of D'Indy shows up in my *melodic* line and also my harmonic structure." In its final incarnation, a third, completely original verse was added. In 1934 the song titled "I Wonder as I Wander" was first published in the G. Schirmer octavo collection *Songs of the Hill Folk* with the following lyrics, and subsequently various choral arrangements were issued, selling forty thousand copies annually for at least a thirty-five-year span.

I wonder as I wander, out under the sky,
How Jesus the Savior did come for to die,
For poor on'ry people like you and like I,
I wonder as I wander, out under the sky.

When Mary birthed Jesus, 'twas in a cow stall,
With wise men and farmers and shepherds and all.
But high from God's heaven a star's light did fall,
And the promise of ages it then did recall.

If Jesus had wanted for any wee thing,
A star in the sky or a bird on the wing,
Or all of God's angels in heav'n for to sing,
He surely could have it, 'cause he was the King.

I wonder as I wander, out under the sky,
How Jesus the Savior did come for to die,
For poor on'ry people like you and like I . . .
I wonder as I wander, out under the sky.[47]

Since "I Wonder as I Wander" was the product of both tradition and transformation, and since it was so widely disseminated, the song served as a lightning rod for Niles concerning the related issues of attributions, royalties, plagiarism, and authenticity. Niles originally called it simply an "Appalachian Carol." Obviously, with this attribution, the song appeared to be in the public domain, and thus no royalties could be due to G. Schirmer or to Niles. Consequently, he altered the attribution to read "Collected by John Jacob Niles" and "Adapted and Arranged by John Jacob Niles." It is unfortunate that the song itself suffered criticism because its composition lay between two worlds and Niles felt compelled to be ambiguous in his claims of authorship. As Ellen Stekert commented, "Ironically, it was not far from the time John Jacob Niles claimed to have collected 'I Wonder As I Wander' and many other superb creations of his own, for to have discovered the natural gem was then far better than to admit to having produced it artificially."[48]

Audiences and critics are unanimous in praising the beauty and strongly affective quality of this plaintive Christmas carol. And yet, many have been troubled by its status as a folk song. "I Wonder as I Wander" certainly stretches the boundaries of most folk-song definitions because, although based on traditional music, it was largely composed and notated. Although it has enjoyed some circulation in oral tradition, it has been largely disseminated through commercial recordings and in concert performance. At the same time, the essential nature of the carol seems to belong to the folk despite its compositional history. This sentiment is seconded by Oscar Brand, the noted folksinger and host of the *Folksong Festival* on New York City's WNYC since 1945. In *The Ballad Mongers*, Brand presents a personal and subjective definition of folk song that contrasts with the International Folk Music Council's definition, and he uses "I Wonder as I Wander" to illustrate his concept of folk song as "simple noise."

> When I refer to "traditional song," I am applying the definition promulgated by the International Folk Music Council, "Music that has been submitted to the process of oral transmission: It is the product of evolution, and is dependent on the circumstances of continuity, variation, and selection." Sometimes, however, I

refer to a "folk song" as a song which does not meet with all the elements of the Council's definition. That is because I use a very subjective rule of thumb in selecting my folk songbag. And since it *is* subjective, it cannot suit anyone but me, and will rarely satisfy anyone else. Nonetheless, as far as I am concerned, a folk song is distinguishable by a special sound, a kind of "simple noise." This sound is the result of an artless, unself-conscious quality in the music and lyrics which commends itself to my critical ear.

John Jacob Niles is an accomplished composer from Boot Hill, Kentucky, now busily at work on a symphony. One day, many years ago, he heard a short poem recited by a little mountain girl. He wrote some additional verses, composed a haunting melody, and published the work as "I Wonder As I Wander." Many authorities include this work in the folk song catalogue because they are unaware of its origin. I would include this work in the charmed circle because it has the "simple sound" I love. Others of Niles' creations would probably be acceptable as well, among them "Venezuela," "The Lass from the Low Countree," and the music for the best-known version of "Black Is the Color of My True Love's Hair."[49]

A more objective theoretical approach to addressing the matter of tradition and transformation is provided in Pauline Greenhill's essay "'Barrett's Privateers' and 'Baratt's Privateers.'" In examining the role of original composition in the folk process, she cites Eleanor Long's "four basic types of folk artistry"—"perseverator," "confabulator," "rationalizer," and "integrator." Niles's conscious transformation of folk material leading to original text would appear to place him in her "integrator" category, particularly since his texts have entered into folk circulation. Greenhill explains:

The performer who makes the fewest changes in the received text Long calls the perseverator, her first type of folk artisan. Often described as "conservative," "weak," "uninspired," "timid," "insensitive," this individual is actually motivated instead by a great respect for the integrity of a traditional text, and insists that it be faithfully reproduced.

Long's second type, the confabulator, generally makes changes in the text that he or she feels would make it a better artistic performance. Creativity is expressed primarily "in style rather than content, drama rather than coherence, and fancy (in the Coleridgean sense) rather than imagination. Of confabulators, Long suggests: "They stand in no particular awe of received tradition; they may add narrative themes . . . ; they may *revise* the text to conform to a tentative notion of 'better sense' or greater appropriateness . . . ; or they may simply *improvise* for the sheer love of improvising."

Long's other two categories include the rationalizer who "makes the text conform to a previously-adopted extra-textual system of values that is of significance to the singer." And the integrator, who "is as aware of the tradition as the perseverator, as innovative as the confabulator, and as conscious of the need for organization and consistency as the rationalizer. He goes beyond all three by creating texts that are unique. An integrator's original texts bear a close relationship to the local song tradition; some may even enter that tradition."[50]

Whether it is classified as folk song, art song, or Niles-as-"integrator" song, when Niles left Ulmann asleep at the Hotel Regal at Murphy and stumbled upon the musical fragment that germinated and flowered as "I Wonder as I Wander," the end result was a thing of great beauty, a song whose strains continue to echo today for "poor on'ry people like you and like I."

Sight and Sound in the Mountains

Niles and Ulmann reluctantly left Brasstown on August 7. During a little over three weeks there, Ulmann had formed a particularly close relationship with Olive Campbell, one that continued to deepen in the next few years. It is evident that Ulmann had quickly grown dependent on the director of the Campbell School for emotional support and guidance in social purpose. She voiced these heartfelt sentiments in a letter written to Campbell on the evening of their departure: "These interesting busy weeks will always remain a landmark in my life and it is such a precious posses-sion to know you. We spoke of you and all the dear people at the school constantly, because you have become part of our lives."[51] As they motored northward, they stopped at the home of Zilla Wilson in Highlands, North Carolina, where Ulmann spent two hours photographing her. Then they went on to Highlands and spent the night at the Highlands Country Club. The next day Niles and Ulmann traveled to Asheville, where they spent the day at a handicraft center called the Spinning Wheel. A letter from Ul-mann to Campbell written on August 14 describes her meeting with Cle-mentine Douglas, the director of the Spinning Wheel: "At Asheville we had the pleasure of meeting Miss Douglas—We saw her attractive cabin and as I had been too busy to try my hand at carding and spinning, I took the opportunity there and tried to work these things myself. I did not take my camera with me when I went to the Spinning Wheel—probably I should have."[52]

From Asheville Niles and Ulmann headed to Marion, Virginia, to experience the third Interstate Music Festival (the White Top Festival). Niles was particularly anxious to meet composer and folk enthusiast John Powell (1882–1963), who, along with Annabel Morris Buchanan (1888–1983), was one of the organizers of the festival. Powell mirrored Niles in many ways, since he was a composer who was also interested in folk music presentation. The White Top Festival drew a vast crowd, estimated at between twelve thousand and twenty thousand, including First Lady Eleanor Roosevelt (1884–1962). While the festival featured traditional performers in the area, such as Horton Barker, there were also more ar-tificial displays of English culture, such as Morris dancing coached by Richard Chase, and Punch and Judy marionette shows.[53] While they were there, Niles collected the ballad "Lady Margot and Love Henry" from "a delightful little white-haired octogenarian," Pete Johnson; "Fair John and the Seven Foresters" from Roscoe Pulsifer; and "Who's Goin' to Shoe Your Pretty Little Foot" from "a yarb [herb] man," Pres Wilcox.[54] Although the festival provided a concentration of traditional singers for Niles, Ulmann found it useless for her purposes and, in fact, was upset by the entire scene. After her time at the John C. Campbell Folk School, where the arts and crafts were inculcated as a natural extension of the community, the whole carnival atmosphere of the festival seemed inappropriate to her. Ulmann's letter to Campbell reveals a sensitive and perceptive understanding of the deleterious effects of altering the traditional context for mountain culture: "We have been at White Top—personally, I think it rather a mess. Those mountain people are at their best when you find them in their homes, speak to them quietly and give them the opportunity to be themselves with you. It was crowded, particularly on Saturday on account of the presence of Mrs. Roosevelt. While the simple mountain singing and playing was going on—the buzz of the reporters' type writers was heard. And what a dissonance!"[55]

After the festival, Niles and Ulmann headed back to New York City, staying at the Harrisburger Hotel in Harrisburg, Pennsylvania, before arriving home on August 15. There was little time to relax, however, because Ulmann immediately began developing proofs to show Allen Eaton. Furthermore, President William J. Hutchins of Berea College had written to Niles inviting Ulmann and him to Kentucky to mount a photography exhibit and perform for the student body.[56]

Niles responded the very next day in a breathless and excited epistle that suggests both exhaustion and exhilaration. Since he had started working with Ulmann, a whole new world of experiences was opening up for him, and he was obviously teeming with ideas and projects, such as the dialect dictionary that would attempt to trace Appalachian expressions to a venerable British lineage.[57] Revealingly, he was simultaneously scheming for ways to make a profit on the art and disingenuously claiming the high moral ground in working only to benefit others. With Ulmann's considerable financial support, his comments about "carrying on somehow" ring a bit hollow and hypocritical: "Its too bad you can't sell this show out and make your self some money. . . . Perhaps you can do this later at some other city where the rich could be caught and impressed with your needs. . . . Don't mind about paying me, or Miss Ulmann, we carry on somehow. . . . My motto is 'OTHERS.'"[58]

Niles and Ulmann left New York City on August 21 and checked into the Hotel Grand in Hazard, Kentucky, the next day. Working with suggestions tendered by "Ma" Hibler, Allen Eaton, and Olive Campbell, they quickly covered quite a bit of territory in East Kentucky. An August 10 letter from Campbell to Lula Hale, director of Homeplace on Troublesome Creek at Ary, Kentucky, provides a revealing portrait of Campbell's impressions of the pair after their initial residence at Brasstown. In addition, it reflects the close communication and common mission that mountain workers shared as they attempted to navigate the difficult situation posed by being sympathetic "outsiders" in a traditional culture.

> Mrs. Ulmann has just been here for three weeks with John Jacob Niles who is, one might say, three quarters mountain in his up-bringing. He helps her and at the same time gathers folk song to sing in his concert work. We have had a beautiful time with them. Mrs. Ulmann looks very exotic in her scarlet silk dress with a natty little red, New York hat on her head. She is quite likely to smoke her gold tipped cigarettes at any moment but would re-frain from it if you asked her to do so. I have felt that our young people might as well realize that there were other standards and other ways of doing things. We have tried to explain as far as we could to the local people and I think in the main they liked her very much. She is a most understanding person and appreci-ates character wherever she sees it. I have also had to explain a good many times that she wants people as they live and work, not dressed up for the photographer's studio. That is sometimes hard for people to understand. They are always crazy about Mr. Niles and his singing of old songs. Get him to the piano and you will certainly have a good time too. He is a character as you will soon see, and we certainly had a good time with them.[59]

Niles and Ulmann went directly to Homeplace, where they photo-graphed Lula Hale, Willie Fay Allen, Emery and Orvie Campbell, and various handicrafts. Lula Hale took them to Quicksand in Breathitt County, where Ulmann posed Enos Hardin, a chair maker. The next week was spent following the narrow creeks, such as Caney, Troublesome, and Ball, up and down the countless branches and forks that cut through the hills of Perry, Knott, Letcher, and Floyd counties in the southeastern cor-ner of Kentucky. They traveled through the small towns of Rowdy, Dwarf, Talcum, Vest, Fisty, Leburn, Garner, Yellow Mountain, and Mousie, to Martin in Floyd County. Martin, twenty-eight long and twisty miles from Hindman, was the farthest they penetrated on this trip; they made the return trip, by way of Waylon, Topmost, Kite, Isom, and Happy, to the village of Viper, located at the crook of a big bend in the Kentucky River in Perry County. Here they visited the family of Balis and Abigail Ritchie, who lived at the mouth of Elk Branch in "Slabtown." Ulmann took photographs of family members, including Balis, a teacher, printer, beekeeper, store clerk, county magistrate, farmer, and musician.

The youngest member of the Ritchie family, eleven-year-old Jean (1922–) was there when Ulmann and Niles visited the home place. Now one of America's most celebrated traditional musicians, Ritchie remembered the visit of Ulmann and Niles to her home, slipping into her excited mountain dialect before the intervening years smoothed the patterns of her speech:

> Well 'twas down about the end of the garden yonder, on the road and coming around that big mud hole. Tall man wearing a suit was carrying a woman and she was riding pig-a-back like a youngin' around a big mudhole and then he let her drap—they were laughing and carrying-on like chillern. Now wouldn't you say that's a quare sight? But—come on up to the house and knocked on the door, was just as proper as any folks you ever saw, spoke nice. The man started the talking, said his name was Johnny Niles and this lady is Miss Doris Ulmann. The lady she butted right in and I could tell by her voice that she was from Off—purty fur off—futherin' him. . . . She said she was a photographer and would like very much to take some pictures of us.
>
> Dad had dabbled in photography himself, so he was interested in her cameras and how she operated. Soon she was posing us all round the place. Took pictures of Mom at her canning, her spinning wheel and her loom; took Dad with his hoe I think, then one of him holding the dulcimer, and another showing it to Johnny Niles. The older girls were home from Berea College, and she did shots of them with their homemade puppets, of my sisters dancing, "Seven Maids in a Ring, Tra-la-la-la," and finally all of us scrouged onto the old shed steps, singing a ballad together. You can only see the top of my head and my ear! I guess I was restless while she got ready. Finally she saw I was jealous . . . and

she had me sit on a tabletop in front of the cellar house, with all the puppets hanging around me. But I had a pair of new saddle-shoes I was right proud of, so at the last minute I stuck one leg out where the shoe could be seen. She didn't like that much but she took the picture anyway, and I guess it still exists, somewhere, the photograph of my new saddle shoes!

Johnny Niles stood around, helped Miss Doris set up things, and twiddled with Dad's dulcimer, looking it over, tapping it here and there, and trying to make tunes on it. I remember that he said that he hadn't ever seen one before—maybe he meant that he hadn't seen one like it. He didn't seem to know much about playing it, though, and when Dad wasn't in the pictures Johnny got him to play some tunes and kept saying how much he liked the sound so Dad would go on playing. They had a good time together. We all remembered that day all our lives—it was something different for us.[60]

That day continued to echo into the future as Niles and Ritchie shared the stage in a variety of folk performances.

From Viper they returned to Hazard and made preparations to move their base of operations to the small city of Cumberland. The drive was a challenging one: back through Whitesburg, up and over the crest of Pine Mountain, down to the little town of Oven Fork, and then down along the Cumberland River. The Kingdom Come country surrounding Cumberland provided fertile ground for both Niles's music collecting and Ulmann's photographic work. They spent several days at the Pine Mountain Settlement School, founded by Katherine Pettit in 1913.[61] Cecil Sharp, who had visited Pine Mountain in August 1917, found it to be a "prime case for songs," collecting close to forty ballads within a week.[62]

Following in the footsteps of Sharp, Niles took down a version of the ballad "The House Carpenter" from Pettit and also consulted with her about his dialect dictionary. He collected "The Riddle Song" from the singing of Wilma Creech, who later trained as a doctor. Ulmann photographed the Creech family, including "Uncle" William and "Aunt" Sally Creech, who provided the land where the school was located; "Granny" Creech; Betty; and Wilma. Afterward, Pettit conducted Niles and Ulmann up Line Fork, a thirty-nine-mile creek that flowed from Kingdom Come to the North Fork of the Kentucky River. Along the way Ulmann took photographs, while Niles collected "The Murdered Boy," a version of "The Twa Brothers," from the singing of Kate Ramsey. Near Cumberland, they spent several days in the fascinating company of "Pencil" Marcum, even though he was not a singer and would not permit Ulmann to take his portrait.[63]

The Dulcimer: Tradition and Transformation

Niles and Ulmann finished up their work in the Kingdom Come region and returned to New York by the end of the second week of September. Despite the manic pace of their travels and work, and despite Ulmann's worsening health, they voraciously printed up the plates in anticipation of a forthcoming trip to Berea, Kentucky. In addition to assisting Ulmann with the developing process, Niles was also busily engaged in the composition of "I Wonder as I Wander" and in developing a new repertoire and format for upcoming solo concerts planned for October in New York, in Richmond, Virginia, and at Berea College in October. With the exception of the "Field, Street, and Jailhouse Cry" set, most of the Niles-Kerby repertoire had been arranged for duet with piano accompaniment. In performing alone, he was forced to recast musical lines as well as the piano accompaniment in order to complete missing harmonies. Further, he had to devise a new stage presence. It is almost impossible to accompany oneself at the piano while also maintaining an intimate connection with the audience; the piano is such a forbidding and unmoving barrier. In attempting to overcome this obstacle, Niles conceived of a brilliant and novel solution—the dulcimer.

He had played a poorly-made instrument as a youth living in Jefferson County, but in his travels through North Carolina and Kentucky, he had encountered skilled instrument makers such as Ben and Nathan Hicks of Beech Mountain, North Carolina, and J. Edward Thomas and Jethro Amburgey of Knott County, Kentucky. He was also introduced to proficient performers, such as Balis Ritchie, who strongly influenced his decision to rely on the dulcimer for his own use.[64]

Niles's adoption of the dulcimer carried with it many assets but also a few disadvantages. The physical presence of the instrument was far more mobile and less intrusive than a piano. The ability to transport his own instruments allowed him to control the performance situation more closely—with a piano one could never trust the condition or tuning of an instrument. The gentle, woody tone of the dulcimer's voice was an ideal complement to Niles's countertenor voice, and it ensured that the diction of the words would never be obscured by the accompaniment. Niles's handcrafted instruments were tailored to his specific vocal timbre and range. He often embroidered on this point at concerts: "Do not be surprised at my high voice. When it's functioning it's extravagantly high. If it's high tonight I can sing my songs without any trouble. It's always been this way, and praise God it remains so, because if it changes, I'd be in an awful fix. I'd have to make my dulcimers all over, because the dulcimers are all geared to the voice. The voice is not geared to anything."[65] Nile's instruments *were* geared to his compositional style. The diatonic scale of a dulcimer perfectly accommodated the modal proclivities of many of Niles's songs—the dulcimer was easily tuned to Aeolian, Dorian, and mixolydian modes.[66]

Visually, using the dulcimer reinforced the notion that Niles's music was folk music of venerable stock. The exotic image of the dulcimer was redolent of bucolic mountain scenes and cabin porches, whereas the piano smacked of art song in concert halls or popular song in vaudeville. By the 1930s the dulcimer was already becoming saddled with cultural associations of domesticity and Elizabethan culture in popular consciousness. According to David Whisnant, "the shadowy and presumably ancient origin of the dulcimer was appealing; its plaintive, simple sound was congruent with prevalent assumptions about 'Elizabethan' culture in the mountains."[67]

Finally, the striking picture of Niles bent over the dulcimer or dramatically cradling it like a lover in "The Hangman" distinguished him from both concert vocalists and guitar-wielding folk musicians. The presence of the dulcimer really created his image as a "tragic troubadour" or "mountain minstrel." Traditional singers like Jean Ritchie, Frank Profitt, and I. D. Stamper were still playing the instrument within a circle of family and friends when Niles introduced the instrument to the public at large on a concert stage.[68] There were instances of the dulcimer's presence at events such as White Top, Asheville's Mountain Dance and Folk

Festival, and the American Folk Song Festival, but it was not until later that both traditional performers and folk revival musicians, such as Paul Clayton (1933–1967) or Richard Fariña (1937–1966), performed in concert with the dulcimer.

A few complications were posed by the use of the dulcimer as well. The more elaborate and Impressionist accompaniment parts that were idiomatic to the piano were ill suited to translation on the dulcimer, so Niles was compelled to become even more economical in his writing. This meant that he had to craft one style for his own performance and compose in a rather different style for the published versions that invariably were set for piano and voice.

There were also some major challenges created by the volume of sound produced by the instrument. The sweet timbre of the dulcimer was designed for solo use in intimate gatherings and did not project well in a large hall. Since electronic amplification had not been effectively developed yet, Niles had to build larger instruments with more strings and to cultivate a unique performance style consisting of sharply strummed chords and drones, rather than the traditional finger-picking or strumming with the use of a "noter" and a goose quill.[69] And since the dulcimer is a diatonic instrument, it was necessary to travel with several different instruments tuned to different scales, to avoid dead time on stage while an instrument was retuned.

Niles acquired his earliest instruments from Jethro Amburgey (1895–1971) of Hindman, Kentucky, and Nathan Hicks (ca. 1900–1945) of Rominger on Beech Mountain, North Carolina. The Amburgey instrument is a classic hourglass shape with heart-shaped cutouts, very much in the tradition and scale of dulcimers made by "Uncle" Ed Thomas of Bath, Kentucky. The Hicks instrument, of more generous dimensions, was typical of those made by Nathan and his Uncle Roby that were eventually sold to people in New York for five dollars.[70] By 1935 Niles began fashioning his own dulcimers, and eventually he developed various hybrid instruments that were better suited to the demands of his unique performance style.

Solo Concerts and Mountain Expeditions

As Niles wrestled with the challenges presented by his new performance directions, he was preparing for the upcoming visit to Berea. A letter to

President Hutchins discusses Niles and Ulmann's current activity and broaches an initiative to establish a permanent exhibit and gallery dedicated to Ulmann's photography at Berea.[71]

Shortly before they were due to travel south again, Niles presented his first solo concert in New York City to a full house at the Greenwich House Music School. Without Kerby for the first time, he sang twenty numbers, accompanying himself with both piano and dulcimer. He also performed the ballad "Pretty Polly" without accompaniment. The successful concert proved to be a testing ground for new material; some older songs were dropped from his repertoire forever.[72]

Several days later Niles and Ulmann left New York, checking in at the Jefferson Hotel in Richmond, Virginia, on October 21. The next day, Ulmann spoke briefly and Niles entertained for a gathering held by the Southern Woman's Educational Alliance at the A. A. Anderson Art Gallery, where some of Ulmann's photographs were displayed.[73] On October 24, they headed back to Hazard, where Niles sent a telegraph to President Hutchins advising him that they would arrive in Berea on October 26. In the short time that they were at the college, Niles performed privately for a small gathering hosted by Hutchins and then for an appreciative audience of 1,550 students, who "jumped up and screamed."[74]

Ulmann was equally delighted with the visit to Berea and most impressed with the mission of the school. A letter to Hutchins makes it clear that she was intent on returning to work in conjunction with Allen Eaton's book. The positive experience enjoyed by both Niles and Ulmann paved the way for Ulmann's generous bequest to the school, stipulated in her will less than a year later.[75]

Niles and Ulmann headed back to New York by the end of the month and, en route, stayed at the Lincoln Hotel in Marion, Virginia, where Niles, in a letter to Rena, rhapsodized about the autumn foliage in the mountains: "A poet said that Autumn was a weaver. . . . When you think you have seen all the possible combinations of red, brown, gold, and green, you see a mountain covered with such colors that you give up. . . . You know that although Nature is seldom right (re Mr Whistler) she is right in the Autumn."[76]

Back in New York by the evening of November 4, Niles returned to his arranging and composing, with the prospect of several fall concerts.

On November 17, in Philadelphia, he performed at a private birthday gathering for Mr. and Mrs. Taylor on Delancey Street, and then he and Ulmann went to Richmond, Virginia, where he sang for the Southern Woman's Educational Alliance. On December 8, Niles gave a performance at the American Dalcroze School (directed by the choral musician Paul Boepple, who directed the Dessoff Choirs for thirty-two years), and the next day he shared a concert with Augustus Zanzig at the New School for Social Research.

On December 11 he appeared at the Cosmopolitan Club, where he "sang fifteen numbers and three encores"; this event was followed by a joint concert at the Barnard Club on December 17 featuring Niles and Sarat Lahiri, a singer of traditional Indian songs. Niles was sharing concerts with different styles of music as he developed his new repertoire and expanded his countertenor vocal delivery, to present a new context for his style.[77]

About a week later, Niles and Ulmann left for Brasstown to spend the Christmas holidays at the John C. Campbell Folk School. They arrived in Murphy on the evening of December 21, and the next day the school held a reception for them in Keith House, followed by a party at which Niles entertained the guests.[78] The next evening was Christmas Eve, and as was customary at the school, the students and staff presented a Nativity play interlaced with traditional carols. This year, in a nod to their guest, they included some of Niles's music. Niles commented that it "was like something out of an old legend." The Community Hall where the pageant took place was a vast, dark wooden room with a huge crackling fireplace and a stone chimney that reached to the ceiling and radiated heat throughout the room. A golden glow was imparted by candles mounted on four large wagon wheels hung from the ceiling by pulleys. One of the highlights of the story was the depiction of the "Cherry Tree Carol," sung by the character Mary (the coveted role of Mary was variously sung by Virginia Howard, Blanche Scroggs, Bernice Stalcup, and Anne Hensley) in which a specially designed tree prop actually bent over to offer its cherries to the virgin mother.[79]

Doris Ulmann's description of the pageant and her entire visit wells over with heartfelt enthusiasm and gratitude. For someone who consistently professed a dislike of the holidays (and was of Jewish heritage),

Ulmann found Christmas at Brasstown a remarkable occasion: "I have never experienced a true Christmas spirit as I did at Brasstown,—they do everything in so beautiful and unique a way that it moves you deeply. The play was a beautiful performance—it reminds you of Oberammergau, but I thought it more vital and moving because it had a strange naïve and primitive quality."[80]

Shortly after Christmas, Niles and Ulmann left Brasstown and wandered through Winston-Salem, North Carolina, and Roanoke, Virginia, before stopping at Charlottesville, Virginia, where they toured Thomas Jefferson's Monticello estate. They arrived in Richmond, Virginia, on New Year's Eve, and on January 2, 1934, they attended a supper and special dress rehearsal of the play *Heaven Bound* arranged for them by Ori Hatcher. The drama, written by Nellie L. Davis and sponsored by the Southern Woman's Educational Alliance, featured an African American cast. Niles, because he had been actively involved in the interpretation and collecting of African American material, was very interested in the production, particularly in the musical elements. While his letter of January 3 to Rena lauds the play, it also edges on racism in the way he broadly characterizes African American culture: "The Negro folk Drama was simply too wonderful. . . . The singing part of the time was devine [*sic*] and part of the time it was bad because the Negro can not [be] depended upon to have excellent taste always. . . . Not even whites have that gift."[81]

After leaving Richmond, Niles and Ulmann drove up to Washington, D.C., arriving on January 4, 1934. The next morning Niles visited Washington National Cathedral and penned an emotional and poetic account of his impressions. Nearly alone amid the vast stone vaulted arches of the cathedral, illuminated by shards of colored light from the three rose windows, and infused with the ethereal strains of choral music and the peals of the vast Skinner organ, Niles experienced a remarkable spiritual moment. On a more mundane level, hearing the choir singing his music prompted an understanding of the critical difference between the Groton School's performance of "Down in Yon Forest" and "Seven Joys of Mary" heard at a carol festival and the singing of this same music at Brasstown on Christmas Eve. The essential nature of the Nativity's earthy stable was better served by the heartfelt singing of mountain children than the polished skill of the Groton choir.[82]

After the cathedral experience, it was back to reality for Niles, who met with Carl Engel at his Library of Congress office about a songbook proposal that Niles dismissed as "this damn song book, which I fear will be all talk, and no profit for me. . . . It is being done for the great wide public." The songbook took the form of a slim octavo collection of twelve songs, including traditional ballads and lyric folk songs as well as original compositions, such as "I Wonder as I Wander." Published in November of that same year under the title *Songs of the Hill Folk,* this was the first of a series of eight similar publications by Niles. *Songs of the Hill Folk* was priced modestly at sixty cents and succeeded at reaching the "great wide public," but contrary to Niles's fears, it and subsequent volumes earned a profit for him, even though he received only a 5 percent royalty, as compared to the 10 percent he was making on his other publications. Once again, Niles's friend Engel demonstrated a real capacity for enlightened support of traditional music, coupled with shrewd financial acumen, in his dual role as director of both G. Schirmer Music Publishing and the Library of Congress's Music Division.

Leaving Washington, Niles and Ulmann returned to New York City, where Niles worked at his songbook and performed at various locations, including the Groton School and the Town Hall Club. Writing about Niles to Olive Campbell, Ulmann commented on the performances and also provided some insight into the nature of their relationship, which was stretched thin by the intensity of their work. Ulmann was probably unaware that Niles was also becoming romantically involved with Rena Lipetz at this time; he may have used his work as a means for escaping meaningful discussion with Ulmann: "Jack had a very successful concert at Groton—but he returned so fatigued and so low that he was hardly himself. . . . Jack and I are so busy when in New York that we do not seem to have time to visit—whenever we see each other we are always doing something and when through with our job or whatever it is (social things are too often jobs of the worst kind) we both run to our work."[83] It was a bitterly cold winter in Manhattan, and Niles and Ulmann remained close to home, engrossed in their work—Ulmann in developing prints from the Kentucky journey and the Brasstown Christmas, Niles in completing the songbook for Schirmer and researching his dialect dictionary in consultation with Professor Charles Fries at the University of Michigan.[84]

By March the winter was on the wane, and Niles and Ulmann returned to the road in Niles's new Chevrolet. They were headed for the nation's capital and a performance on March 22 at the White House for a dinner hosted by President and Mrs. Roosevelt. Ulmann had come into contact with Eleanor Roosevelt through the first lady's involvement with a variety of progressive social causes espoused by women, particularly the Southern Woman's Educational Alliance, and her advocacy of traditional folk arts. Niles and Ulmann had certainly met her at the White Top Festival; they had encountered her more personally at an outdoor clambake hosted by Elinor Morgenthau (Mrs. Henry Morgenthau Jr.) at which Niles had entertained.[85]

This first concert at the White House was exceedingly important to Niles's career. The imprimatur of formal state recognition provided credibility at concert venues and academic institutions; informally, friendship with the powerful first lady could open many social and cultural doors. The evening's concert repertoire followed much the same format Niles and Kerby had used, with a set of African American material juxtaposed with Kentucky mountain songs. However, the balance was now tilted in favor of the mountain songs, and new music arrangements arising from his North Carolina collecting experiences were included. Niles was making the transition from his customary reliance on the piano to the increasing use of the dulcimer as an accompaniment. With the exception of "Three Little Pigs in a Stew," these songs all became part of the central core of his concert repertoire in years to come. By all accounts, it was a most successful evening for Niles, who was invited to the White House on three additional occasions. He maintained close communication with Mrs. Roosevelt, periodically sending letters and gifts, such as handbags, a carved wooden mule, stone-ground white cornmeal, and a dulcimer.[86]

Niles and Ulmann remained in Washington for a few additional days, because he was scheduled to present concerts at a private party for Mr. and Mrs. James E. Dunn (Mrs. Dunn was the socially prominent former Mary Armour of Chicago) and at the home of Mr. and Mrs. William Phillips in honor of Chief Justice Charles Evans Hughes. By March 27 they were back in New York City; they unpacked and packed again in preparation for the extended trip into North Carolina, Tennessee, Kentucky, and the Ozarks that Niles grandly termed "the Niles Ulmann Folk Lore Photographic Expedition."[87]

Niles and Ulmann had been preparing for this expedition in a series of communications with Eaton, Campbell, Hutchins, and B. A. Botkin. First, Ulmann planned on beginning the trip with a return to Brasstown for a short residence at the John C. Campbell Folk School. She met with Allen Eaton in New York City to make plans and draw up lists of subjects to be photographed.[88] In setting up the work at Berea and the excursions into Tennessee, Niles wrote to Hutchins to iron out details of lodging, to request the use of a photographic darkroom, and to let Hutchins know about the exhibition of Ulmann's photographs that Lecester Holland, the curator of fine arts, had mounted at the Library of Congress.[89]

Hutchins responded with a letter and an attached "shooting script," a guide to numerous subjects that he thought Ulmann might wish to photograph. The list included several prominent faculty members, such as former president William G. Frost, Dr. James Watt Raine "in tabernacle," and Seth Romen Huntington "in pulpit." He also suggested many craft and industry sites, including one where pottery was made; the kitchen of the ladies' hall; a bakery and a candy kitchen; a dairy creamery and a poultry plant; students who represented mountain types; an iron works, the Grant House, an old watermill; and the sewing and weaving industry.[90]

In constructing plans for travel through the Ozarks, Niles also corresponded with Benjamin Albert Botkin (1901–1975), an English and folklore professor at the University of Oklahoma, who offered to assist them with their work in the Ozark region following their time at Berea. Like their Appalachian contacts, Botkin was willing to provide a detailed itinerary and suggest guides, such as John Lomax and J. Frank Dobie, to help direct Niles and Ulmann to appropriate sites.[91] While Niles indicated in several letters that he and Ulmann intended to expand their work to the Southwest following their six weeks in Berea, they never actually consummated the plans, for various reasons. Ulmann's rapidly declining health made the prospect of such extended travel problematic. Furthermore, the wide range of regions and unfamiliar cultures was daunting in comparison to the relatively circumscribed area of the Southern Appalachians in which they were working. As Ulmann said in response to Eaton's request that they enlarge the scope of their work in the Southeast:

"I am willing to go to as many of the important places as possible—but it really is impossible to go to every place . . . because it would be too fatiguing and would waste too much time. Besides, personally, I think there is always more value in doing one thing thoroughly and as well as possible than in spreading over a large area and getting just a little of many things. In this way it is impossible to produce the best there is."[92]

In what was becoming almost a routine by now, Niles and Ulmann left New York City early in the morning of Saturday, April 14, and checked into the Raleigh Hotel in Washington, D.C., that afternoon. At this point, they were traveling with two automobiles; Uebler was chauffeuring the Lincoln with all the baggage and equipment, while Niles was driving Ulmann in the new Chevrolet that she had purchased for him. The Chevy may have seemed an extravagant purchase in the depths of the Depression, but the heavy Lincoln was simply not able to traverse many of the small roads that followed creek beds through the mountains—terrain that would prove challenging even for today's four-wheel-drive SUVs. With the luggage necessary for these extended trips away from home and the obstacles posed by the rugged roads, they really required two different vehicles now.

The capital looked gorgeous, since they had fortuitously arrived right at the peak of the cherry-blossom time. The next day, Niles and Ulmann went to the White House for dinner, where Niles once again entertained the guests. This return engagement was a much more relaxed affair than the previous one; now he knew what to anticipate. The Kentucky farm boy, after returning from the war, had grown accustomed to socializing in the most elite circles, so that by now even the president of the United States could be characterized as "simply swell." Niles's letter to Rena written that evening was upbeat and succinct: "Well, I was at the white house a few moments ago and now am home again. . . . The President was simply swell. . . . I sat at his right with Miss Morganthau [*sic*] between us and he talked to me all during dinner. . . . Then they brought in the dulcimers and I played right at the table. . . . A little like the great princes of old it was . . . me being the jester or the count [court] musician."[93]

The next day, Niles met with Waldo Leland, secretary of the Council of Learned Societies, regarding his dialect dictionary, and on the morning of April 19 Niles and Ulmann motored on down to Murphy, North Carolina, and checked into the Hotel Regal. Spring was lovely in the Snowbird Mountains surrounding Brasstown. As Niles noted, "The dogwood and the red bud and the apple and peach and forsythia and all such are doing their best against the occasional frost. But when the sun comes out its as warm as summer."[94]

They were at Brasstown for only a few days, but it was long enough for Niles to collect five new songs, assist Ulmann with her photography, and acquire his new six-stringed dulcimer, crafted specifically for him by Nathan Hicks. Since Hicks lived at Rominger, near Banner Elk, the instrument was probably sent by mail to the Folk School. Niles was in Brasstown less than a week, so he would scarcely have had time to make the difficult journey to Beech Mountain to pick up the instrument himself.

This particular dulcimer is interesting because it represents the forces of both tradition and transformation. The overall shape and design are very traditional, handed down through the extended Hicks family. However, Hicks was willing to alter the traditional design by increasing the dimensions of the instrument and doubling the number of strings according to Niles's specifications. Hicks later proved equally flexible in other cultural negotiations between tradition and the requests of folk collectors such as Maurice Matteson, Mellinger Henry, and Frank and Ann Warner.[95]

Niles and Ulmann became proficient at collecting music and photography from their sources. They were also becoming familiar with both the people and places around Brasstown, so that they were able to cover considerable territory with efficiency. Niles's letter to Allen Eaton lists projects that would account for three very full days of photography work from April 20 to 22:

Anne Miller, quilter, with two little boys
Her husband, Henry, magnificent type with white hair and whiskers.

Friday afternoon april 20th
Martin Family
Pig Carvers, Cotton spinners and weavers, using a hand
cotton jennie. Conditions cold but sunny.
Saturday morning. Bringh [bright] and cold.
John Alexander Meadows, Miller of corn and wheat. He

Operates an overshot wheel. Taken thru Dogwood and apple
Blossoms.
Saturday afternoon. Luch Scroggs, father of Fred O. and scroggs.
Frank Henderson (the jennie man) driving two jenny mules,
Named Low and Roup.
Saturday afternoon. N.N. Rogers 78 years old.
Rock collector. Was rebuilding a mill to grind talke [talcum] and
   graphite. Conditions. Overcast and very cold.

Sunday afternoon, Mrs. Hannah Smith, willscott mountain
Singer etc . . . 67 years old.[96]

They visited separate sites each morning and afternoon. Each visit
necessitated challenging travel, introductory conversation, a shared meal,
songs and conversation, and technical preparation before they finally set
to work on the photographs themselves. This was highly challenging and
specialized work, taxing both physical and emotional resources and de-
manding great personal stamina and tenacity.

On April 24, Niles and Ulmann left the Folk School, heading toward
Knoxville through the rugged and spectacular scenery of the Nantahala
Forest. They wound up through Red Marble Gap and Highland Gap, down
through the western edge of the Smoky Mountains, and into Tennessee.
The next day they headed north along Route 25 to Berea and checked into
the rooms at the Boone Tavern that President Hutchins had reserved for
them.[97] Niles and Ulmann were anticipating the work at Berea, but they
also regretted leaving Brasstown, which was beginning to feel very much
like home for both of them.[98]

After several days of preparation, Niles and Ulmann traveled to Nor-
ris, Tennessee, where they joined up with Berea College sociologist Helen
Dingman (1885–1978), who led them to several Tennessee sites, including
Gatlinburg, where they documented activity at the Pi Beta Phi Settlement
School. On April 28 they were in Knoxville, and there Ulmann organized
a small party at the hotel in celebration of Niles's forty-second birthday.

Two days later, they returned to Berea and set to work methodi-
cally documenting all of the school's traditional craft activities as well as
many of the prominent faculty and staff members of the community. Ul-

mann's subjects included portraits and rural-industry documentary for Hutchins, craft-oriented shots for Eaton, and the occasional still life for purely personal reasons. Niles performed for groups of students at Berea and for Frank McVey, president of the University of Kentucky in Lexington, but he collected no music at all in the hill country around the college. Commenting on this, he noted: "I have taken no music to speak of . . . none of any value at least. Berea was a pain in my neck."[99]

Surely there was music to be found here; Professors Raine and John F. Smith both compiled substantial collections based on research conducted in the region, particularly through students enrolled in the college.[100] Niles, however, failed to locate any music sources, perhaps because his style of fieldwork was at odds with the particular methodology necessary here. He was accustomed to searching for granny women and mountain patriarchs inhabiting remote mountain cabins, whereas a very different sort of technique was necessary for unlocking the cultural wealth contained at the Berea campus and in the surrounding hill country.

On Sunday, June 3, Niles and Ulmann made the drive from Berea to Pine Mountain Settlement School, traveling south to Corbin and then east to Pineville, where they followed the Cumberland River to the school. The last portion of the trip was a particularly daunting drive, as Niles exclaimed: "There never was such a road—never this side of hell or heaven." The next day they took photos of the Creech cabin; William Creech's granddaughters, posed in their Aunt Sallie's clothing; the Day family of weavers; Mrs. Nolan, a weaver; Boone Callahan in the wood working shop; and Grannie Bettie Creech.[101]

This is the heart of Kentucky's coalfields, but Niles chose not to record any occupational songs. A letter to Rena summarily dismissed the notion of miners' protest music: "The idea that the Miners have made over the ballads and written in words about oppressive Mine operators is bunk I believe. . . . Of course it may have happened but my lovely child I did not run into it. . . . In fact I did most of the singing."[102] Despite being situated in "bloody Harlan County," pastoral Pine Mountain School was philosophically very much removed from the gritty scene of labor unrest at Harlan. Whether naive, or perhaps willful on account of his conservative political orientation, Niles remained ignorant of singers such as "Aunt" Molly Jackson and Sarah Ogan Gunning.

"Aunt" Molly Jackson (1880–1960) and her half sister Sarah Ogan Gunning (1910–1983), of Clay County, Kentucky, were prominent union activists associated with songs such as "Dreadful Memories," "I Am a Union Woman," and "Poor Miner's Farewell." After the death of her first husband, Jim Stewart, in Florida, Jackson moved back to Harlan County, Kentucky, in 1917 and worked as a midwife. During the Depression, she became heavily involved in the National Miner's Union. Influenced by a delegation of the National Committee for the Defense of Political Prisoners (including authors Theodore Dreiser and John dos Passos) as well as by advice from folklorist Mary Elizabeth Barnicle, "Aunt" Molly traveled to New York City to promote her cause. In December of 1931, Molly and Sarah appeared at the Coliseum in New York City before an audience of twenty-one thousand, where they performed the protest songs that they had either written in the style of folk music or created in parody by matching topical lyrics to traditional tunes.

Although their political purpose was antithetical to Niles's artistic intent, there was a commonality underlying the basic impulse driving this transformation of tradition. "Aunt" Molly and Niles both believed that the extension of tradition through original artifice actually demonstrated a respect for that tradition. Although he did not share her politics, Niles would surely be in harmony with Jackson's definition of folk song, which situates the role of a traditional singer in the modern world: "This is what a folk song really is. The folks compose their own songs about their own lives and their own home folks that live around them."[103]

Upon leaving Pine Mountain, Niles and Ulmann traveled back toward Knoxville and checked into the Kingmeyer Hotel in Morristown, Tennessee. Niles was fortunate to collect one ballad right away in a gasoline station just across the street from the hotel. While having the Chevrolet washed, Niles started chatting with the African American service station attendant, Eddie Stiles, who sang three verses of "Bangum and the Boar" for Niles.[104] Making the Kingmeyer their headquarters (its stationery boasted "free parking and chicken dinners"), Niles and Ulmann began traveling through the uplands of Kentucky and Tennessee with the skilled assistance of Sarah Dougherty, the director of Shuttle-Crafters, a craft guild located in Russellville, Tennessee.

On June 9 they drove through the Cumberland Gap to the Lincoln

Memorial School (now Lincoln Memorial University) at Harrowgate, Tennessee, where they met with Katherine Pettit during the day. That evening Niles gave a concert at the school. On June 11, they all traveled to Grassy Valley, near Trade, North Carolina, then on to Jonesborough and Mountain City, Tennessee, before motoring to Gatlinburg on June 13, where they checked into the Mountain View Hotel. Gatlinburg, the gateway into the Smoky Mountains, was fertile ground for their work. The Pi Beta Phi Settlement School located there was one of the most active weaving centers in the Southeast, and the annual Old Timer's Day provided a concentrated dose of mountain music and culture for Niles. He collected "Patrick Spenser" from Christopher Bell, "a fun-loving old man with a limp left arm, a wonderful sense of humor, and a poetic understanding of song, who was headed to Old Timer's Day," and "In the Lonely Glens of Yarrow" from Miss Sarah Jane Hadley, a "singer and poet."[105]

On June 24, Niles and Ulmann traveled to Lexington, Kentucky, and stayed at the Phoenix Hotel. During their short stay in Lexington, they continued to cultivate their relationship with President and Mrs. McVey, and they enjoyed a cordial evening at the home of Sarah Blanding, dean of women at the University of Kentucky. Niles also performed "an unusually good concert" at the university, according to Ulmann.[106]

Several days later, they left for Murphy, North Carolina, by way of Knoxville and Chattanooga, Tennessee, and Ringgold, Georgia, where Niles collected a version of "Lord Thomas and Fair Ellen" from Bertha Maypother, a "frail white-haired woman of great dignity and great sorrow," while Ulmann photographed "a very good tufted spread maker," Ethel May Stiles. Finally, after a "rather dangerous trip through the mountains from Chattanooga,"[107] Niles and Ulmann arrived at Murphy, North Carolina, where they settled back in their usual rooms at the Regal Hotel. They returned to the Folk School in Brasstown the next day and worked in the surrounding area during a week highlighted by the July 4th Old Timers Day, at which Niles "expected to record some swell tunes."[108] While at the Campbell School, Niles started teaching local residents to build and learn to play the dulcimer. There was no previous history of dulcimers in the area, so Niles, with the best of intentions, sought to inculcate the folk instrument into the local tradition, in much the same way that the dulcimer was being spread to the outside world through the Hindman Settlement

School woodshop under the direction of Jethro Amburgey. In a letter to Rena Lipetz, he wrote: "Years from now, long after I am put in some shady little dell (where the blackbirds whistle and the flowers smell) Dulcimers will be made and played all because I showed them how to . . . to . . . to . . . God knows what."[109]

By Thursday, July 12, the peripatetic Niles and Ulmann were traveling again, this time to Dalton, Georgia, where they photographed various people occupied in crafting knotted spreads. Niles collected "Robin Hood and the Monk" from the singing of Christian Mathers, who "lived in a shambles of a cabin."[110] Two days later they had moved on to Gainesville, Georgia, where a very weary, yet waggish, Niles groused about a skin ailment, the hotel's poor accommodations, and the unsavory dining.[111]

Niles and Ulmann returned to Brasstown on July 16 for their final residence there before leaving for Asheville on July 24. After a gorgeous moonlit drive, they settled in at the Battery Park Hotel and quickly set to work, with the assistance of Clementine Douglas and Frances Goodrich. Like many other female social workers in the mountains, Douglas and Goodrich were well educated and came from affluent backgrounds. Douglas, inspired by Helen Dingman, established the Spinning Wheel, a cooperative center for weaving and the sale of crafts, in 1925. Goodrich, a Presbyterian missionary who had been working in the mountains for forty-four years now, established the Allanstand Cottage Industries (located seven miles outside Asheville) and was involved with the founding of the Southern Highland Handicraft Guild.

While thoroughly documenting the people and the work of these two institutions with Ulmann, Niles also took this opportunity to aggressively pursue his ballad collection. On July 27, he met with Bascom Lamar Lunsford (1882–1973) in the hotel lobby. Lunsford, a folk enthusiast, collector, and entrepreneur, who had founded Asheville's Mountain Dance and Folk Festival in 1927, had much in common with Niles; and he was undoubtedly helpful in directing Niles to various local ballad singers. Niles collected the text for "Little Matthey Groves" from a preacher's wife who wished to remain anonymous; the text of "Young Collins" from a Swannanoa potter, Charlie Walsh; "Earl Colvin" from Carson Shook; and "Lady Ishbel and Her Parrot" from the singing of Hattie Melton at Allanstand. Melton's amusing comments concerning the treachery of the ballad's plot are instructive: "I tell you a woman-person has just got to watch her step when she's dealing with a man. Nowadays menfolk will promise a woman anything. They'll promise her the moon, and when the woman-person gets the moon, she finds out it ain't even made of green cheese."[112]

On July 29, Niles and Ulmann traveled to Saluda, North Carolina, at the request of Eaton, who wanted them to photograph the Anderson family, makers of hooked rugs, for his book *Handicrafts of the Southern Highlands*. There Niles also recorded "The Murdered Brother" ("Edward") from the singing of "Aunt" Selina Metcalf. Two days later, they returned to Asheville, exhausted after "five days in the mud and underbrush" that seriously threatened Ulmann's health. Niles was now handling the physical aspects of the photography work for Ulmann, who had become too weak to do much more than provide instructions.

Despite the obsessive daily routine, Niles also made a little time for involvement in the concert music that was intertwined with his increasingly remote New York way of life. He attended a performance of the North Carolina Symphony at Asheville and wrote an extended poetic essay on Rimsky-Korsakov's *Scheherazade Suite* for inclusion in a letter to Rena Lipetz. In another letter to Lipetz, Niles rose to a left-handed defense of Richard Wagner, responding to Lipetz's criticism of Wagnerian opera: "To tell you the truth I have always thought that Wagner would be better if a lot of beer was taken with it."[113]

The Flight North; the End of Ulmann's Days

Niles and Ulmann remained in Asheville for another week, while Niles continued collecting music from various sources, including Vital Bean, Sam Gentry, Annie Matesby, and Lige Gaffney. Ulmann's condition had steadily deteriorated despite her recently acquired nurse's efforts, and Niles was compelled to contact Ulmann's physician, Dr. Otto Hensel, who was vacationing at Scranton, Pennsylvania. Hensel advised them to travel north immediately, and so on August 9 Niles drove Ulmann to Winston-Salem, North Carolina, while George Uebler and her nurse followed in the Lincoln. The next day they traveled through Virginia into Pennsylvania and spent the night at the Harrisburger Hotel in Harrisburg.

Writing to Campbell that evening from her bed, Ulmann composed a most self-effacing letter in shaky print, expressing annoyance at herself for failing to complete her work and apologizing for causing such a fuss.[114] Two days later they arrived in Scranton, where they checked into the Casey Hotel and met with her physician at 4:00 P.M. Niles wrote Rena Lipetz a rather terse, cold, and self-centered note concerning the sudden turn of events: "If Doris Ulmann does not get better she will have to go to the local hospital. . . . If she gets better she goes home to New York. . . . If she dies . . . then that is all there is to it."[115]

After several days in Scranton, where the doctor tried to stabilize her condition, they left for New York City and arrived there on August 16. Ulmann lingered in bed at her 1000 Park Avenue apartment for nearly two more painful weeks before passing away early in the morning of August 28, 1934. On the certificate of death, number 19458, issued that day, Dr. Joseph Goldstone reported the cause of death as "a kidney abscess and blood poisoning." Pursuant to her wishes and in harmony with Jewish custom, she was buried the following day in crypt 2 of the Ulmann family mausoleum.[116]

9

Transitions and New Beginnings

During Ulmann's final weeks, several wills were written and discarded, leading to a final will and testament that was dictated to her lawyer, Charles Furnald Smith, on August 21, 1934. This document generously endowed the John C. Campbell Folk School, provided a substantial gift to Berea College for a photography exhibition hall, bestowed an annual stipend on Niles, left the prints and photographic plates in care of Niles, and dispersed smaller gifts to family members and servants. Since this document radically altered the provisions of Ulmann's previous will, of 1927, in which she left most of her estate to her family, the new document was challenged by the Necarsulmers (Ulmann's sister Edna, her brother-in-law, Henry, and her niece, Edith), upon their return from Europe following the funeral.

Uebler allied himself with the Necarsulmers and tried to incite the assistance of Julia Peterkin, Irving Fineman, and Lyle Saxon in contesting the will. However, none of Ulmann's longtime friends cared to get involved.[1] While it seems as though Uebler and Ulmann's friends were most concerned with the endowment provided for Niles in the will, it was the sizable bequest to the John C. Campbell Folk School that apparently distressed the Necarsulmer family the most. Not having been in close contact with Ulmann for the past several years, the family failed to understand the deep affection she had developed for Olive Campbell and the work of the Folk School. They were also unaware of the central role that Niles had played in Ulmann's life and work for the past three years, so naturally they were suspicious of the circumstances accompanying her final bequests. Furthermore, Henry had previously served as her attorney, so he had a professional as well as a personal stake in the contesting of the will.

By November 1934, Niles had been cast adrift from his secure income and accustomed way of life. In addition to his financial uncertainty, he was professionally lost in a transition between his earlier successful performance and compositional career and his more recent folk collecting activity. He was distracted by endless rounds of consultations with lawyers and beset by accusations and innuendo concerning his relationship with Ulmann.

Some of the innuendo carried with it an unpleasant whiff of anti-Semitism. A letter written to Rena Lipetz by Niles, postmarked November 29, 1934, does contain a strongly disparaging statement about Jews, but it must be understood within the specific context of his conflict with Henry and Edna Necarsulmer.[2] Niles's reference to "Jews" here is sparked by anger and is directed solely to the Necarsulmers. This appears to be an isolated instance of such vitriol. In fact, the two women who were at the center of his life and career, Rena Lipetz and Doris Ulmann, were both of Jewish heritage, so his personal relationships were certainly not marked by anti-Semitism.

Finally, after six months of contestation and compromise involving the Necarsulmer family, Berea College, the John C. Campbell Folk School, Niles, and the lawyers representing their respective interests, a final settlement was arrived at on February 7, 1935, in which the essential provisions of the final will were preserved. Under the terms of this settlement, Berea College received $15,000; Niles received $3,500 annually from an $80,000 trust fund; and $10,000 was set aside to print and preserve the photographs; the remainder of the estate provided approximately $200,000 to the Folk School. Subsequently, the Doris Ulmann Foundation was established to ensure the preservation of her photographs and provide for future publications and exhibits. Members of this board included Niles, Allen Eaton, Olive Dame Campbell, Marguerite Butler, and Henry Necarsulmer.[3]

With the Ulmann affair settled at last, Niles was free to move on with the rest of his life—to reassemble the fractured facets of his career.

Through Ulmann's generosity, he was now blessed with financial security; an annual stipend of thirty-five hundred dollars in 1935 represented a substantial income.[4] Despite the economic stability, however, Niles was finding it difficult to refocus his professional direction. He attempted to return to composing "The King of Little Italy," but the gritty, urban setting and his Impressionist writing style were very much at odds with the balladry and rural mountain culture in which he had been steeped for the past several years. Progress on the opera sputtered fitfully and eventually ceased entirely by the fall of 1935, when he fled New York City for the mountains of North Carolina.[5]

Niles also sought to resuscitate his performance career buoyed with the new Appalachian repertoire and his novel dulcimer accompaniment, but here as well, his progress was unsteady. His voice was affected by breathing problems, and it appeared likely that he would require some surgery to ameliorate the condition. Furthermore, without an agent or the assistance of a savvy partner like Kerby, he was unable to negotiate the contacts necessary to schedule concert appearances. Life for Niles at 95 Bedford Street in New York City was adrift in transition, but by late winter things seemed to realign for him once again.

On February 18, 1935, Mrs. J. M. Helm, secretary to Eleanor Roosevelt, wrote Niles and invited him to perform at the White House on March 22.[6] Carl Engel took this opportunity to engage Niles to perform for the Friends of Music at the Library of Congress while he was scheduled to be in Washington. Niles was also asked to present a lecture at the National Training School for Boys and a concert at the nearby Hampton Institute. With his tonsils successfully removed, his breathing problems cleared up, and he was ready to hit the road again.

Staying at the Wardman Park Hotel in Washington, D.C., on Wednesday, March 20, Niles performed a program accompanied by both piano and dulcimer for the Friends of Music. The noted pianist Harold Bauer (1873–1951) introduced the concert, and according to Niles, he "made the most lovely little talk about me and my untireing [sic] effort to establish American folk music as part of the art material of the world's music."[7] This purpose was clearly manifest in Niles's repertoire and performance practice, in which traditional song was removed from "the porch" and repositioned in stylized arrangement within a formal "art music" context.

Further, Niles introduced each song with a little "folk musicology" describing the circumstances under which the music was collected or composed. These "oral footnotes" provided both the historical and cultural background necessary to compensate for the transformation of the original folkloric context.

The location of this concert was certainly no accident. Niles's desire to make American vernacular music into a national art music was in harmony with the efforts of Carl Engel, Robert Winslow Gordon, and John Lomax to enshrine a national collection of folk music at the Library of Congress.[8] In synthesizing the roles of scholar-collector and performer, Niles was perfectly situated to "translate" the original, rough yet authentic, traditional music that Gordon had been collecting into an accessible and popular performance that the upscale Friends of Music could appreciate.

The performance featured the three songs that were most closely identified with Niles throughout his future career: "Go 'Way from My Window," "Black Is the Color," and "I Wonder as I Wander." The other songs, a mixture of ballads and lyric folk songs, largely from Kentucky and North Carolina, completely eschewed the African American material and World War I songs that were so prominently showcased in the earlier Niles-Kerby repertoire. While most of the music on this program became part of Niles's standard repertoire for the next forty-four years of his concert career, "Consuela Lullaby" and "Make Me a Bed in a Shady Little Dell" were gradually phased out in performance and were neither published nor recorded.

Niles was continuing to make the gradual transition from the piano to the dulcimer, using the large Nathan Hicks instrument to accompany himself on "There Was an Old Lord," "I Wonder as I Wander," "See Jesus the Savior," and "You Got to Cross That Lonesome Valley." With increased emphasis on a mountain folk repertoire and the freedom afforded by dulcimer accompaniment, Niles came to rely less and less on the piano.

On Friday Niles went to the White House, where he performed at dinner and then spent the night. The next day he drove to Hampton, Virginia, and presented a concert at the historically black Hampton Institute. His letter to Rena reveled in the audience's reception and glowed with appreciation for the history-suffused countryside.[9]

Rena Lipetz: Soul Mate for Life

Up to this point, Rena Lipetz has entered the narrative as a nearly invisible guest. It is now time for her to introduce herself as the single most influential character in Niles's life. John Jacob met the vivacious, brilliant Rena Lipetz in Greenwich Village on the final day of 1932. Rena clearly recalled her first glimpse of the man who became her husband four years later: "The first time I met Johnnie Niles, he was striding down West Eleventh Street in Greenwich Village (he had recently moved to 259 West 11th) impeccably turned out in white tie and tails with a top hat sitting jauntily on his head, tilted to one side with his right ear bent down to accommodate the rakish angle of the brim."[10]

Niles and Lipetz shared tea and crumpets in Niles's apartment following the 1932 New Years Eve concert, and seven months later she phoned him and asked for a letter of introduction to Charles Scribner's Sons. The irreverent and demeaning letter provided by Niles certainly did not pave the way for a job offer from Scribner's; nor would it seem destined to cultivate any further relationship between the young Wellesley graduate and the middle-aged composer and performer. As Niles gave her the "recommendation," he said: "And if this doesn't get you the job, honey, I suggest you wag your little ass right back to Podunk or wherever you came from, and tell your parents that they're damn well going to have to support you until you find some man to do the job for them."[11]

Rena Lipetz was a persistent young woman, however, in addition to being remarkably intelligent, sophisticated, and lovely. Despite Niles's flippant response, she succeeded in landing a coveted position as assistant editor of the foreign affairs periodical the *Living Age*.[12] One month later, she also had Niles composing very different sorts of letters. Writing to her from Richmond, Virginia, on October 23, 1933, he closed with "I send you kissings, and all such strange things. . . . Write me if you will to the Boone Tavern . . . BEREA Kentucky . . . More later Johnnie . . . love." Niles continued to write Rena nearly every week while he was on the road with Doris Ulmann, and with each letter, the language grew more passionate—it is clear that they were in the first blush of a burgeoning romance. By April 20, 1934, the tenor of the letters makes it evident that they were engaged in an intimate relationship.[13]

The Lipetz Family

Rena, the only child of Alphonse and Basile Lipetz, was born November 7, 1913, in St. Petersburg, Russia. Her father was a brilliant engineer who was a full professor at the Polytechnicum at age twenty-one, having already designed a locomotive.[14] Her mother and her aunt, Florentine Karp, were both physicians, having studied at the University of Geneva, Switzerland, because there were no opportunities for such study available to women, much less women of Jewish extraction, in Russia. During World War I, Alphonse was made director of the Division of Locomotives in the Ministry of Ways and Communications, the agency that ran the Russian railroad system. The czar sent him to the United States in 1915 to purchase rail equipment for the war effort, but the rest of the family remained behind until just before the Bolshevik Revolution of November 6, 1917.

At that point, Rena and her mother embarked on the lengthy, adventurous Trans-Siberian rail ride across the great wintry steppes of Russia. The private train, belonging to Iurii Vladinirovich Lomonsov (1876–1952), the minister of railroads, was guarded by Cossacks who were solicitous of their guests despite the rapidly changing political climate, since Lomonsov was closely connected to the Bolsheviks.[15] Finally, they arrived at Vladivostok, where they boarded a boat to Yokohama and then took another ship to Seattle, arriving in the United States on January 25, 1917.

The family reunited and settled in New York City. Alphonse was now serving there as a consultant for the American Locomotive Company, based in Schenectady, New York. Rena attended a Montessori School until the family relocated to Paris in 1920 when her father was appointed head of the American Locomotive Company's European Division. In Paris, Rena attended a girls' school, Lycée du Ferry, while her mother furthered her medical training at the University of Paris.[16] Five years later, the family returned to the United States, moving into a modest yet lovely home at 38 Willett Street in Albany, New York. Rena graduated from public high school at age fifteen and was accepted at Wellesley, but her acceptance was deferred since she was considered to be too young. So Rena returned to Paris to live with her Aunt Florentine for a year while she studied at the

Sorbonne. She then finished her college career at Wellesley, receiving a
B.A. with a major in English and a minor in French in May 1933.

Although Niles was seldom at home in New York City while Rena
was working at the *Living Age,* they continued to correspond regularly
and got away together for short trysts that whetted their appetite to be
together on a more permanent basis.

Niles: New York or North Carolina

After his March 1935 performances at the White House and the Hampton Institute, Niles drove the Chevrolet along the now-familiar roads to
Brasstown, where on March 28 he settled in at his accustomed apartment
in the Old Mill on the campus of the Folk School. With the exception of
a trip to Knoxville to perform at the Conference of Southern Mountain
Workers on April 2, he remained at the Folk School, building a new dulcimer, continuing his ballad collecting, and participating in the daily communal life of the Folk School.

By April 20 he was on the road again. He performed at Norris, site
of the large Tennessee Valley Authority dam, gave an Easter afternoon
concert at Lincoln Memorial University, and then traveled north to Lexington to perform at the University of Kentucky. Niles's stock had risen
greatly since the time he was a poor clerk in Lexington. Rather than playing piano for his supper at a seedy dive on Limestone Street, he was an
honored performer at soirees held at the home of the president of the
university. Instead of staying in a dingy boarding house, he was now embraced as a cherished guest at the Blanding family's gracious Federal-style
home on Richmond Road. Niles described his reception at the university
in a letter to Rena: "I look at the people whom I knew in 1912, and they do
not remember me at all. . . . I was so unimportant to them then. . . . Now
they fall all over themselves to get at me."[17]

Leaving Lexington, Niles arrived at Berea College and checked into
the Boone Tavern as usual. While there he performed at the college and
attended to business relating to Doris Ulmann's will and the proposed
construction of a building to house her photographs. Niles also celebrated
his forty-third birthday, about which he wrote Rena: "I am much farther
on my way than I was last year, I am much happier than I ever expected

to be, I have much to thank you for, you have been so lovely, so kind, so long suffering with me this past year."[18] After a week at Berea, he pointed the automobile east for a long-awaited assignation with Rena on May 4 at the Broad Street Pennsylvania Railroad Station in Philadelphia.

Niles returned to New York for the summer, courting Rena and attempting to complete his opera, but life in the city made him increasingly restless, and he succeeded only in arranging and publishing *Ten Christmas Carols from the Southern Appalachian Mountains* with G. Schirmer. His heart was still back in the mountains of North Carolina, so in November he packed his car with all his belongings, bade a final farewell to New York City, and journeyed south once again to Brasstown, North Carolina. Olive Campbell welcomed him, gave him a position as director of the music program, placed him in charge of the garden, and provided him with a new little home.[19]

Despite the delights of his cozy new house, Niles had a difficult time making the transition from a lively urban environment to the solitude of rural isolation. After the continual clamor of New York City streets, the solitude of the lonely hills was deafening. Writing to Rena, he expressed his resolve to live and work in the mountains: "The nights are still rather terrifying. . . . I feel so small and weak and the forests are so great and so shocking, so dark and so full of strange sounds. . . . I seem to have developed a new sense, a valuable sense by the way. . . . One that permits me to hear new sounds. . . . They are almost symphonic sounds. . . . I shall write real music yet . . . and down here . . . not in the cities."[20]

Niles eventually grew more comfortable with his surroundings and settled into the tempo of daily Folk School life. He filled the short December days playing virginal, reading, reveling in the beauty of nature, and participating in the daily rehearsals for the Nativity play written by Campbell and based on his carols. Christmas was an exciting and convivial time at Brasstown. Besides the Nativity-play practices, there was the customary 3:30 teatime (almost a "sacred" ritual at the school), and there were also tree trimmings, sleigh rides, music evenings, and celebrations during all the twelve days of Christmas.[21]

By Christmas, a happy and satisfied Jack Niles seemed to be very much at home in Brasstown. It is evident that he meant to settle there permanently, because the day after Christmas he went to inspect one hundred acres of property belonging to Leon Deschamps, a Belgian engineer married to May Ritchie, Jean Ritchie Pickow's older sibling. By the end of January, Niles had bought Deschamps's 108 acres for $432 and was making long-term plans for his farm.

Niles entered into his duties with idealism and enthusiasm, preparing lectures on music history for his students. Doubtless, he approached the classroom as merely a different kind of stage. Unfortunately, his zeal was quickly dampened by the dissonance between his idealistic expectations and the pragmatic response of his students. Teaching was clearly a very different sort of performance art and the classroom a more daunting stage. Just three weeks later he wrote: "My lectures here are a dismal failure. . . . I have had to scrap all my swell ideas and my plans and my records and everything. . . . I have given it up entirely . . . and gone back to the beginning."[22] Despite the problems associated with developing an engaging teaching style, life at the John C. Campbell Folk School was a tonic after his difficult New York City summer.

Niles was free from financial anxiety because of the sinecure provided for him in Ulmann's will. His expenses were few, since his board and bed as well as his telephone, heat, and electricity were all included with his salary. Niles also enjoyed the trust and friendship of Olive Campbell. As he put it, "I shall not desert the school. . . . Mrs. Campbell and I are better friends than ever. . . . She is the most adorable old girl on earth."[23] The only thing missing from his life at this point was . . . Rena Lipetz. And so, despite the miles and the years separating them, Niles began formulating plans to enfold Rena into his utopian life in the North Carolina Mountains. There were many obstacles in the way, however, one of the most formidable being the hostility of Rena's parents. Quite understandably, Alphonse and Basile Lipetz were distraught at the notion that their only child, a twenty-two-year-old, might marry a divorced man exactly twice her age. Further, Niles was a musician— and not even a "real" musician—who threatened to take their daughter to the remote mountains far, far from the civilized world of New York.[24]

Niles and Lipetz made and discarded various long-distance plans for a wedding—everything from eloping in Knoxville to marrying in Bennington, Vermont, where the laws were more relaxed. Finally a narrow window of time and place presented itself as Niles traveled north on an extended publicity jaunt on behalf of the Campbell Folk School.

On February 26, Niles's play *Carrion Crow,* based on the ballad of the same name, was presented at the Folk School.[25] The next morning he left Brasstown; he arrived at Williamstown, Massachusetts, where he was scheduled to perform several concerts at Williams College, and then embarked on an exhausting tour of New England and New York, presenting several concerts each day. From Medford, Massachusetts, on March 13 Niles sent Rena a ring to try on for size. Several days later, on March 17, he wrote her a rather disjointed letter that reflected his agitated state of mind. All the travel, performance, wedding plans, and an increasing reliance on barbiturates to aid his sleep contributed to a strained mental condition.[26]

Just four days after sending that letter, Niles drove through an intense rainstorm from Boston to Albany, New York, in order to wed Rena at a civil ceremony solemnized by the justice of the peace. They shared a simple lunch with a few friends at the Lipetz home, and then the newlyweds traveled south to their new domicile at Brasstown.

The honeymoon was far from perfect. Although Niles was enthusiastic about the musical environment and loved being given responsibility for the garden, he started to chafe at the hierarchical organization and the communal participation of the campus. There was a monastic feel to the place: everyone there shared a common mission, they were largely cloistered away from the rest of the world, there was an orderly daily schedule with specific tasks delegated to each participant, and all the inhabitants took their meals together three times per day at the "refectory."

In the first blush of his enthusiasm, Niles had embraced this way of life, but upon returning to the Campbell School in his married state, it affected him differently; he and Rena found themselves increasingly at odds with Brasstown style. The Nileses greatly enjoyed the company of Leon and May Deschamps, and Niles maintained affection and respect for Olive Campbell, but his relationship with several women on the staff grew contentious. By early summer, he had a difficult time accepting the authority of the assistant director, Marguerite Butler Bidstrup.[27]

An anecdote told by noted musician and instrument craftsman Homer Ledford (1927–2006), then a student at the school, suggests something of the difference in leadership styles of the idealistic Campbell and the pragmatic Bidstrup. Homer was playing on the piano in the large hall when Bidstrup began chastising him, accusing him of damaging the piano or knocking it out of tune. Mrs. Campbell, who entered just in time to hear the exchange, told Homer, so that Bidstrup could overhear it, "Homer, you can play the piano anytime you want to." Homer noted that he was "fond of Marguerite, but loved Mrs. Campbell," who was more given to encouragement than admonition.[28]

Niles was willing to submit to Olive Campbell's direction, but he and Bidstrup developed a mutually antagonistic relationship. Things boiled to a head when she began to dictate how the garden should be administered. Niles regarded the garden as his special charge, and he was justifiably proud of raising the "sugar corn, squashes, tomatoes, peppers, potatoes, cucumbers, lettuce, greens, turnips, green and pole beans, and cabbage" that fed the entire school. Upon being told how to harvest the produce, Niles exploded in rage.[29] Incidents such as this made him increasingly hostile to members of the community and ultimately rendered him bitter about his experience at the school.

For her part, Rena tried to adapt to the very foreign world of Brasstown, but her temperament and upbringing had hardly prepared her, a sophisticated and recently married young woman, for the rural folk school. She loved the scenery and the excitement of novel experiences, but she shared her husband's independent streak, and in private she railed against the rules concerning deportment.[30]

While both Rena and John Jacob strained against the authority imposed by the school's hierarchy, Rena was also probably uncomfortable with another aspect of the school, which she never specifically articulated in her letters and diaries. She was certainly aware of the romantic attachment that Niles had had for Doris Ulmann, and although Doris had passed away, her ghost was a very palpable presence at the John C. Campbell Folk School, where she had spent so much time and invested so much of herself. Rena undoubtedly felt that it was necessary to escape from Ulmann's shadow and make a fresh start with Niles in another place, not associated with Ulmann and the memories associated with her.

Symbolically, it is at this time and through the agency of Rena that Niles's name gradually made the transition from "Jack" to "Johnnie." Jack, a rakish nickname, had been bestowed on Niles by his wartime buddies, and he continued to go by this name throughout his New York days and his time traveling through the mountains with Doris Ulmann. When Rena entered his life, she started calling him Johnnie, claiming him as her own with a more endearing and softer nickname than Jack. In more professional situations, she began referring to him as John Jacob. So while he was still Jack to his pre-1934 friends, his newer associates came to know him as the more domesticated "Johnnie" or the professional "John Jacob."

Study Abroad

As early as a letter of January 27, 1936, Niles had proposed traveling to Europe with Rena to study Scandinavian folk schools for a year. In fact, it was Olive Campbell who suggested the notion to Niles, based on her own formative trip. With things starting to unravel for him at Brasstown, Niles began formulating plans to leave the Campbell School and go to Norway, Sweden, Finland, and Denmark for a year of honeymoon and study. The trip abroad offered him a tactful escape from the school, but it also bore the promise of enhancing his knowledge of balladry and demonstrating a pragmatic model for the integration of folk culture into education and society.

With the intention of leaving Brasstown for good, Rena returned to her parents' home, leaving Niles to finish the next several months at the Folk School without her. She set off early in the morning of July 12 and caught the train from Asheville at 5:00 P.M.; her father met her the next day in Albany. That very evening Rena returned to her element, attending an Albany Symphony Orchestra concert featuring Dukas's *Sorcerer's Apprentice*. Free to wear makeup and dress as she felt appropriate again, she filled her days shopping; socializing with family and friends at lunches, cocktail parties, and dinners; attending a variety of lectures and concerts; and making short excursions to Lake George and Saratoga for the horse races.[31]

Finally, by the end of September, Niles was ready to rejoin Rena and to travel to Europe. Storing his furniture and belongings at the school and packing his luggage into the black Chevrolet, Niles headed north, stopping overnight at the White House, where he entertained the Roosevelts and their family guests after supper. The next day he arrived in Pittsburgh and performed at the Tuesday Musical Club at the Upper Hall of the Soldiers and Sailors Memorial Hall on November 3. Then he drove the rest of the way to Albany, where he and Rena remained while making the final preparations for their European trip. Niles performed at Skinner Hall of Vassar College on November 11, and shortly after that they sailed aboard the *Scanstates*, landing at Helsinki in mid-November.

John Jacob and Rena remained in Finland for four chilly, dark winter months. Niles spent much of his time at the university at Helsinki and visiting folk schools. Rena recalled a musical excursion to the industrial city of Tampere, where they visited a union hall, "a wonderful-looking place all marble and glass," and heard a chorus of female workers who sang both Swedish and Finnish folk songs. Niles had hoped to talk to Jean Sibelius, but the composer was in ill health and declined to meet with him. Perhaps the high point of the visit was a Christmas dinner at which Niles shared his carols on dulcimer and then all were treated to portions of the *Kalevala*, sung by a group of sixteen "rune singers."[32] As the spring thaw returned to Finland, the Nileses returned to the United States earlier than they had planned, landing March 6 in New York City harbor.

Back in the United States: Home to Kentucky

After a hectic few days in the city the Nileses left on March 11, 1937, and spent the night at Vassar College, where they heard a piano recital and were elegantly housed in the Founder's Suite. The next day they had breakfast with a Mrs. McCracken and made arrangements for Niles to perform March 22 for the Lincoln Community Center benefit dinner. Then they drove to Albany, where they remained for the next few weeks with the Lipetz family. On March 21 the family celebrated Rena and John Jacob's first anniversary with a great deal more joy and revelry than had accompanied the wedding itself. Her parents, particularly her mother, had come to a better understanding of their son-in-law, and the frosty relationship that had existed between them seemed to thaw.[33]

The next day the Nileses returned to Vassar College; they enjoyed tea with the faculty at 3:30 in the Main Hall, and in the evening Niles performed at a dinner in the Alumni House. The next day they traveled to New York City and shared dinner with Leah Salisbury, who later became Niles's concert agent. The following day, he presented a concert for the Music Club at Teachers College of Columbia University, and then he and Rena returned to Albany to pack for their next journey—the one that would ultimately take them to their permanent home. After a year of nomadic life wandering between Albany, New York; Brasstown; and Finland, the newlyweds finally decided to alight in Lexington, Kentucky.

10

Life in Lexington

The Nileses' trip to Kentucky took them first to Lancaster, Pennsylvania, and then to Pittsburgh, where they spent Easter with their close friends the Eliots. On Monday, March 29, 1937, they arrived at Wilmington, Ohio, and then spent Tuesday with their friends Ernest and Leona Haswell in Cincinnati. When they arrived at Lexington on Wednesday, they checked into the Phoenix Hotel and had dinner with President McVey and his wife. The next day they located an apartment to rent, the second floor of a house at 231 McDowell in the Chevy Chase neighborhood. With a place to call their own now, the Nileses set off for Brasstown the next day to retrieve their belongings that were stored at the school. Arriving on Saturday, they shared dinner with the Deschampses and caught up on the grumbling and gossip about the Campbell Folk School.

After John Jacob and Rena had spent several days packing, the moving truck arrived on April 7 and was loaded up. By that evening, the pair arrived in Knoxville, where Rena noted that Johnnie was "very gay, very glad to be out of it."[1] On April 9 their belongings were unloaded from the moving van, and the Nileses were now happily ensconced in Lexington. The small and lively city of approximately forty-seven thousand appears to have been a fortuitous choice for the couple.[2] Fresh, yet familiar, Lexington offered a new beginning; they were liberated from the memories of New York City and Brasstown that haunted Niles's past and free of the family entanglements of Albany and Louisville. The couple already had many friends through their relationship with the university, and they enjoyed a lively social life that included an almost-daily round of luncheons, cocktail parties, dinners, and entertainments. Lexington was spirited and sophisticated enough to appeal to Rena's cultured background and yet agricultural enough to appeal to Niles's earthier sensibilities. Located centrally in the bluegrass, it offered easy access to Berea and the mountains of East Kentucky and was within an easy drive of Niles's family in Louisville. The good roads and three railroad lines that were available made it relatively simple for Niles to schedule concert tours throughout the country. The Nileses complemented each other in domestic skills. Rena had not acquired any culinary prowess, but John Jacob loved to cook. Rena loved to shop and decorate, while her husband was content with the most spartan furnishings.

Rural Radio in the Mountains

Right after they moved to Lexington, a novel opportunity presented itself. Through an introduction from President McVey, Niles got to know Elmer Sulzer (1903–1976), the director of the university's radio station. In 1933, Sulzer had begun distributing radios to homes and stores throughout the East Kentucky region. The radios, a gift from the *Courier-Journal* and the *Louisville Times,* represented an attempt to link the mountainous region to the rest of the commonwealth. As Sulzer traveled the region, he developed the idea of establishing an educational radio station that would offer programming appropriate to the people living in the mountain counties.[3]

Since April 1, 1929, WHAS, a large, fifty-thousand-watt clear-channel radio station owned by the Barry Bingham family (who also owned the Louisville *Courier-Journal* newspaper), had cooperated with the University of Kentucky in an attempt to create programming that was both entertaining and educational. Sulzer saw the opportunity for combining the commercial broadcasting power of WHAS, the educational mission of the University of Kentucky's radio studio, and the audience and culture of Kentucky's Appalachian region. In John Jacob Niles, Sulzer found the perfect link. Niles was familiar with radio through his work in Chicago and New York City, he was a highly respected performer who could talk eloquently about the music, and he possessed the Kentucky accent and traditional folk repertoire that would resonate with local mountain communities.

Sulzer also recognized the necessity for remote broadcasting from local listening stations in local mountain communities, so that people could feel as though they had a personal investment in the radio broadcasts. So on May 2, Niles left for Hazard, Kentucky, to do his first radio show the next day. The show was successful, so a concert and radio broadcast tour was quickly assembled, with Sulzer joining Niles and Ted Rannells, head of the university art department, on the road. On May 10, they reached Jackson, Kentucky, and from there they traveled to Hazard; the Consolidated Coal Company camp town of Jenkins; the small Letcher County town of Fleming; Pikeville, the busy county seat of Pike County; Partridge; Middlesboro, near the Cumberland Gap; and finally Lincoln Memorial University, on the other side of the gap, just inside Tennessee. They returned to Lexington May 14, after five days of traveling twisty roads and playing eight concerts at a variety of auditoriums, churches, and gyms.

After his return there was little opportunity for Niles to do much more than unpack and read his mail, because he was suddenly booked to present a series of concerts in Pittsburgh three days later. Leaving May 17, the Nileses spent the evening with their friends the Haswells in Cincinnati and left the next morning for Pittsburgh, where Niles performed at Carnegie Tech, the Pennsylvania College for Women, Duquesne University, the Crippled Children's Home, and a private dinner for the Eliots. On Sunday evening, May 23, free of performance or social obligations, John Jacob and Rena set out to collect music from a local musician and colorful character known as "Old Mrs. English," a "drunken old slut, with a scalded face and a big eye" who played fiddle, sang river songs, and lived on a houseboat. Unfortunately, after they finally tracked her down, they learned she had died a month earlier.[4]

At a time when Niles was removed from the fertile folkloric soil of Brasstown and no longer actively collecting music under the patronage of Ulmann, this little field trip—though unsuccessful—conjured up the excitement of "the good old days" for him. Niles had abandoned the active phase of collecting folk material and was now entering a period of consolidation. Drawing upon the vast reservoir of music he had acquired during the initial forty-odd years of his life, he continued to return to the well for performance material and published arrangements, but by the autumn of 1936 he was scarcely involved in collecting new sources of traditional music.

Returning home on May 29, the Nileses immediately reentered the social whirl of Lexington. That day they also severed their final physical bond with Brasstown by selling their property to Thomas Larkin. Leon and May Deschamps visited for lunch on June 5, and it was then that Niles signed the deed over to Larkin. Then, on Wednesday, June 9, the Nileses, in the company of Elmer Sulzer and Merrill Denison, departed on an action-packed two-day tour of the mountains to do a listening-post radio broadcast from Fouracre in Magoffin County and another broadcast hosted by a Reverend Deaton at the listening station in Wooten, Leslie County.[5] The next day they intended to travel to Lott's Creek and Carcassonne, up and over the mountain from the small Letcher County hamlet of Blackey, but it was raining so hard that they were compelled to spend the day in the county seat of Whitesburg instead.

At lunch in Whitesburg, Niles and Corsia Whitaker, a local assistant, plied Denison with stories about the mountains, which prompted Rena Niles to enter into her diary a frank assessment of her husband's character:

> The most interesting listening posts being inaccessible because of the rain, we decide to make the best of the bargain by showing Denison the mountains, while Johnnie and Whitaker pump him full of fact, legend, and lore. Denison may never get the facts he wants, but he will go away with an impression of the fun and joy and ribaldry that he never expected. But let's hope he doesn't fall into the error of assuming that JJNs grow on every Kentucky greenbrier. True enough, JJN is a typical Kentuckian in many ways; in fact he is so typical he ceases to be representative. He has all the Kentucky characteristics, real and alleged, carried out— deliberately—to such a fine point that it's the old story of something being too good to be true.[6]

Rena clearly articulated the essential nature of Niles's constructed persona. He was at once simple and sophisticated. His simulated Kentucky backwoods charm and charisma were essential to his performance style. Although Niles was highly cultured, musically sophisticated, and socially adept, he could affect aspects of a rustic mountain performer. His artfully arranged and partially composed adaptations of traditional music maintained an air of authenticity because his calculated posture retained a suggestion of the original earthy performance. The fully researched and scholarly stage patter was tempered by engaging anecdotes, so that his stage presentation conjured the image of a folksy storyteller. He reinvented himself as a twentieth-century troubadour, a modern minstrel who was at once entertaining and enlightening.

This affected showmanship style eventually left Niles vulnerable to criticism of his inauthentic performance style. There is no question but that his dramatic ballad interpretation owed as much to the operatic stage as to the mountain porch. However, it is important to temper this criticism with an understanding of Niles as a performer and an actor steeped in the traditions of Chautauqua and vaudeville.

It is essential for any performer or actor to successfully put on the mask that allows him or her to create the role. This is not dishonest dissembling but rather a way of exposing truth through fiction. On the stage, Niles was a most convincing actor—he disguised himself in "all the Kentucky characteristics, real and alleged" in his performance. If there was a weakness in this role, it was only that there was too fine a line separating Niles-the-person from Niles-the-performer over time. Like any actor who becomes too closely associated with a starring role, Niles became unable to untangle his stage persona from his real personality and fell victim to his own myth.

The listening-post entourage left Whitesburg for Partridge, "where the light effects on the mountains are too beautiful for words," and then traveled on to Pine Mountain Settlement School, to Harlan, and finally to Pineville for the night.[7] The next day they stopped at Berea on the way home to Lexington. By the end of three days they had covered quite a bit of terrain, driving over the challenging roads in East Kentucky in the course of presenting several radio shows.

The radio series, dubbed *Salute to the Hills*, appeared to be a success, and for the next three years Niles journeyed into the region to produce the radio broadcasts at twenty-five different stations located in small communities scattered throughout the East Kentucky region. In each case, Niles wrote the script, with the assistance of Corsia Whitaker and with some local information contributed by local radio post directors. In the second year, 1938, he compiled another series of thirteen shows. An excerpt of the script of a June 15, 1938, broadcast from the community of Lott's Creek in Knott County provides a glimpse into the localization of the script and the mix of education and entertainment featured by Niles. After the theme music plays for about fifteen seconds, Niles sings:

> I'm so glad trouble don't last alway
> I'm so glad trouble don't last alway
> Make more room down in your heart for me
> Oh, my Lord, Oh my Lord, what shall I do.

The announcer, Phil Sutterfield, then cuts in:

> The University of Kentucky presents John Jacob Niles Salute to the Hills. . . . In the ensuing half hour you will hear the third of a series of five broadcasts written and edited by Mr. Niles especially for our Listening Centers in the Eastern Kentucky Mountains. . . . Today's broadcast will be directed to Cordia in Knott County . . . in what we call the Lott's Creek neighborhood where Miss Alice Sloan [Slone] is our Listening Center Director. In this programme Mr. Niles will conduct the usual ballad rehearsal, will tell more of his family's legend and will sing a group of native spirituals and classic ballads. . . . It gives me great pleasure to present Mr. Niles.

Niles speaks:

> I do hear tell that last Wednesday was an important day in the life of Soft Shell, Kentucky . . . for on that day . . . a copy of the Sunday edition of the Courier-Journal and Louisville Times arrived. On that day they had a radio programmer directed to them person-ally to say nothing of the arrival of the Radio Woman. . . . That's what we call miss [Corsia] Whitaker. . . . I understand the folks at Soft Shell had a picture of Mrs. Niles and myself up on the wall

during the broadcast . . . a picture taken at Gander during the Carcassonne Community Center Conference. . . . You see, folks, we are living in the twentieth century and things have a habit of happening very rapidly when they happen at all . . . even at Soft Shell. . . .

To be sure that a lot of you good people got the benefit of today's rehearsal, I have sent song sheets to Bolyn, Kentucky . . . to Cordia, Kentucky . . . to Crab Orchard, Kentucky, where we have a little lowland listening group in the Gilbert Henry Community Center, where Miss Ruth Rietveld is conducting the rehearsal . . . and also to my mother down in Louisville. . . . So you all can see that the idea of a wider ballad rehearsal is taking hold . . . and it should be thrilling to you Lott's Creek folk to think that these other folk will be singing along with you at exactly the same time.

When I was in Pittsburgh recently I damaged one of my dulcimers . . . but I have it all repaired now and ready for use again. . . . Listen to the bass string . . . hear that. . . . When the string speaks to you, you know you are being spoken to . . . just like old Uncle Ben the Great Gander . . . the one I told you about last week. . . . And remember Uncle Ben's philosophy. . . . United we fly. . . . Divided we free. . . . Well, folks, here's the dulcimer and here is the ballad. . . . I call it Bonny Farday. . . . Some folks call it Babylon.

At this point Niles performed the ballad "Bonny Farday" live, accompanying himself on dulcimer. The song concluded and he returned to the script.

I recorded this song at Whitesburg, Kentucky . . . on the 9th of July, 1932 . . . from the singing of Aunt Beth Holcum . . . and I might say right here that I consider Aunt Beth to have been the greatest folk singer I have ever seen or heard tell of. . . . She's dead now . . . and whenever I mention her name I say God rest her. . . .

Next week we shall broadcast for the good folks at Handshoe in Knott County . . . and until then I remain your wandering minstrel most sincerely . . . your wandering minstrel who aims to come to Lotts Creek and help you cut some of the best watermelons in 112 counties.[8]

In addition to the run-outs to the rural listening posts, every Wednesday from July 7, 1937, through September 29, Niles went to the university radio station to broadcast a program consisting of a script he had written (narrated by Sarah Blanding) and performances of his musical arrangements of traditional music.[9] Occasionally he also included guests on the program, such as his friend Frank Long, a painter and Works Progress Administration mural artist from Berea, Kentucky. The radio program dictated the flow of each week's activity, so that days spent writing and arranging material culminated in the Wednesday broadcast. As soon as he returned from the fall concert tour, on December 13, his thoughts immediately returned to the radio station, and he closed out the year with four different Christmas programs, broadcast on December 20, 21, 22, and 23. These Christmas programs eventually evolved into a "Nativity play" loosely based on the John C. Campbell Folk School Nativity plays. The programs were presented the next year, and many subsequent years, on Louisville's WHAS radio station.[10]

The First Fall Concert Tour

The fall music tour of 1937 was the prototype of many others that occurred in the succeeding four decades. With Rena serving as his manager, Niles relied on a social network of friends, on acquaintances from his previous Niles-Kerby engagements and from universities, and on recently cultivated connections made by Rena. In each location there would be several informal recitals and social engagements at a club or an elegant home that would culminate in a more formal concert. Woven into the tour were ample opportunities for socializing as well as free time for attending concerts, plays, and movies and going to art galleries. Niles would be called on to perform almost daily—sometimes several times a day—but there was also considerable time devoted to the social graces of good meals and lively conversation.

Leaving October 4, the Nileses arrived at Pittsburgh, where they stayed with the Eliots while Niles performed in an "awful room" at the Pennsylvania Women's College and at the Hotel Schenley for the Southern Women's Club on October 8.[11] Then, after a full day of church-going on Sunday to hear various choirs, Niles presented a major concert at the

Stephen Foster Memorial Hall for the Department of Music Appreciation, which was a financial and critical success. The next day was spent socializing with prominent local musicians Harvey Gaul, Anton Billoti, and Ferdinand Fillion; in the evening a madrigal dinner was presented by the Oriana Singers, conducted by Alfred Hamer. On October 13 Niles presented an afternoon concert in the Architectural Room of Carnegie Tech, and the next day he performed at a hastily organized concert for students at the University of Pittsburgh who were unable to hear him earlier.

After a day spent at an art exhibit at Carnegie Tech and attending a Maxwell Anderson play in the evening, Niles traveled to Dormont to perform at the New Century Club on October 15. That evening, he and Rena enjoyed dinner at a vast home at Fox Chapel and concluded the day with a midnight supper of oysters back at the Eliots' home. The following day, Saturday, Niles performed for the city's music supervisors and then Rena and Niles shared a farewell dinner with the Eliots. After church the next morning, the Nileses departed eastward, where they engaged in another round of entertainments and performances in New York and New Jersey and spent several weeks with Rena's family in Albany.

On November 15, during a residence in New York City, the remaining tour, and even John Jacob and Rena's marriage, nearly unraveled permanently. Niles came within a hair's breadth of driving Rena from his life forever. After installing his dulcimers in a large storefront display at G. Schirmer's Publishers, the Nileses attended Maxwell Anderson's play *Star Wagon*. The play and Niles's return to the city where he had spent such turbulent times strongly affected Niles and drove him into an emotional tirade. As Rena recalled the frightening outburst:

> When the curtain went down in the first and best act, Johnnie was in tears. . . . When we finally left and walked across 48th street to Fifth Avenue, he was weeping bitterly and cursing me, denouncing me, saying I had reduced him to this state, and many other things I shall omit. . . . For the moment my chief concern was to get him home and avoid contact with the police, get him home and to bed . . . and later we would see. . . . That was probably my mistake. . . . I should possibly have left that night. It might have

done us both a great deal of good. . . . I know that I know now that if this ever happens again, no tour, no concerts, no business of mine or his will stand between me and the great open spaces.[12]

The next day things seemed back to normal, with the Nileses sharing lunch at the Parkside with Quincy Howe (editor of *Living Age*), having dinner with the chair of the upcoming National Conference on Educational Broadcasting, and attending the play *Processional*, about a West Virginia coal strike. On Wednesday morning at eleven o'clock, Niles performed at New York University in a concert described by Rena as "one of the really inspired performance[s] of the tour."[13]

Following lunch with Carl Engel, they dashed off to see a matinee performance of the Abbey Theatre production of *Far Off Hills*. Their thirst for theater undiminished, that evening they attended a performance of Fred Finklehoffe's *Brother Rat* at the Biltmore Theatre. Thursday Niles gave another concert at Millbank Chapel of Teachers College of Columbia University. After the concert Rena contemplated her role as manager in her diary: "Strange, this has been a year of success for J. . . . Wonder how much is the result of my work and how much is plain luck and chance. . . . Don't know and it doesn't really matter."[14]

At a late-night reception following the concert, hosted by pianist and teacher Bernice Frost, John Jacob and Rena had an opportunity to chat with Samuel H. Lifshey (the photographer charged with printing the Ulmann plates) at an event that Rena termed "quite a party." Arising late the next day, the Nileses took tea at her aunt and uncle's apartment and then shared drinks and dinner with Merrill Denison and his wife. The elegant Coq Rouge was quite a different setting from the Daniel Boone Hotel restaurant in Whitesburg, Kentucky, where Denison and the Nileses had last shared a meal during the radio listening post tour.

Saturday morning was spent at Aunt Flo's, and that evening the Nileses dined at an Indian restaurant and attended Stanley Young's *Robin Landing*, which had opened two nights earlier at the Forth-sixth Street Theatre. The play, about pioneer days in Kentucky, was a curious choice for the Broadway stage, right in the heart of Manhattan. However, the urban and sophisticated New York audience was clearly attracted to nostalgic portraits of the rural frontier. In some ways it was a manifestation of the same fascination that drew audiences to Niles's recordings and performances in which he laid a polished veneer upon the rough-hewn frame of traditional mountain culture.

Sunday was devoted to family, with numerous children and neighbors. Niles obligingly presented a small informal concert for everyone, following a supper of clams fresh from Long Island Sound. The next day was occupied with shopping and business downtown. That evening, at Helen and Allan Campbell's home, Niles presented a private concert that was followed by a midnight supper. While this kind of evening performance was exhausting and provided no financial gain, the performance was still important because it created a social network that Rena could utilize in booking concerts for her husband.

Tuesday was largely taken up by an interview with journalist John Selby and dinner at the home of booking agent Leah Salisbury and her husband Philip. After dinner they all attended a performance of *Playboy of the Western World* and then returned to the Salisburys' for drinks and conversation about possible tour plans and a scheme for marketing "Go 'Way from My Window" to Hollywood. Business negotiations continued the next day with the Association of American Colleges, which was interested in booking Niles for a tour of midwestern schools in the spring.

Thursday, November 25, was Thanksgiving, but the holiday was not a restful day devoted to sharing a turkey dinner at home with family. Instead, the Nileses spent the day packing and then going to Jack Tarcher's home for a private party arranged by Leah Salisbury. This was yet another opportunity for Niles to showcase his performance in intimate surroundings for wealthy and cultured elites. The next day Rena and John Jacob finally left Manhattan and traveled to Farmington, Connecticut, where they stayed at the Elm Tree Inn—a quaint and venerable establishment founded in 1638. The day after, they explored the town before the evening concert at Miss Porter's School, a boarding school for women founded by Sarah Porter in 1843. Following the concert the Nileses attended a lively reception hosted by the founder's grandnephew Robert Porter Keep and fueled by a bottle of twenty-year-old Sunnybrook Whiskey. Niles's grandfather and father had both been connected at various times with this Louisville distillery.

The next morning John Jacob and Rena drove to Albany, where the couple unpacked and packed again, because John Jacob was scheduled to take the 7:04 P.M. train to Chicago to give a presentation about the Radio Listening Centers project.

After a last-minute scramble at the train station, Niles arrived in Chicago on Sunday, November 28, and he presented his talk on the Listening Centers before the National Conference on Educational Broadcasting on Monday afternoon. Niles gave concerts the next two days—on Wednesday at the grand Drake Hotel at the base of Chicago's "Magnificent Mile" and on Thursday at the Quadrangle Club, the University of Chicago's gracious English manor–styled faculty club on the campus at Fifty-seventh Street. The next day Niles took the train back to Albany, New York, where a letter from J. M. Helm, secretary to the president, awaited them, inviting them to dine at the White House between December 6 and 9. Subsequent correspondence fixed the date for the dinner on December 10. The Nileses then spent a few days with the Lipetz family before traveling down to New York City on Sunday, December 5.

Domestic relations between John Jacob and Rena had certainly been strained as a result of the extreme differences in their family backgrounds. While the couple appeared to successfully negotiate their differences of age and background when they were at home or otherwise by themselves, things became more complicated when they were in the presence of their respective families. During this extended fall trip, while they were based at the Lipetz home, the couple was more prone to discord; it was incumbent on Rena to mollify her husband, as this passage from her diary suggests:

> I find myself constantly expected to shield J. from my family. . . .
> It's more or less expected of me, and I find it easier to shield him,
> at the risk of offending them, than not to—and listen to what he
> has to say thereafter. For, while J has no understanding of them,
> or patience with them, they understand him very well, and real-
> ize that I'm in a rather odd position. . . . I don't think J. ever noted
> the delicacy with which they accept his peculiar attitude . . . all
> in effort to make my task easier. But I cannot help but note it and
> being intensely grateful. For, after all, from a purely selfish point
> of view J. is the one I have to live with and it's important for my

own well being to keep him in good humor. Of course, there is
no parallel to this situation when we're in Louisville. . . . I have
to take his family as they are, and no effort is made to make it
easier on me . . . least of all by the family. Whatever my people
may think of JJN—and I think they treat him with great kindness
and receive him with the cordiality due the honored guest . . . J's
family receive me with toleration. . . . Were it not so amusing,
it would be extremely irritating. As it is, I just know they don't
know any better, and no more can be expected of them than they,
by their very natures, can give.[15]

Niles spent the next few days in New York City, tending to the business aspects of his career. Monday afternoon he participated in a photography session with Carl Nesensohn of the *Times Wide World* and was
interviewed by Wilbur Fauley of the *New York Times*. Later that afternoon, he and Rena rushed over to meet Leah Salisbury at the office of
W. Colston Leigh. Leigh, a successful manager whose clients included Eleanor Roosevelt, listened to Niles sing and then offered him a contract
stipulating a fifty-fifty split, with the agency paying the costs of travel and
publicity.

The next day continued in the same vein: Rena met again with
Colston Leigh while Niles was interviewed by Katherine Lowe of *Time*.
Finally, done with the publicity events, the Nileses left New York and
drove to Philadelphia, spent the night there, and headed to Washington, D.C., where they arrived on Wednesday, December 8. The next day
there was a publicity-photo session in the hotel before they were taken
to the Treasury Art Project, where Niles gave an afternoon concert. On
Friday Niles enjoyed a congenial lunch with Harold Spivacke, director
of the Archive of Folk Culture at the Library of Congress. According
to Rena, the meeting "changed his attitude a bit towards the folk-lore
project of the library, not that he thinks any more of Alan Lomax than
he did before; but even JJN will admit that maybe Alan is all right . . .
though the father [John Lomax] is a palpable SOB."[16] Following lunch,
the Nileses met back at the Raleigh Hotel, where they were staying, before going to the home of Olin Downes to join him for tea. Returning to
the hotel, Niles donned his evening wear and Rena dressed in her "new

white and coral red dress with her squirrel cape" before setting off for dinner at the White House.[17]

There the guests were shown to the rose drawing room. The Nileses introduced themselves to the other guests, and then Mrs. Roosevelt escorted them to the private dining room, where the president was already seated. The guests all shook hands with him before taking their seats. Rena found it all "very informal . . . and very charming." According to her diary account, the meal was "a sort of family supper, with the President carving a delicious Tenn. Ham (Treachery! With Kentuckians present . . .)." Among the guests was Roosevelt's cousin, "the newly appointed interior decorator to the embassies abroad . . . a gay looking gal, with her hair dyed a nice shade of lavender . . . it's really quite amazing."

"After supper," Rena's diary continues, "the President departed, shifting himself with a flick of the hand from his chair to the wheel chair. When he left the room, everyone rose—Mrs. R. being the first one to get up. Meanwhile JJN had already brought the dulcimers to the table, while the rest of us enjoyed our artichokes; and played for the President . . . which President R. seemed to enjoy very much—especially 'John Henry.' The president told about a section near Warm Springs, Georgia, that abounds in folk-lore of every kind. We shall have to go there some time." Later, "we sat in Mrs. R.'s private drawing room, while the First Lady knitted a white sweater and Johnnie sang . . . and all was very merry and delightful."[18]

The following day the Nileses finally departed for home, stopping at New Market, Virginia, for lunch. While there they also bought a quantity of Smithfield hams to give friends and family as Christmas gifts. That night they stayed at the General Lewis Inn at Lewisburg, West Virginia, where Niles took photographs of a six-string dulcimer said to have been crafted 140 years before. The next day the couple drove home through Charleston, West Virginia, to Morehead, Kentucky, where they encountered snow and ice that accompanied them all the way home to Lexington. So ended the fall concert tour, a journey of seventy days; more than twenty concerts and recitals; and scores of social and publicity events, from boarding school campuses to the White House, that helped cement John Jacob's reputation as a nationally renowned balladeer and scholar of folklore.

Boot Hill

John Jacob and Rena chose Lexington as their home in large part because three different rail lines converged there, the C&O (Chesapeake and Ohio), the L&N (Louisville and Nashville), and the Southern. A career as a concert artist dictated a nomadic lifestyle with performances scheduled throughout the nation. Because Niles was on the road so much of the year, it was critical for him to have a clearly defined sense of home—a place whose gravity could draw him back into the embrace of repose, security, family, and spiritual regeneration.

The 231 McDowell Street apartment served the newlyweds perfectly well. There was adequate room for Niles to compose, a cramped but efficient kitchen, and a dining room that sufficed for the continuous social occasions. Scarcely a day passed without a dinner, luncheon, or tea with university guests such as President and Mrs. Frank McVey and Sarah Blanding or artists such as Frank Long, Bert Mullins, and Ted and Doris Rannells. The apartment began to bulge at the seams with such activity, however, and before long John Jacob and Rena were scouring the countryside in search of a home of their own, preferably with sufficient land for farming. Although they looked at several homes in the city, such as one in the lovely Deepwood subdivision, Niles was intent on property with sufficient acreage to support a working farm.

Rena's diary notes frequent visits in the company of real estate agents and friends in search of the ideal domicile. On July 15, 1937, she wrote: "At 4:30 we pick up the widow Barrow and go to Bob's [Bob Jewell]. He takes us down to see a farm that is for sale right down the road from his place—100 acres, with a magnificent old house built in 1805 and belonging once to Daniel Boone's sister. In terrible disrepair, but very lovely. . . . Selling for $20,000 and it would take about $10,000 to recondition it."[19] And later, on March 5–6, 1938, they visited several estates, including Mary Dewitt Snyder's "beautiful, but isolated farm that seems unsuitable for remodeling into a year-long dwelling" and a home on Bryan Station Pike that had "nice stone work, but the worst piece of designing I've ever seen." A month later, the Nileses were still looking at real estate. On April 22, Rena commented, she "went out with Mr. Christian the real estate agent in the morning, while JJN goes to his dentist in Nicholasville. . . . He shows me several places but the only one worth talking about is a ten-acre tract along the Paris Pike. . . . Nice land but not enough trees."[20]

Niles was beginning to despair of ever finding a suitable house with land. While Rena was in Albany visiting her parents in July, he dedicated his time to the search. After several weeks of wild goose chases, he wrote in frustration to Rena: "It has been hot and has rained every day and it is muggy and sticky and the real estate agents have been taking me about showing me things that were no use to anyone. . . . This afternoon I am going on my last roundup. . . . After that I shall put the money in the bank and quit looking."[21] Just as he was about to give up, Mary Snyder steered Niles to a thirty-three-acre farm on the Athens-Boonesborough Road on July 21.

On Sunday morning, July 24, he wrote Rena:

I went out the second time and visited the 37 [actually 33] acres and I looked it over carefully. It is rather thrilling. . . . There is enough rock handy to build the empire state building. . . . I mean right where a house could be built. . . . There are rock fences everywhere. . . . I could find work for three years building and rebuilding dry walls. . . . There is no sign of a house . . . only the foundations where one was. . . . You would not want to live there as it is too near the road. The parts of the land that are tillable are swell . . . the other parts should be left to grass.

There are several building sites, each one better than the other. . . . The price is said to be 2000. . . . I went out to look over the land with the owner and he did not show up. . . . I was irritated. . . .

Here is a place we could play with endlessly. . . . The electricity will be over there soon and the state has already put up a sign saying the road was under construction. . . . That is a rural roads project.

The creek is running and there is a swell spring. . . . I have not seen the spring yet, but they say it is there. . . . The rock fences please me endlessly.[22]

It is easy to see why Niles regarded this acreage with such enthusiasm. The property, perched on the Clark County side of Boone Creek, about a mile and a quarter from the hamlet of Athens, included some scenic bottomland that followed the contour of Boone Creek as well as a small hill. The hilltop was planted with a tobacco crop laid out in a boot-shape pattern to accommodate the shape of the hill, so the Nileses decided to name the farm "Boot Hill Farm" in reference to the contour of the tobacco crop—they did not intend to associate the name with any cemeteries that are colloquially referred to as "Boot Hill."

When Niles looked at the property, there was no house because a tornado had carried off the original frame dwelling the year before, leaving only a small stone foundation. Niles immediately saw the beauty of the setting and the potential for both a home and a sizable garden, but he continued looking for another few weeks before making an offer to purchase the land for two thousand dollars.

The Nileses continued living on McDowell Road, but in the fall they enlisted the assistance of their new African American neighbors Robert and Katie Hicks, who lived just across the road, to prepare their new property. Together, they planted two hundred small trees, provided by the state of Kentucky, as well as strawberries, red raspberries, and an asparagus bed.[23] This activity afforded the couple an opportunity to get to know their land intimately before placing a house on it. Originally, they intended to build their home at the top of the hill, so they constructed a driveway to the crest and commissioned architect Wayne Haffler to design the home. Upon viewing Haffler's blueprints, however, they decided that the proportions in his design were all wrong and that the hillside was not the appropriate site for the house. Instead, the Nileses elected to nestle the dwelling down by the creek to facilitate access to the well.

In the spring of 1939, Rena and John Jacob erected their first home, a Gunnison prefabricated two-bedroom dwelling purchased from Carruthers Coleman.[24] Since the parts of the house merely had to be fitted together, like panels on the steel frame of an automobile, it took less than two weeks for the home to be completed. They moved into their new house on April 17, 1939, and remained there for the rest of John Jacob's life.[25]

Later in 1939 Niles built a garage with a carved oak wooden door that depicted rural Kentucky images, including tobacco leaves, a dogwood blossom, a rooster, and a figure carrying a pail of water. In the ensuing years, Rena and John Jacob gradually added on to the original prefabricated section and built various outbuildings to accommodate their growing family and facilitate their agricultural pursuits. In 1940, with the assistance of the Snowdens, a father and son team of skilled stonemasons from Clark County, Niles built a twenty-five-foot-square "studio" with native limestone quarried from Boone Creek.[26] This addition, really more of a living room, also contained the front entrance to the home and a small office for Rena. There was a large stone fireplace at one end of the room and, facing it, a raised platform that ran the length of the room. The platform accommodated a root cellar below and, more importantly served both as the "shop" where Niles composed at his Steinway "M" model grand piano and as a stage for the salon-style concerts that were presented at home.

Never content with mere pragmatic construction, Niles enhanced the aesthetics of the space by setting ornamental tiles into both the interior and the exterior walls. The room was further graced by three hand-carved doors featuring balladic inscriptions, poems, names of influential composers, and symbols depicting Kentucky's flora. The front door is particularly striking with its massive timber and carving. Hewn from a block of river oak that had long lain on the bottom of the Kentucky River, it bore the inscription, carved by John Jacob himself, "This house, which is the home of John Jacob Niles, Rena Niles, John Edward Niles, and Thomas Michael Tolliver Niles, is dedicated to the balladry of the Anglo-Saxon people, which cheered the halls of our gallant ancestors and, having also cheered us, has gone out from this spot to the ends of the English-speaking world."[27]

In 1943 Niles needed to build an outbuilding to fulfill their needs for a pony barn. Unfortunately, because of World War II, construction materials such as steel, concrete, and lumber were simply unavailable. Consequently, Niles turned to a construction medium found easily at hand—dirt. Conveniently, there was a large pile of soil that had been excavated by Niles's brother Robert to construct a mushroom cellar. Influenced by the *pisé de terre* (rammed-earth) construction Niles had observed in France, he created wooden forms and rammed the earth in between the boards, packing it in tightly. When he was finished with the walls, he removed the forms, plastered over the surface with an inch of concrete, and placed a roof over the structure. It lasted for years and eventually, with the addition of a flagstone floor, served as a snug office during Niles's final years, which were devoted to writing his autobiography.

With the war over in 1945 and building materials available again, Niles turned his attention back to his home. The family was expanding, with the couple's first son, Thomas Michael Tolliver, born September 22, 1939, and a second son, John Edward, on May 21, 1945. Since the house needed to be enlarged to keep pace with the two boys, Niles grafted a new brick bedroom wing, containing a master bedroom, a dressing room, a closet, and a bath, onto the original Gunnison prefab core. The house now consisted of three wings, each constructed of a different material and each lying at a different level.

In 1958 the fourth wing was added onto the house, which finally joined all the sections together to make a harmonious whole. This addition, designed by architect Ernest Johnson,[28] connected the bedroom wing to the entrance and the stone music room. It provided a spacious dining room upstairs, which was connected directly to the kitchen and a back door. Below the dining room, a narrow hallway connected the two wings of the house. Finally, a commodious dry basement was built underneath to serve as storage space. It may have grown gradually with eccentric additions, but Boot Hill was a perfectly modern and comfortable home in which to raise a family.

Double exposure of Niles at piano and with dulcimer, 1951. Photo by Eugene Meatyard. John Jacob Niles Photographic Collection, PAS82M9M9716, Special Collections and Digital Programs, University of Kentucky.

Niles in white tie and tails with top hat in New York City, 1932–1933.
Photo by Doris Ulmann. J. Paul Getty Museum, 87.XM.89.10. Courtesy
of the museum.

Rena Lipetz's high school graduation portrait, Saratoga Springs, New York, 1929. Photo by Gustav Lorey. John Jacob Niles Photographic Collection, PA82M9388.

Portrait of Rena Niles in Finland, 1936. John Jacob Niles Photographic Collection, PA82M9393.

Niles performing at a broadcast of the Radio Listening Center at Lott's Creek, Knott County, Kentucky, 1937. John Jacob Niles Photographic Collection, PA82M9021.

Thomas Michael Tolliver Niles and John Jacob Niles at the front door of Boot Hill Farm. The door was carved by Niles in 1948. John Jacob Niles Photographic Collection, PA82M9441.

Boot Hill, Niles's home in Clark County. The photograph was taken for a Garden Club tour in 1951. John Jacob Niles Photographic Collection, PA82M9006.

Rena, John Jacob, and son Tom, reading together in the living room of Boot Hill Farm, ca. 1941. John Jacob Niles Photographic Collection, PA82M9710.

Tom Niles with his brother John Edward (*seated on pony*) at Boot Hill Farm, ca. 1949. John Jacob Niles Photographic Collection, PA82M9452A.

Niles and a stubborn Jersey cow at Boot Hill Farm, 1955. Photo by Frank Van Deren Coke. John Jacob Niles Photographic Collection, PA82M9224.

Niles holding a cigar and a cabbage in his garden at Boot Hill Farm, ca. 1970s. Courtesy of Thomas Michael Tolliver Niles.

Niles on a tractor with his son Tom in the garden at Boot Hill Farm, 1955.
Photo by Frank Van Deren Coke. John Jacob Niles Photographic Collection,
PA82M9469.

Niles (*right*) working on a dulcimer with Harry Mefford at the wood shop of the University of Kentucky, ca. 1937. John Jacob Niles Photographic Collection, PA82M9511C.

Niles's cello-style G dulcimer under construction with clamps at the University of Kentucky wood shop, ca. 1941. John Jacob Niles Photographic Collection, PA82M9635B.

A "slipper chair" carved in 1631, flanked by two copies carved by Niles ca. 1939–1942. John Jacob Niles Photographic Collection, PA82M9636H.

Table and chairs hand-crafted by Niles and used regularly at Boot Hill Farm. The table is inscribed with names of ballads and songs composed and collected by Niles. Photo by the author. This furniture is a gift from the Niles family to the John Jacob Niles Center for American Music.

Niles surrounded by objects representing his interests, including carving, woodworking, composing, painting, recording, and gardening, 1953. Photo by *Louisville Courier-Journal* staff photographer. John Jacob Niles Photographic Collection, PA82M9220.

John Jacob and Rena Niles, photographed at Boot Hill Farm for a *Life* magazine feature, 1942. Photo by Alfred Eisenstaedt. John Jacob Niles Photographic Collection, PA82M9421. Courtesy of the Alfred Eisenstaedt Estate, J. Paul Getty Museum.

Niles (*second row, right end*) with the other staff of and participants in the Indiana University Folklore Institute, July 1942. John Jacob Niles Photographic Collection, PA82M9516A.

Niles holding his G dulcimer, posed by the portrait painted by
Victor Hammer ca. 1958. John Jacob Niles Photographic Collection,
PA82M9791-F. The painting is in the possession of Thomas Niles; a
preliminary sketch for it is in the John Jacob Niles Center for American
Music.

Left to right: Niles, Jacqueline Roberts, Thomas Merton, and Janelle Pope (*seated*) at a rehearsal of the Niles-Merton songs at Boot Hill Farm, 1967. Photo by Helm Roberts. John Jacob Niles Photographic Collection, PA82M9099a.

The exterior of the John Jacob Niles Center for American Music at the University of Kentucky, 2010. Photo by the author.

Settled in Kentucky

Domestic Life: Family and Farm

While the world war cast its sullen shadow over Europe, the great golden Indian Summer had taken up residence in the heart of Kentucky's bluegrass. With the core of the house construction at Boot Hill Farm complete, Rena and John Jacob settled into the serene routine of a domestic life, interrupted only by the customary fall and spring concert tours.[1]

As though in celebration of this new period of domesticity, Rena gave birth to their firstborn son, Thomas Michael Tolliver Niles, at about two o'clock in the afternoon of September 22, 1939. Rena recalled that "the arrival of Tom was a great event for Johnnie Niles, and he loved him devotedly and spent endless time with him. He would hold him in his lap and sing to him when he was just a tiny baby so that Tom really grew up on the sound of his father's voice singing the old ballads."[2] Eleven years later, this musical nurturing flowered as Tom Niles joined his father on stage at several concerts, demonstrating "the process by which the ballad and the carol has been passed on for centuries of time, passed on from father to son."[3] This precocious beginning also marked the early conclusion of Tom's "professional" musical career, however. Although he retained a lifelong reverence for music, Tom developed more along the lines of his mother's family: he became a highly successful career diplomat with a range of important ambassadorial and attaché postings.[4]

John Jacob's concertizing frequently called him away from home, but he still managed to be a doting and devoted father who loved "the Beezer," as Tom was nicknamed.[5] Observing Niles's affectionate bond with his son, Rena intuited that the relationship revealed the essence of her husband's sensitive nature: "He (Niles) was a natural-born father. He loved children, little babies, toddlers, older children. He loved them as long as they were willing to love him in return: that was his only request. He was a man who needed to live in a continual bath of approval and affection in order to survive. He withered under criticism, and his love of children may have had something to do with his own personal need for approbation."[6]

While Tom Niles and his father shared a warm relationship, Tom also enjoyed the benefits of a companion who was almost like a second father to him. Robert Hicks, who worked for the Niles family, served as a mentor and companion to Tom while his father was on the road, and he generously guided Tom to a compassionate understanding of the natural world at Boone Creek. The expertise, affection, and hard work that "Uncle Robert" and "Aunt Kate" lavished on the family supplied the strong glue that kept Boot Hill humming harmoniously.

Five and a half years after the birth of Tom, Rena bore a second son. After a strenuous concert itinerary that took John Jacob from Michigan to New York to Minnesota to Washington, Oregon, California, and Arizona, he arrived home just before John Edward Niles's entry into the world on May 21, 1945. John Ed followed in his father's steps as a musician. Rena explained that "though Tom had the advantage of being first-born and remaining the only child until he was five-and-a-half, John Ed was clearly the musician of the two and there was no question of his father's devotion to him on that score alone. John Ed's love of music was very obvious from the beginning. John Ed learned piano, clarinet, and cello, in that order, but his great love from the beginning was opera."[7] The father's passion and involvement in opera was consummated at last in the accomplishments of this son, who later became artistic director and conductor of the Opera Theatre of Northern Virginia.[8]

Although John Ed was engrossed in his youthful musical world, he also participated actively in both the chores and the delights of farm life. He was particularly attracted to the Iroquois Fox Hunt, which engraved the hills and rills of the bluegrass upon his heart. Unfortunately, Robert Hicks passed away when the boy was only five years old, but John Ed had the good fortune to grow up in the company of John Simmons, an African American who served as pastor of the nearby Pleasant View Baptist Church and worked for the Niles family. Simmons, along with his wife, Mary Tippy (Taylor), came to work for the Nileses in 1950 and served as a boon companion to John Ed and an astute horse handler who greatly assisted the family with the care of their well-bred hunter horses. Mary Tippy Taylor Simmons (who married Willard Mullins upon the death of her husband) remained a beloved member of the household until Rena left Boot Hill Farm in 1987 to move into an apartment at Richmond Place.[9]

In addition to the new responsibilities of fatherhood, Boot Hill Farm demanded quite a bit of Niles's attention. Driven by childhood memories of his own father's attempt to create a self-subsistence way of life at Inverness Farm, Niles aspired to have his property supply his family with almost everything they needed. Doubtless, the exigencies of the wartime economy also stimulated the family's desire for a self-sufficient lifestyle. By 1940, Boot Hill Farm sustained cows, hogs, chickens, and horses; a substantial vegetable plot; hay and field-corn fields; and a tobacco allotment.[10] Niles was particularly interested in the burley tobacco, the most important cash crop in the bluegrass region. Characteristically, he wed his imagination to the backbreaking labor of tobacco production and composed a cycle of fourteen sonnets devoted to the cultivation of tobacco; he titled it "The Cycle of the Weed." Sonnet 6 of the cycle follows:

A tobacco bed is surely a beautiful thing,
A strip of creamy white against the green,
A strip of cloth to which the rain drops cling,
Protecting tiny plants too young to wean.
When I was small the women-folk would sew,
And stitch and measure most all of a night,
Joining strips of cotton, row on row,
To shade the tender growth from frost and light.
A tobacco bed is like a silent sign,
To those who pass that burley will be grown,
That burley will be given tender care,
That men will curse the rust, that men will pine
For wind and weather, that the seed once sown
May never halt for moisture, mould, or tare.[11]

Farming was unremitting hard work and a wild gamble as well, so despite his vision of self-sufficiency, gradually the Niles family grew less and less dependent on the soil. A ledger of John Jacob's tobacco account reveals how little profit actually accrued from the intensive labor. When all the costs were deducted from the profit, there was but $329.83 to deposit in the bank.[12]

With John Jacob absent for weeks at a time during both the planting and the harvest, much of the burden of work fell on Robert and Katie Hicks, although the daily chores were done by Rena and the boys. When the war ended, the quality and quantity of goods at grocery stores improved, and it simply became more cost-effective to buy produce rather than raising it. By about 1955, the livestock began to be phased out, the tobacco crop was completely relegated to a tenant farmer, and the scale of the garden was diminished. Nevertheless, Niles maintained his love of the earth and remained a "gentleman farmer," tilling at least an acre of garden on his old International Harvester "Farm All" tractor until he was in his eighties.[13]

Music from Boot Hill

The stability of farm and family life provided Niles with a hospitable environment for his composition. He continued consolidating and arranging his ballad collection, by engaging in background research, adapting and collecting verses from multiple sources, arranging the tunes and dulcimer accompaniments, and honing his performance style. Ballad singing is a deceptively complex art couched in a seemingly simple performance style. An extensive narrative poem coupled with an unadorned melodic line, the ballad flourished as intimate conversation within a small circle of family and friends during the eighteenth and nineteenth centuries.

As the agrarian context of the music steadily vanished in the face of twentieth-century industrialization, ballad performance began to disappear, since there was little perceived need for this slow-paced and archaic form of communication. A ballad can successfully communicate only if the audience invests a great deal of its own time and energy into collaborative participation in the performance, in order to allow the imagination to animate the long and convoluted stories. The twentieth-century listener, dwelling in a world of recorded sound, is seldom willing to engage in the tedious and personal relationship necessary to comprehend an art form in which the drama was implied rather than made explicit.

Carl Sandburg (1878–1967), the Pulitzer Prize–winning poet and folk-song contemporary of Niles, noted the difficulties inherent in folk-song interpretation: "Often a song is a role. The singer acts a part. He or she is a story teller of a piece of action. Characters or atmosphere are to be delivered. . . . No two artists deliver a role the same way. Yet all good artists study a song and live with it before performing it. . . . There is something authentic about any person's way of giving a song which has been known, lived with, and loved, for many years by the singer."[14] Niles both studied and lived among his ballads. While he encountered the music in its original context in the rural upland South, he sagely realized that he could not perform the songs just as they had been bequeathed to him. He understood that he needed a new context, a new way of reinvesting the timeworn texts and tunes with a vitality that would speak directly to the heart of a contemporary audience.

With his operatic training and performance experience gleaned in the company of Marion Kerby, Niles was comfortable with projecting a stage presence. What he was struggling to master was a method for serving as a medium between the original singer and the contemporary audience. He was seeking to channel the original context and transform it in a way that would sway a large concert audience. In 1939 he discovered the key to this technique, and consequently his reputation gained luster, his tour schedule filled, and his concert fees began to appreciate. Niles articulated his method of "singing from the heart":

The problem was the projection of personality and the employment of dramatic methods, remembering all the while that every time I sing a single line of one of the great ballads or carols, I must have somewhere in my vision of what I thought a medieval bard looked like, also the personality of the singer whom I knew. Although I had been in the great world of the concert stage as a singer singing alone only a short while, I knew that I had to blend two powerful forces, my person and the personality of my informant. For example, Johnnie Niles, dulcimer and all, and Beth

Holcum, my mature informant. This blending process either makes or breaks a folk singer. If the singer of folk music is to reach the hearts of his listeners, he needs must employ every trick in the book, trying to reach back to the ancient bewhiskered bard, and then to the folk informant, or to the poet and composer. And he must do this without seeming to do it at all.[15]

It is the art that conceals art, the seemingly natural way of conjuring the essence of a Beth Holcolmb without imitating Beth Holcolmb in any discernible way. It is the art of creating a distinctive personal style in which is contained the souls of hundreds of singers, each with her or his own unique personality, and their songs. That was the foundation of Niles's art, which made him one of America's most sought-after performers during the next several decades. Although he was later faulted as an "inauthentic" folksinger, it is clear that his intent was not to *be* the authentic folksinger but rather to *interpret* the essential experience of the original folksinger through the lens of his own personality.

Niles rapidly garnered a reputation as a compellingly dramatic and charismatic ballad singer in live performance, but more importantly, he was able to transmit this presence on recordings as well. It is one thing to be able to present yourself on stage, where your voice can be augmented by dramatic gestures. But it is an entirely different matter to be able to project this quality on a sound recording, without the benefit of any visual impact. Niles's first records evidenced the success of his ability to communicate directly with his voice alone.

In November 1938 Niles traveled to New York City to initiate his recording career with RCA's Red Seal label. On March 15, 1939, he signed a one-year contract with RCA Manufacturing to produce six selections, for which he would receive 10 percent in royalties from the list price. Sandwiched between concert artists such as violinist Yehudi Menuhin (1916–1999) and opera diva Lily Pons (1898–1976) in the prestigious catalog, Niles, described as a "mountaineer tenor with dulcimer accompaniment," released his first set of four 78 rpm recordings, *Early American Ballads*, on November 1, 1939.[16] Charles O'Connell, the music director for RCA Victor, was encouraged by the positive critical reception given the recordings, and he implored Niles to return to the studios to record material for additional recordings.[17]

The critical and commercial success of the first set motivated RCA to record a substantial body of Niles's repertoire. He made three additional trips to RCA's Twenty-sixth Street studio, with the final session on January 8, 1941. RCA released a second set of four 78 rpm recordings, titled *Early American Carols and Folksongs,* in the fall of 1940.[18] In October 1941, a third set of Niles recordings was released, titled *American Folk Lore Volume 3.*[19] As a way of linking all three recordings in the Niles series, RCA assigned the generic title *American Folk Lore* to the three albums while retaining the original titles as subtitles. At this point RCA projected another set of four ten-inch discs featuring the extended ballads "Bonnie Farday," "The Two Sisters," "Love Henry," and "Our Good Man," with a special one-disc release of "That Lonesome Road" coupled with "The Cuckoo" or "Mollie Vaughn," but the recording ban imposed by the American Federation of Musicians on July 31, 1942, prevented Victor from releasing additional material for two years until the firm signed an agreement in November 1944 that ended their dispute with the musicians' union.

Finally, after the ban had been settled and recording companies moved back into production, RCA returned to its interest in Niles, releasing *Songs of the Gambling Man* in 1949.[20] The success of the gambler songs interested RCA in recording more material, particularly the song "Venezuela," but the onset of a second year-long recording ban imposed by the American Federation of Musicians on January 1, 1948, severely disrupted the recording industry again.[21] This ban was lifted on December 13, 1948, but the industry was also in turmoil because of some major technological innovations. In June 1948 Columbia introduced the new vinylite 33⅓ rpm disc, and RCA, which refused to cooperate with Columbia, offered the 45 rpm disc. As a result, no new recordings were made of Niles, but sales were steady enough to warrant the reissuing of his Red Seal recordings as 33⅓ long-playing recordings on RCA's Camden label.[22] Unfortunately, the quality of the packaging and the recordings was far below the standards that Niles was used to on Red Seal—it was a little like being forced to shop in the basement bargain bin after growing accustomed to Brooks Brothers.

RCA did release one final "greatest hits" reissue of Niles's recordings, titled *The 50th Anniversary Album,* in November 1956,[23] but the supportive and genuinely personal tone of Charles O'Connell's letters was gradually supplanted by more terse and businesslike communications from RCA as their eighteen-year relationship dissolved. Concerning the new release, Peter Delheim, Recording Coordinator for RCA, simply noted:

> Please be advised that the orders to date for the John Jacob Niles Anniversary Album total 2,900. This is somewhat below our expectations but we are hopeful that reorders will substantially increase the eventual total.
>
> The two other LP's and two of the three EP's are still on the market. One of the EP's was dropped from the catalog some months ago due to lack of sales.
>
> We have no plans at this time for the reissuance of any further John Jacob Niles material.[24]

In response, Niles terminated his relationship with RCA and began recording in 1957 for the Clancy Brothers' new Tradition label, a recording company that was more in tune with the emerging folk revival.

Before 1940, Niles's compositional efforts had been focused on small song forms—the lyric, the carol, and the ballad—although he had completed a multimovement work, *Africa to Harlem,* for two voices and two pianos, and had labored over the opera "The King of Little Italy," which remained incomplete. With a more stable home environment, Niles finally found himself in a position to attempt more ambitious compositions. Comfortably seated at his black Steinway grand piano in the large stone room of the "shop" and embraced by the genial glow of the fireplace, Niles slipped into the stimulating challenges of constructing large-scale musical architecture.

In December 1940 Niles had met the Louisville poet Cale Young Rice through Rena, who had written an author portfolio on him for publication in the *Courier-Journal.*[25] Niles and Rice's association ripened into collaboration as they developed an orchestral-choral suite of seven movements. It was called *Cities* because it was based on an extended poem of Rice's that symbolically characterized the capital cities involved in the

World War—Paris, New York, Rome, Tokyo, Moscow, London, and Berlin. London was portrayed as "waiting in the rain," while Moscow was personified as "high cheek bones and bloody with proletarian hate," and New York was described as "a young Amazon."[26]

Through his formal study and performance experience, Niles had absorbed an understanding of harmonic theory, but he had not really had occasion to learn the grammar of orchestration. Fortunately, he was able to collaborate with Edward Barret, who had previously helped him produce the Kentucky Nativity plays at WHAS in Louisville. Barret now contributed the orchestration for Niles's piano sketches and assisted him in drawing up the final score and instrumental parts. Shortly before his forty-ninth birthday, the composition was premiered by the Louisville Civic Orchestra, conducted by Robert S. Whitney, at a performance at Louisville Memorial Auditorium on April 21, 1941.

It is relatively easy to receive a premiere, but it is considerably more difficult to receive a second performance, once the cachet of novelty has worn off. While *Cities* held topical interest because of its vivid war-related imagery, the work was marred by a somewhat dogmatic and heavy-handed choral homophony, and consequently it was not accorded additional performances. Thirty years later, Niles accurately assessed his compositional assets and liabilities: "As I look back on my efforts in large-scale composition, I now (at long last) realize that I was talented in the short or small statement." After *Cities* Niles collaborated with Young on several songs, "Fee Simple," "The Cypress Tree," and "Figures on the Hill," which were more successful than the pair's large-scale collaboration.[27]

Ways with Wood

When Niles was not tied up with life on the farm, he frequently drove into town and worked at the University of Kentucky woodshop. In partnership with Harry Mefford, director of buildings and grounds at the university, Niles constructed his dining room furniture, carved doors for his home, and built a large G dulcimer from a cello that had been cut in half. The university workshop offered plenty of space, an arsenal of tools, and the expert guidance of Mefford, who was a master craftsman.

Consonant with his philosophy of self-sufficiency, Niles elected to carve his own furniture for the home. First he concentrated on chairs, crafting two "slipper chairs" in imitation of a seventeenth-century English chair graced with elaborately carved Celtic-knot work. Then he parlayed that experience into creating two thronelike end chairs that were an expansion of the slipper-chair concept. With their high backs and copious amounts of carving, these thrones resembled oversized chess pieces.[28] Next he built a table that would have been at home in a medieval banquet hall. The tabletop was constructed of a single broad oak plank. The sides and braces were decorated with carvings and inscribed with the titles of various ballads and songs closely associated with Niles. Niles even carved names into the bottom brace of the table, saying: "You don't get to see those until you fall drunk under the table, and I think you're not looking very carefully then." The dining room furniture was perfectly functional and suitable for life in a rural farmhouse. At the same time, Niles's eccentric design was redolent of a romanticized past in which Boot Hill was perceived as a bridge between the eighteenth-century chivalry of the ballads and twentieth-century Kentucky on the banks of Daniel Boone's creek. Niles's home and furnishings clearly symbolize his fascination with Chaucer and reflect the Anglo-Saxonism, nativism, and romanticism that energized and informed the collection and presentation of ballads in the hands of folk enthusiasts such as fellow Kentuckian Jean Thomas.[29]

Life at Boot Hill

Growing up in this household, Tom Niles was not really aware of his father's persona and myth construction, but he was aware that his family was different, that they were almost playing a role in the troubadour dream that Niles conceived for his family and farm. It was not until Tom left home that he gained some perspective on the special quality of life at Boot Hill. Tom spoke of his father in 2004:

> We knew he was different. He was always in the process of creating and nurturing this character. The realization came later, I can not date it. I did at some point become aware that he was engaged in creating a public persona of John Jacob. But we were part of it, we were living it as he did it. You did not really sense it until you

were away from it. As long as you were there, [you] were part of it—the clothes, of course the music, other parts of it that were so integral to this composite that he was putting together. The old Boone Creek Boy—which he always referred to himself as, the old Boone Creek Boy—I mean this is a guy that traveled all over the world and lived everywhere and had done everything.[30]

This was the fanciful reality that was presented to the world at large in September 1943, when Niles was featured in a *Life* magazine story written by Roger Butterfield, national affairs editor, and illustrated with photographs by Alfred Eisenstaedt (1898–1995), the "father of photojournalism," who became famous several years later for his "VJ Day 1945" photo.[31] Niles had dinner with the Butterfields in November 1941 and made arrangements for a team from *Life* to visit the next month. Unfortunately, the photographer who had been assigned was killed in a crash, and the intended author of the feature, Eric Schaal, was declared an enemy of the state as war was declared between Germany and the United States. The story was suspended until Butterfield himself could visit Boot Hill in the company of Eisenstaedt. The resulting feature sprawled across six pages and included an action sequence of six shots of Niles at the dulcimer, images of Niles curing country hams and constructing a dulcimer, and a remarkable final photograph of him standing on his head in a yoga pose. Butterfield's generous prose described him as

A jug-eared, blond-haired, ruddy-faced man of 51 who looks much younger than he is, and does acrobatic stunts with the vim and vigor of a lad of 18. He always sits in a chair while singing, with a dulcimer flat on the table in front of him. During a song he tosses his head feverishly and opens his mouth very wide, disclosing a wolfish array of gleaming white teeth. His voice is the most startling and, to his admirers, the most satisfactory thing about him. It is extremely high-pitched, clear and keen, and he can run up above middle C as nimbly as a trained soprano.[32]

Although Niles had developed a national reputation in folk circles, this single article suddenly launched John Jacob Niles as a household name. Building on this momentum, he signed on with the large West-Coast management agency National Concert and Artists Corporation several days later on September 17, 1943.[33] Immediately his agent, Robert Smith, began to book him into attractive, lucrative concert sites and prestigious university residencies. As Rena recalled it, "an affable, cultivated man, Robert Smith had charge of Johnnie. Things went well. He understood exactly what Johnnie was about, and he booked him in the right way in the right places."[34] After decades of hard labor and frustration, Niles began to reap what he had sowed—the world was now very much his oyster.

12

Dean of American Balladeers

Life was simultaneously very ordinary yet also very extraordinary for the Niles family. Domestic life was rather ordinary as Rena and John Jacob were occupied with raising a "baby boomer" family during the prosperous postwar Truman-Eisenhower years. But Niles's flourishing career created an extraordinary lifestyle: the household had to adjust to his frequent absences from home and accommodate his creative lifestyle when he was present. Rena's diary entry of March 27, 1939, communicates the welter of excitement and activity that was typical of daily Boot Hill life.

> The foal is a filly . . . and the mare was as mean as could be during the process . . . nearly killed the foal. . . . The cat also had kittens. . . . We find this all out when we go out there in the morning on the way from our farm. . . . Our own house is coming along very nicely, if we can keep those men from scratching up the floors. . . . Home to lunch and at 3, JJN has to meet some photographers in the shop to let them take his pictures for Hoagland and Country Life—she is still fiddling with that. . . . Then they return and take more pictures here—a Miss Thomas and his sister of Spengler Studios . . . both very buxom et al. . . . The man comes to get my fur coats, Frances Jewell calls to find out if JJN will sing for the preachers, but it seems that it has to be done on April 20th, when he is to be in Danville. . . . The telephone rings like mad, etc.[1]

John Jacob Niles was constantly on the go. The National Concert and Artists Corporation scheduled tours that lasted for weeks at a time, with performances and two-week campus residencies at a host of college venues—from Harvard to UCLA, from the Juilliard to Eastman—and at museums such as the National Gallery of Art and the Cleveland Museum of Art.[2] The recording projects in New York City, first with Victor, subsequently with Moses Asch's Disc label, and finally on the Clancy Brothers' Tradition label, drew him to the New York halls and studios to document his repertoire. Residencies at institutes and conferences, such as the Indiana University Folklore Institute and the annual Music Teachers National Association meeting, provided opportunities for scholarly exchange.[3] In between times, Niles briefly touched down at Boot Hill Farm to tend his farm, his family, and his musical composition. Life was passing by in a whirlwind of activity. By the time the 1950s were over, Niles had turned sixty-seven years old and had seen himself become the "dean of American balladeers."[4]

While the concerts continued in an unbroken parade of passing halls and auditoriums, several performances stood out in stark relief above the mundane.[5] On October 5, 1946, Niles made his debut at New York City's Town Hall. Located at 123 West Forty-third Street, on Manhattan's west side, this wonderful old venue, built as a democratic meeting space for the suffragette League for Political Education, opened on January 12, 1921. Ever since, it has served continuously as a premier concert facility for a diverse range of performance styles. In keeping with Niles's recent status as a Victor Red Seal artist, he was in the company of classical musicians, such as Sergei Rachmaninoff, Lily Pons, Fedor Chaliapin, and others who had once graced this stage. It had been fourteen years since Niles had performed in New York City, though, and his return to the city where he had once lived must have been daunting.

The stage—fifty feet wide, twenty-five feet tall, and just over twenty feet deep—could swallow up a single lonely performer. The storied history of the hall would surely also prove intimidating. But perhaps even more frightening was the nature of the event itself. Niles's performance was an experiment, being scheduled as the debut of a new series billed as "Music at Midnight." Producer Ted Zittel hoped that the late hour might draw a different audience, but no one had any idea who might be in the seats when Niles walked out on stage. Fortunately, it was an enthusiastic audience of nine hundred young folks welcoming Niles back to Manhattan. The *New York Times* review described Niles's performance style, focusing on his eccentric but effective vocal delivery: "Mr. Niles is not a singer of the conventional type. His voice is like an organ with several stops. The listener gets used to it, but at first the way he shifts from one to the other is disconcerting. The lower tones are hoarse and lack body, but the upper ones, that resemble falsetto, grow increasingly lyric, sweet and poignant the higher they go. Sometimes, as in the very high refrain, 'O Sorrow, sing sorrow,' it was almost like a voice crying from another world."[6]

Niles returned to Town Hall on several occasions, most notably for an April 11, 1958, concert at which he shared the bill with urban folk revivalists Susan Reed (1927–) and Oscar Brand (1920–) and again on September 26, 1959, at what was billed as a "folk festival" with Oscar Brand, Jean Ritchie, Leon Bibb, and John Sellers.[7] John S. Wilson's *New York Times* review cited Niles's contributions to folk music and commented on his unique performance delivery:

> White haired, courtly, impeccably turned out in tails, pawing passionately at the strings of his dulcimer and singing in his odd, high-pitched voice, Mr. Niles presented a striking contrast to the casually attired and casually voiced singers who have followed along the path that he blazed.
>
> Most of Mr. Niles' portion of the program was devoted to songs that have become such an accepted part of the folksong repertory that one is apt to forget that he created them—"Go 'Way from My Window," "I Wonder As I Wander," and "Black Is the Color of My True Love's Hair."[8]

Whereas Niles's Town Hall appearances are well documented, unfortunately the facts are inconclusive about his concert history at New York's other famous concert venue, Carnegie Hall. Niles's son John Ed believed that he was there in 1931, but there is nothing to buttress that claim, although Niles was certainly performing with Marion Kerby in venues all over the city at the time. The book *Portrait of Carnegie Hall* boldly stated that Niles was the first musician to present an all-folk concert at Carnegie Hall: "A lean, long-jawed ridge runner named John Jacob Niles appeared in Carnegie Hall the week before Christmas, 1932, and strummed and sang a program of holiday and folk music. Although many vocalists before him had included a folk song or two in their programs, the Niles appearance was the first true folk music event in the main hall."[9] In 1932 Niles was performing concerts in the Chicago area between December 16 and 20, although he did perform on New Year's Eve at Mrs. George Schirmer's home, 212 E. 16th Street, so it is entirely possible that he was back in New York in time for this concert. The publication "Carnegie Hall Then and Now: 100 Years of Excellence 1891–1991" stated: "In 1933, John Jacob Niles became the first folksinger to perform at Carnegie Hall."[10] However, there are no *New York Times* reviews to substantiate any of these dates, the John Jacob Niles Collection at the University of Kentucky contains no sources, and Gino Francesconi, archivist and museum director of Carnegie Hall, has not found any documentation. It is possible that this concert was merely a myth that should have been true yet never was.[11] If Niles did not actually present what was dubbed as the "first folk performance in Carnegie Hall," he did appear there a decade later, when he was at the height of his popularity following the *Life* article, the RCA recordings, and his Town Hall debut. The *New York Times* recorded a "Concert of American Folk Music" as a gala benefit concert for the Greater New York Committee for Russian Relief to be held April 20, 1946, in Carnegie Hall.[12] Niles was featured in the concert along with a virtual "who's who" list of folk-song celebrities, including Josh White, Susan Reed, Woody Guthrie, Edith Allaire, Leadbelly, Pete Seeger, and Carl Sandburg, with Sandburg serving as the honorary chairman. The concert was reviewed in the April 21, 1946, *New York Times*, but the story was focused on the humanitarian aid aspects of the event, and few of the performers were cited by name.[13]

The Newport Folk Festival

While the history of Niles's performance at Carnegie Hall may be ambiguous, Niles was most definitely present for the mythic occasion of the first Newport Folk Festival, held July 11–12, 1959. Robert Shelton's *New York*

Times review characterized the Newport Festival as "perhaps the most ambitious attempt ever made at delineating a cross-section of the nation's folk music. . . . There have been regional events for many years, but the program that sailed into Newport was a full-masted craft with a cargo from all over the country."[14]

George Wein, producer of the six-year-old Newport Jazz Festival, and his partner Albert Grossman conceived of a folk festival that would explore the entire gamut of American folk experience, from the refined academic to the raw authentic, including a remarkable mix of commercial, urban revival, and traditional musicians. A swirl of styles engaged the audience of approximately fourteen thousand, gathered in Newport's Freebody Park to hear twenty-eight acts, including the Reverend Gary Davis, the Kingston Trio, Pete Seeger, the New Lost City Ramblers, Earl Scruggs, Jean Ritchie, Odetta, Joan Baez, and Bo Diddley. Pete Seeger (1919–) led off that Saturday afternoon's inaugural set, accompanying himself on twelve-string guitar and his familiar long-neck banjo. Changing gears quickly, Sonny Terry (1911–1986) appeared on stage with his raucous whooping blues harp, accompanied by Brownie McGhee (1915–1996) on the guitar. Just as suddenly, the mood shifted again as the Kossoy Sisters (identical twins Irene and Ellen) brought their Washington Square–bred southern mountain vocals to the stage.

Carrying two of his signature dulcimers, Niles appeared next, looking every bit the "dean of American balladeers"—at age sixty-seven he was clearly of an older generation than most of the other performers. As at his Town Hall concert, Niles's gently strummed dulcimer and ethereal voice appear to have been ill-suited to the large open space, but his quirky style and dramatic presence still made an impression on the younger audience. Robert Shelton merely observed that "the gracious and delicate work of Jean Ritchie and John Jacob Niles have been heard to better effect in more intimate surroundings or on disks, but their place at a folk festival is undisputed."[15] Ritchie herself provided this personal recollection of Niles's appearance:

> At the first Newport Folk Festival in 1959, he had some competition—not only many of his friends like myself, but a long line of performers from Earl Scruggs to the Kingston Trio. We had a

good visit backstage while waiting our turns to go on, and Niles was much at ease and joking with his friends. Every so often he'd peer out at the big stage, which would be at times almost completely obscured by long trailing wisps of white fog drifting in from the bay, and he'd mutter, "Whew, what a stage set!" Of course he did his act with "The Hangman's Song," and amid the fog the song took on a most mysterious medieval quality; when the fog moved along, he could be seen, sometimes facing his big dulcimer and singing or talking to it, or embracing it, or weeping into it . . . with an occasional rumbly strum across the strings for punctuation. On the resulting Vanguard lp *Folk Festival at Newport, Volume 3*, the notes about him end with, "All too rare in our time—Jonnie Niles, an Original. An unforgettable performance on an unforgettable night."[16]

Viennese-born actress-singer Martha Schlamme (1922–1985) concluded the set with several songs from her vast international repertoire. And so the first set of the first Newport Folk Festival passed into lore.[17]

An Original

Niles's participation in the Newport Folk Festival reveals his ambiguous role within the urban folk revival. He was at once on the leading edge of the revival and not really part of it—an eccentric who was simultaneously embraced and excluded as an "original." Part of this is generational—he was 51 years older than Joan Baez and Bob Dylan, 29 years older than Pete Seeger, and 23 years older than Richard Dyer-Bennet. Only Carl Sandburg (1878–1967) was of his generation.

Another aspect that distinguished Niles from other folk revivalists was his politics. The urban folk revival was associated with labor and leftist politics, and some musicians, such as Pete Seeger and Richard Dyer-Bennet were "blacklisted" as a result. Niles, however, was far more conservative, and he consistently avoided mixing his politics with his music, with the exception of the anti-Communist text of his oratorio *Lamentation*. Although he appeared in the company of fellow folk revivalists in several concerts that had a political agenda, it was clear that

his presence on the program was more about performing than supporting any cause.

Finally, Niles's presentation and context were completely out of step
with those of other revivalists. His stylized dramatic interpretations, histrionic gestures, high-pitched vocal timbre, formal costume attire, unusual dulcimer accompaniment, and extended anecdotes associated with
each song were simply unique. Niles's whole persona and performance
style were in striking contrast to the casual hootenanny style of the folk
revival. He was a concert artist who adapted folk music for his repertoire,
but he was not a folksinger. This career trajectory was mirrored in his own
composition.

The Metropolitan Opera Connection

Even as Niles's music was finding a home in the nation's most important
folk venues, his songs also began to gain a life of their own in the most
celebrated art music halls. From 1945 onward, noted Metropolitan Opera
divas Gladys Swarthout (1900–1969), Eleanor Steber (1914–1990), and
Patrice Munsel (1925–) and baritones Lawrence Tibbett (1896–1960),
John Charles Thomas (1891–1960), and Mack Harrell (1909–1960), the
father of cellist Lynn Harrell, began programming Niles's music for use in
their recitals. Although Niles had created his repertoire for his own use,
the songs were beginning to enjoy a life apart from their creator. While
folksingers had already freely borrowed several Niles songs that they assumed were in the public domain, the art music world was just awakening to the beauty of his music and discovering that it worked very well in
concert settings, particularly as novel encore numbers.[18]

Gustave Reese (1899–1977), the well-known musicologist who had
replaced Carl Engel at G. Schirmer, was most helpful in nurturing Niles's
music within the art music world. A letter written by Reese on October
31, 1945, speaks of the interest in the *Five Gambling Songs* accruing from
his promotional efforts.

The Songs of the Gambling Men made a terrific impression. . . .
John Charles Thomas and Mack Harrell have both decided to use
the entire set. Thomas wishes to introduce them the first week in

December on his West coast tour and I gather from his remarks and the expression in his eye that he would dearly love to put on the program "arranged for John Charles Thomas."

Mack Harrell will sing these songs in his Eastern concert and of course Swarthout is doing "By Low" everyplace in the world she is singing. I am waiting to place the "Lotus" with the right person and am looking forward to receiving the two new manuscripts you mentioned—one having to do with either Spanish words or Spanish fandango. So hurry them along! I am anxiously waiting to see them.[19]

Three baritones were particularly associated with Niles's set of four gambler songs. Lawrence Tibbett, who made his Met debut on November 24, 1923, in *Boris Godunov*, premiered them, and fellow Red Seal artist John Charles Thomas (1891–1960), who was particularly associated with Guion's "Home on the Range," sang them frequently. Mack Harrell, who made his debut at the Met in December 1939, first performed Niles's gambler songs at the Juilliard School July 18, 1946, and thereafter he made them a standard part of his recital fare, recording them for Remington Records in 1953.[20] In more recent times, Met basso Paul Plishka programmed them (he described them as "a special pet of mine") at his Town Hall debut alongside Schubert, Schumann, Tchaikovsky, and Rachmaninoff art songs and operatic arias.[21]

Sopranos were attracted to Niles's songs as well. Gladys Swarthout was a particularly strong champion of Niles's music, and he, in turn, returned the compliment by dedicating "Gambler's Wife" ("By Low") and "I Wonder as I Wander" to her. Swarthout, who made her Met debut in 1929, became closely associated with several of Niles's songs, including "Wild Rider," which she began performing in 1947; "Go 'Way from My Window," her opening number April 21, 1947, on the *Bell Telephone Hour;* and "I Wonder as I Wander," which she performed as an encore for her concert with the Philadelphia Orchestra on May 7, 1949, and subsequently recorded with the RCA Victor Symphony July 20, 1950, for release on the Red Seal label.[22]

Eleanor Steber won first place in the Met audition in 1940 and made her debut that year in the role of Sophie in *Der Rosenkavalier.* Born in

Wheeling, West Virginia, she had some affinity for Niles's folk-tinged songs, and she kept his "The Cuckoo," "Pretty Polly," and "The Lotus Bloom" in her repertoire, performing them most visibly on the *Voice of Firestone* May 2, 1952. Coloratura Patrice Munsel (1925–) was perhaps the most illustrious of the divas who regularly programmed Niles's songs. The youngest singer to ever make her debut, she appeared at the Met as Philine in *Mignon* in 1943. With cinematic roles and her own television variety show, Munsel was in a position to expose Niles's songs to a wide audience, and her correspondence with Niles in 1954–1955 led to her performance of "Black Is the Color" on the *Voice of Firestone* program.[23]

Niles found his particular niche in the intersection of folk music and art music, in the artful adaptation of folk material, and in original composition wedded to traditional style. But he wanted his music to transcend categories and markets—to be accepted simply as music, not just folk music. As he stated in a *New York Times* article: "I should like to set forth the case for folk music as music—as poetry and song. . . . I should like to set forth the necessity for folk-music to be judged on a par with the other arts. It has come of age, at long last. If it's good music; if the poetry thrills our ears, let us listen to it. . . . But let us reject it rather than listen to it because it's quaint, or cute, or old-timey. . . . Let us not shed our critical faculties simply because we happen to approach the subject of folk-music."[24] The fact that some of the most important opera stars of the time chose to perform his songs was vindication for Niles, who wanted his music to live down through the ages alongside the arias, lieder, and chansons that he had studied in his conservatory education. In part through the very public exposure of Swarthout, Steber, Munsel, Harrell, Tibbett, and Thomas, Niles's songs have been embraced by singers within the standard vocal literature, where they continue to be taught in conservatory studios and widely performed on the concert stage to this day.

Niles's music also found its way onto the concert stage in arrangements by several other composers, most notably Weldon Hart (1911–1957), a graduate of the Eastman School who had taught at Western Kentucky University and West Virginia University and was head of the music department at Michigan State University when he died. Hart composed the *John Jacob Niles Suite* as "a sincere tribute to the famous Kentucky folk singer by making available in orchestral form several of his better known songs" in an orchestra composition. The suite premiered at Eastman's annual Festival of Music at Rochester, New York, May 12, 1949, and was subsequently performed at Ohio University on December 7, 1952; by the Atlanta Symphony on March 9, 1956; and by the Michigan State University Orchestra on November 17, 1957.[25]

Composition and Consolidation

As Niles's songs were finding a life of their own on the concert stage, he was busily engaged in arranging his collection for publication and composing several large-scale works. His popularity created a vast market for choral arrangements of his works, and Niles obligingly produced reams of choral arrangements, with the assistance of various arrangers associated with G. Schirmer Inc., including Cyr de Brant, Arthur Warrell, Frank H. Goff, Arthur S. Talmadge, Willis Laurence James, Arrand Parsons, and Hugh Robertson. Niles collaborated with these arrangers through the 1950s, but in 1941 Niles established a long-term working relationship with Lewis Henry Horton (1898–1978), who was responsible for the majority of Niles's collaborative arrangements.

A native of Youngstown, Ohio, Horton was an accomplished musician with degrees from Oberlin College and Ohio State University (1938). After teaching briefly at Oberlin, he moved to Morehead State University, Morehead, Kentucky, where he served as chair of the music program from 1930 to 1942, and then to the University of Kentucky, where he taught for the next five years. After that he served as composer-in-residence at Transylvania University, just across town, for the next six years until he retired. He was well known around central Kentucky, because he served for many years as a music columnist and critic for the Lexington *Herald-Leader*. The collaboration of Horton and Niles was a felicitous marriage of Niles's gift for melody and Horton's musicianship and understanding of the choral medium. Even better, the two musicians shared a common interest in folk sources—Horton had composed two extended works employing rural Southern hymnody, "The White Pilgrim" (1940), written in conjunction with noted Kentucky balladeer Buell Kazee (1900–1976), and a cantata "Appalachian Nativity" (1955), written in consultation with noted Vanderbilt shape-note scholar George Pullen Jackson (1874–1953).[26]

Niles and Horton worked together on projects both small and large, eventually publishing thirty-one choral octavos and the oratorio *Lamentation*, all for G. Schirmer. That first year, a contract dated April 21, 1941, stipulated an even distribution of the royalties, with 5 percent going to Niles and 5 percent to Horton, as was the case with Niles's previous arrangers. In 1942, however, a new contract dated March 20, 1942, increased Niles's share to 6 percent and lowered Horton's share to 4 percent, an arrangement that they maintained until 1944, when Niles began to pay Horton a one-time fee for each arrangement and collected the entire 10 percent of the royalties.

Niles's catalog of choral works published by G. Schirmer Inc. continued to swell during the 1940s and 1950s—the publisher's catalog of Niles's music listed 170 octavos published in various choral formats, including SATB, SAB, SA, SSA, SSAA, TTBB, 2-part, and unison.[27] These arrangements sold very well; they were deftly tailored to satisfy the choral world's enormous appetite for new music that was lyrical, in English, flexible in form, and modern without being modernist. Niles's arrangements were musically challenging enough for choral societies and university ensembles, yet also accessible by high school choirs. The texts were clearly American, rooted in American native folk song with interesting narratives, and couched in direct, yet poetic, verse. The repertoire was suited to both sacred and secular use, with one hundred sacred works appropriate for church choir use (many of them intended for Christmas) and seventy secular works, largely based on Appalachian folk song, intended for concert performance. The arrangements are diverse in format and style, often set in a rhythmically declamatory homorhythmic texture, but they usually build to more polyphonic complexity and often feature a solo voice. The octavos are harmonically interesting without being overly challenging—they completely eschew pungent twentieth-century dissonances that might disturb mainstream audiences and performers. At the same time, Niles's use of modal tonality imbues the works with an original freshness. A review of "O Waly, Waly" provides a fairly representative critique of Niles's arrangements.

Publishers are notoriously squeamish about bringing out choral music for women's voices in anything but three-part SSA arrangement. Here the flavor of four-part writing is made possible, however, by adding a line for either a solo soprano or a few sopranos. Some of the perennial problems of writing for women's chorus a capella are deftly solved by contrapuntally setting cross rhythms between the individual voices, by utilizing the extreme low range of the alto part when dynamics permit, by judicious voice crossing, and by utilizing but not overworking the device of a hummed or "ah-ed" background in three parts to the text sung by the fourth. The combination of Mr. Niles's lovely melody and the tasteful arrangement make a worthy addition to the literature of choral music for women's voices.[28]

With the assistance of some very creative and sympathetic arrangers, Niles was able to establish an extensive choral repertoire that attracted generations of music educators, choral directors, and church musicians. That repertoire continues to appeal to contemporary musicians and audiences, judging by the number of arrangements still in print—the database of choral music in print lists 191 sacred and 45 secular arrangements of Niles's songs published by G. Schirmer, Mark Foster, and Carl Fischer.[29]

Lamentation

In addition to the choral arrangements, Niles collaborated with Horton on the oratorio *Lamentation,* for which Niles composed the text and music and Horton created the orchestration. The roots of the music can be traced to an incident in 1945 when Niles allegedly served as an interpreter at an immigration hearing for some Estonian refugees seeking political asylum in the United States. (It was more likely that his wife, Rena, who was fluent in Russian, was the interpreter.) According to the foreword by Bishop William R. Moody (Episcopal bishop in the diocese of Lexington) to the G. Schirmer edition:

> In 1945 John Jacob Niles acted as court interpreter when a group
> of Estonian refugees made their appeal for admission into the
> United States, after having crossed the Atlantic in a small boat,

fleeing from the Communist terror. The patriarch of the group appealed in these words: "We ask only the simplest things in life for ourselves and for our children, but things without which the soul of man cannot live—a home, clothes, food, and the right to be free." The plea impressed Niles: "It was like listening to a prophet! That man was voicing the eternal struggle of the spirit of man against tyranny, and his determination to be free, through the power of God."[30]

The incident certainly resonated with Niles's political sympathies and complemented those of Rena, whose family had fled Russia during the Russian Revolution. However, this was a particularly volatile time in which to compose and publish a musical work based on an anti-Communist narrative, since the McCarthy hearings were in full swing at the time of the oratorio's publication in 1952.[31] Because of the strong association with labor causes in the 1930s, folk music was accused of communicating anti-American messages. A number of folksingers were involved in House Un-American Activities Committee hearings—most prominently, Burl Ives, who was an informant, and Pete Seeger, who was blacklisted. Despite his prominence, however, Niles gracefully sidestepped any association with the hearings and yet managed to retain personal and professional association with the more leftist-oriented folksingers.[32] This oratorio, which was far removed from his folk music career, constituted his sole public political statement—and that statement barely whispered under the force of the music.

Twenty years later, when asked about folk music as a political tool, Niles responded: "I have managed to make it in folk music without getting into political dissents, without protesting, although I protest to Hell in my heart. Well, I don't believe in the Vietnam War. I don't agree with anyone brow-beaten and consigned to a ghetto. But my job was not liberating them. My job was trying to disseminate the idea of American culture through music."[33]

Lamentation's libretto gently dissembled the political subtext underneath a universal message of exile and hope told in the unimpeachable tones of King James scripture. Niles translated contemporary issues in eternal terms by adapting a Neo-Handelian oratory form in which both

scriptural passages and original poetry used the seventeenth-century lo-
cutions "thee," "thou," and "hast."

The oratorio harked back to Handel in musical ways as well. The tonality is strictly common practice, devoid of any contemporary idioms.
Harmonic effects are limited to devices such as a sudden modal inter-
change (B minor to B major in "By the Waters of Babylon"). The texture
is almost completely homorhythmic, with all four parts usually singing
together in syllabic text declamation. There are no contrapuntal passages
whatsoever—the only instances of textural variety are provided by solo
passages and occasional melismatic sections in texts such as "our mouth
filled with laughter" or "Amen."

Besides the directness of expression, there is little in the oratorio
that suggests Niles's folk settings. One passage, "Babylon hath fallen," has
an opening gesture that echoes W. E. Chute's shape-note hymn "Babylon Has Fallen"; but other than that, there appear to be few overt references to traditional music. Furthermore, there are hardly any instances
of Niles's penchant for modal tonality. Unlike the choral arrangements
that fuse his roles as both performer and composer, *Lamentation* clearly
reveals Niles simply as a composer, and not a particularly innovative one
at that.

The oratorio premiered March 2, 1952, in a performance by the Louisville Chorus and Louisville Orchestra conducted by WHAS Radio director Edward Barret. Subsequently it was performed March 14, 1952,
at Indiana State Teacher's College in Terre Haute, conducted by Ruthann
Harrison, and at West Virginia University on April 21, 1952, conducted
by Bernard McGregor. With the publication of the piano-choral version
of the score by G. Schirmer, performances by amateur choral societies
and churches started to appear, such as the one on October 25, 1952, at
the First Presbyterian Church in Spokane, Washington.

With its musical simplicity and its conservative musical language,
Lamentation seems much better suited to the church choir than the concert hall. Critical reception of the oratorio quite naturally commented on
this fact. James S. Dendy observed in the *Diapason*: "The style of composition used here is that which is today generally regarded as 'old fashioned' and there will be those for whom it has little interest. Yet there are
many passages of musical beauty and the popularity of Mr. Niles' carol

arrangements will arouse audience interest. The work is not difficult and probably could be done satisfactorily with twenty-five voices."[34]

David S. Cooper's review praised the way Niles's text integrated scripture and original poetry, but he faulted Niles for the simplistic musical aspects of the oratorio and criticized its lack of originality:

> Harmonically the work is straight-forward to the point of dullness. Chordal progressions and modulations are of the most obvious nature, and one looks in vain for any contrapuntal interest in voices or accompaniment to relieve the monotonously consistent homophonic framework and plodding bass line. While the *Lamentation* may well appeal to certain choruses by virtue of its unproblematical simplicity, it can not be considered a particularly significant work in the broader sense. One cannot escape the feeling that here is another pretentious choral composition cast in exactly the mold typical of dozens if not hundreds of works in the last 75 years.[35]

The critical reception must have been frustrating for Niles, who craved the respect that was accorded to composers of operas, symphonies, and oratorios but denied to composers of "small form" songs. Rather like Edward "Duke" Ellington, who was a master of blues and thirty-two-bar song form jazz charts but longed to compose suites and concerti, Niles vainly invested years of his life in attempting to craft extended works. He was a consummate songsmith, a master of line, lyricism, text setting, and nuance, but his attempts at large compositions were unsuccessful because he lacked a broad architectural vision and an overarching sense of formal development, and his harmonic imagination had been narrowed by years of conformance with commercial-publishing-house style.[36]

13

Consolidation of a Life in Music

By the mid-1950s the white-haired Niles, at the retirement age of sixty-five, was characterized as the "dean of American balladeers." His collecting days were long past, his concert schedule had slowed somewhat, and he was regarded by a younger audience as something of a curiosity with his high voice and dramatic articulation. At this point Niles began to consolidate his life's work in recordings with Tradition, Disc/Folkways, and Boone Tolliver and in publication of *The Ballad Book of John Jacob Niles* and *The Songs of John Jacob Niles.*

Post–Red Seal Recordings

Although RCA declined to make any new recordings, the firm did elect to reissue a number of them in the new 33⅓ rpm format as both long-play and extended-play albums. Unfortunately, RCA expended little time or money on the production—the old recordings were simply "enhanced" electronically, and the packaging was generic and rudimentary, devoid of program notes, photos, or biographical material on the sleeve or inserts. After the prestige of being a Red Seal artist, it must have been difficult for Niles to see his music released in this string of low-budget offerings, which included *John Jacob Niles Sings American Folk and Gambling Songs, Six Favorite Folk Songs, Folk Songs of Christmas, Folk Songs of Christmas Volume II,* and *John Jacob Niles Sings American Folk Songs.* When Niles's final Camden release, the *50th Anniversary Album,* was issued in November 1956, it marked both fifty years of his performance career and the culmination of his first recording period—eighteen years as a Red Seal and RCA Victor artist. However, the album was really only a "spring cleaning" collection of material from the vault that had been recorded in 1939–1940, with the addition of nine selections that had not been previously released on the earlier 78 rpm discs.

Back in the 1940s, when RCA declined to make any additional original recordings, Niles chose to record with Moses Asch, on a new label that seemed more supportive of his role as a folk artist. There was a certain cachet in being the lone folk artist on the Red Seal label, but on Asch's Disc label, he was embraced as part of "the folkways of the world on records," along with artists associated with the early urban folk revival, such as Richard Dyer-Bennet, Woody Guthrie, and Leadbelly.[1]

All three of Niles's albums for Disc, recorded in 1946, were released in 1947. His *John Jacob Niles—Early American Folk Carols* and *John Jacob Niles Vol. 2—American Ballads and Folk Songs* were both issued as albums with three ten-inch discs, while *John Jacob Niles—Child Ballads* was released as an album containing two twelve-inch discs. A review of the 1947 release of *Early American Folk Carols* lauded Niles's knowledge but avoided any discussion of his characteristic performance style: "Mr. Niles is perhaps the greatest American authority on folk songs, and has spent many years collecting, codifying, singing, and recording these curiously interesting and musically unique expressions of the people from many lands, particularly those of England and the United States."[2] *Time* briefly praised it as the "most beautiful of this year's Christmas albums. Nativity music sung simply and sweetly to a dulcimer by the dean of American balladeers." In this off-handed way, *Time* created the sobriquet "dean of American balladeers," which followed Niles for the remainder of his career.[3]

Unfortunately, Asch was more visionary than pragmatic, and the Disc label folded one year later in 1948. Suddenly Niles was bereft of a label again, so John Jacob and Rena decided to control the recording business themselves. Four years later they established Boone Tolliver Recordings to record and distribute Niles's music. Niles recorded four sessions at Boot Hill Farm on February 5, 7, 11, and 12, 1952. The acoustics in the large stone room were resonant but clean, and Dr. A. E. Clark of

Electronic-Recording Studio in Lexington was able to get a master with which RCA was pleased. According to Rena Niles, "The recording was done under the most favorable conditions. Although every session was followed by great fatigue, every one enjoyed it greatly. It seemed that the tape of [the ballad] "Earl Brand" was the most thrilling and moving."[4]

With the music committed to tape, in March the Nileses negotiated with RCA to press the discs and with the Cole Corporation of Chicago to produce the sleeves. On June 2 RCA shipped five hundred copies of the finished product—*John Jacob Niles: American Folk Love Songs* (BTR-22)—and the next day, to formalize the business, the Nileses incorporated Boone Tolliver Records with a formal "Certificate of Business under Assumed Name" form in Clark County, Kentucky.[5]

Finally, they were ready to begin selling records, but this proved to be the most challenging part of the whole operation. Without the distribution and publication network of a major label, Niles had to find other means for getting his music into the hands of an audience. Rena accomplished all this herself, designing brochures with mail-in order slips; sending out mailings; mailing promotional copies for review; taking out advertising in magazines, such as the *New Yorker* and *Saturday Review*; and seeing that recordings were always available for sale at each of Niles's concert appearances. But Rena realized that this activity would not be sufficient to move a quantity of records, so she signed an agreement with K. O. Asher, a wholesale-distribution-import-export business in Chicago, to distribute recordings in the Midwest and other selected states.[6]

Boone Tolliver released a second recording, *Ballads by Niles* (BTR-23), but the Niles cottage industry was proving to be difficult work that was only marginally lucrative. Rena was constantly occupied with filling mail orders, shipping records, and maintaining the books, so when Irish folksingers Patrick (1923–1998) and Liam (1936–) Clancy offered Niles the opportunity to record with their new Tradition label, the Nileses were more than happy to jump aboard.

July 9, 1957, Niles signed a one-year contract with Patrick Clancy, and on September 19 John Jacob, Rena, and fourteen-year-old John Ed checked in at New York City's Great Northern Hotel across the street from Carl Fischer Hall on West Fifty-seventh Street, where Niles was to commence recording. Rena Niles remembered that "the heat and humidity were beyond belief" and said that after a full day in the studio without air-conditioning, Niles returned to the hotel, lay down in bed, and commented, "You know, my mouth is so dry I don't think I can do it but perhaps I can still spit and hit the ceiling." And he did.[7]

Working closely with sound engineer David Hancock, Niles laid down eighteen usable tracks during the week, and on November 27, 1957, Tradition released *I Wonder as I Wander: Traditional Love Songs and Carols by John Jacob Niles* (TLP 1023), a collection of Niles's best-known songs, recorded for the first time on high fidelity. A year later Niles again spent several days recording in Carl Fischer Hall, adding twenty-nine ballads to the vault. Just in time for the winter 1960 catalog, the label released *An Evening with John Jacob Niles* (TLP 1036) on November 12, 1959. This recording featured "The Carol of the Birds," "You've Got to Cross That Lonesome Valley," and the gambler songs. On October 15, 1961, Tradition released its third and final Niles recording, *The Ballads of John Jacob Niles,* a collection of balladry that was designed to accompany the publication of Niles's *Ballad Book.* The recordings sold reasonably well, although the success of the first release was not matched by the subsequent albums. An accounting made December 1, 1966, when Tradition was in the process of being sold to Elektra, indicated that *I Wonder as I Wander* had sold 3,097 units, *An Evening with John Jacob Niles* had sold 1,383 records, and *The Ballads of John Jacob Niles* had sold 737 units. The recordings were well received, though critics were almost always puzzled by Niles's unique style. This *New York Times* review of *The Ballads of John Jacob Niles* is typical of the response Niles engendered:

> For the general listener and reader, the disk set and book have many appeals. Niles' singing defies categorization; it is an otherworldly voice, a high tenor with trained polish, used in an intensely dramatic fashion. The younger generation, particularly, has had many problems in penetrating the vagaries of Niles' style, yet there are many who find him a remarkable interpreter of folk song.
>
> This listener assumes the uncomfortable posture of a fence-sitter. Niles' singing has a weird melancholia about it and a distinctiveness that puts him in a class by himself, a position Niles

has undoubtedly sought. Meanwhile, for a collection entered upon with serious intent, this is an important set. For the Niles fan, it is his most ambitious effort in a long and rich career.[8]

Unfortunately, the financial uncertainties of an independent label coupled with the Clancy Brothers' flourishing performance career persuaded the brothers to sell their catalog to Elektra in 1966. Niles was once again left without a label to call his home.

Niles's final exposure on a commercial label came in 1964 when Asch's Folkways label reissued material from the original acetate recordings on an LP titled *John Jacob Niles Sings Folk Songs*. With careful and extensive notes by English enthusiast Leslie Shepard, this is a fairly representative collection of Niles's repertoire, although the material was all recorded eighteen years earlier.[9]

The Ballad Book and The Songs of John Jacob Niles

The Disc, Tradition, and Folkways recordings presented a very complete portrait of Niles's career as a concert artist, summarizing his collecting and composition activity of the past seventy-four years. Two music publications served a similar retrospective function, assembling in print his ballads and his lyric folk songs. *The Ballad Book of John Jacob Niles*, published by Houghton Mifflin in 1961, documented his extensive ballad collection, while *The Songs of John Jacob Niles*, published by G. Schirmer in 1975, presented Niles's original and folk-derived songs.

Niles was now a sixty-eight-year-old man—the time was right for a reflective glance into the rearview mirror to relive the vivid memory of ballads, personalities, and experiences garnered in the course of fieldwork carried out between 1905 and 1936. Although Niles had already released a substantial portion of his repertoire through collections such as *Seven Kentucky Mountain Songs*, *Impressions of a Negro Camp Meeting*, and various G. Schirmer collections and arrangements, he delayed presenting most of the balladry in published form because he was concerned that folk enthusiasts and performers might pirate his versions. Ballads were the music dearest to his heart, and he hoarded them as a jealous lover.

Traveling to Boston, Niles met with Paul Brooks, editor-in-chief of the Houghton Mifflin Company, on May 9, 1958. Encouraged by the publisher, Niles sent Houghton Mifflin a preliminary manuscript upon his return to Lexington on May 14. Just a month later, in a letter dated June 10, Brooks confirmed his interest in publishing the work.[10] Encouraged by this response, Niles submitted several other installments over the next few months, and on January 21 Houghton Mifflin offered John Jacob and Rena jointly a contract with an advance of five hundred dollars.[11]

The first "onionskin" typescript of the book slowly emerged from a welter of field notebooks in which Niles had documented ballads and stories experienced over an entire lifetime. Fact and fancy were intertwined as Niles paired colorful stories set down in the notebooks with historical context gleaned from his sizable personal research library. Musical settings that were originally transcribed in smudged pencil on cramped, worn pages were fleshed out in crisp arrangements for piano and voice. As Niles completed a "volume," his wife edited it and sent it to Helen Phillips at Houghton Mifflin.

Phillips was an attentive, skilled, and plainspoken editor who was also musically literate; her musicianship greatly influenced the form that Niles's accompaniments took. After examining the first draft of ballad arrangements, she noted the difficulty of the piano accompaniments and encouraged Niles to simplify his style to complement the skill of his readers. In a July 21, 1959, letter she wrote: "Now that I have finished going over all the ballads I feel more strongly than ever that a great many settings are far too difficult for the public to whom this book is mainly directed." To illustrate her point she set up a pragmatic experiment.

To test my theories I had two separate one-hour sessions with two young women—one is a musical folksong enthusiast with four years of piano study and the other a graduate of Vassar who sang with the Vassar College Choir and therefore has had a considerable amount of experience in music aside from her eight years of piano study. The first girl found the music so difficult to read that she never was able to convey any feeling for the flow of the melodic line of the songs. The second girl, despite her greater experience and training, had difficulty in playing the accompaniments and had to take such slow tempos that,

again, an insight into the musical character of the ballads was
just not possible.[12]

Niles accommodated her requests in the next draft of the manuscript,
submitting new arrangements that were uniformly uncomplicated with
melodies prominently doubled and harmonies stated in a generally ho-
mophonic texture. The new settings were also very pianistic, with only a
rare arpeggiated chord, as in "The Two Old Crows," to suggest Niles's distinctive dulcimer strum.[13] In a September 1959 letter, Phillips expressed
her pleasure with the revisions and focused on minutiae, such as whether
a chord in "The Soldier and His Lady" should be a C minor rather than
the E flat indicated.[14]

By December 1959, Niles and Phillips were going over the first publisher's proofs and sorting through small errors that had crept into the
music, such as a missing time signature or an omitted sharp in a modal
key signature. Phillips wanted to ensure that the pages were absolutely
accurate, and since Houghton Mifflin was not a music publishing house,
she endorsed Niles's suggestion to have J. Stanley Sheppard at St. Mark's
School do the final proofreading. Sheppard, an outstanding musician,
chaired the music department at this venerable preparatory school for
thirty-four years.[15] Recalling his association with *The Ballad Book,* Sheppard said, "Some time in the late '50s he [Niles] asked me to re-do the
guitar chords for his prospective Ballad Book. That job had already been
done by someone in the Harvard Music Dept. whose name was unfamiliar to me. JJN felt that it was all too sophisticated for what was essentially
folk music. Since my own background included a lot of jazz, pop, and folk
music, I was happy to help, and it was my harmonic work that eventually
appeared in the Ballad Book."[16]

After years of typescripts, several sets of edited galley proofs, page
dummies, page proofs, and three sets of music proofs, the final ozalid
process proofs were submitted to Niles for inspection on May 24, 1961. A
May 29 letter from Helen Phillips noted a few last-minute changes made
by Niles and indicated that unbound sales-conference copies were now
available, with the final bound copy projected by the end of July. Finally,
on August 11, 1961, Paul Brooks announced the welcome news in a letter to Niles. "I can hardly believe it but there has just appeared on my

desk, fresh from the press, an advance copy of THE BALLAD BOOK. I hope you agree that it is indeed a handsome volume—that the format, perhaps, even lives up to the contents."[17]

To celebrate the publication, Niles gave a number of interviews and performances on a promotional tour of the East organized by Anne Ford of Houghton Mifflin. On September 27 he left by train for New York and taped music for two volumes of children's educational books built around his songs. He and Helen Louise Smith collaborated on these books, titled *Folk Ballads for Young Actors* and *Folk Carols for Young Actors* and published by Holt, Rinehart, and Winston in 1962. During the next few days he made appearances on WRVR and WBAI radio and gave a concert at Fairleigh Dickinson University before traveling to Boston. While there he gave a concert at St. Mark's School, appeared on the *Boston Herald Traveler Show* on WHDH TV, did a series of radio and television appearances, and performed to a sold-out audience at Harvard University. He returned to New York for appearances on the *Mike Wallace Show* (airing October 18) and the *Jack Paar Show* (October 14). Finally, Niles returned home to Lexington on October 15, weary but elated over the publicity accorded his book.

The Ballad Book was successful in terms of sales; by December 1961, more than half of the run of three thousand books had been sold, and by August 29, 1966, the book was listed as out of print. Rather than commit to another printing, Houghton Mifflin issued the rights to Clarkson Potter Inc. on December 23, 1966, and that company republished the book through Bramhall House.[18] Sales continued strong in the Bramhall House edition until Houghton Mifflin assigned the rights to Dover, which issued a paperback edition in a printing of forty thousand copies in 1970.[19] Most recently, the University Press of Kentucky issued a new edition in 2000.

The Ballad Book's critical reception was more equivocal—the preeminent scholarly journal in the field, the *Journal of American Folklore*, elected not to review it. However, the popular press, less dogmatic concerning issues of "authenticity," was more willing to embrace Niles's efforts. Horace Reynold's *New York Times* review relished the engaging stories and music and was more forgiving of faults that "armchair scholars" would find with the publication:

Mr. Niles has an eye for scene and character and an ear for pic-
turesque speech which make his account of the way he collected
these ballads a truly fascinating document, a record of a vanishing if not already vanished, way of life. . . .

These are the rewards of a ballad hunter, not the armchair
scholar, and in this account of the Southern mountain people in
action Mr. Niles, who is collector, editor, singer, composer, and
lyricist all rolled into one, is surely at his best. . . . In the past Mr.
Niles has admitted making changes in the words and music of
songs he first offered as folksongs. Some singers can't seem to tol-
erate any music not their own. Mr. Niles' reputation for tinkering
will make any student of balladry reluctant to base a theory on
the variants here printed. But that need not interfere with one's
pleasure in Mr. Niles' versions of such ballads as "Edward" and
the "Farmer's Curst Wife." ("The Farmer and the Devil). . . . This
is a major collection, and Mr. Niles' rich evocation of the people
in whom these ballads have their life and continuance greatly
helps us to understand and enjoy it.[20]

Niles was a performer as well as a collector. As such, he wanted exclusive rights to perform the material that he had gathered. According
to Niles, "I had collected it at great pains. No vastly rich foundation had
helped me. I had financed the operation myself. Therefore, I thought I
should have first right to its use."[21] He sought to share his repertoire with
the public through his own performance, but he was reluctant to make
the ballads readily available for others to perform and record until late
in his career because he understandably viewed his repertoire as his private intellectual property. Well-intentioned singers had been recording
his copyrighted material for years, assuming that his songs were purely
folk music and in the public domain.[22] The tangled origins of his songs
coupled with the ambiguous attributions compelled Niles, as a composer
as well as a collector, to engage in lawsuits to validate his claims to "Black
Is the Color," "I Wonder as I Wander," "Go 'Way from My Window," "The
Lass from the Low Countree," "If I Had a Ribbon Bow," "Jesus, Jesus,
Rest Your Head," "The Black Dress," and "Venezuela."[23] A review of Niles's
American Folk Love Songs appearing in the *Journal of American Folklore*

addressed the issue in a way that clarified the distinction between artifice and tradition and yet rendered the difference moot in the appreciation of Niles's music as music, rather than folk music:

> What has continued to disturb many students of folk music is an attitude of proprietorship and a casual feeling for sources that strike them as unconventional, if not actually unsportsmanlike. Is there justification today for his assumptions?
>
> To judge Niles fairly, one must think of him not as a mountaineer singing the songs he learned at his grandparents' knee, but as a professional performer. Like any recitalist, he chooses his materials with great care; and, having some abilities as a composer, he often writes his own music or adapts traditional melodies to his special needs. Seen in this light, his unusual interest in copyright becomes simply good business practice, not a distortion of ethics; moreover, the problem of authenticity disappears, for it is irrelevant in these contexts.[24]

Unfortunately, the marketing of Niles's music *as* folk music was what created the contentious issue—the word "folk" is too prominent in the title—perhaps this album should have been simply called "American Love Songs." Niles was aware of the treacherous ground he was treading between tradition, adaptation, and invention. The sleeve note to the album *American Folk Love Songs* noted: "In this album of Niles' best-beloved folk love songs, we have carefully indicated what is composition, what is adaptation, what is traditional material pure and simple. The truth of the matter is that Niles transforms everything he touches."[25]

Since Niles blurred the line between personal artifice and traditional expression in his "songs in the folk style," by extension, his versions of ballads were also naturally suspect. Folklorists dismissed his work, and important collections, such as Bertrand Bronson's monumental *Traditional Tunes of the Child Ballads* included only Niles's "Lady Ishbel and the Elfin Knight."[26] Bronson chose not to incorporate items from Niles's substantial collection not because of copyright or sales issues. He stated, "There are, besides, precisely six genuine ballad-variants for which permission was denied, which have been cued in alphabetically, those may be left for the curious to identify. I have not, however, felt obliged to take account of the versions of J. J. Niles in this way."[27] Reading between the lines, it appears as though Bronson dismissed the balladry collected by Niles as being simply inauthentic and unreliable.[28] Although there was clearly intentionality on Bronson's part, the issue is somewhat clouded, since even an advance copy of Niles's *Ballad Book* was not published until August 1961, and by that time the first volume of Bronson's collection was in print (1959) and the second volume appeared shortly thereafter (1962). Even if Bronson had wanted to print all of Niles's ballad texts and tunes, it would have proven difficult logistically at this late stage in the completion of his publication. It was also unclear why Bronson chose to include the solitary example of Niles's balladry—an example that seems little different from any of his others.

Niles certainly provided the serious folklorist with ample ammunition for suspicion concerning the accuracy of his transcriptions and the veracity of his attributions. Often Niles's texts sound impossibly Elizabethan; it is difficult to conceive of their being collected from people actually living in the twentieth century in the Appalachian Mountains. Many of his texts present a jarring dissonance between seventeenth-century English language and mountain colloquial language, which is complicated by the misuse of vernacular mountain speech.

Melodically, Niles's versions often stick out egregiously when compared with other versions assembled by Bertrand Bronson. Niles's melodies uniformly bear no relationship to Bronson's carefully constructed tune families. While you would expect to find isolated examples of tunes unrelated to the three or four major tune families for each ballad, in Niles's collection the usual versions are seldom represented. There are also note choices that sound almost impossibly affected, such as the weird presence of A flats in "Three Little Babies." Although Niles was careful to address this in his notes, stating that his informant's "pitch was variable," it seems completely uncharacteristic for a traditional North Carolina singer to sing such a quirky version of a melody. Tonally, while the Niles versions are not exceptional in their use of modes and pentatonic scales, the Vaughn-Williams-like piano accompaniments do make them sound far more British than Appalachian, far more composed than documented.

Finally, the repertoire itself contains some troubling anomalies. Niles collected ballads that were scarcely, if ever, collected anywhere else in oral tradition. Most blatantly, Niles includes *three* different versions of "Judas" (Child No. 23), a ballad detailing the betrayal of Christ by Judas Iscariot. This is more than remarkable, since the thirteenth-century text, the earliest one included by Francis Child, is not known to have ever circulated in oral tradition.[29] At the same time, Niles described in great detail Mayberry Thomas, Harkus and Tillie Whitman, and Pete Mulleneoux, the sources from whom he collected the versions. The version ascribed to Thomas is convincingly documented in field notebook 7 in an entry dated August 12, 1933, at Knoxville, Tennessee,[30] although the other two versions were not substantiated in other notebooks.

The thing that makes this whole issue of authenticity so challenging to unravel is that Niles provided convincing documentation most of the time. There is no doubt that he traveled to the places he described and met the characters he claimed to have met. Ella Wilson of Texana, North Carolina, was a real person, and Texana, an African American community just outside Murphy, was a real place. Regrettably, Wilson has passed away, and it is no longer possible to compare her singing of "Hangman" with Niles's well-known version that he attributed to her.[31] Unfortunately, this is the case with the many sources that have long since taken their music to the grave with them.

Niles's field notebooks record exacting transcriptions of ballads with attention to subtle nuances of intonation and rhythmic complexity. They also frequently document personal information concerning the subjects from whom he culled the music as well as providing comments regarding the location, date, and particulars of the collecting experience. Niles may have influenced the version by causing the informant to repeat and alter the singing to suit Niles's preconceived idea of what the tune should sound like, but he was guilty of only minor changes in the melody or text once they had been set down in the field notebook. Still, these are just transcriptions, subject to the ear of the person making the transcription. Unlike the fieldwork carried out by Alan Lomax, who used a recording device, Niles's collection, as well as that of the many others who collected using only music notation, must be considered subjective at best.[32]

It is difficult to assess Niles's *Ballad Book* in comparison with other ballad collections, because his book was published so late and his fieldwork was accomplished so early. The important collections, such as Cecil Sharp's *English Folksongs from the Southern Appalachians* (1917) and Josiah Combs's *Folk-Songs du Midi des Etats-Unis* (1925), were published long before Niles's *Ballad Book,* and yet Niles's notebooks indicate that he was actively engaged in fieldwork for his collection during the same time frame as Sharp and Combs.

Niles's early folk arrangements closely resemble those published by his contemporaries. His G. Schirmer octavo arrangements, such as *Songs of the Hill Folk* (1934) and *Ballads, Carols, and Tragic Legends from the Southern Appalachian Mountains* (1937) are similar in content and format to other octavo publications, such as Mellinger Henry's *Beech Mountain Songs and Ballads* (1936). Niles's *Seven Kentucky Mountain Songs* (1929) for piano and voice bears a resemblance to the arrangement style of Loraine Wyman and Howard Brockway's *Lonesome Tunes: Folk Songs from the Kentucky Mountains* (1916). And yet, Niles's comprehensive collection, the *Ballad Book,* is really an anomaly because it occurs after the fact—it exerted no influence on volatile contemporary social and political ideologies such as Anglo-Saxonism, nativism, and racism. It exerted no influence on other folk collectors and collections, folk festivals, or education initiatives. In 1961 the *Ballad Book* could be savored for its lovely melodies, dramatic texts, interesting stories of people and places in remote Appalachia, but in 1961 the *Ballad Book* was severed from the immediacy of the world it described. It provided a nostalgic glance back through the rearview mirror rather than a contemporary view straight ahead through the windshield.

Despite that, or rather, because of that, The *Ballad Book* can speak to contemporary audiences with a kind of classic detachment and objectivity. The stories possess timeless truths of love, jealousy, murder, nobility, and avarice told without superfluous details. The melodies, whether traditional or composed—or a product of the two—have a haunting quality tempered by an internal logic.

Niles, quoting Cecil Sharp, in the introduction to the *Ballad Book* articulated the purpose for his book: "The primary purpose of education is to place the children of the present generation in possession of the cultural achievements of the past."[33]

14

Do Not Go Gentle

The locusts have eaten nearly all of my years
And left the husks and hulls of endless days
And now I must discover how to live with the bitter
Husks and tattered fragile hulls
Of days I shall never see again.
So if you see me trying to piece the shards
Of broken days and tiny fragmented moments together
To brighten the dark night of my loneliness,
Be kind, be gentle, be affectionate to an old man
Who has given his years to the locusts: be kind.
—John Jacob Niles, *Brick Dust and Buttermilk*

A white-haired, stern-faced old man, stooped slightly forward at the waist, wearing black tails and a white tie, walked slowly from the wings. He stopped at the center of the stage, where there were three card tables, a dulcimer lying on each. According to an account in the *Cincinnati Enquirer*,

> Slowly, he sat down at one of the tables, reached out and his lean brown fingers began to move lightly across the strings of the dulcimer.
>
> "Do not be surprised at my high voice," he said. "It has always

been a high voice. And may God let it remain a high voice." And he began to sing.

"Black . . . black . . . black . . ."[1]

The time was shortly after eight o'clock on the evening of April 28, 1967, as Johnnie Niles, the seventy-five-year-old "Boone Creek Boy," trilled out the familiar opening line of "Black Is the Color," a song he had performed on stages across the world for the past thirty-five years, a song he had sung in public more than five thousand times. It was his seventy-fifth birthday—a conflagration of candles on the cake of life. In keeping with his longstanding tradition, Niles celebrated the event by performing a concert designed to introduce his most current compositions. The festivities surrounding this particular birthday were really no different, except that this occasion became special in presaging the future rather than lingering on the past.

From the stage at the University of Kentucky's Agricultural Science Auditorium, Niles concluded the evening passionately embracing his large B cello-like dulcimer in a dramatic version of "Hangman," followed by a pensive "Amazing Grace" and then a final formulaic benediction: "It was awfully pretty to be with you all. God bless you and good evening."

Unfortunately, as Niles was entertaining the standing-room-only audience, thieves were ransacking his Boot Hill Farm living room, stuffing several suitcases full of unpublished manuscripts, stealing what Niles had been giving so freely of on stage. Reflecting on the theft, Niles spoke to Norman Nadel of the *Cincinnati Post and Times Star*: "It was somebody who knew a lot about me—maybe a friend. He knew where I live, just where the manuscripts were kept, and what was worth taking, and he obviously knew that my wife Rena and I would be at the university that night. He wasn't an ordinary thief; he passed up an expensive camera lying near the music and other things of value. He'll wait until I'm dead, then let the manuscripts drift onto the market. They'll bring a good price."[2]

The puzzling theft of Niles's songs and poetry was never solved. Niles occasionally grumbled that it was the university that had "set him up." Kenneth Wright, a composition professor at the university who had worked closely with Niles, also thought the theft might have been university-related, characterizing it as a "disgraceful event—was it really a fraternity joke or initiation?"[3] Clearly, it was not a typical robbery, since no jewels, electronics, or other valuables were stolen; the thief or thieves must have been speculating that the manuscripts would someday prove valuable. Perhaps it was only as Wright suggested, something as thoughtless as a fraternity prank.[4]

In one fell swoop, original copies of the music and poetry Niles had been actively working on had vanished—songs, 175 sonnets, choral arrangements, an "Indian Summer Suite" for piano; all disappeared. Rena said, "This is the loss of a lifetime." At seventy-five, Niles must surely have despaired; at that age it must have seemed more than daunting to think of starting anew on days' and months' and years' worth of accumulated work that had not yet made it to publication. But remarkably, Niles embraced this loss as a gift, observing, "[The loss] was a blessing in disguise in some ways. . . . My 75th birthday marked the end of something and the beginning of a new concept of music."[5] The thieves unwittingly provided Niles with an opportunity to start afresh, and ten years beyond the usual retirement age he reinvented himself in challenging new musical and philosophical directions.

A Tale of Two Artists: *The Niles-Merton Songs*

Several weeks after the Boot Hill Farm robbery, Victor and Carolyn Hammer introduced Niles to the poetry of Thomas Merton (1915–1968). Victor Hammer (1882–1967), a noted Viennese artist and printer, and his wife Carolyn Reading had moved to Lexington in 1948 and had become good friends of Rena and John Jacob. The Hammers had also become fast friends of Merton, the celebrated writer and poet who had chosen to live a contemplative life as a Trappist monk at Gethsemani Abbey in Nelson County, near Bardstown, Kentucky. By this time Hammer had completed oil portraits of both men.[6]

At a performance at the Newman Center on the University of Kentucky campus, Niles recounted Hammer's role in introducing him to the transformative force of Merton's poetry: "As it worked out one day a man came to see me—Victor Hammer, the Viennese painter, and his wife Carolyn. They said to me, 'Johnnie, you're wasting your time on a lot of nonsense. This poetry.' I said, 'My dear child, it's my poetry.' 'I know, but have you ever read Tom Merton's poetry?' I said, 'I read his book *Seven Story Mountain.*' 'All right, all right, here's the book, here's the poetry—*Selected Poems* and the other one, *Emblems of a Season of Fury.*' "[7] And Niles began to read, and to read, devoured by the power of Merton's voice in verse.

Thomas Merton was born in Prades, France, but he almost immediately embarked on a peripatetic life that carried him to the United States, back to France, and to Bermuda, England, and Italy before he settled in Kentucky during 1941. Merton studied at Cambridge, England, but completed his B.A. and an M.A. at Columbia University in New York City. He taught for several years at Columbia University and St. Bonaventure College and then briefly engaged in social work at Friendship House in New York City's Harlem district. In 1941, a religious awakening that Merton had experienced in the summer of 1933 at Rome, Italy, eventually led him to become Father Louis, a monk, and to dedicate the remainder of his life to contemplation, prayer, labor, and writing at Gethsemani Abbey in Trappist, Kentucky. Merton succinctly defined the essential nature of his vast body of writing in comments delivered at Bellarmine College in Louisville: "Whatever I may have written, I think it can all be reduced in the end to this one root truth: that God calls human persons to union with Himself and with one another in Christ, in the Church which is his mystical body."[8]

Niles and Merton had settled in Kentucky at approximately the same time, but they had not met each other, nor had they encountered each other's work until Carolyn Hammer slipped Merton's poetry into Niles's hands. Almost at once, Niles digested the poetry, making notes to himself in the book's margins. He responded to the poems by setting a couple of them to music, first "The Messenger" and later "The Nativity."[9]

In late summer of 1967, Carolyn Hammer brought Rena and John Jacob to meet Merton at Gethsemani Abbey. They shared a delicious picnic and good conversation. Although Father Louis did not actively engage in collaborating with Niles on what became known as the "Niles-Merton Songs," Merton did give his blessing to the project.[10]

Niles and Merton shared a strong spiritual bond, even though Niles frequently and vociferously distanced himself from the Roman Catholic faith, claiming that he was a Zen Buddhist or a "Zen Christian."[11] While Rena and John Jacob frequently worshiped at Christ Church, the

Episcopal Cathedral, Niles was more drawn to the aesthetic and cultural aspects of liturgical drama than to theological dogma. Instead of denominational religion, Niles's and Merton's faith really intersected in a deeply spiritual understanding of nature. Monica Weis observed: "For Merton, the stars, the light, the morning mist, a tree, the colors and changing seasons—even walls and windows—provided encounters with the holy. 'All nature is meant to make us think of Paradise.' Merton said."[12] Niles was equally moved by a pantheistic perception of the earth, as evidenced by the thread of nature imagery woven throughout a lifetime of poetry and song and grounded in his own garden. His song "I Sing of the Earth" stands as an example:

> I sing of the earth, the mother who bore me,
> And gave me the hands to dig in her skin
> And bring forth the food for the myriads of people
> Living under the curve of God's blue heaven,
> My brothers under God's heaven.
>
> I sing of the earth, the mother who bore me,
> Who stirs when the bitter winter is past
> And patiently waits through the fogs of April,
> Waiting for the summer sun, when she will be fruitful,
> Beautifully fruitful, fruitful since God's time began.
>
> I sing of the earth, the mother who bore me.[13]

Tune and Text

With only a scant handful of exceptions, Niles had relied on his own poetry or his adaptations of folk expression as the source for his lyrics.[14] Thus, it is surprising that he felt drawn to set someone else's verse to music so late in his career. Furthermore, Merton's verse does not seem initially hospitable to musical interpretation. There are few instances of metric regularity, regular strophic structures, symmetrical repetition, refrains, and recurrent rhyme schemes. The sole exception in the twenty-two songs that Niles eventually set was "A Responsory, 1948," which has a recurrent four-line refrain. Merton's irregular poetic shape dictates a fluid and through-composed musical form without the safety net of preexistent forms and repetitive structures. Each poem asks to be interpreted on its own terms and made to sing in its unique style.

Given Niles's extensive experience with song composition, it proved easier for him to solve the technical issues of form and scansion than to deal with the more challenging task of comprehending the poetry and then imparting that understanding to the listener. Niles believed that it was only when Merton's words were set to music that the poetry's meaning could be truly revealed.

The key to understanding the poetry is to make it understood. Niles realized that it was essential for him to reinforce the lyrical quality of the verse by matching it with an equally lyrical line. Paradoxically, this was achieved by almost completely eschewing the use of melisma in favor of a rhythmically fluid syllabic style that matched the verse like glove to hand. Consider the challenging articulation of phrases such as: "Suppose the dead could crown their wit with some intemperate exercise."[15] The rhythm of the poetry became incarnate in the rhythm of the melody. In this way, Niles ensured that the text declamation would remain remarkably clear.

Textual clarity was also the driving force behind the piano accompaniment. There is an airy and transparent quality in the piano, with runs and rhythmically complex parts only juxtaposed against sustained vocal lines or reserved for filling in space between phrases. The piano for these songs, unlike the piano for his folk-oriented arrangements, seldom thickens the texture by doubling the vocal line; instead the accompaniment parts are often generated in a motivic way or based on a wealth of runs and arpeggios. One song, "The Ohio River—Louisville," conjures up the river's deliberate flow through the use of "black note" sustained cluster chords effected by using a felt-covered ten-and-seven-eighths-inch-long board.[16] Another song, "Evening," is obsessively grounded in a four-note motive that grew out of the call of a whippoorwill heard at Boot Hill. The whippoorwill motive is literally sounded in every measure of the song, just as Niles experienced the bird song itself.[17] He commented on one occasion, "You all recognize the whippoorwill's call—do you all have whippoorwill in this country? Well, we have many of them down there in

Kentucky, and I have counted thirty-five 'whippoorwills' from one bird at a time before he stopped to get his breath. He's a fabulous singer. Has no variations, he only says one thing, but he says it magnificently."[18] Whether sparked by an allusion to nature or a purely musical idea, in each case, the piano part seems to arise organically out of the essential spirit of each song, and there is a collaborative chemistry bonding vocalist to pianist.

The final, and perhaps most significant, factor contributing to the clarity of text expression must be considered the special process through which these songs were brought into the world. Unlike all of his previous music, the Niles-Merton songs were composed in collaboration with the performers, vocalist Jacqueline Roberts and pianist Janelle Pope (and later pianist Nancie Field, after Janelle moved away from Lexington in 1969). Although Niles had written songs expressly for Metropolitan Opera divas, such as Gladys Swarthout, the performers were never involved in the creative process. Here, for the first time, Niles enjoyed the luxury of being able to hear his ideas sight-read on a twice-weekly basis. For the first time, he could tailor the composition to complement the unique vocal and pianistic resources of the performers.[19] For the first time, Niles could revise his sketches based on an actual listening experience, incorporating the critical input of gifted performers whose judgment he trusted.

"The Girls": Jacqueline Roberts and Janelle Pope

Born in the northern Kentucky town of Russell, in Greenup County on the Ohio River, Jacqueline "Jackie" Warnick Roberts (1933–), shared a Kentucky heritage with Niles. Much of her family were musically connected with the Mead Memorial Methodist Church in Russell: her mother was the pianist; at age three Jackie gave her first public performance there, singing "I Will Make You Fishers of Men"; and her sister Jeanine later served as the church's pianist. Jackie's musical ability manifested itself early, and at age thirteen she began taking the bus every week to Huntington, West Virginia, to take vocal lessons with Marguerite Neekamp-Stein and piano lessons with Mary Shepp Mann. Upon graduating from Russell High School, she attended Oberlin Conservatory, where she earned her B.M. degree in vocal performance. She then completed a master's degree at Miami University, Oxford, Ohio, teaching voice as a graduate assistant.

Jackie married architect Helm Roberts in 1955 and lived in Jackson-
ville, Florida, while Helm was serving as a flyer in the U.S. Navy. In 1962
the couple settled in Lexington, where they raised two sons while Jackie
worked as a freelance singer in musical theater and at area churches. She
first met Niles briefly at Christ Church when she sang his "The Little Family" at an Easter service attended by John Jacob and Rena. Shortly thereafter, Jackie was preparing music for a sacred recital at Second Presbyterian
Church. She had decided to dedicate the first half of the concert to European works, but she wanted the second half to represent contemporary
works in English. On impulse, Jackie called Niles and asked him if he might
suggest music for the recital. In response, he graciously invited Jackie and
her accompanist out to Boot Hill to visit and try out some new repertoire.

Jackie and Janelle read through music and Niles picked out two songs
for her recital, "The Flower of Jesse" and "Come Gentle Dark." Then he
asked them a simple question, which completely altered the direction of
their lives. As Jackie recalled the moment:

> "Now may I ask you a favor?" he said, placing a manuscript on
> the piano in front of Janelle. "I have taken a poem by Thomas
> Merton," he explained, "and made it a song for soprano voice.
> Would you sight read it so that I might hear how it sounds?" We
> were pleased to do what he wished, and he listened intently to
> every note. The song was "The Messenger," in which the com-
> ing of spring reminds a sentry of the day of the Annunciation,
> "The morning, the mother of God/Loved and dreaded the mes-
> sage of an angel." I never dreamed, as we read our way through it
> that I would sing this song so many times and in so many places.
> I was perfectly happy that day, to have been received so kindly
> and critiqued so helpfully. But now that I look back on it, there
> was something unusual about the way I acted on impulse, and
> even something portentous about the song itself, and the look on
> Johnnie's face as he listened to it: it was a kind of creative annun-
> ciation that would transform all of our lives.[20]

Rena and John Jacob attended Jackie's recital on May 7, 1967, and Niles
found himself impressed by her keen diction, her sense of drama, and her

rich mezzo timbre. Within a month, Jackie, Janelle, and Niles initiated a regular pattern of meeting twice a week to sight-read new Niles-Merton songs even as Niles was engaged in the composition and revision process.

First with Janelle, and two years later with pianist Nancie Field, Jackie made the half-hour drive out from town to Boot Hill and worked from ten o'clock until noon. Afterward, they all shared a glass of wine or a bloody Mary and some convivial conversation before sitting down to lunch, served by Mary Tippy in the dining room. As they labored, composing, practicing, reading, critiquing, and revising, the songs gradually took shape. Three songs, "Messenger," "Carol," and "A Responsory, 1948," were completed in time for Thomas Merton's first visit to Boot Hill Farm on October 28, 1967.

Mott's biography of Merton depicted the visit:

> On the twenty-eighth they (Merton and Doris Dana) drove to Lexington to visit Carolyn Hammer. Merton had been concerned for her since Victor's death. He was reassured, and had not been expecting the day would bring back the best of earlier Hammer picnics, or a day when he found himself celebrated not as a cult figure, but as a stimulant to other artists. Doris Dana and Carolyn Hammer and Merton went on for luncheon at the farm of the singer and folklorist John Jacob Niles. Merton had been wanting to meet Niles for some time now and they met in the best of situations. The Kentucky sunlight that day seemed to Merton particularly beautiful, and he was fascinated by Boot Hill Farm. After lunch the group was joined by soprano Jacqueline Roberts and the pianist Janelle Pope, and they listened to poems of Merton's that had been set to music: "Messenger," "Carol," and "Responsory." John Jacob Niles explained that he had been working on a musical setting of "Evening," the next in a larger Merton-Niles cycle he was planning. Merton found himself in tears: he was moved by the songs, "but above all by this lovely girl, Jackie Roberts, who put her whole heart into singing them."[21]

Merton's enthusiastic embrace of the songs that afternoon ensured that Niles and "the girls" would continue their creative collaboration.

Niles also asked Jackie and Janelle to perform at Boot Hill for the annual Niles family Christmas gathering. There was a festive dusting of snow outside, but inside, in the great stone living room, a generous fire cheered the company of nearly fifty guests as they gathered in an array of chairs arranged facing the Steinway grand piano. There were cocktails and hors d'oeuvres, but not too many, because Rena did not want to spoil people's appetite for dinner. And then, with guests still arriving Niles introduced "the girls" and announced each of his songs, calling out:

> This afternoon we have Jackie Roberts and Janelle Pope and my son John Edward, who will be here in a few minutes: he's going to play cello and the girls are going to—Jackie's going to sing and Janelle's going to play. Of course you know I am the consummate egotist. I always present people singing my own music and to hell with the hindmost. I know all about Bach, Beethoven, and Brahms: I've been exposed to it ever since I was knee-high to a duck. The first music I ever heard was the great symphonic works of Beethoven and Brahms. Now nowadays, notwithstanding— come on over here, honey, here's a seat for you! Notwithstanding, at this age in my life, I feel that I'm justified in presenting my own material. It's a little bit different from the average run of music. . . . All right—we start with something that I wrote, and I have it down in the low sexy part of this girl's voice. She's a soprano, but when you pitch her down in the low mezzo area, you get something for your money! All right, honey.[22]

Buoyed by the merry company, supported by the living room's resonant acoustics, and embraced by the cordial glow of the evening, Jackie and Janelle performed "I Dare Not Ask"; "My Little Black Star"; "Nativity"; "The Messenger"; a new Niles-Merton song, "A Responsory, 1948"; and closed with "Flower of Jesse" and "Flame Within."

As the last notes died away, Niles invited his guests in to dinner and pronounced his customary histrionic thanksgiving—no brief, perfunctory grace could possibly satisfy Niles's sense of drama and ceremony— even if it meant that the dinner grew cold during the extended blessing.[23] With their appetites sharpened by the salon concert and the lengthy grace, the guests all dined in the best Boot Hill tradition—old Kentucky ham cured and smoked by Niles himself on the farm, beaten biscuits, vegetables preserved from sunnier days, Mary Tippy's velvety corn pudding, and that fragrant, freshly baked bread.[24]

It had been a delightful evening, but what "the girls" did not yet realize was that they had just passed their audition to perform regularly on stage with Niles on his future concert tours. Rena and John Jacob had talked the matter over and had elected to include "the girls" as full partners in forthcoming concerts. Jackie's and Janelle's lives now became thoroughly intertwined with the Nileses', meeting twice a week to read through new Niles-Merton songs, traveling with Rena and John Jacob on performance tours, and participating in the lively social scene that emanated from Boot Hill.

As the composition and rehearsal process continued on the Niles-Merton songs, progress was punctuated by several additional meetings with Merton at Gethsemani. Rena particularly remembered a picnic in the woods "on a memorable, bright, cold February day."[25] By the time Merton visited Boot Hill again in September 1968, the ten songs that made up opus 171 had been completed and were ready for performance at Knight's Hall of Bellarmine College on November 10.[26]

Merton was treated to opus 171, and then they all sat down to lunch. Following the meal, they gathered in a circle in the living room while Merton and Niles shared their poetry aloud. Afterward, the conversation naturally turned to a new gathering of Merton's poetry that Niles intended to set as opus 172. Niles again asked permission to make small changes in the verse as necessary to suit the music, and Merton encouraged him to do so, simply saying, "You're the composer." All too soon, the delightful afternoon was over and Merton had to drive to his doctor's office in Lexington. Unfortunately, this was the final such gathering; Merton traveled to the Orient in October, where he died accidentally in Bangkok, Thailand, on December 10, 1968. Niles and Merton shared a brief but profound relationship, one that strongly shaped the final years of Niles's own life. In recalling Merton, Niles said he was "one of the great men who influenced my life more than anyone I have encountered."[27]

With Merton's incorporeal presence continuing to guide him, Niles continued work on the Niles-Merton songs, and by 1970 he had composed twelve additional songs, grouped as opus 172.[28] The final song Niles composed, "Mosaic: St. Praxed's," imparted a sense of closure to the Niles-Merton songs by returning to several of the themes that permeated the other poems. Merton's translation of a French poem by Raissa Maritain, this verse employed bird imagery ("So like a quiet pigeon"), celebrated the creative force of the Virgin Mary ("In this dim sheltered paradise Mary made of love art and poetry"), and praised the power of art and poetry to transcend evil ("You welcome me refuge pure to see you O Soul's delight"). Niles's comments on a manuscript of "Mosaic" serve as a final resolution and epitaph to the concluding years of his creative life: "I started these two cycles, Opus 171 and 172, with 'The Messenger' 3 years ago, and though it was the most moving and creative experience of my entire life, many times I have never wished I had ever heard tell of this wonderful 'Poetic' material. It taught me a new kind of music composition and the writing of poetry." After signing his name in the usual bold flourish, he added: "P.S. For me nothing has ever been the same."[29]

Despite the differing emotional and philosophical character of the two opuses, these songs all share stylistic cohesion. It is impossible to discern any musical differences separating the songs written before Merton's death from the ones written afterward. It is clear that the songs all belong together; however, they do not constitute a true "song cycle." They were not conceived that way, nor is there a narrative or any other imposed order in which the songs should be presented, although the order in which they were published reflects a possible performance sequence, according to the intent of Jacqueline Roberts and Rena Niles.[30] Jackie characterized the differences between the two opuses this way:

> When I review them now, the songs in Opus 171 are intensely reflective and even apprehensive—facing the "anxieties of void." At the time they were composed there was, as there is now, a sense that the country's spiritual compass had been lost or at least misplaced. Death and dread seemed all the more horrible in a world that seemed unable to give life meaning.
>
> The twelve songs that were written after Thomas Merton's death seem to me to have some different qualities from the first

ten songs, even though the first four songs in this new opus are transitional in that they are meditative and reflect the influence of Zen.[31]

The first time the entire Niles-Merton songs were performed in a single concert was September 17, 1975, at the Newman Center on the University of Kentucky campus. In most performance situations, Jackie freely mixed songs from both opuses according to the context of a specific program. A typical recital or concert would include two sets of Niles-Merton songs, including "A Responsory, 1948," "The Greek Women," "Great Prayer," "Love Winter When the Plant Says Nothing," "The Weathercock on the Cathedral at Quito," and "The Ohio River—Louisville" as one group, and "Cana," "Wisdom," "Autumn," "Lament of a Maiden," "Evening," and "For My Brother, Reported Missing in Action, 1943" as the second group.[32]

Taking the Show on the Road

It was an astute decision to incorporate performances by "the girls" at Niles's concerts for the final ten years of his career. Even though he still presented a charismatic presence onstage, Niles's stamina was greatly diminished. Jackie and Nancie contributed the energy and enthusiasm that allowed Niles to extend his concert schedule until age eighty-six. This concert format also facilitated Niles's desire to introduce the solo art song for soprano voice alongside the popular songs in the style of folk music that his audiences expected to hear. Niles made a genuine effort to integrate the two styles by insisting that Jackie learn to sing the folk songs as well as learning how to accompany herself on dulcimer.[33]

Niles still maintained the central role onstage, however, announcing the songs, interjecting his well-worn tales and anecdotes, and singing—usually the children's songs that he loved, such as "Frog in the Spring" and "I Had a Cat and the Cat Pleased Me." Niles also invariably paraded out several of his vaudeville-style "stage tricks" for engaging the audience. His favorite device was to catch an audience member in the act of taking a photograph during the performance. He would interrupt the song immediately and berate the photographer as a means for drawing the audi-

ence to his side. Author Studs Terkel recounted one such occasion at the
Newport Festival:

> His style of speech is that of an old-time schoolmaster lecturing
> a group of enraptured though at times unruly students. In mo-
> ments of fervor, his mode may be that of W. C. Fields, a circuit-
> riding evangelist, or an old-time medicine man. His ebullience
> overwhelms. I initially encountered him at the first annual New-
> port Folk Festival of 1959. As master of ceremonies, I introduced
> him to the assembled young, who at the moment were discover-
> ing Bob Dylan. As he held the dulcimer in his arms, close to his
> breast, he murmured into the microphone, "She is my love, my
> dear companion." There were audible snickers in the audience.
> Unperturbed, he sang out the tragic ballad. When someone in
> the crowd flashed his Kodak camera, Niles stopped midsong to
> lecture him: "Young sir, would you impinge upon the privacy of
> a man and a maid making love?" Without missing a beat, he re-
> sumed the song.[34]

Rena, John Jacob, Jackie, and Nancie traveled together harmoniously
on tours to New York, Ohio, Kansas, Indiana, and Kentucky, giving performances at venues such as Colgate University, Cincinnati Conservatory, Agnes Scott College, Baker University, Wichita State University, and
Oberlin College. Travel was by plane if necessary, but Niles preferred to
drive, traveling in a gracious style with a well-laden picnic hamper.[35]

Newspaper reviews were highly favorable, glowing about Niles's past
achievements, praising his still charismatic performance, and briefly
lauding Roberts and Field. An excerpt from a 1977 review in the *Kansas
City Star* conveys the flavor of reviews generated by Niles and "the girls"
during the final concert tours:

> Future generations will remember John Jacob Niles as a great
> folklorist, an accomplished composer, and the compiler of sev-
> eral important collections of traditional American songs. . . .
>   The alto voice has grown wispier over the years, but not a
> whit less expressive in its many colorful inflections. Niles is still

the ideal interpreter of his own compositions—some of which, "Black Is the Color of My True Love's Hair" and "Go Way from My Window"—have become folk classics in their own right.

Jacqueline Roberts and Nancie Field, a soprano and pianist long associated with Niles, performed several of his songs attractively on the first half of the program.[36]

Final Compositions

With the Niles-Merton songs behind him, Niles immediately turned his imagination to larger forms again, composing a vast, lumbering forty-minute oratorio for 150 voices, *Golgotha*. It was composed during 1970, a year of extraordinary political unrest and social protest set against the backdrop bookends of the utopian Woodstock and the violent Altamont festivals, the escalating Vietnam War, the Civil Rights movement, and spring-semester student strikes that closed college campuses nationwide and culminated in vast protests at Washington, D.C. Niles responded to the "ridiculous, ridiculous, ridiculous world," the "world gone mad" commenting:

> I think we're in a very desperate state. Vietnam is an utter mistake. Tonkin Bay was nothing but falsehood and fluff. On the other hand, the young militants of the age are woefully immature thinkers, incapable of analysis, they are completely ignorant of history and probably Communist inspired. What they're protesting against needs to be protested against. But their method! I don't think its necessary to do a Marxist upheaval. I believe there is a way to the hearts of these young people. Not by bashing them over the head, but by leading them back to their sources. Their mothers and fathers should talk to them.[37]

Niles was determined to talk to them. With two young sons himself, Tom now thirty-one and John Ed twenty-five, he quickly sketched in a libretto and music designed to "bridge the cataclysmic gap between young and old and between the races, and between the nations."[38] *Golgotha* was performed twice; first by the Lexington Singers, directed by University of

Kentucky faculty member Donald Ivey at Memorial Hall on March 30, 1971, and then on May 23, 1971, in Charleston, West Virginia, at the Baptist Temple, in a concert presented by the Charleston Civic Chorus, directed by Conrad Eaddy.[39]

The oratorio, or cantata, as it also was termed, allowed Niles to expand ideas from the Niles-Merton songs on a larger canvas, while making a "Zen Christian" statement about peace. Unfortunately, the composition was not successful in musical terms; and removed from the political context of its creation today, it appears rather self-indulgent and dated.

Niles's final large-scale work, *The King and the Common Man*, represented the very first paid commission that he ever received. With the 1976 American Bicentennial celebrations building to a crescendo, Immanuel Baptist Church, the largest church in Lexington, asked him to write a cantata for performance on the Fourth of July. Niles recounted the story of his first commission:

> Recently a very important church in Lexington, Kentucky wanted a special piece of music for their Christmas service. And their choir mistress (who is a Minister of Music, incidentally) said, "Johnnie, write me a piece of music that could include children and grownups—two choirs."
>
> I said, "Oh very well. I will try."
>
> "This is a commission: we mean to pay you for this."
>
> "Oh my! Composers are not used to being treated this way! What text do you want me to use?"
>
> "We haven't got any text." I had to write the text and write the tune and do the arrangement for these little voices, and I did it. And to my great surprise, the day I finished the manuscript and handed it to her, she handed me a check! I nearly fell in the street! That's not the way composers are treated, you know. They usually hold the bag.[40]

Niles constructed a libretto that presented a short history of the travails of "the common man" as he traveled from England to the shores of America and journeyed along the Wilderness Road to Crab Orchard and Fort Boonesboro, Kentucky. The opening section begins: "In Early English times we learn that the mind of George III and the mind of his court was weak and low, while the common man was even poorer than poor, while his taxes increased more and more, because the king and his court made merry by dancing the night away, never thinking of the common man, who sweated both night and day."[41]

Instead of being featured as a separate concert, the cantata was liturgically woven into the morning worship service as the "offertory" movement. It was directed by Bill Williams and accompanied by organist Daniel Tilford; the soprano soloist was, as usual, Jacqueline Roberts. The festival work suited the occasion and was well received by the audience, but there was not much of enduring substance in the cantata to command additional performances. Still, the fact that Niles was still writing large-scale compositions at age eighty-four at all was remarkable.

The Sands Run Out: Final Publications, Last Concerts

For one who had wedded music and verse for so many years, it was most appropriate that Niles closed his publication career by releasing a final volume of poetry. Titled *Brick Dust and Buttermilk* after the Shaker formula for that rich shade of red paint, this collection assembled the old and the new, incorporating song texts and recent poems. The first group of verses is focused on love, while the later poems ponder old age. Symbolically, twin photographs framed the collection, with a young, reflective 1932 Jack Niles gazing out of the front cover and a venerable, wrinkle-creased 1977 Johnnie Niles staring out from the back cover. In between are the poems that sing of a long life dedicated to love, to the muse, to the veneration of nature, and to thoughts occasioned by old age and death.[42]

Brick Dust and Buttermilk was published in early 1977 by Jonathan Greene's Gnomon Press, in association with Niles's own Boone Tolliver label. Greene was an artisan literary publisher who took great care with the design work and carried out the printing process himself. Shortly after the release, Niles began reading poetry and signing books at special appearances and at his final concerts, such as at the opening of the Doris Ulmann Gallery at Berea College, at Ohio State University, at a benefit for the University of Kentucky's Art Museum, at the Kentucky Music Weekend in Louisville, and at New Harmony, Indiana.

But time was running out on Niles's long-running act. On Thursday, September 14, 1978, at 7:30 P.M., Niles took to the stage at Warren Wilson College's brand new Kittredge Recital Hall to perform "a program of American Folk Music."[43] His program consisted of two sets that featured many of the songs that had become associated with him over the past seventy years of his concert career: the love songs "Little Mohee," "Lost Love," "Black Is the Color," "The Swapping Song," "The Sea Witch," "Venezuela," "Go 'Way from My Window," and "Fond Affection"; and the ballads "Pretty Polly," "Babylon," The Cruel Brother," "The Knight and the Shepherd's Daughter," "Little Mattie Groves," and "The Hangman." Niles was alone on stage; "the girls" did not accompany him on this trip. Rena recalled the concluding moments of the evening:

> At the end of the concert, Johnnie walked out to a standing ovation. He bowed and—so I thought—was about to go to the tables where the dulcimers lay, to do an encore. Instead, he walked down to the footlights and said: "Ladies and gentlemen, in years to come you will be able to tell your children and grandchildren that you attended John Jacob Niles's last concert, because my friends, this is it. So goodnight and God bless you.
>
> There was a momentary stillness, as if the audience were gasping collectively. Then applause. Johnnie went back to the tables, checked the tuning on one of the dulcimers and sat down to sing "Amazing Grace," which he had made his trademark years before it came into the repertoire of many others. Finally, he sang "I'm Goin' Away."[44]

So ended Niles's extended concert career, which had taken him from an impromptu Chautauqua afternoon in New Albany, Indiana, to Chicago's Westinghouse Radio, to the Cincinnati Opera, to London's Wigmore Hall, to Carnegie Hall, to the Newport Folk Festival, and finally to Warren Wilson College in Asheville, North Carolina. His father once said to him: "If you stick to this old-timey family music and work at it, you may be able to take it a long way . . . maybe as far as Cincinnati."[45] His father was right—John Jacob did, indeed, make it as far as Cincinnati, but Tommie Niles also greatly underestimated the power of this old-timey music in the hands of his enterprising and talented son.

Niles lived long enough to experience widespread recognition of his career as a performer, a composer, a folk music collector, and a Kentucky legend. He lived a curious life within and without the academy. Although universities and colleges provided his most constant venue for concerts and workshops, he was always subject to suspicion by scholars. Thus, Niles was particularly gratified to receive the slew of honorary doctorates that seemingly validated his career as a collector folklorist. On June 2, 1949, he received the doctor of music degree at the University of Cincinnati, where he gave the commencement address at Wilson Chapel. Additional honorary degrees were bestowed at Transylvania University (June 9, 1968), Episcopal Theological Seminary in Kentucky (May 1970), and the University of Kentucky (May 1973).

Other accolades and awards accompanied his twilight years as well. In a more creative sort of tribute, the Walden Theatre in Louisville presented a musical, *My Days as a Youngling,* based on Niles's early life. With a script written by Nancy Niles Sexton, Vaughn McBride, and Martha Harrison Jones, the play depicted formative scenes from Niles's youth—his move from Louisville to the farm, his adolescent love relationships, his performance with the show in Indiana, and the writing of "Go 'Way from My Window." Niles attended the preview performance on October 6, 1978, and took part in the filming of the production for WKPC-TV.[46]

On January 19, 1979, Niles suffered a heart blockage and became wheelchair-bound. Despite weakness and pain, Niles participated in two sets of recordings that Jackie Roberts made—*Niles-Merton Songs* and *Songs by John Jacob Niles.*[47] Although Niles could not communicate in words, his eyes showed that he was following the music closely. Then on Saturday, March 1, 1980, John Jacob Niles quietly passed away. The burial ceremony was held at St. Hubert's Church, the little Episcopalian country chapel for which he had carved the doors many years before. Niles's voice was finally silenced. Symbolically, there was no singing at the funeral service—the only music was the sound of the organ playing "I Wonder as I Wander" as the recessional. Afterward Niles was laid to rest in the Kentucky soil he loved so dearly.

Sunset in Clark County, Kentucky

The sun drops below the shadow-shrouded hills of Kentucky's rolling bluegrass and etches a final image of springtime's freshly verdant trees. From my upstairs porch, you can just make out the silhouette of that first wave of mountains on the other side of the snaky green Kentucky River. Looking out over the rugged fieldstone walls hugging Grimes Mill Road, it is less than a mile to John Jacob Niles's Boot Hill Farm, cradled in a bend of Boone Creek. The same creek that was home to frontiersman Daniel Boone in 1773 was Niles's home from 1939 until his death in 1980.

The twilight casts long shadows over St. Hubert's bucolic graveyard as evening mists settle over the walnut trees and the serene pond. Here John Jacob rests next to his wife, Rena Lipetz Niles, under a simple granite marker that lies flush with the lush bluegrass. The stone reads simply: "John Jacob Niles 1892–1980." Here, at the end, is where the story of John Jacob Niles ends.

> When I am just a whisper in the wind,
> The wind that blows so often east to west,
> When I am just a whisper in the wind
> And all the breath that once did raise my voice
> Has joined the breath that whispers in the wind,
> Even then my song will never die
> And join the ghostly whisper of the wind,
> Even then my song will never be hung on willow trees
> That sway with the wind,
> Torn and tattered as moldering dust.
> Even then my song will swirl and spin
> And find men's hearts to rest therein:
> Even then my song will swirl and spin.[48]

Coda

But the story does not really end. It continues with a birthday party. At just past six thirty on Friday evening, April 28, 2006, exactly 116 years after John Jacob Niles was born, guests begin to arrive at the lovely Lexington home of Jackie and Helm Roberts. Pianist Nancie Field, still keen and spry, is already seated on the sofa chatting with Hannah Shepherd, close confidante of Rena Niles, in the commodious living room that was designed by Helm as a concert space inspired by the Boot Hill Farm "stage."[1] Actress Janet Scott is engaged in animated discussion with Jackie as I and my wife, Hooey, arrive and greet the company. A few minutes later musicologist and vocal coach Tedrin Blair Lindsay arrives in the company of singer Sherri Phelps. Other guests gradually congregate: Reeda and Brad Leasor, Geneva and El Davidson, neighbor Joyce Chan, and Bryan and Nancy Potter. Convivial conversation flows easily among the guests, all longstanding friends of the Robertses and all connected in some way to the long absent, yet very present birthday guest—John Jacob Niles.

After enjoying the opportunity to catch up on news and gossip over a glass of wine and hors d'oeuvres, we are gently shepherded by Jackie into the dining room, where we stand for a moment behind our chairs as Helm eloquently delivers verbatim the lengthy grace that Johnnie Niles customarily gave. We sit down to Boot Hill Farm's traditional Kentucky menu of "old ham," corn pudding, and a green salad, and various toasts are offered to the host and hostess and to John Jacob Niles. The meal is delicious; Jackie cooks as well as she sings. Conversations around the table are generously sprinkled with amusing anecdotes related to Rena and Johnnie. Gradually the animated cacophony subsides, dishes are cleared, and the meal closes with the lustily sung birthday song.

The table is briskly cleared, and back in the living room, the evening continues with a celebration of Niles's life and career in song and word. First Tedrin sits at the piano and accompanies Sherri in a set of Niles's songs. Their ease and style, born of many previous concerts together, are evident as they perform "Jesus, Jesus, Rest Your Head," "The Lass from the Low Countree," and "Black Is the Color of My True Love's Hair." Tedrin remains at the piano and sings and plays "The Rovin' Gambler" and "The Gambler's Lament." It is fascinating how different voices and different interpretations bring out new perspectives in these songs that seem so simple and direct yet are also so elegant and complex.

Next Janet Scott rises and unexpectedly reads aloud several passages from the *John Jacob Niles Cookbook*. Scott, an accomplished actress, invests the lists of ingredients and terse directions with sparkle and humor. Then, with scholarly gravitas, I open an early typescript of this book and declaim from the opening pages: "The sun creeps over the mist-shrouded hills of Kentucky's rolling bluegrass and ignites the amber and scarlet leaves clinging to the autumnal trees. . . ." Finally, it is time for more music, and Jackie moves to the piano and sings four love songs, "My Lover Is a Farmer Lad," "Unused I Am to Lovers," "Go 'Way from My Window," and "The Wild Rider." In a last brief benediction, Jackie brings out her dulcimer and artfully conjures up visions of mist-shrouded valleys, ancient Nativity carols, and playful children's frolics. Her lovely voice and her poise also manifest a healthy dose of showmanship acquired from Niles during her years of concertizing with the old master.[2]

The impromptu concert concludes, the contented guests linger for a few minutes in fond farewells, and they gradually disperse. It was a lovely evening and a sincere tribute, proof that John Jacob Niles, though gone, is far from forgotten in his bluegrass home.

"And not forgotten," I reflected on the ride home. Various recent CD reissues have made his music available to a new generation of listeners, and several new performances have been recorded, allowing the music to live vibrantly in our time.[3] Niles's culminating collection of balladry, *The Ballad Book*, was republished in a new edition in 2000, with a foreword that I wrote, and an unlikely new arrangement of his music has even been recently issued. A manuscript for Arnold Schoenberg's a cappella choral adaptation of Niles's "My Horses Ain't Hungry" was uncovered by Severine Neff in 2004, reconstructed by Allen Anderson, and released in 2007.[4] Niles's legacy has been publicly acknowledged in several ways, including his induction into the Kentucky Music Hall of Fame and Museum in 2006 and the designation of a "star" for him on Lexington's Main Street in 2007.[5] The Graduate String Quartet at the University of Kentucky was named the Niles Quartet in 1990. Various publications and releases have kept Niles's name before the public. Jackie Roberts's memoirs of her years concertizing with Niles were published, along with a CD release of Niles's songs, in time for the dedication of the John Jacob Niles Center for American Music in 2001.[6] Studs Terkel's collection of interviews with musicians, *And They All Sang,* begins with an extended conversation with Niles, and Bob Dylan's autobiographical *Chronicles* includes a vivid paragraph noting the influence Niles had on him: "Niles was nontraditional, but he sang traditional songs. A Mephistophelean character out of Carolina, he hammered away at some harplike instrument and sang in a bone chilling soprano voice. Niles was eerie and illogical, terrifically intense and gave you goosebumps." In addition, the documentary film on Bob Dylan, *No Direction Home,* featured a haunting scene of Niles performing, accompanied by a small chorus.[7]

Niles's personal relationship and professional collaboration with Doris Ulmann remains an intriguing story. Noted author Sallie Bingham wrote a script, *Piggyback,* based on the well-known photographic image of Niles helping Ulmann across Cutshin Creek in 1932. The play was produced at Horse Cave Theatre in Kentucky in 1993, and subsequently several film scripts have been developed around that same theme, although they have never been produced. A more scholarly inquiry into the Niles-Ulmann collaboration took place at a colloquium sponsored by the J. Paul Getty Museum in 1994; an edited version of the discussion was published two years later.[8]

More recently, a Google search of "Niles" on the Internet yielded 149,000 sites and references, from conversational threads on the folk listserv "mudcat," to a *Wikipedia* entry, to a John Jacob Niles Web site (www .JohnJacobNiles.com) containing biographical and discographical material compiled by Barry Alfonso. The Web also reveals an extensive site for the John Jacob Niles Center for American Music.[9] It is here that much of the Niles past lives on into the future at the University of Kentucky.

Niles at age eighty-five. Photo by Tony Leonard. John Jacob Niles Photographic Collection, PA82M9269b, Special Collections and Digital Programs, University of Kentucky.

The Center for American Music proudly bears the name John Jacob Niles in part because of the family's generous gift that allowed the vision of such a center to become a reality. But the name was also chosen because Niles's life and work as a composer, collector, performer, and scholar closely mirrors the mission of the center. As Niles's career included aspects of traditional music, popular music, and art music, so the center seeks to be an inclusive home to all American musics, from bluegrass to jazz to opera. As Niles was a scholar and collector, the center seeks to collect American music manuscripts, letters, books, and recordings, so that future scholarship may be encouraged. As Niles was a performer and a composer, the center seeks to nurture musical art by hosting performances and presentations. As Niles was a Kentuckian, the center intends to support the music that lives closest to home, focusing on the bluegrass, the Commonwealth of Kentucky, the Southeast, and the United States.[10]

The Niles Gallery in the Lucille C. Little Fine Arts Library features, at its entrance, a vast glass display case full of handmade musical instruments, including four large dulcimers handcrafted by Niles. Inside the hall, exhibit cases display books, manuscripts, photographs, recordings, letters, and artifacts documenting the rich and varied life of the Kentucky balladeer, composer, and author. A gorgeous 1864 quilt from Clark County, Kentucky, hangs on the wall behind the stage area and is flanked by two hand-carved interior doors from the Niles home, beautifully framed by noted University of Kentucky craftsman Lynn Sweet. The mahogany walls and hardwood oak floor glow in rich, woody tones. The resonant acoustics of the room allow the space to sing like a full-voiced cello.

Next to the gallery, the Niles Study Room, graced by Niles's hand-carved furniture and paintings, provides a welcoming oasis for scholars using the center's archives, including the John Jacob Niles Collection, the Glenn and Helen Wilcox Collection of American music, the John L. Lair Research Library, the Woodsongs Archives, the Charles Faber Collection of Country Music Recordings, and the Temple Adath Israel Choral Music Collection.[11] There is also a spacious "green room" for performers, a sound digitalization work space, a temperature- and humidity-controlled closed stack area, and an office for the director.

The physical space of the center embraces a wide range of activity, including auditions, recitals, lectures, conferences, and the "Appalachia in the Bluegrass" concert series, which has welcomed musicians such as Mike Seeger, the Carolina Chocolate Drops, Howard Levy, Lee Sexton, J. D. Crowe, Red State Ramblers, Ginny Hawker and Tracy Schwarz, John Cohen, Alice Gerrard, and Homer Ledford.[12] The Niles Gallery opens its doors to all aspects of music, particularly the American music that John Jacob Niles cherished.

Thirty years and more after his death, the cultural work of John Jacob Niles continues to resonate. Music he collected, composed, arranged, and adapted is still widely performed. His performances live on through recordings. His words and ideas still circulate in print. And his life and career still exert unflagging energy that sparks the celebration of America's musical heritage.

Notes

"Autobiography" in the notes refers to the final version of John Jacob Niles's unpublished typescript autobiography, edited by David Burg and currently in the possession of the author. The John Jacob Niles Collection in the Special Collections Library at the University of Kentucky holds other items, here designated "JJNC," followed by a box number, a folder number, and sometimes a place within the folder, indicated by a letter (a, b, c, etc.) or by page numbers within an item, such as a field notebook. For example, JJNC, 45/2 is the second folder in box 45 of the Niles Collection.

Overture

1. Henry Enoch, *Grimes Mill, Kentucky Landmark on Boone Creek, Fayette County* (Bowie, MD: Heritage Books, 2002).

2. Winnifred Madden Morris donated the land where St. Hubert's was built.

3. John Jacob Niles, *Brick Dust and Buttermilk* (Frankfort, KY: Boone Tolliver Press; dist. by Gnomon Press, 1977), n.p.

4. "New Records," *Time,* December 23, 1946.

5. *Life,* September 1943, 57–64. Noted as the "first in a long succession of folk singers to appear at Carnegie Hall; Niles often performed his arrangements of American regional tunes on lutes or dulcimers that he himself had handcrafted." "The Fall and Rise of America's Most Celebrated Stage: 100 Years of Carnegie Hall," *Town and Country* (July 1990): 75. He performed at the White House on at least four occasions: March 22 and April 15, 1934, and March 22 and May 6, 1935.

6. Ellen Stekert defines the term "singer of folksong" (contrasted with "folksinger") as "a person (usually from the city) who learned songs from traditions other than his own, and who performed them in a style other than that of the traditional culture from which the songs came." Ellen Stekert, "Cents and Nonsense in the Urban Folksong Movement, 1930–66," in *Transforming Tradition: Folk Music Revivals Examined,* edited by Neil V. Rosenberg (Urbana: Univ. of Illinois Press, 1993), 105.

7. His first performance was in 1907, when he accompanied performers at a vaudeville-Chautauqua show in New Albany in 1907. His final performance was at Warren Wilson College at Asheville, NC, September 14, 1978.

8. Gene Bluestein, *Poplore* (Amherst: Univ. of Massachusetts Press, 1994), 9.

9. Ibid., 23.

10. Rena Niles, "Recollections," typescript of an oral account recorded September 1985, in possession of the author, p. 11.

1. The Families Gather at the River

1. The city of Portland described here no longer exists; it merged with Louisville in 1852. The city of Portland in Adair County, Kentucky, today is unrelated to the former Jefferson County town.

2. General William Lytle bought three thousand acres of land from Henry Clay and Fortunatus Cosby to build a canal. To raise money for the project, he subdivided his land into lots to be sold. His agent, Joshua G. Barclay, named the prospective town Portland, and his surveyor, Alexander Ralston, laid out the six-block grid of "Portland Proper" between 1812 and 1814.

3. Jacqueline Roberts and Kerstin Warner, *A Journey with John Jacob Niles: A Memoir of My Years with Johnnie* (Lexington: Univ. of Kentucky Libraries, 2001), 68.

4. This information about Engelbert comes from the Louisville Directory of 1832.

5. John B. Graff was born about 1820 in France and had married Mary Louisa Perry January 21, 1845, in Floyd County, Indiana. The Graff family settled on both sides of the Ohio River, in New Albany, Indiana, and Portland, Kentucky. It would appear likely that Sarah was a sister to John B. Graff. See the Graff Genealogy Page on the Web, www.geocities.com/Heartland/Estates/7998/grafftree1 .htm.

6. Unfortunately, a series of floods, in particular the great flood of 1937, seems to have destroyed the last of the pianos built by Adams. John E. Adams died in 1890 and Sarah in 1899. They are buried together at Cave Hill Cemetery on 701 Baxter Road, Louisville, with a joint headstone that simply identifies them as "mother" and "father."

7. The death certificate, vol. 060, no. 29532, notes that he was eighty-eight years of age when he died on December 11, 1925, which would certify his birth in 1837.

8. Kaiser Wilhelm's grandmother was Queen Victoria, and her husband was Prince Albert of Saxe-Coburg-Gotha. There were assassination attempts on Victoria in 1849 and 1850.

9. James Brown Ewell "Jeb" Stuart, a Confederate cavalry general.

10. Niles, "Autobiography," 34–35.

11. Robert Niles, personal correspondence, January 21, 2004.

12. The company is presently the Cumberland Loan.

13. Robert Niles, personal correspondence, January 21, 2004.

14. Jacob's wife, Louisa C. Reisch, was born in 1849 and died on May 2, 1929, at age eighty in Jefferson County, Kentucky.

15. Tommy West, "John Jacob Niles: Balladeer, Woodworker, Maker of Dulcimers, Gentleman Farmer, Storyteller . . . ," *Cincinnati Enquirer,* May 17, 1970.

16. Niles, "Autobiography," 36.

17. Her maiden name is unknown; Niles refers to her as Anna Bell Tolliver.

18. An advertisement in *Carron's Directory* described the Fischer-Leaf Company as "manufacturers of marbleized iron and slate mantels and grates, stoves, air grates, dealers in all kinds of brass goods, and agents for American, English, and French tiles for halls vestibules, and hearths." See *Carron's Directory of the City of Louisville,* 1886, 284.

19. Niles, "Autobiography," 152.

20. Nancy Niles Sexton, interview by the author, Louisville, September 1985. It was the family's belief that Tolliver was John Tolliver Niles's mother's maiden name.

21. I believe this "Mary Niles" is actually Ann Renouf's sister Mary, who was married a year later to Henry Ernst in a ceremony witnessed by John Niles and Ann Elizabeth Niles.

22. Robert Niles, personal correspondence, January 21, 2004.

23. *Louisville Courier-Journal,* March 31, 1890. Eastern Cemetery is not maintained, and graves were regularly "re-used" after 1870, but the Day Books do list burials for both Anna E. Niles and John Renouf on March 30, 1890. Philip DiBlasi, staff archaeologist, Univ. of Louisville, personal correspondence, December 13, 1996.

24. All of Tommie and Lula's children were born in rooms that the family occupied over the grocery and bar except the last one, Charles, who was born at the farm on Inverness Avenue.

25. Noel Coppage, "John Jacob Niles," *Stereo Review* 84:1 (January 1975): 58.

26. Niles, "Autobiography," 44–46. According to an 1884 Portland map, the Duncan Street School was on the block bounded by Seventeenth and Eighteenth streets and Duncan and Columbia.

27. Niles, "Autobiography," 69–71. Frank Villella, archivist for the Rosenthal Archives of the Chicago Symphony Orchestra, noted that it was "quite possible that the Orchestra performed a run out in Louisville in 1900." There were no Mahler performances recorded during Thomas's tenure; the first performance was by Frederick Stock in the 1906–7 season and was the Mahler Fifth symphony. Frank Villella, personal e-mail communication, November 24, 2003.

28. JJNC, 45/2a.

29. Niles, "Autobiography," 74–76.

30. Stephen Foster, "American Experience," www.pbs.org/wgbh/amex/foster/sfeature/sf_minstrelsy_1.html.

31. See Fred E. Cox, John Randolph, and John Harris, "Jug Bands of Louisville," *Storyville* 159 (September 1994); 161 (December 1994). These are excerpts from "The Jug Bands of Louisville," an unpublished 1978 manuscript written by Fred E. Cox in 1978.

32. He noted that on one occasion he "tried to play dance music" on "a rather terrible piano." He "played only when the jug band was resting and drinking some throat-scorching moonshine." Niles, "Autobiography," 143.

33. "Vaudeville," http://xroads.virginia.edu/~ma02/easton/vaudeville/vaudevillemain .html. The same site explains that

> problematically, the term "vaudeville," itself, referring specifically to American variety entertainment, came into common usage after 1871 with the formation of Sargent's Great Vaudeville Company of Louisville, Kentucky, and had little if anything to do with the vaudeville of the French theatre. Variety showman, M. B. Leavitt claimed the word originated from the French "vaux de ville" "worth of the city, or worthy of the city's patronage," but in all likelihood, as Albert McLean suggests, the name was merely selected "for its vagueness, its faint, but harmless exoticism, and perhaps its connotation of gentility." Leavitt and Sargent's shows differed little from the coarser material presented in earlier itinerant entertainments, although their use of the term to provide a veneer of respectability points to an early effort to cater variety amusements to the growing middle class.

34. JJNC, 45/2a.

35. Niles, "Autobiography," 4–23. This account is also discussed in JJNC, 45/2a.

36. For example, "Black Is the Color of My True Love's Hair" was noted as collected at "Airy [*sic*] on Troublesome Creek, Perry County, KY." In fact, he did collect a version of the text and tune from the Combs family at Ary, but the version he published in *More Songs of the Hill Folk* (New York: G. Schirmer, 1936) couples the Ary version of the text with a tune that was completely composed by Niles. By the time G. Schirmer published *The Songs of John Jacob Niles* in 1993, the attribution for "Black Is the Color of My True Love's Hair" appropriately stated, "Text collected and adapted by John Jacob Niles. Music by John Jacob Niles."

37. Niles, "Autobiography," 77–79. The essential points of this account are corroborated through an October 12, 2006, entry in JJNC, 45/2/24, that provides a map of the Graham family's location and notes: "Words of Graham family's song copied from mother's note book—it was kept in the piano bench with my song manuscript for many years." A subsequent entry in the same notebook (December 24, 2006) says: "Mother asked for some kind of singable version

of the Graham family song, so I am trying to finish it off." The autobiography account wrongly states that it was nine years before he completed a version of the song. See field notebook, JJNC, 45/2.

2. The Move to Rural Jefferson County

1. Niles, "Autobiography," 94.

2. Ibid., 104–105. R. E. Olds is Ransom Eli Olds (1864–1950), who released the first Olds automobile in 1897. However, it was Henry Martin Leland, whose design had been rejected by Olds, who released the first Cadillac through Henry Ford on October 17, 1902. By 1906 there were fifty model H Cadillacs manufactured. Thus, Niles's letter to R. E. Olds might have been inspired by the sight of these early Cadillacs, but R. E. Olds had nothing to do with the Cadillac plant. Credit for the automatic turn signal and brake light is generally attributed to the actress Florence Lawrence, who designed an "auto signaling arm" attached to the rear bumper of a car by 1914. Kelly R. Brown, *Florence Lawrence, The Biograph Girl: America's First Movie Star* (Jefferson, NC: McFarland, 1999).

3. DuPont Manual High School, www.dupontmanual.com/about.htm (accessed March 27, 2010).

4. Niles, "Autobiography," 106, 116. Niles was not a tall person as an adult; he reached a height of 5 feet 9 inches, according to the generous record on his 1935 New York driver's license, which also noted his weight as 160, his eyes as blue, and his hair as grey.

5. Niles later introduced the song in concerts by describing it as an early protest song recorded in 1642 in which Oliver Cromwell was parodied through comparisons to a hog and other animals.

6. Niles, "Autobiography," 150–151. The account is also included in John Jacob Niles, *The Ballad Book* (New York: Houghton Mifflin, 1960; rev. ed., Lexington: Univ. Press of Kentucky, 2000), 122.

7. JJNC, 45/2/51–52.

8. Lila W. Edmands's groundbreaking "Songs from the Mountains of North Carolina," *Journal of American Folklore* 6:21 (April–June 1893): 131–134, and an article by Katherine Pettit (cofounder of Hindman Settlement School) in the *Journal of American Folklore* (1907) were among the earliest efforts at folk collection, but it was not until Cecil Sharp's visits to the southern mountains between 1915 and 1917 and the subsequent publication of his influential *English Folk Songs from the Southern Appalachians* (1917) that folk collection activity began to accelerate.

9. *Five Gambling Songs* was published by G. Schirmer in 1941 and recorded on Camden CAL 219 (*John Jacob Niles Sings American Folk and Gambling Songs*) and Tradition TLP 1036 (*An Evening with John Jacob Niles*).

10. JJNC, 45/2/42.

11. The two songs are both versions of "The Elfin Knight," Child ballad 2.

12. Niles, "Autobiography," 175–176. I have edited this account.

13. Niles, *Ballad Book,* 17–19.

14. For instance, see David Reed Parker, "John Jacob Niles and Revisionist Folklore: The Corpus Christi Carol/"Down in Yon Forest," *Southern Folklore* 49:2 (1992): 147–156.

15. Cecil Sharp, Maude Karpeles, and Olive Dame Campbell, *English Folk Songs from the Southern Appalachians: Comprising Two Hundred and Seventy-four Songs and Ballads, with Nine Hundred and Sixty-eight Tunes, Including Thirty-nine Tunes Contributed by Olive Dame Campbell* (London: Oxford Univ. Press, 1932), preface, xviii. Cecil Sharp was the pioneering British folklorist who founded what became the English Folk Dance and Song Society (1911) and collected English-derived balladry in the United States during 1916–1918. Maude Karpeles (1885–1976) was the British dance folklorist who collaborated with Sharp on his 1916–1918 American folk collecting trips. Generally Karpeles had responsibility for the lyrics while Sharp notated the music.

16. JJNC, 45/1.

17. John Jacob Niles, "The Passing of the Street Cry," *Scribner's Monthly* 87:3 (September 1929): 265–271. For the "several others," see JJNC, 46/4/161, 164–165. RCA Red Seal recordings, 1939; the arrangement was later re-released on Camden CAL 219.

18. Ray Brown, former rector of Holy Trinity Church, Georgetown, Kentucky, in conversation with the author in December 1997, said that of the three great original branches of Christianity, "the Anglican Church is the church of the Nativity; the Roman Catholic Church is the church of the Passion; and the Orthodox Church was the church of the Resurrection." With his abiding interest in the Christmas story, Niles clearly felt most comfortable with the Episcopal Church. In addition, he was a close personal friend of Bishop William R. Moody of the Episcopal Diocese of Lexington. Niles's gravesite is just a few yards away from Bishop Moody and his wife's plot at St. Hubert's Cemetery.

19. JJNC, 45/4.

20. JJNC, 45/2/81–82.

21. Niles, "Autobiography," 124–127, edited by the author. An interesting conflation of the dual role of woman as "Whore of Babylon" and as "Madonna" is revealed in a sketch of Niles's "Jesus, Jesus Rest Your Head" contained in JJNC, 45/2a. Here, between stanzas of the text, Niles interjects a graphic observation of Bridgett's charms, just as though it was a line of the song text:

Jesus, Jesus rest your head
You has got a manger bed
All the evil folk on earth
Sleep in feathers at your birth

Jesus, Jesus rest your head
You have got a manger bed

Bridgett's titties are so lovely—the down between her legs is dark brown

Have you heard about our Jesus
Have you heard about his fate
How his mother went to that stable
On Christmas Eve so late.

22. Coppage, "John Jacob Niles," 58.

23. Niles, "Autobiography," 143–144. "Objerall" is probably a misspelling of "overall."

24. JJNC, 45/1. Although Niles notes this as 1908 in various accounts, it is possible that the date of this first record of the tune is considerably earlier, since it is contained within other notebook entries of 1905–1906, such as the brake-light diagram.

25. JJNC, 45/2a.

26. JJNC, 45/2/84.

27. JJNC, 45/2/82.

28. John Jacob Niles, *The Songs of John Jacob Niles* (New York: G. Schirmer, 1993), 6–7.

29. JJNC, 45/2/71–72.

30. JJNC, 45/22/70.

31. JJNC, 45/4.

32. Niles usually ended the introduction by reporting Blanche's statement this way: "She said I was no composer, no singer, and no poet." After a pregnant pause, Niles then would add: "She was mistaken, of course."

33. Niles, "Autobiography," 165–166.

34. The song's popularity is manifest in recordings by diverse artists such as Joan Baez (Vanguard VSD 79160), Burl Ives (United Artists VAL 3060), and Harry Belafonte (RCA LPM1927) as well as the continuous sales of arrangements for choral ensembles by G. Schirmer/Music Sales.

35. In 1588 a license was granted to print a blackletter ballad, "Goe from My Window." There is a discussion of this song in James Johnson, William Stenhouse, Robert Burns, Stephen Clarke, and Henry George Farmer, *The Scots Musical Museum* (Hatboro, PA: Folklore Associates, 1962), 498, 501–502, with both Scottish and English versions of the song.

36. *Folk Song and Minstrelsy,* Vanguard SRL 7624. Ronnie Gilbert's performance is on side 2, band 2.

37. *Another Side of Bob Dylan,* Columbia CS 8993, 1964.

38. JJNC, 45/2/68.

3. Independence and Adventure

1. JJNC, 45/2/28.

2. Brunsviga Type B mechanical adding machines were first manufactured in 1894 and were made until 1925.

3. The Burroughs Adding Machine Company traced its founding to William Seward Burroughs, who invented and patented the first workable adding and listing machine in St. Louis, Missouri, in 1885. To produce and market his machine, Burroughs and three other men (Thomas Metcalfe, R. M. Scruggs, and W. C. Metcalfe) formed the American Arithmometer Company on January 20, 1886. The company's product "line" consisted of a single model, a straight adding and listing machine that sold for $475.

4. Michael Hancock, "History, 1857–1953," Burroughs Adding Machine Company, www.dotpoint.com/xnumber/hancock7.htm.

5. JJNC, 45/2/92.

6. Niles, "Autobiography," 198.

7. Ibid., 198–200. The annual "Court Days" held in county seats drew folks from outlying farms into the bustling community of the town for a few days of trading and entertainment while the circuit court was in session. Jean Thomas, founder of the American Folksong Festival, discovered fiddler William Day ("Jilson Setters") at Court Days in Ashland, Kentucky. Today, the Court Days tradition has all but disappeared in Kentucky except for the Mount Sterling celebration in Montgomery County.

8. JJNC, 45/2.

9. JJNC, 45/2; 45/2/65, 77.

10. Niles, "Autobiography," 203.

11. Ibid., 212.

12. JJNC, 45/1, unpaginated (last two pages).

13. Hibler later owned the large Hibler Hotel at the base of Main Street, right beside the bridge over the Kentucky River.

14. Niles, "Autobiography," 222.

15. Ibid., 229–230. Niles collected the carol "No Shelter for Mary" in Index, KY, in May 1913. In his notebook he mentions simply "a tall, beautiful dirt poor woman deserted by her husband." JJNC, 45/2. Niles published "No Shelter for Mary" in his collection *Ten Christmas Carols from the Southern Appalachian Mountains* (New York: G. Schirmer, 1935), under the title "See Jesus the Saviour."

16. JJNC, 45/2/26.

17. JJNC, 45/2/20.

18. In *More Songs of the Hill Folk,* Niles attributed this song to "Airy on Troublesome Creek, Perry County, KY."

19. JJNC, 45/2.

20. JJNC, 46/4.

21. JJNC, 45/2.

22. The song and its origins still have the power to excite contemporary discussion. For an extensive conversation thread concerning "Black Is the Color," see the Mudcat Web site, www.mudcat.org/thread.cfm?threadid=32248.

23. *Sing Out!* 12 (December 1962): 41.

24. Cecil Sharp, *English Folk Songs from the Southern Appalachians* (New York: Putnam's, 1917), 255. Also printed in Alan Lomax, *The Folksongs of North America* (Garden City, NY: Doubleday, 1960), 206–207. Interestingly, Sharp collected his version on September 15, 1916, more than a month later than Niles's versions. Jean Ritchie, *Folk Songs of the Southern Appalachians as Sung by Jean Ritchie* (New York: Oak Publications, 1965; reprint, Lexington: Univ. Press of Kentucky, 1997).

25. Troublesome Creek flows through the town of Ary in Perry County, KY, where Niles collected his version. The Clyde River rises in the Lowther Hills of South Lanarkshire, flows northwest through the heart of Glasgow, and then widens to form the Firth of Clyde.

26. Ritchie, *Folk Songs*, 94. Jean Ritchie said, in personal correspondence on January 22, 2004:

Funny you asked about "Black Is the Color." Elektra, via Warner Brothers and Rhino, are reissuing three of my early records, the first two Elektra ones and the WB one done much later, as a set. I have been going over the old notes, and my note on EKLP-2 (Elektra's first folk recording) says about "Black . . ." that we learned it at Brasstown, and that Cecil Sharp had found it in NC in 1916. In another note I credited it to Lizzie Roberts, as I had seen it in one of Sharp's books. Anyway, us Ritchies have known it since about mid-1930s when Edna, Jewel, and Kitty were attending the summer short courses in folk music and dance at the John C. Campbell Folk School. I started going too, when I was in high school, and later was on the staff there.

Maybe one of the reasons we loved that song, aside from the wonderful harmonies we enjoyed when singing it, was that some very similar lyrics were in an old banjo picking song we had. One of the verses:

O that pretty little girl, sixteen years old,
Hair just as yeller as the flamin' gold,
The sweetest face and the neatest hands,
God bless the ground on where she stands.

We called it the "Poor and Rambling Boy." The language is much more down-to-earth and easy to understand, and I always wondered, and still do, which came first, the chicken or the egg?

27. Kelly's Hall was in Louisville at the intersection of Taylor and Bluegrass Roads.

28. JJNC, 45/2.

4. Jack Niles Goes Off to War

1. Roberta Voorhies was buried next to her father in Louisville's Cave Hill Cemetery, lot 93, section 9.

2. JJNC, 45/5.

3. Niles, "Autobiography," 246.

4. On August 1, 1907, the Army Signal Corps established an Aeronautical Division, and on July 18, 1914, it organized the Aviation Section of the Signal Corps. It was not until the National Security Act of 1947 that the U.S. Air Force was established as an independent branch of the armed services.

5. See Niles, "Autobiography," 102–103; and JJNC, 45/4/4–5, for an account of the glider that Niles constructed and flew in 1905.

6. Niles, "Autobiography," 255–256. "Rudolph's narrative" was from Puccini's opera *La Bohème*; "Rogers" refers to James Hotchkiss Rogers (1857–1940), who wrote a song cycle and other art and lyric songs; "There Is a Long, Long Trail . . ." was Zo Elliott and Stoddard King's popular song from 1914.

7. American Expeditionary Force air squadrons located at Issoudun included the 10th, 21st, 26th, 30th, 31st, 32nd, 33rd, 35th, 37th, 43rd, 101st, 149th, 158th, 173rd, 257th, 369th, 372nd, 374th, 640th, 641st, 642nd, 644th, 801st, 802nd, and 1104th. Information concerning Issoudun is from www.worldwar1.com/dbc/issodun.html. Dwight Messimer provided much of the material for this Web site.

8. JJNC, 45/6.

9. Bert Hall and John Jacob Niles, *One Man's War* (New York: Henry Holt, 1929; reprint, New York: Ayer, 1980).

10. The commandant at Foggia was Captain Fiorello LaGuardia, formerly a flyer with the Lafayette Escadrille and later the mayor of New York City from 1934 to 1945.

11. The Alberto Dei Piccoli hotel is located at 15 Villa Borghese in Rome.

12. "Carol of the Polish Grenadiers" was published as Carl Fischer 30505.

13. Niles noted the different aircraft included Spads, Sopwith Camels, Salmsons, Breguets, Caudrons, Bats, Snipes, Libertys, Hadley-Paiges, Dolphins, and Snarks. A complete list with commentary is found in his "Autobiography," 303–304.

14. Niles, "Autobiography," 306–307.

15. Ibid., 354, 356.

16. Special Order 121 succinctly notes only that as of October 14, 1918, Niles was "relieved of further treatment at this hospital as of Class A and will return to his proper replacement unit." JJNC, 57/3.

17. Niles, "Autobiography," 383.

18. I have not successfully identified a member of the faculty at the Schola Cantorum with the name of Clothilde Marcel.

19. Douglas Moore also studied with d'Indy at this time, so it is possible that Niles and Moore became acquainted musically through d'Indy. Moore and Niles later collaborated on several projects.

20. Niles, "Autobiography," 392.

21. Niles said of this studio, "Never had I grown so attached to a place as I have that studio—but all my life I have been leaving places which I thought were each ever better than the one before." JJNC, 45/8.

22. JJNC, 45/8.

23. The list includes the songs "Swan" (Ibsen); Grieg, "Prayer" (Morike); Hugo Wolf, "All Souls Day"; "Allah" (Chadwick); "Dedication" (R. Strauss); "Morning of the Year" (Cadman); "Il Mio Tesoro Intanto" (Don Giovanni); "Benedictus" (J. S. Bach B Minor Mass); "Chanson triste" (Duparc); "My Lord, What a Mornin'"; "Danny Boy"; "L'invitation au voyage" (Duparc); "I Stood on the Ribber ob Jordan" (Burleigh); "Les Roses d'Ispahan" (Faure); "Carry Me Back to Old Virginny"; "I Love Thee" (Grieg); "To an Ancient Picture" (Wolf); "When Thou Goest to Thy Flowers" (Wolf). JJNC, 45/7.

24. Niles's trip to France was on the first voyage of the *Covington* (formerly the *Cincinnati*), and he returned on the final voyage of the *Cap Finisterre*.

5. Life after the War

1. Niles's honorable discharge and service papers are located in his Personal Memorabilia Box, JJNC, 57/3.

2. The conservatory, formerly on Highland Avenue at Oak Street, is now the College-Conservatory of Music of the University of Cincinnati and is on Corry Street off Jefferson Avenue.

3. Rockdale Temple is the familiar name for K. K. Ben Israel, the oldest Jewish congregation west of the Allegheny Mountains, founded in 1824. The temple was then at Rockdale and Harvey avenues, near the Cincinnati Zoo. The Jewish seminary is Hebrew Union College, the first permanent Jewish institution of higher learning in the New World, founded in 1875. Rabbi Mark Goldman, K. K. Ben Israel, personal correspondence, February 17, 2004.

4. JJNC, 98/1, concert program.

5. Ralph Lyford founded the Cincinnati Opera Company in June 1920. Nicknamed the "Zoo Opera" because it performed "downwind of the elephants" at the Cincinnati Zoo, it is the nation's second-oldest opera company. Niles, "Autobiography," 436.

6. Dan Beddoe was primarily an oratorio singer who appeared as a tenor soloist in large-chorus productions of the *Messiah*. He also made

test pressings singing in *Les Troyens* for the Edison Cylinder Company in 1912–1913.

7. Niles, "Autobiography," 443. Edgar Stillman Kelley studied in Chicago and at Stuttgart Conservatory in Germany. In 1910 he was appointed professor of composition at Cincinnati conservatory, where he remained until his death in 1944. He was best known for incidental music to a stage production of *Ben Hur*. Cincinnati Conservatory Web site, www.libraries.uc.edu/Libraries/ccm/kelley .html.

8. The Chicago Stockyards, bounded by Pershing, Halsted, Forty-seventh, and Ashland, contained 475 acres served by 130 miles of tracks and 50 miles of roads, according to the Chicago Historical Society.

9. Niles, "Autobiography," 466, 472.

10. Ibid., 467. The Chicago Grand Opera Association had been presenting opera from 1915 to 1922 when the company was re-formed as the Chicago Civic Opera. In 1956 this company became the Lyric Opera of Chicago. Mary Garden was the last director of the Chicago Grand Opera Association.

11. Joseph E. Baudino, a talk given on September 24, 1975, at the Broadcast Pioneers meeting held in the KYW Transmitter Building in Whitemarsh, PA.

12. Niles, "Autobiography," 476–477.

13. Ibid., 480.

14. Mount Auburn is a hillside neighborhood just north of downtown, close by the University of Cincinnati.

15. *The 1920 Federal Population Census: A Catalog of National Archives Microfilm* (Washington, DC: National Archives and Records Administration, 1991); Robert Niles, personal correspondence.

16. The signed collection is now housed in the Special Collections Library of the University of Kentucky. Years later Niles enjoyed a visit by Francis Child's daughter Henrietta to Boot Hill Farm.

17. John Brophy and Eric Partridge, *Songs and Slang of the British Soldier* (London: E. Partridge, 1931). This collection was later revised and republished as *The Long Trail: What the British Soldier Sang and Said in the Great War, 1914–1918* (New York: London House and Maxwell, 1965).

18. Helen Babbitt was born in Des Moines, IA, on December 12, 1896.

19. The Little Theatre Movement was a reformist and progressive trend that attempted to counter the commercialism of movies with live theater, presenting challenging drama in small "alternative" theater spaces. See Dorothy Chansky, *Composing Ourselves: The Little Theatre Movement and the American Audience* (Carbondale: Southern Illinois Univ. Press, 2004).

20. Rena Niles diary, JJNC, 128/1. The diary is now located in the unprocessed Rena Niles Collection, Special Collections and Digital Programs, Univ. of Kentucky; the box is still cataloged as JJNC, 128/1. It is also possible that they met as early as 1918 in France during the war. Joanne Gardner claims that they

met in Europe during the war and that they were married in 1920 and divorced in 1932, although there is no documentation for this. See Joanne M. Gardner, "The Appalachian Troubadour" (bachelor's thesis, College of Notre Dame of Maryland, 1992).

21. Notes contained in JJNC.

22. Niles to Society for the Advancement of the Colored Races, June 20, 1927, NAACP Papers, box C-219, Library of Congress.

23. *Syracuse Post Standard,* January 27, 1929.

24. Niles first met Haswell in World War I. "Pharaoh's Army" was dedicated to Haswell in *Impressions of a Negro Camp Meeting.*

25. Niles noted in his diary: "1932. To Europe to sing spring concerts—separated from Hélène." JJNC, 46/2.

26. Roy Flanagan was a personal friend and the author of *Amber Satyr* (Garden City, NY: Doubleday, Doran, 1932).

27. JJNC, 33/1 (general correspondence series).

28. JJNC, 2/1.

6. Creating a Life in the Big Apple

1. Gustave Schirmer was president of G. Schirmer. His father, also named Gustave Schirmer (1829–1893), had founded the music publishing firm in 1866. Niles's work for Schirmer finally resulted in a catalog of 478 compositions and arrangements. See the sixteen-page G. Schirmer catalog "The Music of John Jacob Niles," in the possession of the author.

2. Alberto Bimboni (1882–1960), a pianist and composer, was a member of the faculty at the Juilliard School. He had accompanied Eugene Ysaÿe and John McCormack, with whom he recorded. As a composer, Bimboni was noted for his songs and for operas such as *Winona* (1926) and *In the Name of Culture* (1949).

3. Coppage, "John Jacob Niles," 58.

4. Niles, "Autobiography," 491.

5. Ronald D. Scofield, "John Jacob Niles Sings Sweet, True," *Santa Barbara News-Press,* October 23, 1953.

6. Oscar Brand, "Review of Boone-Tolliver Recordings," *Saturday Review,* August 29, 1953, as cited in *Current Biography* (Bronx, NY: H. W. Wilson, 1959), 19.

7. Paul Hume, "The Ballad of a Great Vocalist: John Jacob Niles," *Washington Post,* May 4, 1980.

8. Gerard Sheedy, "Southern Accent Distinguishes Niles at Station WFBH," *New York Times,* 1925, clipping in JJNC, 113/1.

9. Chez Helen Morgan opened on September 27, 1927, at the site of the old Club Anatole. It was raided on December 30, 1927, just before the New Year's Eve revels and several days after Morgan's premier as Julie in *Show Boat.*

10. *The Dybbuk* followed the Follies, opening on December 15, 1925.

11. *Abie's Irish Rose,* a burlesque on Anne Nichol's play about interfaith marriage between the Jewish Abie and the Roman Catholic Rosemary, was eventually made into a 1946 film featuring Nancy Carroll.

12. James Weldon Johnson and John Rosamond Johnson, *The Book of American Negro Spirituals* (New York: Viking Press, 1925); *The Second Book of American Negro Spirituals* (New York: Viking Press, 1926).

13. Harry Burleigh, *Negro Spirituals Arranged for Solo Voice: "De Gospel Train"* (London: G. Ricordi, 1931). The "New Negro" movement, which was launched March 21, 1924, at a Civic Club Dinner in New York City, brought together African American writers and white publishers.

14. Foreword to *Impressions of a Negro Camp Meeting,* by John Jacob Niles (New York: Carl Fischer, 1925) (my italics).

15. "Hebrew Children" is a camp-meeting tune attributed to Peter Cartwright in *Sacred Harp,* by B. F. White and E. J. King (Bremen, GA: Sacred Harp, 1971), 133.

16. Niles, *Impressions of a Negro Camp Meeting,* foreword.

17. Magazines such as *Scribner's Monthly, Harper's New Monthly Magazine,* and *Lippincott's* featured entertaining "documentaries" based on "exotic" people and places written for consumption by a middle-class audience. See Henry D. Shapiro, *Appalachia on Our Mind—the Southern Mountains and Mountaineers in the American Consciousness, 1870–1920* (Chapel Hill: Univ. of North Carolina Press, 1978). John Jacob Niles, "Hillbillies," *Scribner's Monthly* 82:5 (November 1927): 601–605.

18. The location of "Sam'l Bradley's island" is certainly based on Niles's familiarity with the various islands and sandbars at the falls of the river between Portland and Louisville.

19. In his autobiography, Niles mistakenly recorded that "In Defense of the Backwoods" was published in 1925 in *Scribner's Monthly* 33:6. In fact, it appeared on pages 738–745 of *Scribner's* 83:6 in June 1928. Ulmann's photos appear in a photo-essay titled "The Mountaineers of Kentucky" on pages 675–681.

20. Niles, "In Defense of the Backwoods," 745.

21. John Jacob Niles, "The Sixth Hangar" *Scribner's Monthly* 84:1 (July 1928); "Hedge Hoppers," *Scribner's Monthly* 85:3 (March 1929): 311–315; "Eleven a.m.," *Scribner's Monthly* 87:1 (January 1930).

22. John Jacob Niles, "Shout, Coon, Shout!" *Musical Quarterly* 16 (October 1930): 516–530.

23. A letter from Charles Scribner's Sons to Niles on May 28, 1929, was accompanied by a check for $175 to reimburse him for "all serial rights to his contribution."

24. The date is from a diary entry by Hall contained in Niles, *One Man's War,* 291. Niles noted in his autobiography that the initial meeting occurred in late December 1928.

25. E. R. Van Gorder, "Bert Hall: Soldier or Scoundrel?" *Cross and Cockade Journal* 4:3 (October 1963), called Hall "America's Bad Boy Ace"; J. David Truby, *Air Classics* (March 1978): 61–65.

26. Lafayette Escadrille, www.acepilots.com.ww1/Lafayette.html (accessed March 28, 2010).

27. Bert Hall, *En L'Air! (In the Air) Three Years on and above Three Fronts* (New York: New Library, 1918).

28. AFI Catalog Silent Films, www.afi.com/members/catalog/DetailView.aspx?s=1&movie=17233.

29. John Jacob Niles, "War Takes to the Air," *Collier's*, April 27, 1929. A *New York Times* column of April 6, 1928, announced, "War Flier Will Try Globe-Girdling Hop," and noted that there was a $27,500 award being offered for the forty-seven-hundred-mile flight that Hall was attempting to make between Seattle and Tokyo in his plane that had been specially designed by Charles A. Levine.

30. Linda Robertson, *The Dream of Civilized Warfare* (Minneapolis: Univ. of Minnesota Press, 2003), 298.

31. The two reviews are from a Henry Holt and Company publicity digest, 2:6 (May 15, 1929), JJNC, 113/1.

32. *One Woman's War* (New York: Macaulay, 1930), v.

33. Niles, "Autobiography," 531.

34. Ibid., 561.

35. Niles, *One Man's War*, 349–350.

36. Botrel had been commissioned by M. Millerand of the French Ministry of War to compile songs, poems, and illustrations as a patriotic gesture. There was a much earlier antecedent, Union officer Thomas Higginson's article on African American songs collected during the American Civil War, published in *Atlantic* in June 1867. Niles was evidently unfamiliar with this article, which reproduced song texts (without tunes) and provided some commentary concerning each song.

37. Detailed information concerning African American involvement in World War I is provided in Emmett J. Scott, *Scott's Official History of the American Negro in The World War* (1919; reprint, New York: Arno Press, 1969).

38. *Singing Soldiers* is not dissimilar in tone and intent to DuBose Heyward's novel *Porgy* (1925) and his play, also named *Porgy*, which became the basis of Gershwin's opera *Porgy and Bess*.

39. NAACP Papers, box C-219, Library of Congress.

40. John Jacob Niles, *Singing Soldiers* (New York: Scribner's, 1927), 59.

41. Olin Downes, "A Study of Soldier Songs," *New York Times*, May 8, 1927, 6.

42. Robert A. Simon, "Some A.E.F. Blues and Tin-Pan Ditties," *New York Evening Post*, April 9, 1927.

43. S. T. Williamson, "Colored Songsters of the A.E.F.," *New York Times*, June 12, 1927, 6–7.

44. John W. Thomason Jr., "Negro War Songs," *New York Herald Tribune*, May 22, 1927.

45. "Negro War Songs Yield Rich Harvest," *Hartford (CT) Courant*, April 3, 1927.

46. "Cast and Forecast," *New York Times*, September 1, 1928.

47. George S. Kaufman—Broadway's Greatest Comic Dramatist, www .georgeskaufman.com/pages/internas.php?SECCIONPAS=Biography.

48. Niles, "Autobiography," 494.

49. The largest artillery in the war was actually German. The "Big Bertha" gun manufactured by Krupps, with a range of over seventy-five miles, shelled Paris from a distance of approximately sixty-six miles away. The German "Amiens Gun" had a barrel that alone weighed forty-five tons.

50. John Jacob Niles, *The Songs My Mother Never Taught Me* (New York: Macaulay, 1929), 104.

51. Niles to Wally Wallgren, February 20, 1929, currently in the possession of the author.

52. A copy of the contract signed by Niles, Wallgren, and A. Lee Furman, president of Macaulay, is contained in JJNC, 33/1.

53. Niles, "Autobiography," 496.

54. The *Stars and Stripes* enjoyed a large circulation of 156,000.

55. Niles, *Songs My Mother Never Taught Me*, 12.

56. Ibid., 209. Language describing African Americans has changed a great deal from the early 1900s. While "colored" possesses demeaning connotations in the twenty-first century, it was a generally accepted polite term at the time. The paternalistic-sounding "colored boys" was essentially no different from "white boys," used frequently by the authors throughout the book. The more highly charged "nigger" was used only once in the book, and that was in the lyrics for "Sally Brown."

57. While *Songs My Mother Never Taught Me* is not a "scholarly edition" with careful attributions and critical notes, there is a list of names under the heading "In Appreciation" that constitutes a partial list of contributors.

58. "Quand La Guerre Est Fini," 57; and "Jamais de la Vie,"184, in Niles, *Songs My Mother Never Taught Me*.

59. *Songs My Mother Never Taught Me*, 13.

60. Ibid., 131, 151.

61. John Jacob Niles, "My Precarious Life in the Public Domain," *Atlantic* 182:6 (December 1948): 130–131.

62. The National Prohibition Act, better known as the Volstead Act, after its sponsor, Republican congressman Andrew Volstead, prohibited the manufacture, transport, and sale of alcohol in the United States. The act was passed in 1919 after the ratification of the Eighteenth Amendment to the Constitution on January 16, 1919.

63. In 1900 Sonneck compiled the *Bibliography of Early Secular American Music* and published it at his own expense. In honor of Sonneck's many bibliographic and scholarly contributions, a gathering of American music scholars joined together to establish the Sonneck Society in 1975. The organization, now named the Society for American Music, is devoted to the study of all aspects of American music.

64. "Library of Congress Plans to Preserve American Folk-Songs in National Collection," *Washington (DC) U.S. Daily,* April 21, 1928, C2.

65. See Carl Engel's early advocacy of jazz in his "Jazz: A Musical Discussion," *Atlantic Monthly* 130:2 (August 1922): 182–189.

66. In addition to Niles's two works, the collections in this series devoted to American music contained American-English folk songs, "bayou ballads" from Louisiana, North Carolina mountain songs, four books of African American songs, songs from the Vermont mountains, Hispanic songs of California, and spirituals from South Carolina.

67. For a comprehensive discussion of industrialization in Appalachia, see Ronald Eller, *Miners, Millhands, and Mountaineers: The Industrialization of the Appalachian South, 1880–1930* (Knoxville: Univ. of Tennessee Press, 1982).

68. John Jacob Niles, *Seven Kentucky Mountain Songs* (New York: G. Schirmer, 1929), 5.

69. Jim Wayne Miller's glossary, in *Southern Mountain Speech,* by Cratis Williams (Berea, KY: Berea College Press, 1992), indicates no use of "mammy" and "pappy" in mountain speech. The word "hit" is defined as "a pronoun. Old fashioned form of 'it,' used usually for emphasis (hit's the one I mean!)."

70. Preface to Niles, *Seven Kentucky Mountain Songs,* n.p.

71. JJNC, 47/5, pp. 43, 51.

72. These songs do not appear in any of the Kentucky collections that were contemporary with Niles's work. See Hubert G. Shearin, *Syllabus of Kentucky Folk-Songs* (Lexington, KY: Transylvania, 1911); Loraine Wyman and Howard Brockway, *Lonesome Tunes: Folk Songs from the Kentucky Mountains* (New York: W. H. Gray, 1916), and *Twenty Kentucky Mountain Tunes* (Boston: Oliver Ditson, 1919); Josephine McGill, *Folk Songs of the Kentucky Mountains* (New York: Boosey and Hawkes, 1917); and Josiah Combs, *Folk-Songs du Midi des Etats-Unis* (Paris: Presses Universitaires de France, 1923).

73. John Jacob Niles, *Seven Negro Exaltations* (New York: G. Schirmer, 1929), 13.

74. The only listing for this song in *Index to Negro Spirituals* (Chicago: Center for Black Music Research, 1991) is attributed to Niles.

75. See *Index to Negro Spirituals;* Kathleen A. Abromeit, *An Index to African-American Spirituals for the Solo Voice* (Westport, CT: Greenwood Press, 1999); Guthrie Meade, *Country Music Sources: A Biblio-Discography of Commercially Recorded Traditional Music* (Chapel Hill, NC: Southern Folklife Collection,

Univ. of North Carolina at Chapel Hill Libraries, 2002); and Robert Dixon, John Godrich, and Howard Rye, *Blues and Gospel Records, 1890–1943* (Oxford: Clarendon Press; New York: Oxford Univ. Press, 1997).

7. Kerby and Niles Present Folk Music on the Concert Stage

1. *Social Notes, New York Times,* March 11, 1926, 14.

2. "A Joint Recital," *New York Times,* May 5, 1927, 30.

3. "Benefit Is Given at Southampton," *New York Times,* August 24, 1927, 28; "Openings of the Week on Broadway," *New York Times,* January 15, 1928, 105; "Cissie Loftus Gives Portraits," *New York Times,* August 15, 1929, 20.

4. *Musical America,* April 14, 1917, 33; "Oscar Seagle Returns," *New York Times,* November 25, 1917, 15.

5. Mrs. H. H. A. Beach to Marion Kerby, January 2, 1929, JJNC, 33/1.

6. Lila Edmands, "Songs from the Mountains of North Carolina," *Journal of American Folklore* 6:21 (April–June 1893): 131–134.

7. Hubert G. Shearin, *British Ballads in the Cumberland Mountains* (Sewanee, TN: Univ. Press at the Univ. of the South, 1911), 15.

8. See, for instance, John Lomax and Alan Lomax, *American Ballads and Folk Songs* (New York: Macmillan, 1934), with melody line and text notation; compared with Alan Lomax, *Folksongs of North America* (Garden City, NY: Doubleday, 1960), with piano arrangements by Matyas Seiber and Don Banks and guitar chords by Peggy Seeger; Alan Lomax, *Folk Song U.S.A.* (1947), with arrangements by Ruth Crawford Seeger; and John Avery Lomax, Alan Lomax, Charles Seeger, and Ruth Crawford Seeger, *Folk Song U.S.A.* (New York: Duell, Sloan, and Pearce, 1947).

9. Howard Brockway, "The Quest of the Lonesome Tunes," *Art World,* June 1917, 229.

10. "Songs from Kentucky," *New York Times,* October 30, 1916, 3.

11. Olin Downes, "Mrs. Hoover Guest at Music Festival," *New York Times,* October 9, 1929, 4.

12. "Give Songs of the South," *New York Times,* January 16, 1930, 26.

13. *Syracuse Post Standard,* January 26, 1930.

14. Niles, "Autobiography," 574; Herbert Hughes, *Daily Telegraph* (London), May 1, 1930.

15. Ibid., May 27, 1930.

16. Basil Maine, *Morning Post* (London), May 27, 1930.

17. JJNC, 33/1. Dorothy Scarborough received her Ph.D. from Columbia with a thesis titled "Supernatural in Modern English Fiction." She taught literature at Columbia but became involved in research in folk music. She published *On the Trail of Negro Folk Songs,* with transcriptions by Ola Lee Gullege, and then turned her attention to Appalachian music; her *A Song Catcher in the Southern*

Mountains: American Folk Songs of British Ancestry, based on her collecting experiences in the mountains, was published posthumously in 1937. In the feature film *Songcatcher* (2001), the title of her book and aspects of her career were conflated with those of Katherine Pettit of Hindman and Pine Mountain Settlement Schools and Olive Dame Campbell of the John C. Campbell Folk School.

18. *Evening Telegram* (Toronto), December 12, 1930.

19. JJNC, 46/2.

20. *San Francisco News,* February 9, 1931.

21. *Evening Telegram* (Toronto), March 26, 1931.

22. Anton Mayer's critique is translated in Kerby and Niles's publicist's typescript of a translation of the review; two other translations of reviews of the Berlin and Holland concerts are contained in JJNC, 46/1.

23. JJNC, 46/1A; *Daily Telegraph* (London), May 15, 1931.

24. Niles, "Autobiography," 629–630.

25. "Joseph E. Widener Palm Beach Host," *New York Times,* January 31, 1932, N5.

26. "Palm Beach Group Gives 'June Moon,'" *New York Times,* February 3, 1932, 6.

27. M.L.S., "Marion Kerby and John Jacob Niles," *Musical Courier,* April 2, 1932. The American Women's Club was an association founded in 1922 for female professionals. In 1932 the membership, consisting of professional women, was listed as numbering four thousand. The clubhouse facility contained a swimming pool, two gyms, five roof gardens, twelve hundred private rooms, and five roof gardens.

28. JJNC, 46/2.

29. JJNC, 46/2.

30. "A French Holiday in Old New Orleans," JJNC, 19/1/g. Niles noted on the manuscript of the final movement, "Night Club," that the work was "finished by the grace of what men call God and my own imagination at 155 W. Twelfth St. on the 14th of October 1931 at 1:04 P.M. Wednesday—cloudy, rainy, warm." JJNC, 19/1/c.

31. "The King of Little Italy," act 1, scene 1, JJNC, 22/1/a.

32. Irene Kuhn, "'Mister Johnnie' Niles Sings Songs with a Dulcimer; Sees Revival of Interest in That Ancient Instrument," *New York World-Telegram,* March 2, 1933.

33. JJNC, 46/2.

34. Niles, "Autobiography," 656. Vilnoorde today is a northern suburb of Brussels.

35. Niles, "Autobiography," 659.

36. JJNC, 46/2.

37. L. von S., "Marion Kerby and John Jacob Niles: Sensational Success in

Holland," *Algemeen Handelsblad* (Amsterdam), April 23, 1933, as translated by the Imperial Concert Agency in London.

38. Niles, "Autobiography," 661.

39. Krishna Kripalani, *Rabindranath Tagori* (New York: Oxford Univ. Press, 1962).

40. Niles, "Autobiography," 664.

41. JJNC, 33/1.

42. Doris Ulmann to Olive Dame Campbell, August 1933, John C. Campbell Folk School Archives, Brasstown, NC.

43. "Camp Fire Benefit Set," *New York Times*, October 31, 1933, 25.

44. Kerby lived at 1722 West Stanley Avenue, Hollywood, CA.

45. "Marion Kerby Sings Spirituals Program," *New York Times*, January 27, 1947, 17.

46. Niles to Kerby, March 30, 1951, JJNC, 34/9.

47. Susan Reed recorded both "Black Is the Color" and "Go 'Way from My Window" on the Elektra LP titled "Susan Reed" (EKL 116).

48. Marion Kerby to John Jacob Niles, and Rena Niles to Kerby, JJNC, 34/9.

49. "America Singing," *New York Times*, June 2, 1957, 132. Marian Anderson (1897–1993) was a contralto who broke many "colored barriers" through her concert performance at Lincoln Center in 1939 and her debut at the Metropolitan Opera in 1955. See letters from Kerby to Anderson in the Marian Anderson Collection, Van Pelt Library, Univ. of Pennsylvania.

8. Doris Ulmann

1. A full biographical account of Doris Ulmann may be found in Jacobs, *Life and Photography of Doris Ulmann*.

2. Philip W. Jacobs, *The Life and Photography of Doris Ulmann* (Lexington, KY: Univ. Press of Kentucky, 2001), xv.

3. John Jacob Niles, introductory essay in *The Appalachian Photographs of Doris Ulmann*, by Doris Ulmann (Penland, NC: Jargon Society, 1971).

4. Clarence White, quoted in *In Focus: Doris Ulmann*, edited by Judith Keller (Malibu, CA: J. Paul Getty Museum, 1996), 107; Allen Eaton, *Handicrafts of the Southern Highlands* (New York: Russell Sage Foundation, 1937), 9; Julia Peterkin to Irving Fineman, ca. May 16, 1932, from Mobile, Alabama, Irving Fineman Papers, Department of Special Collections, Syracuse Univ. Library, Syracuse, NY; Olive Dame Campbell to Lula Hale, August 10, 1933, Doris Ulmann Collection, Special Collections, Southern Appalachian Archives, Hutchins Library, Berea College, Berea, KY. Lula Hale was director of a community center at Homeplace, Perry County, KY. Her photograph by Ulmann was reproduced as plate 52 in Ulmann, *Appalachian Photographs*.

5. Niles, "Autobiography," 512.

6. The "Blue Notebook" (JJNC 46/4) is largely devoted to music collecting from the 1930s. However, an earlier field notebook, JJNC 45/6a, has a brief chronology from 1919–1930 that notes under the year 1925 "Grand Street Follies, Doris Ulmann, Kerby and Alexandrovna."

7. Niles, "Autobiography," 513. The two articles were Niles, "In Defense of the Backwoods"; and Doris Ulmann, "Mountaineers of Kentucky," Scribner's Monthly 83:6 (June 1928): 675–681.

8. Keller, In Focus, 84. The photographs are dated between 1926 and 1930.

9. Niles, "Autobiography," 513.

10. Doris Ulmann to Cammie Henry, August 23, 1931, Melrose Collection, Cammie G. Henry Research Center, Watson Memorial Library, Northwestern State Univ. of Louisiana, Natchitoches.

11. Ulmann biographer Philip Walker Jacobs places their association somewhat later, noting that while they may have met in the mid-1920s through Scribner's, there is little evidence to document a working relationship before spring 1932. Jacobs's assessment of the 1932 date is buttressed by the fact that Niles is not mentioned in any extant letters to or from Ulmann before summer 1932. The first reference to Niles appears in a letter from Ulmann to Dr. Orie Latham Hatcher on June 12, 1932. Records for the Alliance for Guidance of Rural Youth, Rare Book, Manuscript, and Special Collections Library, Duke Univ., Durham, NC. See Jacobs, Life and Photography of Doris Ulmann, 36–38.

12. Their final concert was June 29, 1933.

13. Niles, "Autobiography," 510; Jacobs, Life and Photography of Doris Ulmann, 97; Julia Peterkin to Irving Fineman, January 6, 1932, Irving Fineman Papers.

14. George Uebler to Lyle Saxon, September 10, 1934, Melrose Collection.

15. Peterkin to Cammie Henry, September 1934, Melrose Collection.

16. Niles, "Autobiography," 516.

17. Ulmann to Orie Latham Hatcher, June 12, 1932, Records for the Alliance for Guidance of Rural Youth, Rare Book, Manuscript, and Special Collections Library, Duke Univ., Durham, NC.

18. Personal correspondence, manuscripts, books, and other materials relating to Jean Thomas and the American Folksong Festival are located in the Jean Thomas Collection in the Dwight Anderson Music Library of the Univ. of Louisville, Louisville, KY.

19. Jean Thomas to Niles, August 11, 1932, JJNC, 33/1.

20. Niles, "Autobiography," 527.

21. This structure is still standing on Main Street, though no longer operating as a hotel.

22. JJNC, 1932 notebooks.

23. Some of these musicians were also photographed by Ulmann, including Solomon and Beth Holcomb, James Duff, and Tillie Cornett.

24. Minutes of the Eighteenth Annual Executive Board Meeting of the Southern Woman's Educational Alliance, St. Regis Hotel, New York City, October 31–November 1, 1932, Alliance for Guidance of Rural Youth Papers.

25. Keller, *In Focus*, 40.

26. Ibid., 86. Blanche Scroggs, a sixteen-year-old student at the John C. Campbell Folk School, was the granddaughter of Lucius Scroggs, who donated seventy-five acres of his wife's land for the grounds of the Folk School.

27. Julia Peterkin to Irving Fineman, August 1933, Irving Fineman Papers, box 7.

28. Susan Millar Williams, *A Devil and a Good Woman Too: The Lives of Julia Peterkin* (Athens: Univ. of Georgia Press, 1997), 235.

29. Julia Peterkin to Irving Fineman, October 4, 1934, Irving Fineman Papers, box 7.

30. The Russell Sage Foundation was established in 1907 by Margaret Olivia Sage in memory of her husband, for "the improvement of social and living conditions in the United States."

31. Eaton, *Handicrafts of the Southern Highlands*, 242.

32. Ulmann to Lyle Saxon, July 5, 1933, Melrose Collection.

33. The school's archives contain numerous donation cards that list the contributions of money, property, livestock, and labor that community members pledged to the school.

34. Niles, "Autobiography," 632.

35. Allen Eaton to Olive Campbell, July 13, 1933, John C. Campbell Folk School Archives, Brasstown, NC.

36. See Ulmann to Lyle Saxon, July 20, 1933, Melrose Collection.

37. Ulmann to an unnamed faculty member at Berea College, July 25, 1933, Doris Ulmann Collection, box 1, folder 1, Hutchins Library, Berea College.

38. Mercer Scroggs, interview by author, May 25, 2004, John C. Campbell Folk School.

39. There are still many members of the Stalcup family living near Brasstown. Mercer Scroggs, who accompanied many of Niles and Ulmann's trips from the Campbell School, commented: "We called it little Brasstown or Stalcupville, a community; everything up there's a Stalcup or married." Scroggs interview, May 25, 2004, John C. Campbell Folk School.

40. Niles, "Autobiography," 675–679.

41. Nelson Stevens, review of *Folksong U.S.A.*, by John A. and Alan Lomax, *Arizona Quarterly* 4:3 (Autumn 1948): 276.

42. Recall that Jean Thomas first encountered William Day in the courthouse square of Morehead, KY. "Court Days," when the circuit court was in session in the county seat, were particularly active days in the community life, serving as a magnet for entertainers and traders.

43. That fountain was moved from its original central location to a small yard

in front of the former library, which now serves as the Cherokee County Historical Museum.

44. JJNC, 46/4.

45. JJNC, 45/2, p. 53.

46. JJNC, 45/2, p. 54.

47. John Jacob Niles, *Songs of the Hill Folk* (New York: G. Schirmer, 1934), 9.

48. Ellen Stekert, "Cents and Nonsense in the Urban Folksong Movement: 1930–66," in *Transforming Tradition: Folk Music Revivals Examined*, edited by Neil V. Rosenberg (Urbana: Univ. of Illinois Press, 1993), 100.

49. Oscar Brand, *The Ballad Mongers* (New York: Minerva Press of Funk and Wagnalls, 1962), 10–12.

50. Pauline Greenhill, " 'Barrett's Privateers' and 'Baratt's Privateers,' " in Rosenberg, *Transforming Tradition*, 155–156.

51. Ulmann to Olive Dame Campbell, August 7, 1933, John C. Campbell Folk School Archives.

52. Ulmann to Campbell, August 14, 1933, John C. Campbell Folk School Archives.

53. For an insightful critique of the White Top Festival, see David Whisnant, *All That Is Native and Fine: The Politics of Culture in an American Region* (Chapel Hill: Univ. of North Carolina Press, 1983), 181–252.

54. Niles, *Ballad Book*, 228, 169.

55. Ulmann to Campbell, August 14, 1933, John C. Campbell Folk School Archives.

56. Dr. William Hutchins to Niles, August 11, 1933, Doris Ulmann Collection, Hutchins Library, Berea College.

57. JJNC, Personal Series, 47/7.

58. Niles to President Hutchins, August 16, 1933, Doris Ulmann Collection, Hutchins Library, Berea College.

59. Olive Campbell to Lula Hale, August 10, 1933, John C. Campbell Folk School Archives.

60. Jean Ritchie, personal communication by e-mail to the author, September 3, 2005.

61. Katherine Pettit, who was born in Lexington, KY, and May Stone had founded the Hindman Settlement School in 1902.

62. Cecil Sharp to John C. Campbell, September 2, 1917, John C. Campbell and Olive Dame Campbell Papers, Southern Historical Collection, Univ. of North Carolina, Chapel Hill.

63. Niles, "Autobiography," 673–674.

64. For example, Jean Ritchie's playing eschews a simple melody line in favor of a countermelody that frequently changes throughout the song in relation to the meaning of the lyrics.

65. Roberts and Warner, *Journey with John Jacob Niles*, 95.

66. The fret board of a dulcimer is diatonic in its arrangement of whole and half steps, rather than chromatic, like the guitar. Niles actually refretted traditional instruments to make them conform to his different harmonic needs. See the instruments archived at the John Jacob Niles Center for American Music, Univ. of Kentucky, Lexington.

67. Whisnant, *All That Is Native and Fine,* 98.

68. Jean Ritchie's first performance was at an alumni tea at New York University in 1947. Subsequently she appeared May 15, 1948, at the Fourth Annual Festival of Contemporary Folk Music at Columbia University.

69. Traditional dulcimer performance often used a "noter" or "fretter," consisting of a short rod that slid along the melody string of the fretboard, like a "bottleneck slide" of a guitar. In the time before tortoise-shell or plastic plectrums were readily available, musicians strummed with quills or twigs.

70. Two of Niles's instruments are archived at the History Center of the John C. Campbell Folk School; others are displayed in the Gallery of the John Jacob Niles Center for American Music at the University of Kentucky.

71. Niles to William Hutchins, September 20, 1933, Doris Ulmann Collection, Hutchins Library, Berea College.

72. Notice of the concert, including the mention of his use of the dulcimer, was given in the *New York Times,* October 20, 1933, 15.

73. Niles to Rena Lipetz, October 23, 1933, JJNC, 2/1.

74. Niles to Lipetz, October 29, 1933, JJNC, 2/1.

75. Ulmann to William Hutchins, November 3, 1922, Doris Ulmann Collection, Hutchins Library, Berea College.

76. Niles to Lipetz, October 31, 1933, JJNC, 2/1.

77. The *New York Times* mentions the concert in *Music Notes,* December 18, 1933, 25.

78. Niles to Lipetz, December 23, 1933, John C. Campbell Folk School Archives.

79. Mercer Scroggs, interview by author, May 25, 2004, John C. Campbell Folk School.

80. Ulmann to Lyle Saxon, December 31, 1933, Cammie C. Henry Research Center, Watson Memorial Library, Northwestern State Univ. of Louisiana, Natchitoches. The Oberammergau Passion Play has been performed in Oberammergau, Germany, once each decade, beginning in 1633.

81. Niles to Lipetz, January 3, 1934, JJNC, 2/1.

82. Niles to Lipetz, January 5, 1934, JJNC, 2/1. The Groton School is a boarding academy founded in 1884 and located in Groton, Massachusetts. Twining Lynes, the music teacher and choral director, received Niles's music for "Down in Yon Forest," "Seven Joys of Mary," and "From the Manger to the Throne of God" for use in a festival of lessons and carols performed by the boys' choir on the last day of the fall semester.

83. Ulmann to Campbell, January 25, 1934, John C. Campbell Folk School Archives.

84. Ulmann to Campbell, February 28, 1934, John C. Campbell Folk School Archives.

85. The Morgenthaus were old family friends of the Ulmanns through a mutual association in the Ethical Culture Society. The invitation to Niles read: "We are having the white house correspondents and Mrs. Roosevelt to a clambake on the farm Saturday evening August twenty third if you would be willing to sing for us we would be very happy to have you and Miss Ulmann come up Saturday afternoon and spend the night. Please wire answer collect beacon kindest greetings." Western Union Telegram to Niles c/o Ulmann, August 18, 1933, JJNC, 33/1.

86. See Ulmann to Campbell, March 22, 1934, John C. Campbell Folk School Archives. The carved animals were made at Brasstown. At the White House gathering Niles also presented the Roosevelts with copy number one of *Roll Jordan Roll*. *Roll Jordan Roll* was a collaborative publication devoted to stories and images of southern African Americans, mostly based at Lang Syne Plantation in South Carolina. The book was published in a limited edition by Robert Ballou, and each of the 350 copies of the edition was signed by both Ulmann and Peterkin.

87. Niles to Hutchins, March 11, 1934, Doris Ulmann Collection, Hutchins Library, Berea College.

88. Ulmann to Campbell, April 14, 1934, John C. Campbell Folk School Archives.

89. Niles to Hutchins, March 11, 1934, Doris Ulmann Collection, Hutchins Library, Berea College.

90. "Possible Program for Miss Ulmann and Mr. Niles," n.d., Doris Ulmann Collection, Hutchins Library, Berea College.

91. B. A. Botkin to Niles, November 22, 1933, JJNC, 33/1. B. A. Botkin later became the national folklore editor for the Federal Writers Project and curator of the Archive of Folksong at the Library of Congress.

92. Ulmann to Eaton, July 9, 1934, JJNC, 51/1.

93. Niles to Lipetz, April 15, 1934, JJNC, 2/2.

94. Ibid., April 23, 1934, JJNC, 2/2.

95. The instrument that Hicks made for Niles is now archived at the John Jacob Niles Center for American Music, Univ. of Kentucky, Lexington. See Lucy Long, "The Negotiation of Tradition: Collectors, Community, and the Appalachian Dulcimer in Beech Mountain, North Carolina" (Ph.D. diss., Univ. of Pennsylvania, Philadelphia, 1995).

96. Niles to Eaton, June 5, 1934, facsimile copy in author's collection.

97. Boone Tavern is still owned by Berea College and staffed by students enrolled in Berea's distinctive work-study program.

98. Ulmann to Campbell, April 23, 1934, John C. Campbell Folk School Archives.

99. Niles to Eaton, June 5, 1934, facsimile copy in author's collection.

100. See the John F. Smith Traditional Music Collection (SAA5) and the James Watt Raine Ballad Collection (SAA6), Special Collections and Archives, Berea College Library, Berea, KY.

101. Niles to Lipetz, June 8, 1934, JJNC, 2/2.

102. Ibid. See Archie Greene's *Only a Miner: Studies in Recorded Coal-Mining Songs* (Urbana: Univ. of Illinois Press, 1972) for a discussion of mine and unionization singers and songs.

103. Molly Jackson, quoted in John Greenway, *American Folksongs of Protest* (Philadelphia: Univ. of Pennsylvania Press, 1953; reprint, New York: Octagon Books, 1977), 8. I have altered some of the grammar and spelling in the Jackson quotation.

104. Niles, *Ballad Book,* 80.

105. Ibid., 133–136, 294–295.

106. Ulmann to Eaton, July 1, 1934, JJNC, 51/1.

107. Ibid.

108. Niles to Lipetz, July 3, 1934, JJNC, 2/1.

109. Ibid., July 8, 1934, JJNC, 2/1.

110. Niles, *Ballad Book,* 234–236.

111. Niles to Lipetz, July 14, 1934, JJNC, 2/2.

112. Niles, *Ballad Book,* 25–27.

113. Niles to Lipetz, July 31, 1934, JJNC, 2/2.

114. Ulmann to Campbell, August 11, 1934, John C. Campbell Folk School Archives.

115. Niles to Lipetz, August 13, 1934, JJNC, 2/2.

116. The Ulmann crypt is located in plot 15 of section 6 of Mt. Pleasant Cemetery, Hawthorne, Westchester County, NY. A more complete discussion of the will contestation and settlement may be found in Jacobs, *Life and Photography of Doris Ulmann,* 148–165. Niles wrote at least three accounts of Ulmann's final weeks. The most detailed narrative is an outline typescript on Western Union telegram forms spanning the dates August 2–28. A prose version is contained in the "Remembrance" in *The Appalachian Photographs of Doris Ulmann,* by Ulmann. A particularly poetic version, tinged with much revisionist history, is contained in a typescript composed in January 1975 for Niles's "Autobiography."

9. Transitions and New Beginnings

1. Julia Peterkin to Irving Fineman, October 4, 1934, Irving Fineman Papers, Department of Special Collections, Syracuse Univ. Library, Syracuse, NY.

2. JJNC, General Correspondence, 33/1.

3. This information is from notes for the meeting made by Campbell School board member J. R. Pitman on behalf of the parties present at the legal office of Ralph Rounds in New York City. A copy of this document is found in the John C. Campbell Folk School Archives, Brasstown, NC.

4. According to the Consumer Price Index formula, $3,500 in 1936 is the equivalent of $54,700 in 2009.

5. Niles summarized the basic idea of the opera this way: "Can an evil doer give up his evil ways? Can Pietro Salmaggio return to his family and give up being a small time underworld figure? Will the underworld let him go? Will his family take him back? Can he live the simple life of his childhood once he has lived in comparative ease and had the thrill of power?" The incomplete manuscript and sketches for "The King of Little Italy" can be found in JJNC, Large Scale Works, 22/1, 2, 3.

6. Mrs. J. M. Helm to Niles, February 18, 1935, JJNC, General Correspondence, 33/2.

7. The English-born Harold Bauer was a pianist, a teacher, and the head of the piano department at Manhattan Conservatory. Niles to Rena Lipetz, March 21, 1935, JJNC, 2/3.

8. In 1928 Robert Winslow Gordon (1888–1961) was appointed the first director of the Archive of American Folk Song at the Library of Congress. In 1934 John Avery Lomax (1867–1948) was appointed "honorary consultant" and curator of the archive.

9. Niles to Lipetz, March 23, 1935, JJNC, 2/3.

10. Rena Niles, oral history typescript, Script 1, in possession of the author.

11. Rena Niles, "In the Fall of 33," *Bluegrass Woman* 1:9 (Winter 1976): 11–13, 47.

12. The *Living Age*, a foreign-affairs monthly journal edited by Quincy Howe, presented European articles translated into English. Rena Lipetz served at the journal for two years and eventually became associate editor.

13. Niles to Lipetz, April 23, 1934: "I'll bet you were 'snatch-weary' all day Friday . . . as I was slightly 'rod-weary' but what the hell. . . . Its worth something to be properly 'bestial.' . . . That's what they call it in books about what every young woman should know." JJNC, Correspondence Series, 2/2.

14. Alphonse Ilya Lipetz was born in Poland December 9, 1881, and was a consulting engineer, an inventor, and the designer of the "Decapod" locomotive. He was also the author of books such as *Diesel Engine Potentialities and Possibilities in Rail Transportation.*

15. Rena Niles, oral history typescript, Script 1, in the possession of the author.

16. Basile Lipetz, who was already a physician specializing in pediatrics, earned her psychiatry degree at the University of Paris. She eventually retired as a full professor of psychiatry at Albany Medical College, Albany, NY.

17. Niles to Rena Lipetz, April 24, 1935, JJNC, 2/3.

18. Ibid., April 28, 1935, JJNC, 2/3.

19. Ibid., December 13, 15, 1935, JJNC, 2/4.

20. Ibid.

21. Ibid., December 20, 1935, JJNC, 2/4.

22 Ibid., January 21, 1936, JJNC, 3/1.

23. Ibid., January 4, 1936, JJNC, 3/1.

24. Rena described the situation in her oral history typescript, 8.

25. The typescript of the play *Carrion Crow* is in JJNC, Manuscript series: Plays, box 77.

26. Niles to Rena Lipetz, March 17, 1936, JJNC, 3/2.

27. Marguerite Butler married Georg Bidstrup.

28. Homer Ledford, personal conversation, May 30, 2004.

29. Niles to Rena Lipetz, July 16, 1936, JJNC, 3/2.

30. Rena Niles, oral history typescript, 13–14.

31. Rena Niles, diary on "The Beverly," Saratoga, NY, stationery, July 12, 1936–August 2, 1936, JJNC, 3/2.

32. Niles, autobiography typescript, 18–19, in possession of the author. The *Kalevala* is a nineteenth-century epic poem and book consisting of 22,795 verses compiled from Finnish and Karelian folklore sources. The title can be translated as "Lands of Kaleva."

33. Rena Lipetz diary, JJNC, 128.

10. Life in Lexington

1. Rena Niles diary, Wednesday, April 7, 1937, JJNC, box 128. The diary is now located in the unprocessed Rena Niles Collection, Special Collections and Digital Programs, Univ. of Kentucky. The box is still cataloged as JJNC, 128/1.

2. The 1930 population was 45,736 and the 1940 population was 49,304.

3. Sulzer had a special interest in the folk music of the region; he published *Twenty-Five Kentucky Folk Ballads* in 1936.

4. Rena Niles diary, May 23, 1937, JJNC, 128/1.

5. In June 1930 the University of Kentucky established the first "Radio Listening Center," designed to transmit broadcasts from the university directly to community centers, since a census revealed a lack of radio access in the East Kentucky mountains. Under the direction of Elmer Sulzer, more than eighty such listening centers were established in a program that continued until the mid-1940s.

6. Rena Niles diary, June 10, 1937.

7. Rena Niles diary, June 10, 1937, JJNC, 128/1.

8. *Salute to the Hills*, Radio Script 3, series 2, June 15, 1938, 1:00 P.M., from University of Kentucky studios WHAS, WLAP, and others, JJNC, 81/4.

9. The station was originally assigned the call letters WBKY because it was based in Beattyville, KY; its call letters were changed to WUKY in 1989.

10. The radio script for two versions of the Nativity play, dated December 21 and 23, are in JJNC, 81/1. A recorded version of the Nativity play of 1938 is archived in the Special Collections Library, Univ. of Kentucky, Lexington.

11. Rena Niles diary, October 7, 1937, JJNC, 128/1.

12. Rena Niles diary, November 15, 1937, JJNC, 128/1.

13. Ibid., November 17, 1937.

14. Ibid., November 18, 1937.

15. Ibid., December 5, 1937.

16. Ibid., December 10, 1937.

17. Olin Downes was an influential American music critic who wrote for the *Boston Globe* and the *New York Times*.

18. Rena Niles diary, December 10, 1937, JJNC, 128/1.

19. Ibid., July 15, 1937.

20. Ibid., April 22, 1938.

21. John Jacob Niles to Rena Niles, July 21, 1938, JJNC.

22. Ibid., July 24, 1938.

23. At the time of this writing, the raspberry patch and the asparagus bed are still producing, and many of the trees still survive.

24. Gunnison Magic Homes of Louisville, KY, produced prefabricated houses, made by U.S. Steel. They consisted of modular four-foot sections of laminated plywood affixed to a steel frame.

25. In 1987 Rena Niles sold Boot Hill Farm to the Bluegrass Christian Camp, which was just across Boone Creek from the farm. At this point Rena Niles moved into the retirement community of Richmond Place, on Rio Dosa Drive, Lexington.

26. This room was variously referred to as the "studio," the "shop," or the "music room" by the Niles family.

27. The door is currently set inside a mahogany frame and resides in the Gallery of the John Jacob Niles Center for American Music at the University of Kentucky.

28. Ernest Johnson (1911–1972) was a Bauhaus-trained architect who designed many buildings in Lexington, including the Memorial Coliseum and the Fine Arts Building at the University of Kentucky campus. See Byron Romanowitz, *Issues and Images: Fifty Years as an Architect in Kentucky* (Lexington, KY: Lynn Imaging, 2007).

11. Settled in Kentucky

1. Niles averaged between forty-five and sixty concerts each year during his active solo concert career (1937–1970).

2. Rena Niles, Recollections, 27, original typescript, in the possession of the author.

3. Concert program notes for the program at the Dushkin School, Winnetka, IL, November 24, 1950, JJNC, 99/4. Tom Niles sang "The Little Mohee," "I'm Goin' Away," "I Heard a Maiden Mother Sing," "I Wonder as I Wander," and "Mary Hamilton" with his father at a concert for the National Teachers of English at the Hotel Schroeder in Milwaukee, WI, and at the Dushkin School in Winnetka.

4. Tom Niles's postings included Belgrade, 1963–1965; Washington, DC (Department of State), 1965–1967; Garmisch-Partenkirchen, Germany (Russian Language School), 1967–1968; Moscow, 1968–1971; U.S. NATO, Brussels, 1971–1973; Moscow, 1973–1976; Washington, DC (National War College), 1976–1977; and Washington, DC (Department of State), 1977–1985. Subsequently he held positions as ambassador to Canada, 1985–1989; ambassador to the European Union, 1989–1991; assistant secretary of state for Europe and Canada, 1991–1993; ambassador to Greece, 1993–1997; and vice president, National Defense University, 1997–1998.

5. Thomas Niles was nicknamed "the Beezer," a corruption of "boozer," because of an eye condition that caused his right eye habitually to water as an infant.

6. Rena Niles, Recollections, 27.

7. Ibid., 28.

8. Located in Arlington, VA, the Opera Theatre was organized in 1961 and incorporated as a professional company in 1967. See its home page at www.novaopera.org/about.html (accessed July 1, 2005).

9. Mary Tippy lived in Winchester, KY, until her death in 2002. She was buried at Pleasant Hill Baptist Church, just down the road from the Niles home on Athens-Boonesboro Road.

10. In 1940 Niles noted that two brood sows, Annabelle and Frances, produced seventeen shoats and that the yield of field corn was 105 bushels per acre.

11. Niles, "Autobiography," 75.

12. Carhart Farm Account Book, JJNC, 47/8.

13. Boot Hill Farm was justifiably celebrated for its prime asparagus bed, its fine raspberry patch, and a garden that boasted many varieties of greens and lettuces.

14. Carl Sandburg, *The American Songbag* (New York: Harcourt, Brace, Jovanovich, 1927), ix.

15. Niles, "Autobiography," 86.

16. *Early American Ballads,* M 604-1 through M 604-8, contained "Barberry Ellen" (parts 1 and 2), "Gypsy Laddie," "I Wonder as I Wander," "Lulle Lullay," My Little Mohee," and "Seven Joys of Mary" (parts 1 and 2).

17. Charles O'Connell to Niles, November 30, 1939, JJNC, 21/1.

18. This second album, M-718, contained "Jesus, Jesus Rest Your Head,"

"Down in Yon Forest," "See Jesus the Savior," "Who Killed Cock Robin," "The Frog Went Courting," "When Jesus Lived in Galilee," "Jesus the Christ Is Born," "The Cherry Tree," "The Old Woman and the Pig," and "The Carrion Crow." The list price was $3.50.

19. *American Folklore Volume 3*, M-824, contained "You Got to Cross That Lonesome Valley," "The Lass from the Low Countree," "Black Is the Color," "Go 'Way from my Window," "One Morning in May," "The Wife of Usher's Well," "The Death of Queen Jane," and "Little Mattie Groves."

20. *Songs of the Gambling Man* contained "Gambler Don't Lose Your Place at God's Right Hand," "My Little Black Star," "Gambling Song of the Big Sandy," "Gambler's Lullaby," "I'm a Roving Gambler," and "Street, Field, and Jailhouse Cries" (two sides).

21. Richard A. Mohr, Artists and Repertoire Department of RCA Victor Division of RCA, to Niles, July 9, 1949, JJNC, 21/5.

22. CAL 219, *American Folk and Gambling Songs;* CAL 245, *American Folk Songs;* and CAL 330, *50th Anniversary Album.*

23. It is perhaps titled the *50th Anniversary Album* because Niles first collected "Jesus, Jesus Rest Your Head" in 1906.

24. Peter Delheim to Rena Niles, February 1, 1958, JJNC, 21/4.

25. Young was the husband of Alice Hagan Rice, who wrote the novel *Mrs. Wiggs of the Cabbage Patch.*

26. The manuscript and parts for *Cities* are in JJNC, 17/1/a; 17/2/a, b; 17/3a; 17/4/1–r.

27. "Fee Simple" was published by G. Schirmer Inc.; "The Cypress Tree" and "Figures on the Hill" are in manuscript form in JJNC.

28. For a description of the furniture, see Niles, "Autobiography," part 2, 125.

29. An original 1631 slipper chair, Niles's imitation, his table, and other chairs and benches are all displayed in the Study Room of the John Jacob Niles Center for American Music, Univ. of Kentucky, Lexington.

30. Tom Niles, personal conversation, May 2004.

31. Roger Butterfield, "Folk Singer," *Life,* September 6, 1943.

32. Ibid., 60.

33. The one-year General Management Contract with National Concert and Artists Corporation made the corporation Niles's sole agent in return for a 10 percent fee for radio engagements and 20 percent for concert appearances.

34. Rena Niles, Recollections, 23.

12. Dean of American Balladeers

1. Rena Niles diary, 1938–1939, Monday, March 27, 1939, JJNC, 128/1. The diary is now located in the unprocessed Rena Niles Collection, Special Collections and Digital Programs, Univ. of Kentucky.

2. The Juilliard "Anglo-American Folk Ballad and Carol" two-week summer school class was pretty typical of Niles's guest residencies. The course was described in the 1945 Juilliard Summer School catalog:

> The aim of this course is to provide the student with a working knowledge of that part of our folk music inherited from English sources. The course will emphasize the American survivals of fifteenth century carols and the "Child" ballad as found in the United States. Available teaching materials will be studied, and the students will be expected to sing a reasonable amount of this published material. The ballads and carols studied will be taken from Mr. Niles' personal collection. The course will also include folk plays based on the ballad for use in little theatre groups, schools, and colleges.

The residency also featured a public concert and several lecture recitals.

3. The Indiana University Folklore Institute was held at the Bloomington campus of Indiana University from June 29 to August 22, 1942, and featured a resident staff as well as visiting lecturers, including Niles (July 13–25) and Alan Lomax (June 29–July 11). See Thelma James, "Report on Indiana University Folklore Institute," *Journal of American Folklore* 55:218 (October 1942): 247–248.

4. "Music: New Records," *Time*, December 23, 1946, Time Archive, www .time.com/time/magazine/archives (accessed August 23, 2005).

5. A typical concert of this time consisted of four large segments performed without intermission: love songs ("My Little Mohee," "Go 'Way from My Window," "Black Is the Color of My True Love's Hair," and "The Irish Girl"); carols ("Matthew, Mark, Luke, and John," "The Carol of the Angels," "The Seven Joys of Mary," "The Carol of the Birds," "My Little Lyking," and "I Wonder as I Wander"); folk tales ("The Suffolk Miracle," "The Restless Dead," "The Pendennis Club," and "The Frederick Road"); and ballads ("Edward," "The Farmer's Curst Wife," "The Gypsy Laddie," and "Barbry Ellen").

6. R.P., "Folk Singer Gives Midnight Program," *New York Times*, October 7, 1946, 22.

7. Oscar Brand, in a personal communication of May 9, 2004, made these comments:

> I spent only a few hours with Niles . . . on several occasions. He was a consummate gentleman and a dedicated composer of serious music. I always thought that his reserve was self-imposed, a grudging acceptance of the failure of his fine creations and the success of his folk music. But he was always pleasant with me, even though he knew that I greatly admired his folk melodies and his truly remarkable performances. He never talked or sang down to his audiences and he was a great guide to audiences in the acceptance and understanding of simple songs. His transmutation of cellos and wooden

basses into "dulcimers" was amusing to me, but audiences were entranced. He knew I respected and admired him and we were friends for that reason. When my first son was born he learned about it through mutual friends and immediately sent a box of ceramic plates—child sizes—with the message, "A son of Oscar Brand should eat from good Kentucky earthenware." I was proud and quite honored. He was a gracious and perceptive host and friend. It's too bad that Schirmer's never found his serious music impressive. I did.

8. John S. Wilson, "John Niles Heard in Folk Recital," *New York Times*, September 28, 1959, 36.

9. Theodore O. Cron and Burt Goldblatt, *Portrait of Carnegie Hall* (New York: Macmillan, 1966), 171.

10. "Carnegie Hall Then and Now: 100 Years of Excellence: 1891–1991," www .carnegiehall.org/pdf/CHnowthen.pdf (accessed April 15, 2010).

11. Gino Francesconi, archivist and museum director of Carnegie Hall, personal correspondence, 2003–2005.

12. "Three Charity Events," *New York Times*, March 29, 1946, 17.

13. "Russian Aid Concert Raises $13,000 Here," *New York Times*, April 21, 1946, 40.

14. Robert Shelton, "Folk Joins Jazz at Newport," *New York Times*, July 19, 1959, X7.

15. Ibid.

16. Jean Ritchie, personal e-mail correspondence, October 3, 2005.

17. Niles's performance is represented by the song "Hangman" on the Vanguard recording *Folk Festival at Newport Vol. 3*, Vanguard VRS 9064.

18. Contemporaneously, American musical expression was being accorded a new respect by the concert world, as manifested in the New York City Opera's two "All American" seasons, 1958–1959, initiated by music director Julius Rudel and funded by the Ford Foundation. See Tedrin Blair Lindsay, "The Coming of Age of American Opera: New York City Opera and the Ford Foundation, 1957–1960" (Ph.D. diss., Univ. of Kentucky, 2009.)

19. Gustave Reese to Niles, October 31, 1945, JJNC, 23/3.

20. Remington CD 1333, reviewed by John Briggs in the *New York Times*, January 21, 1953, X9.

21. Robert Sherman, "Met Basso Tests the Concert Waters," *New York Times*, February 4, 1977, 48.

22. Her song collection publication *Gladys Swarthout Album of Concert Songs and Arias* (New York: G. Schirmer, 1946) included "I Wonder as I Wander."

23. Patrice Munsel hosted her own television series, *The Patrice Munsel Show*, during 1956–1957 and starred in several films, including *Melba*, the story of Australian-born opera diva Nellie Melba.

24. John Jacob Niles, "The Folk Music of America," *New York Times*, April 21, 1940, 126.

25. Weldon Hart's *John Jacob Niles Suite* contained three movements: "Black Is the Color" and "The Cuckoo," "I Wonder as I Wander" and "Carol of the Angels," and "The Frog Went Courtin'" and "Frog in the Spring." It was published by G. Schirmer in 1952. Patrick McCarty based a string orchestra work on "Black Is the Color"; it was premiered by the Oklahoma City Symphony on March 28, 1954, and recast as a string quartet published by G. Schirmer in 1953. Ken Wright (1913–2008), who joined the University of Kentucky as a professor of composition in 1949, also collaborated with Niles on various orchestral arrangements, including "The Kentucky Serenade for Strings," "Cumberland Carols," and "The Seven Joys of Mary," all of which were performed throughout Kentucky during the mid-1950s.

26. Information concerning Horton is found in "Living Kentucky Composers," compiled by the Department of Community Services, College of Adult and Extension Education, Univ. of Kentucky, 1955; and *ASCAP Biographical Dictionary* (New York: Jacques Cattell Press, 1980).

27. "The Music of John Jacob Niles," a catalog of works available from G. Schirmer Inc., n.d. [probably 1960s].

28. David S. Cooper, review of "O Waly, Waly," *Music Library Association Notes* 9:3 (June 10, 1952): 490.

29. The database of choral music in print is Emusic Quest, www.emusicinprint .com (accessed August 11, 2005).

30. William R. Moody, foreword to *Lamentation*, by John Jacob Niles (New York: G. Schirmer, 1952), 1.

31. Senator Joseph McCarthy (1908–1957) began his attacks on Communists in February 1950 and in 1953 became chair of a senate subcommittee for government operations. His power waned in 1954 during the televised hearings investigating subversion in the U.S. Army, and his colleagues censured him in December 1954.

32. Niles grew up surrounded by his father and his father's many "political conspirators," who were all politically conservative. John Thomas was a Republican island adrift in a tide of Democrats—a fact that probably drove him to embrace an even more resolute stance. Naturally, John Jacob's early views were strongly shaped by his father's active participation in electioneering and politics. He even accompanied his father to political meetings, such as the Law and Order League meeting chaired by General Simon Bolivar Buckner on March 29, 1908, at McCauley's Theatre in Louisville.

John Thomas's strong influence was tempered somewhat by John Jacob's education at duPont Manual High School. John Jacob's autobiography reveals the salutary effect of education on the formation of a more independent political consciousness. His deeply ingrained conservative background continued to provide the benchmark against which new ideas were tested, but his burgeoning interest in philosophy, his war years abroad, and his personal association with President and Mrs. Roosevelt in the 1930s certainly opened him up to a world of ideas. By the late 1950s and the 1960s, he might be characterized as a fiscal conservative and a social liberal with a vehemently anti-Communist stance.

33. West, "John Jacob Niles," 3-F. Elsewhere, in an interview with *Lexington Herald-Leader* columnist Don Edwards, Niles commented: "But I am a protest singer! I protest in favor of our Lord and Master Jesus Christ and I sing the carol—the most powerful protest in the world." "Critic Calls Niles Genius; Composer, 73, Works Farm," *Lexington Herald-Leader*, December 24, 1965, 2.

34. James S. Dendy, "New Music for Choir," *Diapason* 43 (June 1941): 7.

35. David S. Cooper, "Choral Music," *Notes* 9:3 (June 1952): 489–490.

36. It is revealing to compare the adventurous Impressionistic harmonic palette of Niles's early works, such as *Impressions of a Negro Camp Meeting*, with the simplicity of harmonic style of later works intended for commercial publication by G. Schirmer.

13. Consolidation of a Life in Music

1. "The folkways of the world on records" was the slogan used to publicize Disc records and the source of Asch's subsequent "Folkways" label. The *Saturday Review* described the new Disc label in glowing terms: "One of the most enterprising and idealistic of the smaller record companies is the group known as Disc, supervised by Moe Asch. Asch specializes in what might be called Authenticity, and notably where the Authentic is contrasted to the Commercial. His recordings are homespun . . . and genuine."

2. J.D.C., "Hot Wax: Records Reviews News/John Jacob Niles: Seven Joys of Mary," *Opera, Concert, and Symphony*, February 1947, 28.

3. "Music: New Records," *Time*, December 23, 1946.

4. Rena Niles, report of activities associated with Boone Tolliver Records, JJNC, box 29.

5. The cost of the first set of recordings was $340, including $105 for the recordings, $120 to RCA for the mastering and the discs, and $115 to Cole for the artwork and the sleeves.

6. Under the terms of agreement with K. O. Asher, signed on June 13, 1952, the distributor would buy the Boone Tolliver records for "list price (less excise tax) less 55% plus excise tax." In practical terms this amounted to slightly under 50 percent of retail cost, i.e., a $4.00 record for $1.88. Asher maintained the exclusive rights to distribute in Ohio, Pennsylvania, West Virginia, Illinois, Indiana, Michigan, Wisconsin, Missouri, Kansas, Iowa, Nebraska, Minnesota, the Dakotas, and Kentucky, with the exception of a few stores in Lexington and Louisville.

7. Rena Niles, liner notes to *The John Jacob Niles Collection*, Gifthorse Records, 1092, G4–10008.

8. Robert Shelton, "A Pair of Durable Folk Singers," *New York Times*, December 31, 1961, X12.

9. *John Jacob Niles Sings Folk Songs*, in a custom-produced CD (FW 02373), may be obtained from Smithsonian-Folkways, www.folkways.si.edu/index.html. Shepard also wrote the introduction to the 1968 republication of Niles's *Singing Soldiers*.

10. Paul Brooks to Niles, June 10, 1958, JJNC, 60/1.

11. Rena signed the contract along with John Jacob and shared in the royalties, in light of her service as his personal editor.

12. Helen Phillips to Niles, July 21, 1959, JJNC, 60/1.

13. See the opening and closing measures of "Two Old Crows," in Niles, *Ballad Book*, 104.

14. Helen Phillips to Niles, September 14, 1959, JJNC, 60/1. Phillips was correct; it should have been a C minor.

15. Niles met Sheppard through performances at St. Mark's School in Southborough, MA, and collaborated with him on numerous choral arrangements published by G. Schirmer, including the shape-note hymns "Kedron," "Warrenton," "Wondrous Love," and "How Firm a Foundation" and folk tunes such as "The Devil's Questions," "I Gave My Love a Cherry," "King William's Son," "The Old Lord by the Northern Sea," "Tiranti, My Love," "The Lass from the Low Countree," and "The Rambling Boy." Niles gave several concerts at the school, including one on October 7, 1961, while on a promotional tour for the *Ballad Book*. Sheppard recollected his collaboration on the arrangements: "All of these publications carry the imprint "Arranged by JJN and JSS. So far as I know, JJN did none of the arranging. I would do the work and send the manuscript to JJN. He would then add his name as part of the 'Arranged by. . . .' I have no way of checking this as I did not keep copies of my original arrangements." J. Stanley Sheppard to the author, September 12, 2005.

16. Ibid.

17. Paul Brooks to Niles, August 11, 1961, JJNC, 60/2.

18. Margaret Minaha, secretary to Paul Brooks, to Niles, August 29, 1966; Ernest F. Elliott to Niles, December 23, 1966, both in JJNC, 60/2.

19. Marcia Legru of Houghton Mifflin to Niles, May 15, 1970, JJNC, 60/2.

20. Horace Reynolds, "Southern Singers," *New York Times*, November 26, 1961, BR14.

21. Niles, *Ballad Book*, xv–xvi. Niles's statement is true in part, although he was the recipient of Doris Ulmann's support in this endeavor.

22. Although the whole issue of intellectual property regarding orally transmitted folk music is a complex web, musicians can establish ownership to a particular *version* of a folk song through family inheritance, through collection and transcription, or, as in the case of A. P. Carter, simply by putting one's name on it. Niles viewed the ballads as in the common domain, but he wanted credit for collecting, adapting, and arranging his specific versions.

23. Affidavits for these songs are contained in JJNC, 24/11–16.

24. Claude M. Simpson Jr., "Review of American Folk Love Songs," *Journal of American Folklore* 66:262 (October 1953): 365.

25. Sleeve note for *American Folk Love Songs,* Boone Tolliver records, BTR-22.

26. Bertrand Bronson, *The Traditional Tunes of the Child Ballads* (Princeton, NJ: Princeton Univ. Press, 1959), 1:4.96, p. 78.

27. Preface to volume 2 of Bronson's *Traditional Tunes of the Child Ballads* (1962), 2:x–xi.

28. Bronson, *Traditional Tunes of the Child Ballads,* vol. 1.

29. "Judas," Child No. 23, was taken from a manuscript held by Trinity College, Cambridge, MS B. 14.39.

30. JJNC, 46/4, 70.

31. Information based on the author's visit to Texana, NC, in 2004 and conversation with David Brose, archivist and folklorist at John C. Campbell Folk School, Brasstown, NC.

32. A letter from Niles to Gustave Reese on October 24, 1944, clearly articulates Niles's own position on what is original and what is traditional in his collection for the purposes of protecting copyrights on his G. Schirmer publications. Niles simply notes that on the one hand, ballads, such as "Riddles Wisely Expounded," The Wife of Usher's Well," "The Two Corbies," "The Cruel Mother," and "Lord Thomas and Fair Ellender," are all folk music. On the other hand, he provides extensive histories on pieces that he claims to have adapted. For instance, consider his description of "The Water Cresses":

> The "Water Cresses" [w]as sung by various members of my family and some of the employees at my father's race horse barn. It was a matter of assembly. I think I can say that none of the verses ever existed completely. It required a juggling about and some considerable guessing on my part. As is the case so many times, after I had put the thing all together, I would sing it to some of the original singers and ask them what they thought about it. If I should be placed under oath, I could not tell you exactly where I began and where the original singer stopped. It is safe to say that some parts of it are adaptation. The song exists in Canadian tradition and is very unlike the material offered you.

33. Niles, *Ballad Book* (1961), xvi.

14. Do Not Go Gentle

1. West, "John Jacob Niles," 3-F.

2. Norman Nadel, "John Niles of Lexington Reconstructs KY ballads, Thief Gets Manuscripts," *Cincinnati Post and Times Star,* March 2, 1968.

3. Kenneth Wright, personal correspondence, September 13, 2005.

4. Fortunately, most of the older notebooks and manuscripts were not stolen, and there were facsimile copies of the more recent unpublished works, such as "Flower of Jesse." In the intervening years, several of these manuscripts have reappeared from time to time, but it has been impossible to trace the source or identify the location of the remaining items. Rena Niles and the University of Kentucky made it a policy to accept any missing manuscripts without question, but they refused to pay for the return of any of the stolen items.

5. Warren Wintrode, "Boot Hill Tragedy: Balladeer Begins Life Anew on 75th Birthday," *Lexington Herald-Leader,* June 28, 1970.

6. The preliminary sketch for the Niles painting is hung in the study room of the John Jacob Niles Center for American Music at the University of Kentucky. The oil portrait of Niles at age sixty-six was completed in 1958. Today it graces a wall in the study at Thomas M. T. Niles's home. Unfortunately, the Merton portrait burned and is no longer extant. The Hammer portraits of both Niles and Merton adorn the cover of the Niles-Merton songs' publication.

7. Niles quoted in Roberts and Warner, *Journey with John Jacob Niles,* 31–32.

8. Michael Mott, *The Seven Mountains of Thomas Merton* (Boston: Houghton Mifflin, 1984), 392.

9. Originally called "Carol" by Merton, but renamed by Niles to celebrate the Nativity and supposedly to avoid confusion with his daughter-in-law Caroll Ehringhaus Niles's name.

10. Since the poetry was already written, there was little that Merton could contribute to the songs. He did give Niles permission to make small alterations of text, such as repeating words, as necessary for the musical composition.

11. Merton was increasingly attracted to Buddhism as well; his poem "Wisdom" and others seem to be very much an expression of Zen thought. Merton was in Bangkok, Thailand, on a journey of rapprochement between Catholicism and Buddhism when he died of an accidental electrocution on December 10, 1968.

12. Monica Weis, quoted in Art Jester, "Landscapes Is a Merton Essential," *Lexington Herald-Leader,* June 11, 2005, H3.

13. Niles, *Brick Dust and Buttermilk,* n.p.

14. Exceptions include Cale Young Rice's poetry in *Cities* and, in the Niles-Young songs, "Fee Simple," "The Cypress Tree," and "Figures on the Hill." Niles also adapted an English translation of an anonymous Chinese poem for "Lotus Bloom" and James Ryman's fifteenth-century poem for "The Flower of Jesse."

15. The opening line from "A Responsory, 1948," in John Jacob Niles, *The Niles-Merton Songs, Opus 171 and 172* (Champaign, IL: Mark Foster Music, 1981), ix.

16. Niles commented:

Charles Ives came up to me one day and said: "Now this is what you want to use, boy. Give up that right-hand business of using all your fingers in the right hand. Just take this board—it's got a piece of felt on the bottom of it, and jam it down on all the black keys every now and then, and then you've got a lot of music." Well, I got ahold of a board and tried it and I wasn't ready for it, you see—I was only a Boone Creek boy in the great world—I did my best. And Charles died and I went on with folk music. But when I got around to these compositions, I realized it was time to listen to someone as great as Charles Ives.

Roberts and Warner, *Journey with John Jacob Niles*, 58.

17. As Merton employs bird imagery in lines such as "So like a quiet pigeon in a hollowed out rock," so Niles weaves whippoorwill song into the music of "Evening" and the call of the bobwhite into "O Sweet Irrational Worship." It is unclear whether Niles had any exposure to the music of Olivier Messiaen (1908–1992), who also used bird calls within his music. See Messiaen's compositions.

18. Roberts and Warner, *Journey with John Jacob Niles*, 46.

19. For instance, Niles once commented regarding Jackie's voice: "The advantage I have in the case of Jackie's voice is that I know where her voice is—the high G—this is her greatest note." Roberts and Warner, *Journey with John Jacob Niles*, 111.

20. Roberts and Warner, *Journey with John Jacob Niles*, 13.

21. Mott, *Seven Mountains*, 501.

22. Roberts and Warner, *Journey with John Jacob Niles*, 14–15.

23. In the 1987 Appalshop film *John Jacob Niles*, Niles's character gave this long blessing:

Oh God, our heavenly father, into thy hands do we commit ourselves. Have mercy upon us, have mercy upon us, have mercy upon us. We thank thee, oh God, for the food on this table, for the many hands engaged in the production of this food, from the fields to the kitchen and to the tables. Bless our cooks, bless the master and mistress of this house, and the guests within our gates. And give us the power, the willingness, the imagination, and the guts to go forward with whatever task is immediately before us. Into thy hands do we commit ourselves, have mercy upon us. Amen.

24. The Boot Hill smokehouse was located near the house, next to the pony barn. See the *John Jacob Niles Cookbook: With Special Recipes by Mary Tippy Mullins* (Lexington, KY: Watersign Press, 1996).

25. Rena Niles, "As I Remember," in Niles, *The Niles-Merton Songs, Opus 171 and 172*, v.

26. The completed opus now included "The Messenger," "The Nativity," "A

Responsory, 1948," "Sundown," "When You Point Your Finger," "The Weather-cock on the Cathedral at Quito," "Evening," "Great Prayer," "Love Winter When the Plant Says Nothing," and "Lament of a Maiden for the Warrior's Death."

27. Sara Holroyd, "John Jacob Niles: Renaissance Man," *Bluegrass Music News* 23:4 (April–May 1972), 9.

28. Opus 172 contained the songs "O Sweet Irrational Worship," "Autumn," "Wisdom," "The Mirror's Mission," "For My Brother: Reported Missing in Action, 1943," "The Greek Women," "Cana," "The Ohio River—Louisville," "Original Sin," "Birdcage Walk," "Jesus Weeps into the Fire," and "Mosaic: St. Praxed's." Niles considered the Niles-Merton songs complete at twenty-one songs, but then he added "Mosaic" to make the total come to the more harmonious number twenty-two. Niles had long considered twenty-two *his* number, because Rabin-dranath Tagore had told him "he was a twenty-two."

29. From a manuscript copy in the possession of Jacqueline Roberts. The only manuscript of "Mosaic" in the JJNC is a four-bar unsigned sketch, JJNC 28/8/m3.

30. See David E. Little, "An Historical and Analytical Study of the Origin of Texts, Melodies, and Performance Practices of the Niles-Merton Song Cycles" (D.M.A. thesis, Indiana Univ., 1994), for a performance-based analysis of the songs. Note the error in Little's title, identifying the opera as "cycles."

31. Roberts and Warner, *Journey with John Jacob Niles,* 50–51.

32. The Niles-Merton songs have been recorded in their entirety twice, once by Jacqueline Roberts and Nancie Field on cassette in 1981, and most recently in 2006 by Chad Runyon (baritone) and Jacqueline Chew (piano) on the CD *Sweet Irrational Worship: The Niles-Merton Songs,* by MSR Classics (MS 1174). The most recent complete performance of the complete Niles-Merton songs was by Runyon and Chew at the International Thomas Merton Society meeting in San Diego, June 2005.

33. Jackie commissioned her cousin Charles Simpson to craft three dulcimers for her use, one of which is modeled after Niles's E instrument.

34. Studs Terkel, *And They All Sang* (New York: New Press, 2005), 1–2.

35. See Rena Niles, "On the Road with John Jacob Niles," *High Roads Folio* 11 (1986): 33–36.

36. Harry Haskell, "Music in Mid-America," *Kansas City Star,* November 13, 1977, 44A.

37. Bryan Wooley, "Portrait of a Balladeer," *Louisville Courier-Journal and Times,* June 28, 1970.

38. Ibid.

39. The Charleston concert was arranged by Jackie's sister Ruth Trumbo, who was living in Charleston, West Virginia.

40. Roberts and Warner, *Journey with John Jacob Niles,* 116–117.

41. Worship bulletin for Immanuel Baptist Church, Lexington, KY, July 4, 1976.

42. There is an interesting notebook from 1969–1972 that contains a number of poems and elegiac writings by Niles. A gift of Thomas M. T. Niles to the JJNC, it is currently in the possession of the author and is uncataloged.

43. Warren Wilson College is at Swannanoa, North Carolina, near Asheville. Concert program in JJNC.

44. Rena Niles, "On the Road with John Jacob Niles," 38.

45. Holroyd, "John Jacob Niles," 8–9.

46. The Niles family was closely connected to the production, with Niles's niece Nancy Niles Sexton contributing to the script and her son Charles Niles Sexton playing the role of young John Jacob. *My Days as a Youngling* received the Children's Theatre Association Distinguished Play Award in 1982. The script is available from Anchorage Press Inc.

47. Jackie Roberts and Nancie Field made these recordings for Rena Niles and released them in cassette format.

48. Niles, *Brick Dust and Buttermilk*, n.p.

Coda

1. Helm Roberts (1931–), an accomplished architect, designed the celebrated Vietnam War Memorial in Frankfort, KY, and also designed this home on New Street in Lexington, KY.

2. Details concerning the birthday party were informed by Jackie Roberts's Daybook (in Roberts's possession) and by Tedrin Blair Lindsay, e-mail communication, June 29, 2009.

3. Recent reissue compact disc recordings include *John Jacob Niles: I Wonder as I Wander, Carols and Love Songs*, Empire 545 450 802–2; *The Ballads of John Jacob Niles*, Essential Media Group 942 311 018–2; *An Evening with John Jacob Niles*, Empire 545 450 832–2; and *John Jacob Niles: My Precarious Life in the Public Domain*, Revola CD REV 138. Recent new recordings include *Sweet Irrational Worship: The Niles-Merton Songs*, performed by Chad Runyon, baritone, and Jacqueline Chew, piano, MSR Classics MS 1174; and *Lass from the Low Countree*, performed by Hope Koehler, Albany Records Troy 1015.

4. "My Horses Ain't Hungry," by Arnold Schoenberg, reconstructed and completed by Allen Anderson (Los Angeles: Belmont Music, 2007).

5. The Lexington Downtown Corporation sponsors the "Star" recognition ceremony.

6. Roberts and Warner, *Journey with John Jacob Niles*; and the CD *Jacqueline Roberts Sings the Music of John Jacob Niles*.

7. Terkel, *And They All Sang*; Bob Dylan, *Chronicles: Volume One* (New York: Simon and Schuster, 2004), 239. The film was aired on a *Folk Sound* television broadcast June 16, 1960, sponsored by Revlon. See *No Direction Home*, directed and produced by Martin Scorsese, 2005.

8. Keller, *In Focus.*

9. Barry Alfonso was the producer of the Gifthorse cassette reissue *The John Jacob Niles Collection,* in 1992. The Niles Center Web site is at www.uky.edu/FineArts/Music/Niles.

10. The mission statement reads:

The John Jacob Niles Center for American Music is a collaborative effort of the University of Kentucky School of Music, College of Fine Arts, and the University Libraries. It is named for Kentucky musician John Jacob Niles. The Center seeks to provide a comprehensive focus for the research and performance of American music, embracing both vernacular and cultivated aspects of the field, from the early Colonial period through the present, with special emphasis on the indigenous culture of the southeastern United States. The Center's mission is both archival and programmatic. It serves as a repository for primary and secondary research materials and it actively supports the dissemination of scholarly research in American Music. John Jacob Niles Center for American Music, www.uky.edu/FineArts/Music/Niles/.

11. See the Niles Center Web site for a description of the collections.

12. See the Niles Center Web site for a description of the "Appalachia in the Bluegrass" concerts.

Bibliography

Books, Articles, and Unpublished Manuscripts by Niles

Cogswell, Theodore, and John Jacob Niles. "The Roper." *Science Fiction* 23:2 (August 1964): 88–89.

Hall, Bert, and John Jacob Niles. *One Man's War.* New York: Henry Holt, 1929. Reprint, New York: Ayer, 1980. Page references are to the 1929 edition.

——. "War Takes the Air." *Collier's Weekly* 83 (April 27, 1929): 18, 20, 34, 36.

Niles, John Jacob. "Autobiography." Edited by David Burg. A 703-page typescript in possession of the author.

——. *The Ballad Book of John Jacob Niles.* See "Music Collections."

——. "Black Is the Color." *Sing Out!* 12 (December 1962): 41.

——. *Brick Dust and Buttermilk.* Boone Tolliver Press. Distributed by Gnomon Press, Frankfort, KY, 1977.

——. "Deft Hands Carve the Dulcimer." *Louisville Courier-Journal Magazine,* January 20, 1952, 26–28.

——. "Eleven a.m." *Scribner's Monthly* 87:1 (January 1930): 35–37.

——. "Faire L'Ecole Buissonière." *Seven Seas* (April 1931): 11.

——. "Folk Ballad and Carol." In *The Great Smokies and the Blue Ridge,* edited by Richard Peattie, 217–238. New York: Vanguard Press, 1943.

——. "The Folk Music of America." *New York Times,* April 21, 1940.

——. "Gossip from English Inns." *Seven Seas* 7:5 (July 1931): 17–19.

——. "Hedge Hoppers." *Scribner's Monthly* 85:3 (March 1929): 311–315.

——. "Hillbillies." *Scribner's Monthly* 82:5 (November 1927): 601–605.

——. "In Defense of the Backwoods." *Scribner's Monthly* 83:6 (June 1928): 738–745.

——. "In the Beginning." *Sing Out!* 11 (February 1961): 19–20.

——. *John Jacob Niles Cookbook: With Special Recipes by Mary Tippy Mullins.* Lexington, KY: Watersign Press, 1996.

——. "John Jacob Niles/Louisville Poetry." *Kentucky Poetry Review* 15:2–3 (Summer–Fall 1979): 2–6.

——. *Mr. Poof's Discovery.* Lexington, KY: Bur Press, 1947.

——. "My Precarious Life in the Public Domain." *Atlantic* 182:6 (1948): 129–131.

——. "The Passing of the Street Cry." *Scribner's Monthly* 87:3 (September 1929): 265–271.

——. "Remembrance." In *The Appalachian Photographs of Doris Ulmann,* by Doris Ulmann. Penland, NC: Jargon Society, 1971.

——. Review of *Folksingers and Folksongs in North America. Music Educator's Journal* (November–December 1965): 107.

——. Review of *Southern Mountain Folksongs and Ballads. Journal of American Folklore* 71:280 (April 1958): 182.

——. *Rhymes for a Wince.* Lexington: Univ. of Kentucky Library Press, 1971.

——. "Shout, Coon, Shout!" *Musical Quarterly* 16 (October 1930): 516–530.

——. *Singing Soldiers.* New York: Scribner's, 1927. Reprint, with a new introduction by Leslie Shepard, Detroit: Singing Tree Press, 1968.

——. "The Sixth Hangar." *Scribner's Monthly* 84:1 (July 1928).

——. "Traveling Carpenters." *Seven Seas* 8:2 (October 1931): 13–14.

——. "Villeneuve les Avignon: The Versailles of the 14th Century." *Seven Seas* 8:6 (February 1932): 4–5, 20.

——. "White Pioneers and Black." *Musical Quarterly* 18 (January 1932): 60–75.

——. "Woman . . . on a Good Man's Mind." *Mentor-World Traveler* 18 (March 1930): 12–15.

Niles, John Jacob, Douglas Moore, and Abian Wallgren. *The Songs My Mother Never Taught Me.* New York: Macaulay, 1929.

Niles, John Jacob, Helene B. Niles, and Bob Dean. *Hinky Dinky Barley Brew: A Cry from the Heart: Being the Reincarnation of the Justly Famous Song Entitled Mademoiselle from Armentières.* New York: Old Grist Mill Press, 1932.

Music Collections by Niles

Niles, John Jacob. *The Anglo-American Ballad Study Book.* New York: G. Schirmer, 1945.

——. *The Anglo-American Carol Study Book.* New York: G. Schirmer, 1948.

——. *The Ballad Book of John Jacob Niles.* New York: Houghton Mifflin, 1961. Rev. ed., Lexington: Univ. Press of Kentucky, 2000.

——. *Ballads, Carols, and Tragic Legends from the Southern Appalachian Mountains.* New York: G. Schirmer, 1937.

——. *Ballads, Love Songs, and Tragic Legends.* New York: G. Schirmer, 1938.

——. *Five Gambling Songs.* New York: G. Schirmer, 1941, 1946, 1964.

——. *Four American Carols for Organ.* New York: G. Schirmer, 1950.

——. *Impressions of a Negro Camp Meeting.* New York: Carl Fischer, 1925.

——. *More Songs of the Hill Folk.* New York: G. Schirmer, 1936.

———. *The Niles-Merton Songs, Opus 171 and 172.* Champaign, IL: Mark Foster Music, 1981.

———. *Seven Kentucky Mountain Songs.* New York: G. Schirmer, 1929.

———. *Seven Negro Exaltations.* New York: G. Schirmer, 1929.

———. *The Shape Note Study Book.* New York: G. Schirmer, 1950.

———. *Singing Campus.* New York: G. Schirmer, 1964.

———. *Song Book for Guitar.* New York: G. Schirmer, 1963.

———. *The Songs of John Jacob Niles.* New York: G. Schirmer, 1975. Rev. ed., containing 8 additional songs and a preface by Rena Niles, 1993.

———. *Songs of the Hill Folk.* New York: G. Schirmer, 1934.

———. *Ten Christmas Carols from the Southern Appalachian Mountains.* New York: G. Schirmer, 1935.

Other Books and Articles

Abromeit, Kathleen A. *An Index to African-American Spirituals for the Solo Voice.* Westport, CT: Greenwood Press, 1999.

"America Has Its Carols Too." *Louisville Courier-Journal,* December 22, 1946.

Anthony, Stewart B. "The Sun Shines Bright on Kentucky." *National Geographic* 82:1 (July 1942): 83.

Asbury, Eslie. "Kentucky Biographical Notebook: John Jacob Niles." *Filson Club Quarterly* 64:2 (April 1990): 277–281.

"A Balladeer Nears His 83rd Year." *Louisville Courier-Journal,* April 19, 1975, A5.

Batiuk, Taras. "The Art of John Jacob Niles." *East Magazine* (1958).

Bernstein, Burton. "Carnegie Hall Takes a Bow." *Town and Country* (July 1990): 69–75.

Billings, Dwight, Gurney Norman, and Katherine Ledford. *Confronting Appalachian Stereotypes: Back Talk from an American Region.* Lexington: Univ. Press of Kentucky, 1999.

Bingham, Barry, Sr. "John Jacob Niles." *Kentucky Review* 15:1 (October 1983).

Bingham, Sallie. "Piggyback." A play produced at Horsecave Theatre, Horsecave, KY, 1994. Typescript in author's collection.

Birney, Andrew. "John Jacob Niles." In *The Lubricator.* Wheeling, WV: Rotary Club, 1945.

Blomstedt, Erik R. "John Jacob Niles (1892–1980): The Dean of American Balladeers." *Dulcimer Player News* 8:3 (Summer 1982).

Botkin, B. A. Review of *The Anglo-American Ballad Study Book. Notes* 2:4 (September 1945): 295–296.

Botrel, Théodore. *Les Chants du Bivouac.* Paris, France: Libraire Payot, 1914. In French.

Brand, Oscar. *The Ballad Mongers.* New York: Minerva Press of Funk and Wagnalls, 1962.

Brown, Roger Lyle. *Ghost Dancing on the Cracker Circuit: The Culture of Festivals in the American South*. Jackson: Univ. Press of Mississippi, 1997.

Bunce, Alan. "'Getting Used to' Niles." *Louisville Courier-Journal*, May 1, 1972.

Burg, David. "John Jacob Niles." *Kentucky Review* 2:1 (1980): 3–10.

Butterfield, Roger. "Folk Singer." *Life*, September 6, 1943.

Campbell, John C. *The Southern Highlander and His Homeland*. New York: Russell Sage Foundation, 1921. Reprint, Lexington: Univ. Press of Kentucky, 1969.

Carey, George. Review of *Singing Soldiers*. *Journal of American Folklore* 82:326 (October 1969): 391.

Cason, Jane. "The Niles-Merton Songs." *NATS Bulletin* (March–April 1983).

Caudill, Harry. *Night Comes to the Cumberlands: A Biography of a Depressed Area*. Boston: Little, Brown, 1962.

Chambers, Virginia. "The Hindman Settlement School and Its Music." *Journal of Research in Music Education* 21:2 (Summer 1973): 135–144.

Cohen, Ronald. *Rainbow Quest: The Folk Revival and American Society, 1940–1970*. Amherst: Univ. of Massachusetts Press, 2002.

Cooper, David. Review of *Lamentation*. *Notes* 9:3 (June 1952): 489–490.

Coppage, Noel. "John Jacob Niles." *Stereo Review* 84:1 (January 1975).

Creason, Joe. "Radio: Niles to Air Original Version of Nativity Play over WHAS Thursday." *Louisville Courier-Journal*, December 19, 1943.

Curran, Thomas J. *Xenophobia and Immigration, 1820–1930*. Boston: Twayne, 1975.

Dixon, Robert, John Godrich, and Howard Rye. *Blues and Gospel Records, 1890–1943*. Oxford: Clarendon Press; New York: Oxford Univ. Press, 1997.

Dugaw, Dianne. *The Anglo-American Ballad: A Folklore Casebook*. New York: Garland, 1995.

Dylan, Bob. *Chronicles: Volume One*. New York: Simon and Schuster, 2004.

Eaton, Allen. "The Doris Ulmann Photograph Collection." *Call Number* 19:2 (Spring 1958).

———. "Handicraft of the Southern Highlands." *Scribner's* (June 8, 1937): 4–11.

———. *Handicrafts of the Southern Highlands*. New York: Russell Sage Foundation, 1937.

Edmands, Lila W. "Songs from the Mountains of North Carolina." *Journal of American Folklore* 6:21 (April–June 1893): 131–134.

Eller, Ronald. *Miners, Millhands, and Mountaineers: Industrialization of the Appalachian South, 1880–1930*. Knoxville: Univ. of Tennessee Press, 1982.

Enoch, Henry G. *Grimes Mill, Kentucky Landmark on Boone Creek, Fayette County*. Bowie, MD: Heritage Books, 2002.

Feintuch, Burt. *Kentucky Folkmusic: An Annotated Bibliography*. Lexington: Univ. Press of Kentucky, 1985.

Filene, Benjamin. *Romancing the Folk: Public Memory and American Roots Music*. Chapel Hill: Univ. of North Carolina Press, 2000.

Filson Club. "Kentucky Biographical Notebook: John Jacob Niles." *Filson Club Quarterly* 64:2 (April 1990): 277–281.

Fischer, David Hackett. *Albion's Seed: Four British Folkways in America.* New York: Oxford Univ. Press, 1989.

Gardner, Joanne M. "The Appalachian Troubadour." Bachelor's thesis, College of Notre Dame of Maryland, 1992.

Goldsmith, Peter D. *Making People's Music: Moe Asch and Folkways Records.* Washington, D.C.: Smithsonian Institution Press, 1998.

Grant, Madison. *The Passing of the Great Race.* New York: Scribner's, 1922.

Hall, Bert. *En L'Air! (In the Air) Three Years on and above Three Fronts.* New York: New Library, 1918.

Halpert, Herbert. Review of *Ballads, Love Songs, and Tragic Legends. Journal of American Folklore* 55:215–216 (January 1942): 103–104.

———. Review of *Songs of the Hill Folk; More Songs of the Hill Folk; Ballads, Carols, and Tragic Legends from the Southern Appalachian Mountains. Journal of American Folklore.* 52:203 (January 1939): 128–129.

Hardy, Owen. "John Jacob Niles: Before Homogenization." *Louisville Courier-Journal,* October 13, 1978, C4.

Harkins, Anthony. *Hillbilly: A Cultural History of an American Icon.* New York: Oxford Univ. Press, 2004.

"He Combines Simplicity and Sophistication." *Kansas City Times,* November 25, 1967.

Henry, Mellinger. "Still More Ballads and Folk-Songs from the Southern Highlands." *Journal of American Folklore* 45:175 (January–March 1932).

Higham, John. *Send These to Me: Jews and Other Immigrants in Urban America.* New York: Atheneum, 1975.

Hinckle, Harry L., and Monica Weiss. *Thomas Merton's Gethsemani: Landscapes of Paradise.* Lexington: Univ. Press of Kentucky, 2005.

Hing, Bill Ong. *To Be an American: Cultural Pluralism and the Rhetoric of Assimilation.* New York: New York Univ. Press, 1997.

Hinshaw, Donald G. "Contemporary Composers: John Jacob Niles." *Journal of Church Music* 18:8 (October 1978).

Holroyd, Sara. "John Jacob Niles: Renaissance Man." *Bluegrass Music News* 23:4 (April–May 1972): 8–9.

Howes, Frank. Review of *Singing Soldiers. Musical Times* 110:1521 (November 1969): 1145.

Index to Negro Spirituals. Chicago: Center for Black Music Research, 1991. Reproduced from an original 1937 edition in the Cleveland Public Library.

Jacobs, Philip Walker. *The Life and Photography of Doris Ulmann.* Lexington: Univ. Press of Kentucky, 2001.

———. "Light Days, Dark Nights: The Carolina Photographs of Doris Ulmann. *Carologue* 13:3 (Autumn 1997): 13–16.

James, Thelma. "Report on Indiana University Folklore Institute." *Journal of American Folklore* 55:218 (October 1942): 247–248.

Jameson, Gladys. "Mountain Ballads." *Southern Mountain Life and Work* (October 1925): 12, 19.

"John Jacob Niles." *Washington Post,* April 12, 1954.

"John Jacob Niles to Present Gala 77 Birthday Concert." *Louisville Courier-Journal,* April 27, 1969, F16.

Johnson, Helen Shea. "John Jacob Niles—the Minstrel of Boone Creek." *Music Journal* (January–February 1980).

Johnson, Randi, and Stephanie Waxman. "Morning Light." Auintillion Productions, 1994. Typescript of a film, in author's collection.

Jones, Dorothy, and William E. Studwell. "Propagators of the Christmas Carol." *American Organist* 27:11 (November 1993): 77.

Jones, Loyal. *Minstrel of the Mountains: The Story of Bascom Lamar Lunsford.* Lexington: Univ. Press of Kentucky, 1984. Reprint, 2002.

Jones, Maldwyn Allen. *American Immigration.* Chicago: Univ. of Chicago Press, 1960.

Keller, Judith, ed. *In Focus: Doris Ulmann.* Malibu, CA: J. Paul Getty Museum, 1996.

Kidd, Andrew Jason. "A True Son of Kentucky: John Jacob Niles." *Kentucky Heritage, Convention Issue* (1981).

Kirk, Elise K. *Music at the White House.* Urbana: Univ. of Illinois Press, 1986.

Kirkpatrick, Haden. "Folk Singer Represents Mountain Music on Radio." *Lexington Herald-Leader,* September 5, 1937.

Knobel, Dale T. *America for the Americans: The Nativist Movement in the United States.* New York: Twayne, 1996.

Kowalski, Shelley Kara. "Fading Light: The Case of Doris Ulmann." Ph.D. diss., Univ. of Oregon, 2000.

Kuhn, Irene. "'Mister Johnnie' Sings Songs with a Dulcimer; Sees Revival of Interest in That Ancient Instrument." *New York World-Telegram,* March 2, 1934.

Lamuniere, Michelle Chesbro. "*Roll, Jordan, Roll:* The Gullah Photographs of Doris Ulmann" (African Americans). Master's thesis, Univ. of Oregon, 1994.

Lancaster, Thomas. "John Jacob Niles on Choral Participation in Folk Music." *American Choral Review* 8:4 (June 1966).

Landess, Thomas. *Julia Peterkin.* Boston, MA: Twayne, 1976.

Lawless, Ray M. *Folksingers and Folksongs in America.* New York: Duell, Sloan, and Pearce, 1965.

Lewis, Helen, ed. *Colonialism in Modern America: The Appalachian Case.* Boone, NC: Appalachian Consortium Press, 1978.

Little, David Earle. "An Historical Overview and Analytical Study in the Origin of Texts, Melodies, and Performance Practices of the Niles-Merton Song Cycles." D.M.A. thesis, Indiana Univ., 1994.

Livingston, Carolyn. *Charles Faulkner Bryan: His Life and Music.* Knoxville: Univ. of Tennessee Press, 2003.

Long, Lucy. "The Negotiation of Tradition: Collectors, Community, and the Appalachian Dulcimer in Beech Mountain, North Carolina." Ph.D. diss., Univ. of Pennsylvania, 1995.

Lyon, George Ella, ed. *A Kentucky Christmas*. Lexington: Univ. Press of Kentucky, 2003.

Mamaluk, Darla. "John Jacob Niles, 1892–1980." *Sing Out!* 28 (September 1980).

McEwen, Melissa A. *Seeing America: Women Photographers between the Wars*. Lexington: Univ. Press of Kentucky, 2000.

McNeil, William K. *Appalachian Images in Folk and Popular Culture*. Knoxville: Univ. of Tennessee Press, 1995.

———. Review of *John Jacob Niles* (film). *Journal of American Folklore* 92:366 (October 1979): 521.

Meade, Guthrie. *Country Music Sources: A Biblio-Discography of Commercially Recorded Traditional Music*. Chapel Hill, NC: Southern Folklife Collection, Univ. of North Carolina at Chapel Hill Libraries, 2002.

Metfessel, Milton. *Phonophotography in Folk Music: American Negro Songs in New Notation*. Chapel Hill: Univ. of North Carolina Press, 1928.

Mootz, William. "Niles Hailed on His 83rd Birthday, Holds His Young Audience Spellbound." *Louisville Courier-Journal*, April 30, 1975, B6.

Mott, Michael. *The Seven Mountains of Thomas Merton*. Boston: Houghton Mifflin, 1984.

Nash, Alanna. "John Jacob Niles: His Legend Lives On." *Frets Magazine* 2:6 (June 1980).

———. "A Song from the Heart." *Beaux Arts* (Summer 1981): 16–19.

Niles, Rena. "Inner Spirit." *High Roads Folio* 8 (1986).

———. "In the Fall of '33." *Bluegrass Woman* 1:9 (Winter 1976): 11–13, 47.

———. "On the Road with John Jacob Niles." *High Roads Folio* 11 (1986): 33–39.

———. "The Songs of John Jacob Niles." *NATS Bulletin* (September–October 1982): 17–21.

Niles, Thomas. "Great Escapes." *Kentucky Humanities* 1 (2000): 28–29.

Nolan, Irene. "John Jacob Niles." *Louisville Courier-Journal*, April 16, 1972, G30.

O'Connell, Charles. *The Other Side of the Record*. New York: Alfred A. Knopf, 1947.

Palcewski, John. "Veteran Performer Niles Plays to Packed House." *Lexington Herald-Leader*, April 29, 1967.

Parker, David Reed. "John Jacob Niles and Revisionist Folklore: The Corpus Christi Carol/'Down in Yon Forest.'" *Southern Folklore* 49:2 (1992): 147–156.

Pen, Ronald. "John Jacob Niles: Intersection of Folk, Popular, and Elite Music." *Kentucky Review* 12:1–2 (Autumn 1993): 3–11.

———. "The Life and Works of John Jacob Niles." Ph.D. diss., Univ. of Kentucky, 1987.

Porterfield, Nolan. *Exploring Roots Music: Twenty Years of the JEMF Quarterly.* Lanham, MD: Scarecrow Press, 2004.

Pudup, Mary Beth, Dwight Billings, and Altina Waller. *Appalachia in the Making.* Chapel Hill: Univ. of North Carolina Press, 1995.

Reed, Billy. "Mountain Minstrel: John Jacob Niles Sings the Folks' Songs." *Louisville Courier-Journal,* November 11, 1976.

Rehder, John B. *Appalachian Folkways.* Baltimore: John Hopkins Univ. Press, 2004.

Roberts, Jacqueline Warnick. "In Memoriam: John Jacob Niles." *Bluegrass Music News* 31:4 (May 1980).

Roberts, Jacqueline, and Kerstin Warner. *A Journey with John Jacob Niles: A Memoir of My Years with Johnnie.* Lexington: Univ. of Kentucky Libraries, 2001.

Said, Edward. *Orientalism.* New York: 1st Vintage Books, 1979.

Scott, Emmett J. *Scott's Official History of the American Negro in the World War.* 1919. Reprint, New York: Arno Press, 1969.

Sexton, Nancy Niles. *My Days as a Youngling.* New Orleans: Anchorage Press, 1982. A musical scripted with songs composed by John Jacob Niles; produced at the Walden Theatre, Louisville.

Shapiro, Henry D. *Appalachia on Our Mind: The Southern Mountains and Mountaineers in the American Consciousness, 1870–1920.* Chapel Hill: Univ. of North Carolina Press, 1978.

Shearin, Hubert G. *British Ballads in the Cumberland Mountains.* Sewanee, TN: Univ. Press at the Univ. of the South, 1911.

———. *A Syllabus of Kentucky Folk-Songs.* Lexington, KY: Transylvania, 1911.

Simpson, Claude, Jr. Review of *American Folk Love Songs. Journal of American Folklore* 66:262 (October 1953): 365.

Sloane, Joseph. Review of *The Appalachian Photographs of Doris Ulmann. Art Journal* 31:3 (Spring 1972): 352.

Smith, L. Allen. *A Catalog of Pre-Revival Appalachian Dulcimers.* Columbia: Univ. of Missouri Press, 1983.

Smith, Ralph Lee. *Appalachian Dulcimer Traditions.* Lanham, MD: Scarecrow Press, 1997.

———. *The Story of the Dulcimer.* Cosby, TN: Crying Creek, 1986.

Smith, Ralph Lee, and Madeline MacNeil. *Folk Songs of Old Kentucky.* Pacific, MO: Mel Bay, 2003.

Stevens, Nelson. Review of *Folk Song U.S.A.,* by Alan Lomax. *Arizona Quarterly* 4:3 (Autumn 1948): 274–276.

Stoddart, Jess, ed. *The Quare Women's Journals: May Stone and Katherine Pettit's Summers in the Kentucky Mountains and the Founding of the Hindman School.* Ashland, KY: Jesse Stuart Foundation, 1997.

Terkel, Studs. *And They All Sang.* New York: New Press, 2005.

Thiersten, Eldred. *Cincinnati Opera: From the Zoo to Music Hall.* Hillsdale, MI: Deerstone Books, 1995.

Tiencken, Charlotte Marie. "Development of *My Days as a Youngling: John Jacob Niles, the Early Years* and Its Production at the University of Texas at Austin." M.F.A. thesis, Univ. of Texas at Austin, 1985.

"Tragic Troubador." *Coronet* (July 1951): 118–124.

Travis, James. "A Voice from Kentucky." *Southern Living* (June 1969).

Ulmann, Doris. *The Appalachian Photographs*. Penland, NC: Jargon Society, 1971.

Warner, Kerstin P. "'For Me Nothing Has Ever Been the Same': Composing the Niles-Merton Songs, 1967–1970." *Kentucky Review* 7:2 (Summer 1987): 29–43.

Warren, Dale. "Doris Ulmann: Photographer-in-Waiting." *Bookman* 72 (October 1930): 129–144.

Weller, Jack. *Yesterday's People: Life in Contemporary Appalachia*. Lexington: Univ. Press of Kentucky, 1966.

West, Tommy. "John Jacob Niles: Balladeer, Woodworker, Maker of Dulcimers, Gentleman Farmer, Storyteller." *Cincinnati Enquirer,* May 17, 1970.

Wheeler, Edward, ed. "Hunting the Lonesome Tunes in the Wilds of Kentucky." *Current Opinion* 65:2 (February 1917).

Whisnant, David. *All That Is Native and Fine: The Politics of Culture in an American Region*. Chapel Hill: Univ. of North Carolina Press, 1983.

Whittlesey, F. L. "John Jacob Niles: An American Tradition." *Choristers Guild Letters* (1970).

Wilentz, Sean, and Greil Marcus. *Rose and the Briar: Death, Love, and Liberty in the American Ballad*. New York: Norton, 2005.

Wilgus, D. K. *Anglo-American Folksong Scholarship since 1898*. New Brunswick, NJ: Rutgers Univ. Press, 1959.

Williams, Cratis. *Southern Mountain Speech*. Berea, KY: Berea College Press, 1992.

———. "The Southern Mountaineer in Fact and Fiction." Ph.D. diss., New York Univ., 1961.

Williams, Melanie. "John Jacob Niles's Settings of the Early Poetry of Thomas Merton in the 'Niles-Merton Songs,' Op. 171 and 172." D.M.A. thesis, Louisiana State Univ. and Agricultural and Mechanical College, 1998.

Williams, Susan Millar. *A Devil and a Good Woman Too: The Lives of Julia Peterkin*. Athens: Univ. of Georgia Press, 1997.

———. "A Devil and a Good Woman Too: The Lives of Julia Peterkin." *Catalogue* 13:3 (Autumn 1997): 8–12, 22–23.

Windland, Lorraine. "A Luncheon with John Jacob Niles." *Kentucky Monthly* 1:2 (October 1979).

Wintrode, Warren. "Boot Hill Tragedy: Balladeer Niles Begins Life Anew on 75th Birthday." *Lexington Herald-Leader,* June 28, 1970.

Wooley, Bryan. "Portrait of a Balladeer." *Louisville Courier-Journal and Times,* June 28, 1970, B4.

Young, William. *Young's History of Lafayette County.* Vol. 2. Indianapolis: B. F. Bowen, 1910.

Folk Collections

Bidstrup, Marguerite. *Singing Games and Folk Dances.* Brasstown, NC: John C. Campbell Folk School, 1941.

Boni, Margaret, and Norman Lloyd. *Fireside Book of Folk Songs.* New York: Simon and Schuster, 1947.

Botsford, Florence. *Botsford Collection of Folk-Songs.* New York: G. Schirmer, 1929.

Bronson, Bertrand. *The Traditional Tunes of the Child Ballads.* Vols. 1–4. Princeton, NJ: Princeton Univ. Press, 1959–1962.

Cambiare, Celestin Pierre. *East Tennessee and Western Virginia Mountain Ballads (The Last Stand of American Pioneer Civilization).* London: Mitre Press, 1934.

Campbell, Olive Dame, Richard Chase, and Marie Marvel. *Songs of All Time.* Delaware, OH: Cooperative Recreation Service, 1946.

Chappell, Louis. *Folk-Songs of Roanoke and the Albemarle.* Morgantown, WV: Ballad Press, 1939.

Chase, Richard. *Old Songs and Singing Games.* Chapel Hill: Univ. of North Carolina Press, 1938.

Child, Francis James. *The English and Scottish Popular Ballads.* 10 vols. Boston: Houghton, Mifflin, 1864.

Combs, Josiah. *Folk-Songs du Midi des Etats-Unis.* Paris: Presses Universitaires de France, 1925.

———. *Folk-Songs from the Southern Highlands.* New York: G. Schirmer, 1939.

Combs, Josiah, and Hubert Shearin. *A Syllabus of Kentucky Folk-Songs.* Lexington, KY: Transylvania, 1911.

Cox, John Harrington. *Folk Songs of the South.* Cambridge, MA: Harvard Univ. Press, 1925. Reprint, Hatboro, PA: Folklore Associates 1963.

———. *Traditional Ballads Mainly from West Virginia.* Works Progress Administration, Federal Theatre Project, Publication No. 75-S. New York: National Service Bureau, 1939.

Davis, Arthur Kyle. *More Traditional Ballads of Virginia.* Chapel Hill: Univ. of North Carolina Press, 1960.

Farnsworth, Charles, and Cecil Sharp. *Folk Songs, Chanteys, and Singing Games.* New York: H. W. Gray, 1909.

"Folksongs from East Kentucky." Collected by the Folk Song project of the Federal Music Project in Kentucky, Works Progress Administration. 1939. Typescript, Univ. of Kentucky Special Collections, Lexington.

Ford, Ira. *Traditional Music of America.* New York: E. P. Dutton, 1940. Reprint, Hatboro, PA: Folklore Associates, 1965.

Fuson, Harvey. "Ballads of Harlan County." Paper presented to the Harlan Historical Society, Harlan, KY, September 5, 1931.

———. "Ballads of the Kentucky Highlands" (before 1931). Special Collections and Digital Programs, Univ. of Kentucky, Lexington.

———. Ballads of the Kentucky Highlands. London: Mitre Press, 1931.

Henry, Mellinger. Beech Mountain Songs and Ballads. New York: G. Schirmer, 1936.

———. Folk Songs from the Southern Highlands. New York: J. J. Augustin, 1928.

Hudson, Arthur Palmer. Folksongs of Mississippi and Their Background. Chapel Hill: Univ. of North Carolina Press, 1936.

Jewell, James William. Kentucky Mountain Melodies. Lexington, KY: Lang, 1950.

Kincaid, Bradley. My Favorite Old Time Songs and Ballads. Chicago: S. N., 1931.

Korson, George. Minstrels of the Mine Patch. Philadelphia: Univ. of Pennsylvania Press, 1938.

Lomax, John. Cowboy Songs and Other Frontier Ballads. New York: Macmillan, 1910.

Lomax, John, and Alan Lomax. American Ballads and Folk Songs. New York: Macmillan, 1934.

Lomax, John Avery, Alan Lomax, Charles Seeger, and Ruth Crawford Seeger. Folk Song U.S.A. New York: Duell, Sloan, and Pearce, 1947.

McGill, Josephine. Folk Songs of the Kentucky Mountains. New York: Boosey and Hawkes, 1917.

Miles, Emma Bell. The Spirit of the Mountains. 1905. Reprint, Knoxville: Univ. of Tennessee Press, 1975.

Pettit, Katherine. "Record of the Settlement of the State Federation of Women's Clubs at Hazard, Perry Co., Kentucky Summer of 1899." Special Collections and Digital Programs, Univ. of Kentucky, Lexington.

Raine, James Watt, and Cecil Sharp. Mountain Ballads. Berea, KY: Berea College Press, 1923.

Randolph, Vance. Ozark Folksongs. Urbana: Univ. of Illinois Press, 1982. Originally published in four volumes by the State Historical Society of Missouri in 1946–1950.

Richardson, Ethel Park. American Mountain Songs. Edited by Sigmund Spaeth. New York: Greenberg, 1927.

Ritchie, Jean. Folk Songs of the Southern Appalachian Mountains as Sung by Jean Ritchie. New York: Oak Publications, 1965. Reprint, Lexington: Univ. Press of Kentucky, 1997. Page references are to the 1965 edition.

Sandburg, Carl. The American Songbag. New York: Harcourt, Brace, Jovanovich, 1927.

———. New American Songbag. New York: Broadcast Music, 1950.

Scarborough, Dorothy. A Song Catcher in Southern Mountains. New York: Columbia Univ. Press, 1937.

Sharp, Cecil. *American-English Folk-Ballads.* New York: G. Schirmer, n.d.

———. *American-English Folk-Songs.* New York: G. Schirmer, 1918.

Sharp, Cecil, and Olive Dame Campbell. *English Folk Songs from the Southern Appalachians: Comprising 122 Songs and Ballads, and 323 Tunes.* New York: Putnam's, 1917.

Sharp, Cecil, Maude Karpeles, and Olive Dame Campbell. *English Folk Songs from the Southern Appalachians: Comprising Two Hundred and Seventy-four Songs and Ballads, with Nine Hundred and Sixty-eight Tunes, Including Thirty-nine Tunes Contributed by Olive Dame Campbell.* London: Oxford Univ. Press, 1932.

Smith, Betty. *A Singer among Singers: Jane Hicks Gentry.* Lexington: Univ. Press of Kentucky, 1998.

Sulzer, Elmer. *Twenty-Five Kentucky Folk Ballads.* Lexington, KY: Transylvania, 1936.

Thomas, Jean. *Ballad Makin' in the Hills of Kentucky.* New York: Henry Holt, 1939.

———. *Devil's Ditties.* Chicago: W. Wilbur Hatfield, 1931.

The United States Songster. Cincinnati: U. P. James, 1836.

Warner, Anne. *Traditional American Folk Tunes.* Syracuse, NY: Syracuse Univ. Press, 1984.

Wetmore, Susannah, and Marshall Bartholomew. *Mountain Songs of North Carolina.* New York: G. Schirmer, 1926.

Wheeler, Mary. *Kentucky Mountain Folk-Songs.* Boston: Boston Music, 1937.

White, Alice, and Janet Tobitt. *Dramatized Ballads.* New York: E. P. Dutton, 1937.

White, Newman Ivey, ed. *The Frank C. Brown Collection of North Carolina Folklore.* Durham, NC: Duke Univ. Press, 1952.

Wyman, Loraine, and Howard Brockway. *Twenty Kentucky Mountain Songs.* Boston: Oliver Ditson, 1919.

———. *Lonesome Tunes: Folk Songs from the Kentucky Mountains.* New York: W. H. Gray, 1916.

Films

John Jacob Niles. Directed by William Richardson, produced by Appalshop Headwaters Films (VHS format), AF 6027, 1978.

No Direction Home. Directed and produced by Martin Scorsese. A documentary of Bob Dylan, distributed by Paramount Pictures (DVD), 03105, 2005. Contains original footage of Niles performing on *Revlon's Spring Festival of Folk Music,* CBS television, June 16, 1960.

Interviews by Author

Barret, Edward, Louisville, KY.
Field, Nancie, Lexington, KY.
Ivey, Donald, Lexington, KY.
Jones, Loyal, Berea, KY.
Ledford, Homer, Winchester, KY.
Mullins, Mary Tippy, Clark County, KY.
Niles, John Ed, Lexington, KY.
Niles, Rena Lipetz, Clark County, Lexington KY.
Niles, Thomas M. T., Scarsdale, NY.
Pope, Janelle, Lexington, KY.
Rannels, Molly, Lexington, KY.
Richardson, Bill, Whitesburg, KY.
Roberts, Jacqueline, Lexington, KY.
Scroggs, Mercer, Brasstown, NC.
Sexton, Nancy Niles, Louisville, KY.
Shepherd, Hannah, Lexington, KY.

Sound Recordings of John Jacob Niles's Music

Recorded by Niles

Marion Kerby (contralto) and John Jacob Niles (tenor), with piano accompaniment. *Negro Exaltations*, Roycroft 172 (78 rpm disc), ca. 1930–1933.

> He's Got the Whole World in His Hands
> Just Like a Tree Planted by the Water

Early American Ballads, "Collected and Arranged by John Jacob Niles, Mountaineer Tenor with Dulcimer accompaniment," RCA Red Seal M 604-1 through M 604-8 (an album of four 78 rpm discs, Victor 2016, 2017, 2018, 2019, with booklet of notes and texts), November 1, 1939.

> The Gypsie Laddie (2016-A)
> My Little Mohee (2016-B)
> I Wonder as I Wander (2017-A)
> Lulle Lullay (The Coventry Carol) (2017-B)
> The Seven Joys of Mary—Part 1 (2018-A)
> The Seven Joys of Mary—Part 2 (2018-B)
> The Ballad of Barberry Ellen—Part 1 (2019-A)
> The Ballad of Barberry Ellen—Part 2 (2019-B)

Street Cries, RCA Red Seal label (later expanded and re-released as *John Jacob Niles Sings American Folk and Gambling Songs*), 1939.

> Gambler Don't Lose Your Place at God's Right Hand
> My Little Black Star
> Gambling Song of the Big Sandy
> Gambler's Lullaby

I'm a Roving Gambler
Street, Field, and Jailhouse Cries (two sides)

Early American Carols and Folksongs, "Collected and Arranged by John Jacob Niles, Mountaineer Tenor with Dulcimer accompaniment," M 718 (an album of four 78 rpm discs, Victor 2119, 2120, 2121, 2122, with booklet of notes and texts), fall 1940.
   Jesus, Jesus Rest Your Head
   Down in Yon Forest
   See Jesus the Savior
   Who Killed Cock Robin
   The Frog Went Courting
   When Jesus Lived in Galilee
   Jesus the Christ Is Born
   The Cherry Tree
   The Old Woman and the Pig
   The Carrion Crow

John Henry/Jack O' Diamonds, RCA Victor 2051 (78 rpm disc), 1940.
   John Henry
   Jack O' Diamonds

American Folk Lore Volume 3, "Collected and arranged by John Jacob Niles, Mountaineer Tenor with Dulcimer accompaniment," Red Seal label M-824 (an album of four 78 rpm discs, Victor 2171, 2172, 2173, 1807, with booklet on songs and texts), October 1941.
   You Got to Cross That Lonesome Valley
   The Lass from the Low Countree
   Black Is the Color
   Go 'Way from my Window
   One Morning in May
   The Wife of Usher's Well
   The Death of Queen Jane
   Little Mattie Groves

John Jacob Niles—Early American Folk Carols, Disc 732 (three 10-inch 78 rpm discs with 8-page booklet), 1946.
   Seven Joys of Mary (6040 A)
   Seven Joys of Mary, Part Two (6040 B)
   The Little Liking (6041 A)
   Matthew, Mark, Luke, and John (6041 B)

I Wonder as I Wander (6042 A)
Carol of the Birds (6042 B)
Carol of the Angels (6042 B)

John Jacob Niles—Child Ballads, Disc 665 (two 78 rpm discs), 1947.
Barbara Allan
Edward
Mattie Grove

John Jacob Niles, Vol. 2—American Ballads and Folk Songs, Disc album 733 (three 78 rpm discs, with notes and text), in the 1947 catalog.
John Henry (6014 A)
Who Killed Cock Robin (6014 B)
Frog Went a-Courtin' (6015 A)
Lass from the Low Countree (6015 B)
Jack O' Diamonds (6016 A)
Go 'Way from My Window (6016 B)

Six Favorite Folk Songs, Camden CAE-197 (7-inch extended-play 45 rpm disc), 195?
Black Is the Color
The Ballad of Barberry Ellen
I Wonder as I Wander
The Old Woman and the Pig
The Frog Went Courting
The Carrion Crow

Folk Songs of Christmas, Camden CAE 205 (7-inch extended-play 45 rpm disc), 195?
The Twelve Days of Christmas
The Kentucky Wassail Song
Jesus, the Christ Is Born
The Seven Joys of Mary
See Jesus the Saviour

Folk Songs of Christmas Volume II, Camden CAE 206 (7-inch extended-play 45 rpm disc), 195?
Sing We the Virgin Mary
The Cherry Tree
Lulle Lullay
Jesus, Jesus Rest Your Head

John Jacob Niles: American Folk Love Songs, Boone Tolliver Records BTR 22 (10-inch 33⅓ rpm disc), recorded at Boot Hill February 5–12, 1952, released November 5, 1952.

> The Little Mohee
> The Lass from the Low Countree
> The Cuckoo
> Go 'Way from My Window
> Black Is the Color of My True Love's Hair
> Oh Waly, Waly
> The Rosy Peach
> The Turtle Dove
> I'm Goin' Away

Ballads by Niles, Boone Tolliver Records BTR-23 (10-inch 33⅓ rpm LP disc), recorded at Boot Hill February 5–12, 1952, released November 5, 1952.

> Little Mattie Groves
> The Gypsy Laddie
> Mary Hamilton
> Barberry Ellen

John Jacob Niles Sings American Folk and Gambling Songs, Camden CAL 219 (33⅓ rpm LP disc), 1956.

> The Two Sisters
> The Old Woman and the Pig
> The Frog Went A-Courtin'
> The Carrion Crow
> Edward
> The Hangman
> I'm in the Notion Now
> The Farmer's Curst Wife
> The Three Hunters
> Who Killed Cock Robin
> Jack O' Diamonds
> The Roving Gambler
> Gambler Don't Lose Your Place at God's Right Hand
> The Gambler's Lullaby
> The Gambling Song of the Big Sandy River
> Little Black Star
> American Street, Field, and Jailhouse Cries

John Jacob Niles Sings American Folk Songs, Camden CAL 245 (33⅓ rpm LP disc), 195?

> You Got to Cross
> The Lass from the Low Countree
> Black Is the Color
> Go 'Way from My Window
> One Morning in May
> Wife of Usher's Well
> Death of Queen Jane
> Little Mattie Groves
> The Gypsy Laddie
> My Little Mohee
> I Wonder as I Wander
> Lulle Lullay
> Seven Joys of Mary
> Ballad of Barberry Ellen

50th Anniversary Album, Camden CAL 330 (33⅓ rpm LP disc), November 1956.

> Cuckoo
> Lord Bateman and the Turkish Lady
> Jimmy Randal
> John of Hazel Green
> Carol of the Birds
> That Lonesome Road
> John Henry
> The Wife Wrapt Up in Wether's Skin
> The Cruel Brother
> Down in Yon Forest
> Molly Vaughan
> Mary Hamilton
> Earl Brand

I Wonder as I Wander: Traditional Love Songs and Carols by John Jacob Niles, Tradition TLP 1023 (33⅓ rpm LP disc), November 27, 1957.

> Little Mohee
> The Sea Witch
> The Irish Girl
> Go 'Way from My Window
> In That Lovely Far-Off City
> Look Down That Lonesome Road
> I Wonder as I Wander
> When Jesus Lived in Galilee

Lulle Lullay
Black Is the Color
Venezuela
I Had a Cat
The Lass from the Low Countree
John Henry
I'm Goin' Away

An Evening with John Jacob Niles, Tradition TLP 1036 (33⅓ rpm disc), November 12, 1959.

Carol of the Birds
Turtle Dove
I'm in the Notion Now
Sing We the Virgin Mary
Black Dress
Cuckoo
O Waly, Waly
When I Gets Up into Heaven
Frog in the Spring
Seven Joys of Mary
Roving Gambler
You Got to Cross That Lonesome Valley

Folk Festival at Newport, Volume 3, Vanguard VSD 2055 (33⅓ LP disc, side 1, track 6), 1959.

The Hangman (Maid Freed from the Gallows)

The Ballads of John Jacob Niles, Tradition TLP 1046 (two 33⅓ rpm discs), October 15, 1961.

Bowie, Bowerie
Brother's Revenge
Jimmy Randall
The Murdered Brother
Bonny Farday
Old Bangum
The Cherry Tree
Lardy Margot and Love
Who's Goin' to Shoe Your Pretty Little Foot
Little Mattie Groves
Barb'ry Ellen
The Hangman
The Shepherd's Daughter and the King

Fair John and the Seven Foresters
The Fency King and the English King
The Death of Queen Jane
Mary Hamilton
The Lady and the Gypsy
The Dreary Dream
The Good Old Man
The Unwilling Bride
The Old Woman and the Devil
The Weep Willow Tree
John of Hazel Green

Folk Song and Minstrelsy, Vanguard SRL 7624 (anthology of four 33⅓ rpm LP discs, side 7/7), 1962.
The Hangman

John Jacob Niles Sings Folk Songs, Folkways FW 02373 (33⅓ rpm LP disc, reissue of Disc recordings made by Moses Asch), 1964.
Frog Went A-Courting
I'm So Glad Trouble Don't Last Always
Who Killed Cock Robin
John Henry
Go Find My True Love
I Had a Cat
The Frog in the Spring
Posheen, Posheen, Posho
The Lass from the Low Countree
Jack O' Diamonds
I Wonder as I Wander
Go 'Way from My Window

John Jacob Niles: Folk Balladeer, RCA V513 (33⅓ rpm disc, reissue of RCA Red Seal recordings of 1939–1940), 1965.
Love Henry (Young Bunting)
Our Goodman (Old Cuckold)
The Maid Freed from the Gallows
Edward
Jimmy Randal
The Ballad of Barberry Ellen
Bonnie Farday (Babylon)
The Cherry Tree
The Gypsy Laddie
Mary Hamilton

The Best of John Jacob Niles, Tradition, released on Everest S-2055 (33⅓ rpm LP disc), 1967.

> The Hangman
> Mary Hamilton
> The Dreary Dream
> Jack O' Diamonds
> The Roving Gambler
> Frog Went A-Courting
> Little Mohee
> Go 'Way from My Window
> I Wonder as I Wander
> Black Is the Color

The Asch Recordings Vol. 2, Folkways AA 004, 1939–1945 (recorded in 1939 and released on two 33⅓ rpm LP discs), 1967.

> Little Mattie Groves

The John Jacob Niles Collection, Gifthorse G4-10008 (cassette), 1992.

> The Hangman
> The Rovin' Gambler
> Venezuela
> I Wonder as I Wander
> The Black Dress
> Barb'ry Ellen
> Go 'Way from My Window
> Froggie Went A-Courtin'
> You've Got to Cross That Lonesome Valley
> Jack O' Diamonds
> Black Is the Color of My True Love's Hair
> Carol of the Birds
> Little Mattie Groves
> Goin' Away
> 1964 Interview with Studs Terkel

John Jacob Niles: My Precarious Life in the Public Domain, Revola REV 138 (CD), 2006.

> Love Henry
> Our Goodman
> The Maid Freed from the Gallows
> Edward
> Jimmy Randal
> The Ballad of Barberry Ellen

Bonnie Farday
The Cherry Tree
The Gypsy Laddie
Mary Hamilton

An Evening with John Jacob Niles, Empire 545 450 832-2 (CD, digital reissue of Tradition Recordings), 2006.
The Carol of the Birds
Jack O'Diamonds
The Turtle Dove
I'm in the Notion Now
Sing We the Virgin Mary
Lulle Lullay
The Black Dress
The Cuckoo
O Waly, O Waly
When I Gets Up into Heaven
The Frog in the Spring
The Seven Joys of Mary
The Roving Gambler
You Got to Cross That Lonesome Valley

John Jacob Niles: I Wonder as I Wander, Carols and Love Songs,
Empire 545 450 802-2 (CD, digital reissue of Tradition recordings), 2006.
Waken Little Shepherd
Jesus, Jesus, Rest Your Head
Frog Went A-Courtin'
Little Mohee
The Sea Witch
The Irish Girl
Go 'Way from My Window
In That Lovely Far-Off City
Look Down That Lonesome Road
I Wonder as I Wander
When Jesus Lived in Galilee
Lulle Lullay
Black Is the Color of My True Love's Hair
Venezuela
I Had a Cat
The Lass from the Low Country
John Henry
I'm Goin' Away

The Ballads of John Jacob Niles, Essential Media Group 942 311 018-2
(two CDs, digital reissue of Tradition recordings), 2007.

> Bowie, Bowerie
> Brothers Revenge
> Jimmy Randal
> The Murdered Brother
> Bonny Farday
> Old Bangum
> The Cherry Tree
> Who's Goin' to Shoe Your Pretty Little Foot?
> Little Mattie Groves
> Barb'ry Ellen
> The Hangman
> The Shepherd's Daughter and the King
> Fair John and the Seven Foresters
> The Fency King and the English King
> The Death of Queen Jane
> Mary Hamilton
> The Lady and the Gypsy
> The Dreary Dream
> The Good Old Man
> The Unwilling Bride
> The Old Man and the Devil
> The Weep Willow Tree
> John of Hazel Green

Selected Recordings by Others

Jacqueline Roberts (soprano) and Nancie Field (piano). *Songs by John Jacob Niles*,
Mrs. John J. Niles, Lexington, KY, TR 1608234 (cassette), recorded at Track 16
studio, Lexington, KY, January 24, 1980.

> Go 'Way from My Window
> The Lass from the Low Countree
> Ribbon Bow
> My Lover Is a Farmer Lad
> Little Black Star
> The Gambler's Wife
> Wild Rider
> Unused I Am to Lovers
> The Lotus Bloom
> Written in the Stars

A Flame Within
Its I Have Lived So Constantly with Sorrow
Calm Is the Night
Fond Affection
Symbol
Figures on a Hill
The Flower of Jesse
Come Gentle Dark
Sweet Little Jesus
Songs of the Earth
The Robin and the Thorn
Softly Blew the East Wind
What Songs Were Sung
The Blue Madonna

Jacqueline Roberts (soprano) and Nancie Field (piano). *The Niles-Merton Songs, Op. 171 and 172,* self-produced cassette, 1980.

The Messenger
The Nativity (Carol)
A Responsory, 1948
Sundown
When You Point Your Finger
The Weathercock on the Cathedral of Quito
Evening
Great Prayer
Love Winter When the Plant Says Nothing
Lament of a Maiden for the Warrior's Death
O, Sweet Irrational Worship
Autumn
Wisdom
The Mirror's Wisdom
For My Brother: Reported Missing in Action, 1943
The Greek Women
Cana
The Ohio River—Louisville
Original Sin (A Memorial Anthem for Father's Day)
Birdcage Walk
Jesus Weeps into the Fire
Mosaic: St. Praxed's

Jacqueline Roberts (soprano), Janelle Pope (piano), and Nancie Field (piano). *Jacqueline Roberts Sings the Music of John Jacob Niles*, self-produced for the University Press of Kentucky (CD), 2001.

> The Flower of Jesse
> Written in the Stars
> Ribbon Bow
> My Lover Is a Farmer Lad
> I Have a Flame within Me
> Figures on a Hill
> Come Gentle Dark
> The Blue Madonna
> Little Black Star
> The Wild Rider
> A Responsory
> The Weathercock on the Cathedral of Quito
> Evening
> Great Prayer
> Love Winter When the Plant Says Nothing
> Lament of a Maiden
> The Greek Women
> The Ohio River, Louisville
> For My Brother, Reported Missing in Action 1943

Chad Runyon (baritone) and Jacqueline Chew (piano). *Sweet Irrational Worship: The Niles-Merton Songs*, MSR Classics MS 1174 (CD), 2006.

> The Messenger
> The Nativity
> A Responsory, 1948
> Sundown
> When You Point Your Finger
> The Weathercock on the Cathedral at Quito
> Evening
> Prayer
> Love Winter When the Plant Says Nothing
> Lament of a Maiden for the Warrior's Death
> O Sweet Irrational Worship
> Autumn
> Wisdom
> The Mirror's Mission
> For My Brother Reported Missing in Action, 1943
> The Greek Women
> Cana

The Ohio River—Louisville
Original Sin
Birdcage Walk
Jesus Weeps into the Fire
Mosaic: St. Praxed's

Hope Koehler (soprano) and James Douglass (piano). *The Lass from the Low Countree: Hope Koehler Performs the Songs of John Jacob Niles*, Albany Records TROY1015 (CD), 2008.

The Lass from the Low Countree
Go 'Way from My Window
Black Is the Color
The Wild Rider
The Black Dress
Ribbon Bow
Unused I Am to Lovers
My Lover Is a Farmer Lad
Little Black Star
The Gambler's Wife
Carol of the Birds
Jesus, Jesus Rest Your Head
I Wonder as I Wander
What Songs Were Sung
Sweet Little Jesus Boy
Gambler, Don't You Lose Your Place
The Robin and the Thorn
When I Get Up into Heaven

Index

Niles, John Jacob *(cont.)*
  honorary doctorates, 277
  hunting, fox, 4, 218, *A2*
  inventive nature, 26–27, *A7*
  local color writing, 45, 81, 83
  mask, myth, persona, 164–166, 201,
    221, 226–227
  Heidy Moore, relationship with, 35
  musical training, 19–24, 28–29,
    51–53, 61–63, 65–67, *A13*
  music publishing, 22, 75, 79, 102–
    110, 170, 190, 238–240, 249–252
  and Rena Niles, 4, 7, 34, 60, 73, 132,
    167, 169–170, 173, 176, 179–181,
    184, 187–200, 204–214, 217–220,
    229, 240–241, 246–248, 250, 260–
    262, 266, 268–272, 276, 278–279,
    B3, B4, B8, B18
  "Niles Ulmann Folk Lore
    Photographic Expedition," 172
  Objerall Jacket (*see* "Go 'Way from
    My Window")
  performance, 6, 11, 19–20, 28,
    32, 42, 46, 162–167, 171, 173,
    178–179, 185–186, 189, 195, 203,
    205, 210, 220, 222, 225, 227, 231,
    233–235, 246, 251, 259–260,
    271–272, 276, 280, 283
  poetry, 3, 54, 60, 63, 219, 237, 243,
    260–264, 269–270, 275
  political viewpoint, 3–4, 19, 177,
    234
  pony barn, 214–215
  radio, 6, 67–69, 77–78, 198–204,
    208, 252, *B5*
  religious views, 19, 34, 262–263, *A1*
  singing style and vocal quality, 6,
    76–77, 118, 122, 165, 222, 227,
    231, 248
  storytelling, 22, 29–32, 83, 90, 201,
    221
  street cries, 33, 290

  tenor voice, 66
  touring, 117, 121–125, 127–130,
    192, 199–200, 204–208, 217, 230,
    252, 272
  Doris Ulmann, relationship with,
    71, 73, 82, 101–102, 103, 125–182,
    305, *A21*
  vaudeville, 6, 20–21, 51, 54, 76, 112,
    117, 165, 201, 271–272, 288
  voice descriptions, 51, 76–78, 118,
    122, 165, 227, 231, 248, 272
  voice recovery, 69, 72, 76–77
  Roberta Voorhies, relationship with,
    34, 53–54
  war service, 53–63
  White House, at the, 5, 171–173,
    185–186, 189, 194, 208–210, *A24*
  wild animals, playing to, 127
Niles, John Jacob, and Marion Kerby
  concert reviews, 113, 117, 118–123,
    125, 128–129
  concert tours, 117–121, 121–123,
    124–125, 127–130
  final concert, 130
  first concert, 117
  first meeting, 111
Niles, John Jacob, and opera, 32,
    51–52, 54, 62, 65–71, 75–76, 78,
    201, 218, 221, 243
  King of Little Italy, 126–127, 224
  Metropolitan Opera connections,
    235–238
Niles, John Jacob, compositions of
  carols, 35, 43, 44, 107, 168–169, 190,
    195, 221, 223, 246, 248, 252, 257,
    280, 316
  choral arrangements, 57, 155, 169,
    224–225, 238–243, 261, 280, 320
  extended compositions, 126–127,
    185, 224–225, 240–243, 273–274
  Impressionist influence, 80, 90–91,
    96, 103, 166, 185, 319